*Environmental
Politics
and Policy*

Environmental Politics and Policy

Seventh Edition

Walter A. Rosenbaum
University of Florida

CQ PRESS

A Division of Congressional Quarterly Inc.
Washington, D.C.

CQ Press
1255 22nd Street, NW, Suite 400
Washington, DC 20037

Phone: 202-729-1900; toll-free, 1-866-4CQ-PRESS (1-866-427-7737)

Web: www.cqpress.com

Cover design: Mike Grove, MG Design

♾ The paper used in this publication exceeds the requirements of the American National Standard for Information Sciences—Permanence of Paper for Printed Library Materials, ANSI Z39.48-1992.

Printed and bound in the United States of America

11 10 09 08 07   1 2 3 4 5

Library of Congress Cataloging-in-Publication Data

Rosenbaum, Walter A.
    Environmental politics and policy / Walter A. Rosenbaum. — 7th ed.
        p. cm.
    Includes bibliographical references and index.
    ISBN 978-0-87289-440-2 (alk. paper)
 1. Environmental policy—United States.   I. Title.

    GE180.R66 2008
    363.7'0560973—dc22

                                                          2007021686

Contents

Tables, Figures, and Boxes

Tables

Figures

Boxes

Preface

We are just past the threshold of the twenty-first century, and any author with a social conscience who writes a book about environmentalism should do so with deliberation. It is a time to measure distances: How far have we come? How far must we go? It is a time to talk about time and change: What have we lost? What have we gained? This book is addressed to an audience who will live well into the new century, a generation with its ambition and imagination resolutely fixed on tomorrow, so it is also a time to talk about what might be: What will this generation accomplish? What ideas and visions will challenge its imagination and come to fruition? In short, an author should write accurately and responsibly not only about what has happened but also about its meaning in social and historical time. Therefore, this is a book about the more enduring institutions and processes of American environmental policy making as well as their ongoing transformation and implications.

Readers familiar with *Environmental Politics and Policy* will recognize a continuity with previous editions in conceptual framework and substantive policy concerns. They will also notice some significant editorial improvements. The foundational chapters that explain and illustrate the essential components of the policy-making process (chapters 2 and 3) still cover these key areas, but they have been carefully reorganized for greater clarity and continuity. Chapter 2 now focuses entirely on the policy-making process, whereas chapter 3 covers the institutions and politics of policy making. Throughout the book, case studies and other examples have been updated comprehensively, where appropriate, to ensure timeliness and relevance. Each chapter has been edited rigorously to eliminate material from previous editions that is no longer essential. The result is a more concise narrative that does not sacrifice such fundamentals as the conceptual design, the careful explanation of substantive policy, and the abundant illustrations that have appealed to the readers of previous editions. As always, a major subtext is the continuing challenge, inherent to environmental policy making, of reconciling sound science with practical politics.

This edition also records the significant events and illuminates the strategic transformations that have taken place in domestic environmental politics and policy since the previous edition appeared. These include:

• *The substantial impact of the George W. Bush administration on virtually every aspect of current domestic environmental policy.* Every chapter of this edition reflects some aspect of the administration's influence. The discussion of command-and-control air pollution regulation in chapter 6 describes the ongoing national debate over the Bush administration's initiative to relax air pollution emission standards by changing "New Source Review" standards for coal-burning electric utilities. Chapter 4 discusses the controversy over White House efforts to influence science policy making at the U.S. Environmental Protection Agency. Chapter 9 considers energy policy conflicts involving renewed presidential efforts to open the Arctic National Wildlife Refuge to more petroleum exploration and the Energy Policy Act of 2005.

• *The shifting texture and discontinuities of public opinion about the environment and its impact on environmental policy making.* Chapter 2, for example, examines a number of potentially significant aspects of public opinion trends since the 2000 presidential election. These include a gradual but ongoing erosion of public conviction about the importance of pollution control and the continuing failure of environmentalism to become a salient factor in presidential voting. At the same time, public support for environmental advocacy groups continues to be robust, and public involvement in environmental activism seems to be increasing. Equally important, evidence now suggests that racial differences concerning environmental pollution and environmental activism may no longer be significant—if, in fact, they ever were.

• *The continuing change in environmental trends and indicators.* The shelf life of environmental data is short. Data need continual updating and pruning to remain relevant. Tables and figures from earlier editions that are no longer useful have been removed. The remaining tables and figures involving the most essential data—current trends in national air pollution emissions, water quality, and toxic waste discharges, for example—have been updated as much as possible.

• *The emergence of new issues and the evolving status of others.* The introductory and concluding chapters bracket the entire narrative with an increasing emphasis on the importance of global issues in understanding both our domestic environmental politics and our international environmental diplomacy. In both chapters, the substance and politics of sustainability receive more attention than in previous editions. Elsewhere, the discussion of water pollution regulation in chapter 6 includes a description of the technically complex, economically expensive problem now confronting the states in determining the "Total Maximum Daily Loading" for contaminants in runoff water from agriculture and other sources of nonpoint pollution. The description of regulatory risk analysis in chapter 4 updates the continuing controversy over the human cancer risk associated with exposure to the chemical dioxin and to chemical plasticizers in materials used in making children's toys.

I have tried to keep faith with colleagues, students, reviewers, and others who have found the narrative design informative, accessible, and durable. That includes an implicit commitment to material that is interesting as well as balanced and teachable—in the end, a book that is both a good read and a fair read.

Acknowledgments

As usual, the talents of many other people were enlisted in the writing of this new edition, and I am deeply indebted to them for the continuing acceptance of this book. Like most teachers, I recognized long ago that my students are often my best instructors and critics. To them I express my continuing gratitude. A number of reviewers made constructive suggestions during the revision and writing of this edition. I want to thank Glen Krutz, University of Oklahoma; Dennis Pirages, University of Maryland; and Daniel Press, University of California, Santa Cruz, for their thorough reviews. To CQ Press, a special appreciation: This edition marks my thirtieth year of very rewarding collaboration with its talented staff. To my current editors Charisse Kiino, Dwain Smith, and Debbie Hardin, I offer a well-deserved thanks for the many hours of planning, reviewing, and patience invested in the work. Faults of omission and commission—alas!—are my own.

—Walter A. Rosenbaum

Environmental
Politics
and Policy

Chapter 1

After Earth Day:
American Environmentalism in Transformation

> *The difficulty of converting scientific findings into political action is a function of the uncertainty of the science and the pain generated by the action.*
> —William D. Ruckelshaus, former administrator
> of the U.S. Environmental Protection Agency

In early October 2006 one of the defining moments in the combatative Texas gubernatorial campaign occurred in a Dallas auditorium. For the only time, incumbent Republican governor Rick Perry confronted all five of his opponents in a public debate. The confrontation was a statewide media event, broadcast live by major television stations statewide, carried simultaneously on the Web site of the Dallas *Morning News*, and covered by all major Texas newspapers. While attention focused almost exclusively on the encounter inside the auditorium, one of the campaign's more prophetic environmental incidents was commencing almost unnoticed outside.

Across the street from the auditorium, "Rick Perry's Smokestack Love Tour" had arrived. Downwinders at Risk, a small Texas environmental group, had parked a traveling editorial cartoon intended to track Governor Perry's campaign across the state. The cartoon was a Styrofoam tableau, mounted high atop a hay wagon, portraying a giant mockup of the governor kissing an 8-foot smokestack adorned with the logo of the TXU Corporation, Texas' largest electric utility. TXU was not amused. With billions of dollars at risk, TXU was then mired in an acrimonious statewide environmental battle over its power plants that had transformed its smokestacks into a public icon for air pollutants.[1]

1

In a moment of remarkably bad judgment, giant TXU publicly threatened to sue the Downwinders to compel them to remove the TXU logo from their smokestack. Environmentalists were delighted. TXU's threat turned what should have been a political sideshow into a statewide media event, cast TXU in the role of corporate bully, and forced more attention on TXU's smokestacks and the profound environmental implications they had assumed for Texas, other states, and ultimately the world. Quite unintentionally, the Downwinders also sent a message about the ongoing transformation of American environmental politics.

In 2005 the TXU corporation, worth $25.5 billion and serving 2.2 million customers, had confidently proposed to power Texas into the future on a scale prodigious even by Texas standards. TXU requested state regulators to approve the largest coal-based electric utility project ever constructed in the United States. Everything about it was supersized: eighteen coal-burning power plants costing $10 billion, generating more than 3.5 percent of all the coal-fired electricity in the United States, producing more than half of Texas's entire electric power within a decade. In 2006 Gov. Rick Perry, then running for reelection, was confident enough in TXU's plan to send it on an administrative fast track to hasten its approval by state regulators. Instead, the proposal plunged TXU, Texas, and his own gubernatorial campaign into the mainstream of a global environmental battle.

A Texas Bet with Global Stakes

The political conflict over the TXU proposal exemplified a major transition in America's clean air politics. Besides the mix of pollutants long associated in Texas and other states with coal-burning controversies—nitrogen oxides, sulfur oxide, soot, mercury, and other airborne toxics—the TXU conflict was prophetic because carbon dioxide, a chemical strongly implicated in worldwide climate change, was also a high-profile concern. A decade earlier, climate warming was politically marginal and scientifically problematic as a public issue. Texas was early evidence of how pervasively global climate warming, often called "the greenhouse effect," had moved into the mainstream of environmental politics by transforming the traditional domestic political struggle over coal combustion at all governmental levels. In many respects, the Texas experience was not unique. But the Texas CO^2 issue had escalated into a high-stakes, big-risk controversy on an international scale.

There were global environmental stakes. Texas was already the national leader in annual statewide CO^2 emissions. Had it been a nation, Texas would have ranked seventh internationally in CO^2 production, producing annually more CO^2 than the combined emissions of the United Kingdom, Canada, and Italy. The eighteen proposed new electric facilities were expected to more than double that state production by adding 78 million additional tons of CO^2 yearly—an amount equal to the annual production of 14 million cars. Texas' emissions alone would then exceed those of twenty-one other states and exceed 7 percent of global climate-warming emissions.

Texas's economic future was also an issue. That Texas needed more electric power was indisputable. Six million new residents requiring electric power were expected within a decade. TXU asserted that Texas faced the probability of rolling blackouts and tenuous electric power reliability unless new power-generating plants were soon constructed. Moreover, TXU asserted, new coal-fired facilities would reduce utility demand for increasingly costly and diminishing natural gas that was better used elsewhere in Texas. The TXU facilities also promised to produce relatively cheap power and create hundreds of new jobs. Texas communities could anticipate millions of dollars in new tax revenue from TXU—one reason more than forty local governments endorsed the TXU project.

And Texas's environment was deeply implicated. TXU predicted that the new plants' advanced pollution controls would reduce TXU's total smog-creating emissions by 20 percent and reduce demand for Texas's increasingly costly, diminishing, and essential natural gas.[2] Consultants for the Texas Environmental Quality Commission, TXU's state regulators, were expected to find the TXU plan mostly acceptable. But TXU's new facilities would still emit approximately 4,000 pounds of airborne mercury annually and possibly keep the state's two largest cities, Dallas and Houston, in violation of air quality controls required by the Clean Air Act—one reason both city mayors joined more than forty-one other urban governmental leaders in opposing the plan. In addition, one environmental health group cited a consultant's report that the new plant's CO^2 and toxic emissions would cause 240 additional deaths annually. The controversy appeared to involve no simple and sovereign solutions, only edgy but inevitable choices.[3]

Then, quite unexpectedly, the TXU controversy took an improbable turn even an optimistic environmentalist would not have predicted. A group of investors bought TXU for $32 billion—the largest leveraged buyout ever in U.S. corporate history—and, as a condition of the sale, TXU suspended its efforts to build eight of its eleven proposed new plants and committed to installing highly advanced pollution control technologies in the remaining planned utilities. An important actor in shaping this buyout was the national environmental organization, Natural Resources Defense Council, which had waged an unrelenting national campaign against TXU's predicted new climate warming emissions. In the end, one lesson, at least, seemed clear: climate warming was now virtually inseparable from any future debate over TXU's future.

The CO^2 controversy further agitated a mix of issues and interests already familiar to environmental policy making and guaranteed to produce a volatile politics: difficult decisions among expensive and contested policy alternatives, environmentally critical implications, disputed science, politically potent factions, and a governmental imperative to act. Predictably, the dispute next shifted to the Texas courts, where environmentalists hoped the judges would disrupt TXU's fast track. Meanwhile, the climate-warming issue continued to reshape environmental policy making in many other states.

From Greenhouse to White House to State House

Until the first decade of this century, climate warming and its entailed controversies involved primary federal agencies and laws. However, the states themselves are major producers of the climate-warming chemicals now predicted to create significant environmental changes and risks among the states themselves. "If the fifty states were to secede and become sovereign nations," notes environmental policy scholar Barry Rabe, "thirteen of them would rank among the top forty nations of the world in emissions." [4] Coal-fired power plants in the states already produce more than 40 percent of the nation's climate-warming emissions. By 2007, more than 150 new coal-fired electric power plants had been proposed among forty-two states. If a substantial number of these facilities were constructed and their CO_2 emissions were left uncontrolled, total U.S. climate-warming emissions would increase significantly.

Climate warming is predicted to have a profound impact on many states. In the Northeast, for example, scientific panels have estimated that moderate climate warming is likely to shift the range of many plant and animal species further northward, accelerate coastal erosion and wetlands losses, increase storm surge along the Eastern coast, and perhaps alter the agricultural growing seasons. In the West, many scientific experts believe that climate warming may result in longer, warmer summers; shorter winters with reduced snowfall; and gradual loss of important plant and animal species. This scientific discourse has drawn the states into active engagement—at times contentious struggles—with Washington about national climate policy.

While the George W. Bush administration was retreating from national and international efforts at governmental regulation of climate-warming emissions, the states were demonstrating initiative on the issue. Barry Rabe notes,

> By the middle of the current decade, more than half of the American states could be fairly characterized as actively involved in climate change, with one or more policies that promised to significantly reduce their level of greenhouse gas emissions. Virtually all states were beginning to at least study the issue and explore very modest remedies and some—such as California, Connecticut, New Jersey, and New York—were every bit as engaged on multiple policy fronts as international counterparts in European capitals. [5]

Just how rapidly climate-warming awareness and its political ramifications have permeated all levels of American government is suggested by the coincidence of two events in late 2006. In Washington, D.C., nine Supreme Court justices were deciding whether climate warming was imminent enough to justify a lawsuit by eight northeastern states intended to compel Washington to regulate CO^2 emissions. Thousands of miles westward in Arizona, representatives of fifty-five Native American nations met at the first Tribal Lands Climate Conference to discuss with environmental organizations the impact of climate warming on Native American lands. The politics of climate warming, like other issues on the agenda of the environmental movement, had become seamless from national to local governmental levels.[6]

Climate warming and the TXU controversy exemplify an ongoing political and scientific struggle, now global in scale, to mitigate the growing evidence of human-induced, severe environmental degradation manifest in practically every ecological domain. The remainder of this chapter is a snapshot from that struggle, a brief and candid illumination of the environmental movement's current ecological and political legacy. It is both a retrospective accounting of the strategic achievements, failures, and uncertainties that define contemporary American environmentalism and shape its ongoing agenda and a preview of the issues and ideas to be explored with greater depth and detail in later chapters.

The Environmental Legacy

In more than three decades since its inception, America's environmental movement has transformed the nation's environment in many significant ways. The evidence of important gains in environmental quality is substantial. One influential report card on international environmental performance, for example, commended the United States for continuing improvement in environmental management between 1996–2004, especially in regulating air, water, and pesticide pollutants during a period when the U.S. economy was vigorously growing. The report noted, in addition, that although the United States was disengaging from international negotiations to regulate climate warming during the George W. Bush administration, the United States still continued support of numerous other international programs.[7]

Perhaps most impressive has been the improvement of the nation's air quality. Ambient concentrations of sulfur oxides, carbon monoxide, nitrogen oxides, and particulates—all associated with serious human health disorders—have been reduced significantly; and many more acutely dangerous ambient air toxics, especially formaldehyde and lead, have been reduced drastically or virtually eliminated. Dangerous chemical and biological pollutants of major U.S. waterways, such as the Mississippi, Potomac, and Ohio Rivers, have been reduced sharply. Aggressive regulatory programs have reduced significantly the number of abandoned hazardous waste sites across the United States and, for the first time, compelled manufacturers and distributors of hazardous or toxic chemicals to comply with national standards for their transport and disposal. National testing programs now require more rigorous screening and testing of newly manufactured chemicals to protect human health and the environment. Numerous plant and animal species threatened with extinction, including the American bald eagle and the American panther, have been protected and, in some instances, restored to vitality. Equally important, the United States is committed to numerous regional and international treaties, such as the Montreal Protocol to reduce the global "ozone hole," testifying to a growing recognition that the quality of the nation's domestic environment and global environmental quality have become interdependent. Most important politically, these transformations are grounded in a durable national consensus that environmental protection must now be a first-order public concern—a remarkable emergence of a national ecological consciousness nonexistent a few decades ago.

Substantial though these transformations may be, the American environment remains significantly degraded in critical respects. More than 52 percent of the U.S. population—approximately 152 million Americans—live in 390 counties where unhealthful levels of either ozone or particulate pollution still prevail.[8] More than half the total area of the nation's biologically essential estuaries and almost half the nation's river miles are considered unacceptably polluted. The primary cause of this water degradation is still largely unregulated. Although testing may now be required to assess the public health risk from newly manufactured chemicals, surprisingly little information is available about the extent to which Americans are exposed to thousands of existing chemicals or about the possible health risks involved. Recent federal government estimates suggest that information on public exposure is available for less than 6 percent of more than 1,400 naturally occurring and manufactured chemicals considered to pose a human health threat.[9] The Environmental Protection Agency (EPA) has been able to assess the public health risks for an even smaller proportion of about 700 new chemicals introduced annually into commerce and industry. "EPA's review of new chemicals provides only limited assurance that health and environmental risks are identified," according to a report by the U.S. General Accounting Office, "because the agency has limited information with which to review them." In fact, one of the most compelling national environmental problems is the pervasive lack of reliable scientific information about current environmental quality and human exposure to environmental contaminants—data absolutely essential for sound environmental policy making. When environmental scientists convened in 1998 to create the first comprehensive, detailed assessment of the nation's environmental conditions, they discovered that they lacked sufficient information for almost half of the indicators considered essential to adequately characterize national environmental quality.[10]

It is increasingly apparent that the scope and scale of this ecological degradation was often gravely underestimated and the social and economic costs of pollution regulation frequently miscalculated badly when the nation's major environmental policies were enacted. For instance, Congress wrote legislation in 1976 requiring the EPA to ban or regulate any chemicals posing an unreasonable risk to human health but was unable to anticipate that more than 62,000 chemical substances might have to be evaluated to determine their toxicity. Nor could Congress predict when it wrote the Comprehensive Environmental Response, Compensation, and Liability Act of 1980 (CERCLA, popularly known as Superfund) to clean up the nation's worst abandoned chemical waste sites that more than 40,000 sites would be discovered by 2007, that 500 new sites would be identified annually, and that the initial funding would be virtually exhausted by the mid-1990s, thus requiring annual additional appropriations of $1.2 billion through at least 2010.[11] Similar examples of this sort are found in every domain of environmental concern. We know now that the seemingly inexorable expansion in the scale and cost of environmental restoration is often the consequence of better environmental monitoring and research revealing, often to considerable surprise, the true reach and complexity of environmental problems. When the U.S. environmental movement began, acid precipitation and ozone holes were scarcely imagined and global climate warming sounded like science fiction.

Improved understanding of environmental problems also comes at a political price, in the form of public frustration when existing policies fail to meet unrealistic predictions; rancorous debate over which parties or presidents are responsible for real or alleged policy failures; impatience with the pace of environmental restoration; and disputes over the credibility of scientific evidence linked to emerging environmental issues. These issues, and more, are inevitable yet essential to policy making in a democratic society. Thus, environmental protection is a work in progress. Today's environmental policy making is grounded in a legacy of past failure and success at environmental restoration mixed with a substantial measure of ambiguity and uncertainty about the implications for the future.

The Political Legacy: From Ronald Reagan to George W. Bush

Environmental quality today is also a political creation, as much a product of politics as it is of science or regulation. Embedded in the design of contemporary environmental policy is a political history that shaped, and still shapes, the evolution of these policies as surely as do environmental research or technology. Much of the history that matters has been written during the turbulent White House years since the presidency of Ronald Reagan.

The Reagan presidency rises like a great divide between American environmentalism in the 1970s and the early twenty-first century. On the far side lies what has been called environmentalism's political ascension, beginning in the 1960s and reaching into the early 1980s. The first Earth Day, in April 1970, launched the Environmental Decade, as the 1970s were styled. These ten years were especially important in creating the legal, political, and institutional foundations of the nation's environmental policies. That decade promoted an enduring public consciousness of environmental degradation and fashioned a broad public agreement on the need for governmental restoration and protection of environmental quality that has become part of the U.S. public policy consensus. It mobilized, organized, and educated a generation of environmental activists. The environmental movement prospered in a benign political climate ensured by a succession of White House occupants tolerant, if not always sympathetic, to its objectives.

All this changed with the advent of the Reagan administration. Reagan and his advisers believed he had been elected to bring regulatory relief to the U.S. economy, and environmental regulations were an early priority on the hit list of laws "needing" reform. Thus began a decade of regulatory revolt. The environmental movement regarded the Reagan administration as the most environmentally hostile in a half century and the president's regulatory reform as the cutting edge of a massive administrative assault on the institutional foundations of federal environmental law. The environmental movement, thrown on the defensive, expended most of its energies and resources through the 1980s in defending the legislative and administrative achievements of the Environmental Decade from the onslaught of Reagan's regulatory relief. The Reagan years severely tested the foundations of the environmental movement. The foundations held, but little was done to advance the implementation of existing policy or to address new and urgent environmental issues. To environmental leaders, the Reagan years meant, above all, dangerous drift and indecision, almost a decade of lost opportunities and intensifying environmental ills.

President George H. W. Bush awakened expectations of major reform from the environmental movement and brought to the White House a more sympathetic and active environmentalism. The senior Bush's performance never vindicated his promise to be the "environmental president," but his administration ended the pernicious impasse of the Reagan years with important, if episodic, new policy initiatives and administrative reforms. The EPA's morale and resources improved, the Bush administration actively promoted the most important reform in federal air pollution law since 1972—the Clean Air Act Amendments of 1990—and the U.S. Department of Energy (DOE) finally ended decades of federal deception and negligence by acknowledging publicly the federal government's responsibility for the appalling environmental contamination at military nuclear weapons facilities.

Nonetheless, the backside of Bush environmentalism was equally conspicuous: a reluctance to address global environmental issues such as climate warming or the preservation of biodiversity, a progressively hardening resistance to any new domestic environmental regulation, a failure to increase the EPA's staff and budget commensurate with its growing responsibilities, and low priority for environmentalism on the policy agenda, to name a few shortcomings. By the end of Bush's single term, it was apparent that his administration had restored only partially the resources essential for governmental management of the environment and had enacted only a few urgently needed policy initiatives. But the rush of history, abetted by science, politics, and economics, was carrying the nation into a new decade for which the crabbed pace and cramped vision of Bush environmentalism seemed inadequate.

Sometime deep in the twilight of the 1980s the political winds shifted again, eventually bringing back to the White House in the 1990s a presidency friendly to the environmental movement and aggressively committed to environmental regulation even if that involved tough rethinking about its goals and accomplishments. The environmental movement expected much of President Bill Clinton, especially since then-vice president Al Gore was an outspoken environmentalist and Clinton had cultivated environmentalist votes. In the end the Clinton administration was distinguished more by its ambitions than its accomplishments. Clinton generally reinvigorated environmental regulation and installed aggressive environmentalist administrators in strategic executive agencies such as the Department of the Interior and the EPA. He revived U.S. engagement in international environmental policy making, eventually committing the United States to the Kyoto Protocol to control global climate warming (which the Senate, however, refused to ratify). But Clinton confronted throughout most of his administration a hostile Republican congressional majority that thwarted most of his legislative initiatives. Clinton's turbulent two terms nonetheless resonated with a vision of environmental governance akin to the ambitious environmentalism of the 1970s, even as the mood of discontent with the existing regulatory regime hardened.

Then came Republican George W. Bush. To the wary environmental movement, Bush's succession to the White House seemed to announce a profoundly unsettling new regime emerging from the shadows of the bitterly remembered Reagan administration and enthusiastically embracing its environmental attitudes. The environmental movement, and most passionate environmentalists, vigorously opposed Bush's election, even though

Bush strongly rejected any implication that he would renew Reagan's assault on environmental regulation. Instead, Bush represented himself as a moderate environmentalist, a prudent reformer rather than an antienvironmental zealot. Nonetheless, Bush's relationship with the environmental movement was confrontational from the outset. His appointment of individuals closely associated with energy production and natural resource consumption to strategic leadership positions in the executive branch, especially in the Department of the Interior and the DOE, and the close association of Vice President Dick Cheney with the oil and gas industry, provoked deep misgiving among environmentalists. Subsequent events, including the president's energy plan; his persistent efforts to open federal lands, particularly the Arctic National Wildlife Refuge, to energy exploration; and his repudiation of an earlier commitment to an international agreement abating global climate warming seemed to confirm the dark suspicions about his environmental sensibilities already pervasive among environmental organizations.[12]

During the Bush administration, the EPA did strengthen national air pollution controls on particulates and mercury emissions, but to environmentalists these, and other administration initiatives, were too laggard and limited. Environmentalists also complained that the Bush administration routinely suppressed or rewrote scientific data to satisfy its ideological prejudices on environmental issues. As U.S. involvement and public frustration with the war in Iraq escalated, environmental affairs seemed increasingly marginalized in the Bush White House—Republican strategists, in any case, had largely conceded the environmentalist vote to Democrats. Bush's first EPA administrator, Christie Todd Whitman, had complained at the end of her term that the Bush administration seemed condemned to "an eternal fistfight" with environmental groups.[13] Her remark become prophetic. "George W. Bush will go down in history as America's worst environmental president," snapped a leading environmentalist spokesperson, as if to confirm Whitman's prediction.[14]

Whoever is president and whatever his policy course, the White House will be at center stage of environmental policy making. Congress, the courts, and the bureaucracy will play their part. Still, presidential activism or inactivism profoundly affects the style and impact of environmental decision making throughout government. This effect will be evident again in Chapter 3, in which we examine more closely the strategies and tactics of this presidential influence.

Ongoing Challenges: Present and Future

The first Earth Day in 1970 was the Big Bang of U.S. environmental politics, launching the country on a sweeping social learning curve of ecological management never before experienced, or attempted, by any nation. No challenge has been more fundamental to American environmentalism since Earth Day 1970 than the constructive adaptation of that original vision of environmental conservation and renewal, once written into law and embedded into the political and economic structure of American life, to continuing domestic and global changes. On that first Earth Day almost half the Americans living today had not been born, and the new movement's youthful leaders are now well into middle age. A whole new generation has since matured, and with that generation, U.S. environmental politics has been, and continues to be, transformed. Several years into the twenty-first century, Americans now have almost four decades' collective experience of unprecedented experiment in environmental management. The ultimate test of the United States's ambitious regime of environmental regulation will be not how well it was conceived but how well it endures. That endurance depends largely on how well American science, political culture, and environmental leadership can learn from past experience and creatively apply the lessons learned to several profound problems now recognized as inherent in all environmental policy making—issues that run like deep and defining themes throughout every chapter in this book.

Implementation Issues

The character and pace of policy implementation changes continually in response to shifting public moods; to ebbs and flows in crucial resources such as money and personnel invested in carrying out environmental policies; to changes in political party control of Congress, the White House, and state governments; and to other changes discussed in later chapters. In short, policy implementation is an unfolding and variable thing, powerfully driven by economic, political, and cultural forces. Practically every important environmental ill has been targeted by a major federal law, but delay and difficulty in program implementation routinely impede enforcement. The majority of important environmental laws have been implemented at a plodding pace, and portions of all the laws exhibit regulatory rigor mortis. Although practically all factions agree on the need for a remedy, a laggardly pace is the norm.

One reason for this plodding pace is the growing complexity of the regulatory process. The average size of major environmental statutes has inflated from about 50 pages in the 1970s to more than 500 pages currently. The original Clean Air Act (1970) was 68 pages, the Clean Air Act Amendments of 1990 weighed in at 788 pages, and the regulations required for their implementation will exceed 10,000 pages. To create the elephantine regulations necessary to implement these complex laws and to apply the procedures in the appropriate instances can consume an enormous amount of time, as subsequent chapters reveal. Regulation of toxic substances provides an illustration. The average time required by the Toxic Substances Control Act (1976) for the complete testing of sixteen common chemicals (a small fraction of the total that must be evaluated under the law) from their initial selection through final EPA review of the test data has been eight years.[15]

Another important source of regulatory delay is the increasing mismatch between the responsibilities assigned to environmental agencies and the budgetary resources required for their accomplishment. Although the EPA's workload increased enormously in the 1980s, its budget failed to keep pace. At the beginning of George W. Bush's administration, for instance, the EPA's annual appropriations were below that of 1980, when measured in constant dollars (that is, after adjustment for inflation).[16] Many deficiencies in current program implementation are the legacy of a decade of underfunding. In early 1993, for instance, the EPA was overwhelmed by the scientific and administrative complexity of its task and was able to reassess and register only thirty-one of more than 20,000 older pesticides whose reevaluations had been ordered by Congress as long ago as 1972 and again in 1988. Despite a congressionally mandated deadline of 1997 to complete the job, the General Accounting Office reported that "the program may not be completed until 2006"—and it wasn't completed even then. Meanwhile, "most of these products may continue to be sold and distributed even though knowledge of their health and environmental effects is incomplete." Enforcement of most environmental legislation also depends on voluntary compliance by regulated interests, public and private, but the responsible federal and state agencies often lack the resources to monitor compliance with the law. Few states, for example, routinely inspect public and private drinking water systems, even though such inspections are required by the Safe Drinking Water Act (1974). Half of the nation's 59,000 large water systems and one fifth of the 139,000 small ones are not monitored to ensure that water is not contaminated by sewage or runoff with pesticides.[17] Quite often, information essential to effective regulation is missing or fragmentary, and the available information is often surprisingly haphazard. Many states, for instance, lack the technical resources to develop numerical standards for many groundwater contaminants and instead depend on evidence of environmental damage or public health risks before acting to control these substances.

Economic growth and population expansion often diminish the effectiveness of pollution controls over time. The automobile emission controls and reduced lead levels in gasoline required by the Clean Air Act together have lowered the average new car's hydrocarbon and carbon monoxide emissions significantly But the number of automobiles in the United States has increased nearly 71 percent, from 80.4 million in 1970 to 137 million in 2006, with an additional 60 million new trucks since 1970. This vehicle population explosion counteracts the emission reductions achieved for individual vehicles and leads eventually to widespread urban violations of federal air quality standards.

Other potent impediments to program implementation include the litigation virtually predestined for any major regulation, difficult coordination between state and federal governments, bureaucratic infighting, and much else that will become apparent in later chapters. Collectively these implementation problems constitute one of the most urgent, and daunting, political and administrative tasks of the twenty-first century.

Rising Costs

By most estimates the national cost of environmental regulation does not seem excessive or likely to inhibit healthy economic growth. Currently the United States spends about $120 billion annually for environmental control, or about 2 percent of the gross national product.[18] Overall, the annual proportion of national expenditures invested in pollution control appears to have decreased since 1990.[19] Although aggregate expenditures increased only moderately after 2000, these expenditures conceal troublesome details. The cost of individual regulatory programs is soaring, often inflicting heavy unanticipated costs on specific economic sectors, depleting regulatory resources, and compelling a search for scarce new funding sources. For example:

• *Superfund,* created to clean up the nation's numerous abandoned hazardous waste sites. After originally authorizing $1.6 billion for the project, Congress was compelled in the mid-1980s to increase spending to $15.2 billion, and estimates now suggest the program will require annual congressional supplements of at least $1.2 billion until at least 2010.[20]

• *Diesel fuel regulations for school buses,* soon to be proposed by the federal government and already required in some states. Meeting the standard can cost from $7500 to $100,000 per bus. California, the first state to require stricter standards, will spend $715 million to implement them.[21]

• *Federal storm water runoff regulations* will require the District of Columbia to spend $1.9 billion to completely renovate its antiquated sewer system.[22]

• *Groundwater samples for water pollution control* can exceed $200,000 for digging a required well while soil samples may cost from $500 to $5000, depending on the number of contaminants present.

The roster of inflationary programs has become a virtual catalog of the nation's major environmental laws.

Unanticipated environmental problems, unexpected scientific complexities, and inexperience with new regulations are common causes of massive cost overruns. Proponents of regulatory programs, particularly the congressional committees and staff writing the laws, are often ignorant (sometimes intentionally) about hidden costs. When Congress ordered the EPA to issue regulations requiring communities to filter and chlorinate their drinking water—a safeguard against giardiasis, a waterborne intestinal disease—it did not specify that the cost might approach $5 billion plus $500 million to $700 million in annual operating expenses.[23] In another instance, the unanticipated difficulties in controlling the formation of low-level ozone and the emission of nitrogen oxides by trucks and automobiles are two major reasons why achieving the goals of the Clean Air Act is estimated to have cost at least $80 billion more than the $60 billion already spent by federal, state, and local governments before the act was amended in 1990.[24] The litany of other inflationary provocations includes administrative delay, litigation, bureaucratic bungling, waste, missing information, and political obstruction. Whatever the reasons, excessive costs divert public and private capital from more productive investment, promote economic inefficiency, impair competitiveness in some industries, and increase consumer costs. And bloated budgets become a cudgel in the hands of opponents eager to beat back demands for essential improvements in environmental management.

Environmentalists traditionally have approached discussions about the cost of environmental regulation with considerable wariness. They suspect, often correctly, that estimates of regulatory costs produced by business or other regulated interests are inflated deliberately. (However, they are not equally dubious about the considerably lower estimates they usually produce.) They also believe that benefit-cost comparisons applied to environmental policies are usually biased because it is much easier to monetize the costs of regulation than the benefits. Even more controversial is the problem of ecological valuation—assigning a value to wetlands, for example, when deciding whether to convert them to commercial development or to protect an endangered species whose habitat is threatened.

Moreover, many environmentalists consider it ethically irresponsible to allow economic costs to weigh heavily in making environmental regulations. Protecting human health and safety, and preserving environmental quality for future generations, are assumed to be preeminent values when compared with any monetary costs that might be attached to their achievement.

But spiraling costs are changing traditional environmental attitudes. Leaving aside predictable and usually unresolvable arguments over the "real" cost of environmental regulations, the fact of sharply rising costs has compelled many major environmental leaders to seek creative strategies for reducing the expense and to collaborate in this effort with the businesses and industries being regulated. This search for creative new approaches has affected the current policy debate in several ways. First, proposals to shift the primary objective of many current pollution laws, such as the Clean Air Act, from eliminating pollution to reducing exposure to the pollutants have become a major reform issue. This debate is explored in Chapter 4. Suffice it to note here that the proponents of reform believe that reducing the risk of exposure, rather than attempting to eliminate pollutants, is a far less expensive and more technologically feasible objective. Second, rising regulatory costs have focused more attention on eliminating pollutants (referred to as pollution prevention) in production processes as an alternative to "end of the pipe" pollution treatment. Third, rising costs have encouraged all sides to give more attention to identifying the trade-offs between regulatory costs and benefits in an effort to identify where the limits of acceptability may be—in short, to identify the threshold of unacceptably high costs. Fourth, many environmental leaders and organizations have become more receptive to economic incentives and other market strategies as substitutes for traditional administrative procedures in securing compliance with environmental regulation on the assumption that market approaches may be more economically efficient and environmentally effective. Recently, national and international trading in "emission rights" has become an increasingly popular proposal by those favoring market-oriented strategies for pollution control.

Still, any debate about the importance of economic considerations in environmental regulation excites an ideological passion among many environmental leaders and groups who profoundly believe environmental values must never be compromised by marketplace logic. The environmental movement likely will remain divided over the wisdom of economic reform. Reform will come anyway, slowly and divisively.

Evolving Science and Technology

When the political leadership of American environmentalism set out its initial policy agenda following Earth Day 1970, the ozone hole, global climate warming, genetically altered foods, endocrine disrupters, leaking underground toxic storage tanks, ionizing radiation, indoor air pollution, and a multitude of other environmental issues—as well as many thousands of chemicals now common to U.S. commerce and industry—were unimagined or unknown. All these matters, and many more currently on the environmental movement's priority list, are largely the product of scientific research in the past several decades. Later chapters observe how science contributes constructively to environmental management through, for example, the discovery of environmentally benign substitutes for more harmful chemicals such as chlorofluorocarbons (CFCs). But the relentless evolution of scientific research can also frustrate, confuse, and discredit existing environmental policy by producing all sorts of new and unexpected discoveries. For example, twenty-five years after the EPA set the original air pollution standard for airborne particulates, a serious public health problem, the agency had to revise the standard, making it significantly more stringent. The result was enormous new public and private costs, attended by a nasty political backlash, largely because later research convincingly demonstrated that the earlier standard was based on insufficient data—although it was the best available at the time.

Ironically, the environmental movement's success often contributes inadvertently to this disruptive research: environmental advocacy has greatly enlarged the resources and productivity of U.S. environmental science, thereby accelerating the pace of new discoveries that often reveal deficiencies in the scientific basis of existing environmental policy. The environmental movement has caused the United States to consider basic and applied environmental research as a much higher scientific priority and to invest vastly more human and material resources in environmental science than existed prior to 1970. In fact, as political scientist Lynton Caldwell observed,

> [E]cology was regarded by many biologists as a dubious candidate for serious scientific status; indeed, some biologists sympathetic to the objectives of ecology preferred the term "environmental biology," responding to the opinion of some prestigious biologists that ecology was not a science.[25]

The rising scientific priority of ecology has had at least four important practical consequences: the initiation of basic research into the human and environmental consequences of exposure to thousands of chemicals and chemical compounds, the establishment of baseline data on the ecological status of natural resources, the discovery of new ecological laws, and the evolution of new theories that advance ecological understanding.

This rising tide of ecological science poses several continuing challenges to environmental scientists and policy makers. First, it can produce new data indicating that prior policy decisions may have been based on inadequate information and must be revised—perhaps with great political or legal difficulty and at considerable expense. Policy makers can easily and unjustly appear to have been ignorant, or impetuous, for having made decisions—often based on the best currently available information and frequently under strong public pressure—which later and better research shows were incorrect. For example, to meet the public health standards of the Clean Air Act, the EPA in 2006 slightly lowered the short-term threshold for public exposure to particulates (soot) as a result of scientific research conducted since the original standard was set several decades previously. Although the new standard, described by the EPA as "the most health-protective in U.S. history," is assumed to create from $9 billion to $70 billion in long-term health and visibility benefits, it is also estimated to cost electric utilities alone about $400 million yearly to implement.[26]

Scientific research can also produce ambiguous, fragmentary, or contradictory data concerning the existence or extent of an environmental problem—especially at an early stage in the research—at a time when policy makers nonetheless feel compelled to do something about the issue. Sometimes a solution—or the appearance of one—seems so urgent that policy makers believe they cannot wait for additional research, or perhaps additional research may never satisfactorily resolve the issue. Sometimes the scientific evidence about the impact of an environmental regulation may also be inconclusive. Thus, science sometimes seems to frustrate the task of fashioning and evaluating environmental policy. The continuing scientific ambiguity about the ecological impact of manmade chemicals mimicking human hormones (often called "endocrine disrupters"), or the persisting controversy about the ecological impact of species loss, illustrates this sort of science problem.

Science is also slowly, sometimes painfully, teaching the public and its policy makers that ecological reality is often more complex than had been assumed. And it can surprise. Consider an outbreak of cryptosporidiosis, a potentially severe human intestinal infection caused by a waterborne parasite, that occurred in Milwaukee in 1997, infecting 403,000 people and killing more than 50 of them. At the time, Milwaukee's public water supply complied with all federal drinking water standards intended to protect the public from such well-known health hazards, and public officials were initially perplexed by the disease outbreak. Subsequent research implied that Milwaukee's epidemic of cryptosporidiosis was related to the turbidity (the concentration of sediment) of the city's drinking water, although turbidity in large public water systems had not previously been associated with microbial contamination. "Milwaukee was a wake-up call," observed one of the EPA's drinking water experts in explaining why the agency would carefully reevaluate its drinking water standards for turbidity from that point on.[27] Milwaukee's problem reveals characteristics common to the ecological surprises that often challenge policy makers. It involved a complex web of causality spanning great geographic distances, embracing different environmental media, and posing many alternative modes of explanation. Cause and effect could not easily be documented and sometimes spanned years or decades. The puzzle also implied related problems not yet discovered, reminding those involved that ecology remains a science rich with uncertainty. In addition, it appeared almost thirty years after the nation's so-called environmental era began in 1970. It is now clear that no simple and sovereign explanations for the nation's continuing environmental problems will suffice. Most ecological ills are the product of several factors in different, often interacting, combinations involving technology, government, science, and the inherent nature of the environment itself.

Finally, scientific research can complicate environmental policy making and, in the process, drive up the cost and time involved in remedying environmental ills by disclosing, instead of timely solutions or quick answers to an ecological problem, the unanticipated need for new information. Pentagon planners call these discoveries the "unk-unks"—the unknown unknowns, the kinds of information one doesn't know are needed until a problem is investigated. Consider, for instance, the experience of scientists trying to explain the sudden, dramatic increase in fish kills between 1991 and 1993 within North Carolina's vast estuaries. Unprecedented millions of fish were floating to the water surface with large bleeding sores, often accompanied by a strange smell that burned the eyes and throat—not the smell of decaying fish. At first, investigators assumed the familiar explanation: lack of dissolved oxygen in the water, a seasonal deficiency in the estuarine environment that sometimes becomes severe enough to kill fish. Additional study disclosed no severe oxygen deficiency. But extensive fish biopsies gradually revealed something wholly unexpected: the presence of enormous quantities of a tiny one-celled creature, a dinoflagellate of the species *Pfiesteria piscicida,* an apparently harmless organism seldom studied and never associated with extensive fish kills. So biologists began to observe *Pfiesteria* habits intensively. They discovered that when estuarine nutrient levels of nitrogen and phosphorous increased significantly, *Pfiesteria* could transform into a murderous little organism with a personality akin to the star of the science fiction movie *Alien,* multiplying to staggering numbers and aggressively attacking and consuming huge fish populations. The *Pfiesteria,* in turn, were stimulated to multiply by the high nutrient levels in the water, apparently caused by agricultural and animal feedlot runoff. Thus, an unk-unk—in this case, the complete life cycle of *Pfiesteria*—unexpectedly uncovered in the course of investigating a fish kill, became a critical component in understanding and eliminating the problem itself.[28]

Sustainable Development and Ecosystem Management

Between the Florida Keys and Orlando, Florida, is presently under way what is predicted to be the largest, most expensive, and most scientifically complex environmental restoration project ever attempted anywhere. The South Florida Ecosystem Restoration Project, popularly called the Everglades Restoration, intends to restore and protect for future generations the ecologically endangered Everglades, a globally unique, irreplaceable subtropical ecosystem gravely damaged by urban development and agricultural cultivation. The project embraces 25,000 square miles of Florida's interior, coastal lands, and water. It will cost more than $10.9 billion and require at least thirty years to complete—if the plan is successful. The Everglades Restoration is one of a half dozen massive federal ecosystem management projects under way across the United States. These projects are markers along the way of a profound transformation in environmental policy associated with the growing importance of "sustainable development" as a foundation for environmental management.

The Challenge of Sustainability

The 1987 publication of *Our Common Future* by the World Commission on Environment and Development (WCED; often called "the Brundtland Report") rapidly advanced an already growing concern with "sustainable development" into a transcendent goal for the international environmental movement. The WCED's definition of sustainable development as "meeting the needs of the present without compromising the ability of future generations to meet their own needs" has become virtually synonymous with the concept itself.[29] Over time, as international environmental scholar Jonathan M. Harris observed, this definition has been interpreted to include three components:

• *Economic:* "An economically sustainable system must be able to produce goods and services on a continuing basis, to maintain manageable levels of government and external debt, and to avoid extreme sectoral imbalances which damage agricultural and industrial production."
• *Social:* "A socially sustainable system must achieve distributional equity, adequate provision for social services including health and education, gender equality, and political accountability and participation."
• *Environmental:* "An environmentally sustainable system must maintain a stable resource base, avoiding over-exploitation of renewable resource systems . . . and depleting non-renewable resources. . . . This includes maintenance of biodiversity, atmospheric stability, and other ecosystem functions."[30]

A multitude of governmental entities, private institutions, and advocacy organizations worldwide, most created since 1990, testify to the expanding impact of sustainable development as a strategic goal for environmental policy and politics. In 1992 the United Nations Commission on Sustainable Development was created, and the next year President Clinton signed an executive order creating the President's Council on Sustainable Development, directed by then–vice president Gore. In 1996 the EPA created its Sustainable Communities Network. The global salience of sustainability as an environmental concern was reaffirmed in 2002 by the UN World Summit on Sustainable Development in Johannesburg, South Africa. By 2007, an international directory listed 51,500 organizations claiming some concern for sustainable development. A U.S. national directory cited more than 2,700 private or public entities involved with environmental sustainability.

The concept of sustainable development is loaded with ambiguities that can reduce it to a cliché and weighted with goals that can seem competitive, even contradictory. Protection of nonrenewable resources, for instance, may appear inconsistent with sustained economic production. Adequate provision of health and education services may appear to require reduction of public spending to protect biodiversity. Thus, there is ample opportunity for disagreement over how sustainability should be defined, how it should be institutionalized, and which among a bounty of desirable goals ought to receive national and international priority. Some of the most divisive political controversies within the environmental movement arise over these issues.

Implementing Sustainability: Ecosystem Management

Despite the difficulties, policies intended to promote sustainability are being created and implemented through public policy at all U.S. governmental levels. One significant illustration is the growing importance of ecosystem management in federal resource planning. The rapid development of environmental science and increasing experience with environmental policy making has compelled a realization that greater emphasis must be given to the inherent ecological value of natural resources and that successful ecological restoration often requires planning on a vast spatial and temporal scale never previously attempted.[31]

A fundamental principle of ecosystem management is that wise resource use must involve "the integration of ecological, economic, and social principles to manage biological and physical systems in a manner safeguarding the long term sustainability, natural diversity, and productivity of the landscape." This means that the primary goal of natural resource planning should be "to develop and implement management that conserves, restores and maintains the ecological integrity, productivity, and biological diversity of public lands."[32] In short, a natural resource should not be managed primarily to satisfy human economic interests nor valued mostly in dollar terms. From this perspective, forests, rivers, wetlands, and other natural resources such as the Everglades should be administered in a manner protecting *all* their natural benefits, including habitat for fish and wildlife; clean drinking water for communities; wood, fiber, forage, and ecological functions; as well as human recreational and economic uses.

A second premise of ecosystem management is that large, endangered natural systems such as river valleys, forestlands, and wetlands—often the most ecologically valuable natural resources—should be restored or protected as whole, interrelated ecosystems, even if they are geographically enormous, rather than divided geographically and managed by different agencies and governments with different missions and often conflicting policies. Another essential principle is that protecting natural systems requires not just sound scientific strategies but also a partnership in planning between scientists and all the important economic, political, and cultural interests (the stakeholders) affected by the natural system. Equally significant, the ultimate objective of both approaches is to sustain the resilience and productivity of natural resources well into the future: the planning horizon is deliberately cast in terms of decades or centuries rather than a few years. Although both approaches require ambitious, often untested policy initiatives, they have substantially elevated the level of creative thinking among policy makers and have encouraged more soundly conceived environmental planning.

Sustainable development through ecosystem management is also politically contentious and inherently risky in the United States. It seems to defy two hundred years of past federal, state, and local natural resource planning with its deeply embedded assumption that government should manage natural resources primarily for their economic value and human utility. Powerful private interests, such as energy producers, timber companies, livestock managers, land developers, recreation industries, and their allies compete relentlessly for access to natural resources administered by public agencies. Indeed, almost every economic interest associated with natural resource consumption strives persistently to preempt competing claims on such resources. Furthermore, numerous governmental bureaucracies responsible for public resource management, agencies whose historic mission has been to facilitate private access to resources in the public domain, cannot easily adapt their deeply rooted organizational cultures to the newer ideas of ecosystem management and sustainable development. Moreover, many states are at best ambivalent about the new planning principles because the traditional economic exploitation of their natural resources, however ecologically disruptive it might be, also brought new jobs, increased tax revenues, and accelerated local economic development. For these and other reasons to be explored in later chapters, the political and economic future of ecosystem management and sustainable development policies promises to be turbulent and problematic.

Plan for the Book

This chapter has introduced, broadly and briefly, the major themes that later chapters will explore in more depth and detail. It has also provided a review of many significant events since Earth Day 1970 that define the political setting for environmental policy making today, thus creating a present sense of place in the rapidly evolving politics of American environmentalism. The following chapters progress from a broad overview of the major governmental institutions, private interests, and political forces shaping all environmental policy today to an increasingly sharp focus on the distinctive issues, actors, and interests involved with specific environmental problems.

Chapter 2 (Making Policy: The Process) describes the phases of the policy cycle that shapes all major environmental policies. Included is an exploration of the influence of the Constitution and U.S. political culture on this process. Also discussed are the nature of environmental pressure groups and other stakeholders in the policy process and the important role of public opinion and the scientific community in policy making.

Chapter 3 (Making Policy: Institutions and Politics) describes the specific U.S. governmental institutions, private interests, and political forces engaged with environmental policy making. The narrative includes a discussion of the presidency, the important bureaucracies, Congress, and the courts. Also discussed is the importance of political events such as changing congressional majorities, economic growth or recession, shifting public moods, and other related occurrences.

Almost all environmental policy making entails some common issues. Chapter 4 (Common Policy Challenges: Risk Assessment and Environmental Justice) explores two of the most scientifically contentious and politically controversial of these issues: risk analysis and environmental justice. Risk analysis is concerned with determining whether specific chemicals, industrial processes, consumer products, and environmental contaminants, among many other things, pose a significant threat to public health or the environment and, if they do, how they should be regulated. Environmental justice investigates whether various social groups, particularly minorities of color and economically disadvantaged individuals, are disproportionately exposed to environmental risks or denied reasonable opportunity to protect themselves from such risks.

Among the longest running and least resolvable conflicts in environmental policy making is contention over the economic cost and fairness of environmental regulations. Chapter 5 (More Choice: The Battle over Regulatory Economics) looks at two major aspects of this issue: the use of benefit-cost analysis to evaluate environmental regulations, and proposals to replace current methods of environmental regulation with policies that rely on market forces to achieve results. Discussed are the major arguments and interests aligned on different sides of these issues, together with evidence about the impact of proposed economic reforms when they have been instituted.

Chapter 6 (Command and Control in Action: Air and Water Pollution Regulation) describes the nation's major air and water pollution control laws and evaluates their impact. The chapter explains how these laws illustrate the command-and-control style of regulation now common in the United States. Also described are the substantive elements of the Clean Air Act (1970) and the Federal Water Pollution Control Act Amendments (1972). Reviewed are accomplishments and deficiencies resulting from these major air and water pollution laws, together with characteristic policy-making challenges created by the scientific and economic requirements of air and water pollution control.

Chapter 7 (The Regulatory Thicket: Toxic and Hazardous Substances) focuses on the major regulatory legislation to control environmental dangers posed by chemical, biological, and radioactive agents. The major laws examined include the Toxic Substances Control Act (1976), the Resource Conservation and Recovery Act (1974), and Superfund legislation. The chapter briefly describes the major elements of these important laws and examines their impact in the context of determining whether these laws have accomplished their purpose to control the manufacture and distribution of ecologically harmful chemicals and to safely regulate toxic waste from the cradle to the grave.

Chapter 8 (Energy: Nuclear Dreams, Black Gold, and Vanishing Crude) describes the nation's primary energy resources and increasing reliance on fossil fuels, together with the ecological, economic, and political risks entailed. The chapter focuses special attention on diminishing petroleum supplies, the attractions and environmental dangers associated with increased coal production, and the environmental problems linked to nuclear power. Also explored are future energy policy options and the ecological implications, especially in the contentious trade-off between coal and nuclear power as future energy sources and the challenges created by greater reliance on energy conservation and energy efficiency as alternatives to major reliance on traditional energy sources.

Chapter 9 (635 Million Acres of Politics: The Battle for Public Lands) focuses on the historic political battle over the use of more than 700 million acres of public land, mostly controlled by the federal government. The narrative examines the major economic and environmental interests engaged in a century-long battle over access to timber, natural gas, petroleum, grazing land, hydroelectric power, and other important resources on federal land. Described are the major federal agencies caught in the middle of these conflicts, such as the Department of the Interior and the U.S. Forest Service. The chapter also discusses the major legislation these agencies are expected to implement in managing these resources and the resulting problems, including the obstacles to achieving ecosystem management on federal lands.

Chapter 10 (The United States and Climate Diplomacy: The Emerging Politics of Global Environmentalism) explains why the United States can no longer satisfactorily regulate or protect its own environment without a growing engagement in regional and international environmental policy making and then reviews the nation's erratic involvement in global environmental policy making. Discussed are the ozone hole, acid precipitation, global climate warming, and sustainable development, to illustrate the compelling need for this international involvement and to illuminate some of the major political opportunities and difficulties posed for the United States by international environmental diplomacy. Finally, the chapter identifies the implications of U.S. environmental diplomacy for achieving sustainable national and international development.

Conclusion

In calendar time, the presidential election of George W. Bush introduced the fourth decade of the environmental era proclaimed in the 1970s. In political time, it commenced an uncertain season for environmentalists now deep into that era, a season of conflicting implications and richly contradictory experiences. From the perspective of policy making, a sense of frustration and impasse nurtured by the bitterly divisive conflict between organized environmentalism and the White House has permeated the era, yet evidence is abundant that environmental leaders have enormously enlarged the temporal and geographic scope of their policy vision to embrace sustainable development, ecosystem management, and global ecological restoration. Improvements in environmental quality have become increasingly apparent, sometimes impressive, yet regulatory achievements often fall gravely below expectations. Environmentalism has matured to the point where its organizational advocates can reflect critically on past experience and accept the need for rethinking and reforming their policy agenda, especially the need to moderate the escalating cost of environmental protection and to find more effective ways to implement pollution regulation. At the same time, the rapid progress of environmental science reveals with increasing acuteness the need to improve significantly the quality of the science base on which environmental policy is grounded. Environmentalism is now firmly rooted in U.S. political culture, yet its electoral force often seems surprisingly feeble.

In many ways, it is the best of times and the worst of times for environmentalism. In no other period has environmentalism seemed more politically potent, armed with powerful organized advocacy, legislative authority, public approval, and scientific credibility and seasoned with political experience. Nevertheless, as this chapter amply demonstrates, at no time have the scientific and political challenges confronting the environmental movement seemed more formidable.

Suggested Readings

Davies, J. Clarence, and Jan Mazurek. *Regulating Pollution: Does the U.S. System Work?* Washington, D.C.: Resources for the Future, 1997.

Graham, Mary. *The Morning after Earth Day: Practical Environmental Politics.* Washington, D.C.: Brookings Institution Press, 1999.

Hayes, Samuel P. *Beauty, Health, and Permanence: Environmental Politics in the United States, 1955–1985.* New York: Oxford University Press, 1987.

Lomborg, Bjorn. *The Skeptical Environmentalist: Measuring the Real State of the World.* New York: Cambridge University Press, 2001.

Mazmanian, Daniel A., and Michael E. Kraft. *Toward Sustainable Communities: Transition and Transformations in Environmental Policy.* Cambridge, Mass.: MIT Press, 1999.

Ophuls, William, and A. Stephen Boyan Jr. *Ecology and the Politics of Scarcity Revisited: The Unraveling of the American Dream.* New York: W. H. Freeman, 1992.

Simon, Julian L. *Hoodwinking the Nation.* Washington, D.C.: Cato Institute, 2000.

Vig, Norman J., and Michael E. Kraft, eds. *Environmental Policy: New Directions for the 21st Century.* 5th ed. Washington, D.C.: CQ Press, 2000.

Notes

1. The TXU controversy is summarized from Matthew L. Wald, "Texas Utility Plans 11 Plants Even as Tough Emission Rules Seem Inevitable," *New York Times,* November 7, 2006, 1A; Environmental Defense, "How Big is Big?" www.environmentaldefense.org/mediacenter.cfm (September 5, 2006); Associated Press, "U.S. Coal Plant Boom Poses Major Ecological, Economic Questions," *Dallas Morning News,* October 16, 2006, A1; Public Citizen Litigation Group, "Public Citizen Defends Environmental Nonprofit from Texas Energy Company," www.citizen.org/litigation (October 24, 2006); Donna Mottola, "Coal's Body Count," *Austin Chronicle,* December 1, 2006, 1; Eric Griffey, "Taking Lumps over Coal," *Fort Worth Weekly,* December 12, 2006, 7.
2. TXU Corporation, "Texas Air Quality Improves Dramatically in Past 20 Years," www.reliabletexaspower.com (December 14, 2006).
3. "New Analysis Tallies Premature Deaths From New Coal-Fired Power Plants," www.cleartheair.org (December 14, 2006).
4. Barry G. Rabe, "Second Generation Climate Policies in the American States: Proliferation, Diffusion, and Reorganization," *Paper Presented at the Wilson Center Conference on Climate Change Politics in North America* (Washington DC: The Wilson Center for Scholars, 2006), 1.
5. Ibid., 2.
6. Corinne Purtill, "Tribes See Effect of Climate Change," *Arizona Republic,* December 7, 2006, 1.
7. Norman J. Vig, "Making the Grade? OECD Environmental Performance Reviews: United States," *Environment* 48, no. 7 (September 2006): 40–43.
8. American Lung Association, "State of the Air 2005: Executive Summary," http://lung action.org/reports/sota05exec_summ.html (January 3, 2007).
9. U.S. General Accounting Office, "Chemical Risk Assessment: Selected Federal Agencies, Procedures, Assumptions and Policies," Document No. GAO 01-810 (August 2001), 16.
10. Robert O'Malley, Kent Davender-Bares, and William C. Clark, " 'Better' Data: Not as Simple as It Might Seem," *Environment Magazine* (March 2003): 9–18.
11. Katherine Probst and David Konisky, *Superfund's Future: What Will It Cost?* Executive Summary (Washington, D.C.: Resources for the Future, 2001).
12. The environmentalist indictment of George W. Bush's administration is summarized in Natural Resources Defense Council, *Rewriting the Rules, Year-End Report 2002: The Bush Administration's Assault on the Environment* (Washington, D.C.: Natural Resources Defense Council, January 2003); and U.S. Congress, House of Representatives, Committee on Government Reform—Minority Staff, Special Investigations Division, *Politics and Science in the Bush Administration: Prepared for Rep. Henry W. Waxman* (August 2003).

13. Katherine Q. Seelye, "Whitman Quits as E.P.A. Chief," *New York Times*, May 22, 2003, 1A.
14. Robert F. Kennedy Jr., "Crimes against Nature, www.rollingstone.com/politics/story/5939345/crimes_against_nature/ (March 12, 2007).
15. U.S. General Accounting Office, "Status of EPA's Reviews of Chemicals under the Chemical Testing Program," Report No. GAO/RCED 92-31FS (October 1991), 27.
16. Gerald Andrews Emison, "Patterns of National Environmental Strategy: Political Alignment, Leadership and Administrative Choice in EPA 1980–2000," paper presented at the annual conference of the American Political Science Association, August 30, 2002, Boston, Mass., 14.
17. Michael Decourcy Hines, "Survey Finds Flaws in States' Water Inspections," *New York Times*, April 15, 1993, A14; U.S. General Accounting Office, "Widening Gap between Needs and Available Resources Threatens Vital EPA Program," Report No. GAO/RCED 92-184 (July 1992).
18. U.S. Department of Commerce, Bureau of the Census, *Statistical Abstract of the United States, 1996* (Washington, D.C.: Government Printing Office, 1997).
19. For estimates on national pollution expenditures and their impact, see William A. Pizer and Raymond Kopp, "Calculating the Costs of Environmental Regulation" (Washington, D.C.: Resources for the Future), Discussion Paper 03-06 (March 2003); and U.S. Environmental Protection Agency, Office of Policy Planning and Evaluation, *The Costs of a Clean Environment* (Washington, D.C.: Environmental Protection Agency, 1990), v–viii.
20. Katherine Probst and David Konisky, *Superfund's Future*.
21. Janet Wilson, "Aging U.S. School Buses Still Fouling Air," *Los Angeles Times*, May 25, 2006, A14.
22. Lisa Rein, "As Pressure Increases, So Do Ways to Control Pollution," *Washington Post*, May 23, 2006, A01.
23. John Cushman, "Efficient Pollution Rule Under Attack,"*New York Times*, June 28, 1995.
24. "Cost of Clean Air Bill Assailed," *New York Times*, March 8, 1988.
25. Lynton K. Caldwell, *Science and the National Environmental Policy Act: Redirecting Policy through Procedural Reform* (Tuscaloosa: University of Alabama Press, 1982), 39.
26. Adrea Fischer, "EPA Tightens Particulate Matter Rule; Manufacturers Concerned with Costs," *Transport Topics*, October 2, 2006: 4, 35.
27. Denise Grady, "Turbid Tap Water May Be Source of Unexplained Intestinal Ailments," *New York Times*, November 4, 1997, A10.
28. Chris Reuther, "Microscopic Murderer: Pollution May Be Motivating *Pfiesteria* to Kill Fish by the Thousands," Academy of Natural Sciences, Philadelphia, www.acnatsci.org/research/kye/pfiester.html (August 1998).
29. World Commission on Environment and Development (Brundtland Commission), *Our Common Future* (New York: Oxford University Press, 1987), 43.
30. Jonathan M. Harris, " Basic Principles of Sustainable Development," Working Paper 00-04 (Medford, MA: Global Development and Environment Institute, 2000).
31. For a comprehensive description of the South Florida project, see Working Group of the South Florida Ecosystem Restoration Task Force, *Success in the Making: An Integrated Plan for South Florida Ecosystem Restoration and Sustainability* (Washington, D.C.: U.S. Government Printing Office, 1998); the Clinton administration's ecosystem management initiative is discussed in U.S. General Accounting Office, "Ecosystem Management: Additional Actions Needed to Adequately Test a Promising Approach," Document No. GAO/RCED 94-111 (1994).
32. U.S. Department of the Interior, Bureau of Land Management, *Ecosystem Management in the BLM: From Concept to Commitment,* Publication No. BLM/SC/Gi-94/005 (1994), 1736.

Chapter 2

Making Policy:
The Process

*"Prof. Sharon L. Smith, an expert on arctic marine ecology at the
University of Miami . . . received a call from the White House.
She had been nominated to take a seat about to open up on the Arctic
Research Commission, a panel of presidential appointees that helps
shape research on issues in the far north, including the debate over oil
exploration in the Arctic National Wildlife Refuge. The woman calling
from the White House office of presidential personnel complimented
her resume, Dr. Smith recalled, then asked the first and—as it turned
out—only question. "Do you support the president?". . . She
responded that she was not a fan of Mr. Bush's economic and foreign
policies. "That was the end of the interview," she said. "I was
removed from consideration instantly."*

> *New York Times*, October 14, 2004[1]

James E. Hansen is a senior scientist at the National Aeronautics and Space
Administration (NASA), Director of NASA's Goddard Institute for Space
Studies, and one of the nation's most well-known and respected atmospheric scientists. One October day in 2004, Hansen sent an angry message
from Iowa to the White House and received a predictably disagreeable
response. It was the opening public round in an acrimonious battle between
Hansen and the White House that prevailed throughout the George W. Bush
administration over the federal government's response to the issue of climate

warming. The struggle exposed deep, persistent, and fundamental disagreements within the federal government over which institutions and officials should shape the government's environmental policies.

The White House and the Greenhouse

From its beginning, the George W. Bush administration's approach to climate change policy was contentious. Soon after his inauguration, Bush retracted an earlier pledge to restrict power plant discharges of carbon dioxide (CO^2), the major gas associated with climate warming. The administration also rejected participation in Kyoto Protocol, the 1997 global treaty in which 149 other nations had pledged to a scheduled reduction in their CO^2 emissions. Bush strongly promoted voluntary industrial cutbacks in CO^2 emissions, endorsed a gradual and moderate decrease in national greenhouse gas reductions, and repeatedly emphasized the scientific uncertainties involved in predicting future climate change—actions provoking vigorous opposition from segments of the scientific community, sharp Congressional debate, and division among policy experts.

A Public Challenge

That October day, Hansen directly contradicted the White House position by assuring the University of Iowa audience that the scientific community generally agreed that temperatures on Earth are rising because of the greenhouse effect—emissions of CO_2 and other materials into the atmosphere that trap heat. Moreover, he noted, scientists believed these rising temperatures could damage crops and human health, cause sea levels to rise, and trigger other problems.[2]

Hansen's presentation seemed designed to infuriate the White House. Hansen told his audience that the George W. Bush Administration only wants to hear findings that "fit predetermined, inflexible positions" and that the Bush Administration "consistently downplayed" information confirming global climate warming. In addition, Hansen asserted, reports that outline potential dangers of global warming were edited by Bush administrators to make the problem appear less serious "in direct opposition to the fundamental precepts of science." If these remarks were not sufficiently inflammatory, Hansen turned to the forthcoming November presidential election between Bush and John Kerry. "Speaking as a private citizen," he said, he believed "John Kerry has a far better grasp than President Bush on the important issues that we face, as far as the area for which I have expertise, climate change and its relation to energy use."[3]

The Bush administration responded by further increasing its already substantial pressure on the administration's political appointees to control the flow of scientific information from NASA by delaying or altering public documents released by the agency. Until mid-2004, however, the simmering conflict between Hansen and the Bush White House seldom erupted publicly. In fact, Hansen had earlier been twice invited to brief the Bush cabinet on climate issues, and the president himself had cited Hansen's research on occasion. By late 2004, however, the White House-Hansen relationship had frayed badly. The Iowa speech revealed the widening depth of their disagreement about climate warming.

"Dire Consequences"?

Rising White House irritation at Hansen's continuing, outspoken views on climate warming policy throughout 2005 culminated in December. That month, Hansen warned the American Geophysical Union that without leadership in the United States, climate change would eventually leave earth "a different planet" and, later, released information that 2005 was probably the warmest year in at least a century. Hansen soon received telephone warnings from NASA's public affairs office that "dire consequences" might follow if his statements continued, including the possibility that public affairs officials might stand in for him at news media interviews. About the same time, a novice NASA public affairs officer, remarking that his job was to "make the president look good," rejected a request from National Public Radio to interview Hansen. Hansen insisted, however, that he had an obligation to speak out because part of NASA's official mission was "to understand and protect our home planet."[4]

Conflict between the White House and agency scientists over where science ends and politics begins was not peculiar to the Bush administration, however. Hansen and other NASA scientists had sparred with both the previous Clinton and Bush administrations over climate warming data and policies. However, Hansen reported to several national newspapers, "nothing in 30 years equated the push made since early December to keep him from publicly discussing what he says are clear-cut dangers for further delay in curbing carbon dioxide."[5] What followed revived public controversy over two of the enduring issues in American environmental policy making: which government institutions and leaders should shape the nation's environmental policies and what role science, and the scientific community, should assume in this process.

Competing Interests and Institutions

Hanson found important allies. Shortly after the revelation of "direct threats," NASA administrator Michael D. Griffin issued a message to NASA's 19,000 employees reassuring them it was not the job of NASA's public affairs officers "to alter, filter or adjust engineering or scientific material produced by NASA's technical staff." [6] The public affairs officer who wanted to "make the president look good" was fired. Sherwood Boehlert, the influential chair of the House Science Committee, himself a Republican, warned that the Hansen affair revealed "NASA is clearly doing something wrong" because "good science cannot exist in an atmosphere of intimidation." [7] And the prestigious American Association for the Advancement of Science hastily convened a crowded session at its 2006 annual conference to denounce political interference in governmental science.

Others saw the controversy differently. "It seems that Dr. Hansen, once again, is using his government position to promote his own views and political agenda, which is a clear violation of governmental procedure in any administration," said a spokesperson for James M. Inhofe, the Republican chair of the Senate Committee on the Environment and Public Works. [8] NASA's deputy assistant administrator for public affairs noted that public affairs officials routinely reviewed the public statements of employees in most federal agencies and such reviews were essential to ensure an orderly flow of information and to avoid surprises. And, he added—in words heard often among Bush White House officials and agency leaders— "while governmental scientists were free to discuss scientific findings, policy statements should be left to policy makers and appointed spokesmen." [9]

None of these actions, however, could eliminate the deep disagreement between governmental institutions, public officials, and scientists over their appropriate role in environmental policy making. These conflicts arise from the many divisions of power embedded in the U.S. Constitution and the ambiguities of authority that result from these divisions. The White House-Hansen dispute, for example, fed on historic controversies over the limits of the president's power as the nation's chief executive and major public policy maker and on conflicting understandings about the responsibility of federal administrators to the White House and to their own professions or agency mission. In addition, to many scientists inside and outside Washington, the Hansen controversy was the raw edge of the always contentious dispute over how much policy makers should defer to scientific data and opinions.

Policy Making Is a Process

The Hansen controversy exemplifies the multitude of actors and institutions; the complex fabric of decisions; and the sometime glacial, disjointed, and frequently contentious sequence of events involved in the making of national environmental policy.

Although environmental policies usually develop less tumultuously, this incident featured some characteristics common to environmental policy making. First, policy making is a process that involves a number of related decisions originating from different institutions and actors ranging across the whole domain of the federal government and private institutions. As policy analyst Hugh Heclo observed, policy is "a course of action or inaction rather than a specific decision or action."[10] Moreover, policy making is continuous; once made, decisions rarely are immutable. Environmental policy is in some respects fluid and impermanent, always in metamorphosis. Second, policy makers—whether of the legislative, White House, or bureaucratic type—can seldom act without restraint. Their discretion is bounded and shaped by many constraints: constitutional separations of power, institutional rules and biases, statutory laws, shared understandings about the "rules of the game" for conflict resolution, political realities, and more. These constraints collectively are a given in the policy setting, which means government resolves almost all issues in a predictable style. Third, environmental policy making is a volatile mixture of politics and science that readily erupts into controversy among politicians, bureaucrats, and scientists over their appropriate roles in the process as well as over the proper interpretation and use of scientific data in policy questions.

One useful way to understand public policy, and environmental policy specifically, is to view the process as a cycle of interrelated phases through which policy ordinarily evolves. Each phase involves a different mix of actors, institutions, and constraints. Although somewhat simplified, this approach illuminates particularly well the interrelated flow of decisions and the continual process of creation and modification that characterizes governmental policy development. This chapter begins by describing the significant phases of environmental policy making and then examines important constitutional and political influences, deeply embedded in U.S. political culture, that continually animate and shape the environmental policies emerging from this policy cycle.

The Policy Cycle

Public policies usually develop with reasonable order and predictability. Governmental response to public issues—the business of converting an issue into a policy—customarily begins when an issue can be placed on the governmental agenda. Successful promotion of issues to the agenda does not ensure that public policies will result, but this step initiates the policy cycle. An environmental issue becomes an environmental policy as it passes through several policy phases.

Agenda Setting

Political scientist Charles O. Jones aptly called agenda setting "the politics of getting problems to government."[11] It is the politics of imparting sufficient importance and urgency to an issue so that the government will feel compelled to place the matter on the official agenda of government—that is, the "set of items explicitly up for the serious and active consideration of authoritative decision-makers."[12] This means getting environmental issues on legislative calendars, before legislative committees, on a priority list for bill introduction by a senator or representative, on the schedule of a regulatory agency, or among the president's legislative proposals. In brief, getting on the agenda means placing an issue where institutions and individuals with public authority can respond and feel a need to do so. Especially if an environmental issue is technical and somewhat esoteric, its prospects for making the agenda are bleak unless political sponsors are attracted to it. Former Environmental Protection Agency (EPA) assistant administrator and environmental activist Clarence Davies observed, "New technical information by itself does not significantly influence the political agenda. It must be assisted by some type of political propellant"—an interest group, congressional committee, or the president, for example.[13] Thus, discovery of the stratospheric ozone hole, and the ability of scientists to portray it in the most literal way—scientific photography enabled the public to *see* a hole—immensely hastened the Montreal Protocol to completion.

Formulation and Legitimation

The governmental agenda also can be a graveyard for public problems. Few issues reaching the governmental agenda, environmental or otherwise, reach the phase of policy formulation or legitimation. Policy formulation involves setting goals for policy, creating specific plans and proposals for these goals, and selecting the means to implement such plans. Policy formulation in the federal government is especially associated with the presidency and Congress. The State of the Union address and the avalanche of bills introduced annually in Congress represent the most obvious examples of formulated policies. Policies once created must also be legitimated—invested with the authority to evoke public acceptance. Such legitimation usually is done through constitutional, statutory, or administrative procedures, such as voting, public hearings, presidential orders, or judicial decisions upholding the constitutionality of laws—rituals whose purposes are to signify that policies have now acquired the weight of public authority.

Implementation

Public policies remain statements of intention until they are translated into operational programs. Indeed, the impact of policies depends largely on how they are implemented. What government is doing about environmental problems relates primarily to how the programs have been implemented. Policy analyst Eugene Bardach compared implementation of public policies with "an assembly process." He wrote that it is

> as if the original mandate . . . that set the policy or program in motion were a blueprint for a large machine that has to turn out rehabilitated psychotics or healthier old people or better educated children. . . . Putting the machine together and making it run is, at one level, what we mean by the "implementation" process.[14]

Policy implementation involves especially the bureaucracy, whose presence and style shape the impact of all public policies.

Assessment and Reformulation

All the procedures involved in evaluating the social impact of governmental policies, in judging the desirability of these impacts, and in communicating these judgments to government and the public can be called policy assessment. Often the federal courts assume an active role in the process, as do the mass media. The White House, Congress, and the bureaucracy continually monitor and assess the impacts of public policy. As a consequence, once a policy has been formulated, it may pass through many phases of reformulation. All major institutions of government may play a major role in this process of reformulation.

Termination

The "deliberate conclusion or succession of specific governmental functions, programs, policies or organizations" amounts to policy termination, according to political scientist Peter deLeon.[15] Terminating policies, environmental or otherwise, is such a formidable process that most public programs, in spite of intentions to the contrary, become virtually immortal. Policies usually change through repeated reformulation and reassessment.

Policy Making Is a Combination of Phases

Because policy making is a process, the various phases almost always affect each other, an important reason why understanding a policy often requires considering the whole development pattern. For instance, many problems encountered by the EPA when enforcing the Federal Water Pollution Control Act (1956) arose from congressional failure to define clearly in the law what was meant by a "navigable" waterway to which the legislation explicitly applied. Congress deliberately built in this ambiguity to facilitate passage of the extraordinarily complicated legislation. In turn, the EPA sought early opportunities to bring the issue before the federal courts—to compel judicial assessment of the law's intent—so that the agency might have reliable guidance for its implementation of the provision. Also, many aspects of environmental policy may occur simultaneously. While the EPA was struggling to implement portions of the Superfund legislation allocating grants to the states for cleaning up abandoned toxic waste sites, Congress was considering a reformulation of the law to increase funding authorization to support more state grants.

Constitutional Constraints

The design of governmental power intended more than two centuries ago for a nation of farmers still rests heavily on the flow of policy making in a technological age. Like other public policies, environmental programs have been shaped, and complicated, by the enduring constitutional formula.

Checks and Balances

The Madisonian notion of setting "ambition against ambition," which inspired the constitutional structure, creates a government of countervailing and competitive institutions. The system of checks and balances disperses power and authority within the federal government among legislative, executive, and judicial institutions and thereby sows tenacious institutional rivalries repeatedly encountered in discussions of specific environmental laws. Yet, as former presidential adviser Richard E. Neustadt observed, these are separated institutions sharing power; effective public policy requires that public officials collaborate by discovering strategies to transcend these institutional conflicts.[16]

The U.S. federal system disperses governmental power by fragmenting authority between national and state governments. Despite the growth of vast federal powers, federalism remains a sturdy constitutional buttress supporting an edifice of authority—shared, independent, and countervailing—erected from the states within the federal system. "It is difficult to find any governmental activity which does not involve all three of the so-called 'levels' of the federal system."[17] No government institution monopolizes power. "There has never been a time when it was possible to put neat labels on discrete 'federal,' 'state' and 'local' functions."[18]

Regulatory Federalism

Federalism introduces complexity, jurisdictional rivalries, confusion, and delay into the management of environmental problems. Authority over environmental issues inherently is fragmented among a multitude of governmental entities. Moreover, almost all new federal regulatory programs since 1970 permit, or require, implementation by the states. Thirty-five states, for instance, currently administer water pollution permits under the Clean Water Act. State implementation of federal laws may vary greatly in scope and detail. Management of water quality in the Colorado River basin, for instance, is enormously complicated because seven states have conflicting claims on the quantity and quality of Colorado River water to which they are entitled. No overall plan exists for the comprehensive management and protection of the river, and none can exist in this structure of divided and competitive jurisdictions. The federal government often attempts to reduce administrative complications in programs administered through the states by the use of common regulations, guidelines, and other devices to impose consistency in implementation. However, the practical problems of reconciling so many geographic interests within the arena of a single regulatory program often trigger major problems in implementing the programs.

Federal and state collaboration in environmental regulation is often amiable but just as often contentious. Many state authorities believe that numerous environmental problems now federally regulated are best managed by state and local governments. Many such state authorities also resent the expense and administrative difficulty they must endure to implement the numerous environmental laws and regulations they believe the federal government has negligently piled on them. During the 1980s, for example, almost a third of all major federal legislative mandates affecting the states related to environmental issues. During that decade, EPA regulations to implement these laws are estimated to have cost the states more than $24 billion in state capital expense and operating costs, while federal financial support for these state activities was diminishing.[19]

Organized Interests

The Constitution encourages a robust pluralism of organized interests. Constitutional guarantees for freedom of petition, expression, and assembly promote constant organization and political activism at all governmental levels among thousands of economic, occupational, ethnic, ideological, and geographic interests. To make public policy in the United States requires public officials and institutions to reconcile the conflicting interests of organized groups whose claims not only to influence but also to authority in making public policy have resulted in an unwritten constitutional principle. The constitutional architecture of the U.S. government also provides numerous points of access to public power for such groups operating in a fragmented governmental milieu. The political influence broadly distributed across this vast constellation of organized private groups clouds the formal distinction between public and private power.[20]

Instead, the course of policy making moves routinely and easily between public institutions and private organizations mobilized for political action.

These constitutional constraints have important implications for environmental policy. It is easier to defeat legislation and other governmental policies than to enact them, to frustrate incisive governmental action on issues than to create it. Further, most policy decisions result from bargaining and compromise among institutions and actors all sharing some portion of diffused power. Formulating policy usually means coalition building in an effort to engineer consensus by reconciling diverse interests and aggregating sufficient strength among different interests to support effective policies. As economist James V. DeLong observed,

> Agencies like to achieve consensus on issues and policies. If they cannot bring everyone into the tent, they will try to get enough disparate groups together so as to make the remainder appear unreasonable. If the interested parties are too far apart for even partial consensus, then the agency will try to give everybody something.[21]

Bargaining and compromise often purchase consensus at the cost of disarray and contradiction in the resulting policies. "What happens is not chosen as a solution to a problem but rather results from compromise, conflict and confusion among officials with diverse interests and unequal influence," noted presidential adviser Graham Allison.[22]

Incrementalism

Public officials strongly favor making and changing policy incrementally. "Policy making typically is part of a political process in which the only feasible political change is that which changes social states by relatively small steps," wrote social analyst Charles A. Lindblom. "Hence, decision makers typically consider, among all the alternative policies that might be imagined to consider, only those relatively few alternatives that represent small or incremental changes from existing policies."[23] In general, such incrementalism favors relying on past experience as a guide for new policies, carefully deliberating before changing policy, and rejecting rapid or comprehensive policy innovation.

Incrementalism is politically seductive. It permits policy makers to draw on their own experiences in the face of unfamiliar problems and encourages the making of small policy adjustments "at the margins" to reduce anticipated, perhaps irreversible, and politically risky consequences. But incrementalism also can become a prison to the imagination by inhibiting policy innovation and stifling new solutions to issues. Especially when officials treat new policy issues as if they were familiar ones and deal with them in the customary ways, a futile and possibly dangerous repetition of the past can result in the face of issues requiring a fresh approach.

The Clean Air Act (1970), the National Environmental Policy Act (NEPA) of 1970, and the other innovative legislation of the early 1970s came only after Congress repeatedly failed in dealing with environmental issues incrementally.[24] For more than thirty years previously, and despite growing evidence of serious environmental degradation, Congress continued to treat pollution as a "uniquely local problem" requiring a traditional "partnership" between federal and state governments in which Washington gently prodded the states to deal more effectively with pollution. This deference to the states was a prescription for inaction. Despite three major new federal air and water pollution laws between 1950 and 1970, all appealing to this governmental partnership, few states voluntarily wrote or enforced effective pollution controls, to the mounting frustration of environmentalists and public health advocates. Finally, Congress put an end to this incrementalism with the avalanche of new, forceful federal environmental laws in the 1970s mandating national pollution standards and regulations that compelled state compliance and enforcement. To many observers, this was a sudden outburst of environmental reform. In fact, its rise to the national policy agenda had been achieved by years of increasingly skilled, patient, and persistent promotion by a multitude of groups. The Clean Air Act, for instance, had been supported for almost five years by a national environmental alliance, the Clean Air Coalition, before it achieved national attention. Nonetheless, time consumed in attempts to attack problems incrementally, the degree of environmental damage necessary to convince Congress that new approaches are needed, and the effort invested by the environmental movement in political action all testify to the tenacity of incrementalism in the policy process.

Interest-Group Liberalism

It is an implicit principle in U.S. politics, assumed by most public officials as well as those groups seeking access to them, that organized interests affected by public policy should have an important role in shaping those policies. Few special interests enjoy such a pervasive and unchallenged access to government as business, for reasons to be elaborated in the next section, but almost all major organized groups enjoy some measure of influence in public institutions. Many officials, in critic Theodore Lowi's terms, conduct their offices "as if it were supposed to be the practice of dealing only with organized claims in formulating policy, and of dealing exclusively through organized claims in implementing programs."[25]

Structuring Groups into Government

Arrangements exist throughout governmental structures for giving groups access to strategic policy arenas. Lobbying is accepted as a normal, if not essential, arrangement for ensuring organized interests a major role in lawmaking. More than one thousand advisory committees exist within the federal bureaucracy to give interests affected by policies some access and voice in agency deliberations. Hundreds of large, quasi-public associations bring together legislators, administrators, White House staff, and private group representatives to share policy concerns, thereby blurring the distinction between public and private interests. The National Rivers and Harbors Congress, for example, looks after water resource projects; the Highway Users Federation for Safety and Mobility diligently promotes the interstate highway system; and the Atomic Industrial Forum pursues the interests of commercial nuclear power corporations. Successful, organized groups so effectively control the exercise of governmental power that, in historian Grant McConnell's words, significant portions of U.S. government have witnessed "the conquest of segments of formal state power by private groups and associations." [26] In effect, group activity at all governmental levels has been practiced so widely that it has become part of the constitutional order.

Business: An Unusual Kind and Degree of Control

No interest has exploited the right to take part in the governmental process more pervasively or successfully than has business. In environmental affairs, the sure access of business to government assumes enormous importance, because business is a major regulated interest whose ability to represent itself and secure careful hearing before public agencies and officials often delays or complicates such regulation. But historically and institutionally the influence of business on government has transcended the agencies and officials concerned with environmental affairs. Business traditionally has enjoyed what Lindblom called a "special relationship" with government.

Business weighs especially heavy in the deliberations of public officials because its leaders collectively manage much of the economy and perform such essential economic functions that the failure of these businesses would produce severe economic disorder and widespread suffering. According to Lindblom,

> Government officials know this. They also know that widespread failure of business . . . will bring down the government. A democratically elected government cannot expect to survive in the face of widespread or prolonged distress. . . . Consequently, government policy makers show constant concern about business performance. [27]

So great is this concern that public officials usually give business not all it desires but enough to ensure its profitability. Out of this grows the privileged position of business in government, its widely accepted right to require that government officials often "give business needs precedence over demands from citizens through electoral, party, and interest-group channels."[28]

Business also enjoys practical political advantages in competition with other interests for access and influence within government: far greater financial resources, greater ease in raising money for political purposes, and an already existing organization available for use in political action. These advantages in strategic resources and salience to public officials do not ensure uncompromised acceptance of business's demands on government, nor do they spare business from defeat or frustration by opponents. But business often, if not usually, is able to exploit its privileged status in U.S. politics to ensure that its views are represented early and forcefully in any policy conflicts, its interests are pursued and protected carefully at all policy phases, and its forces are mobilized effectively for long periods of time. These are formidable advantages, often enough to give a decisive edge in competitive struggles with environmental or other interests that do not have the political endurance, skill, or resources to be as resolute in putting pressure on government when it counts.

Environmentalism's Enlarging Access

Prior to the 1970s, environmentalists were at a considerable disadvantage in achieving effective access to government when compared with environmentally regulated interests, particularly business. The environmental lobby could claim, with considerable justification, to be political outsiders when compared with business. However, environmental groups—along with public interest groups, consumer organizations, and others advocating broad public programs—were quick to promote a number of new structural and legal arrangements that enlarged their governmental influence. Indeed, Congress and administrative agencies often created these structural and legal arrangements deliberately for the advantage of environmental interests. These new arrangements, defended ferociously by environmental organizations against continuing assaults by their political opposition, have diminished greatly the disparities in political access and influence that once so conspicuously distinguished environmentalists from their political opponents. The political season has turned. In the rough calculus of governmental influence, environmentalists may not yet claim parity with organized business, but environmentalism no longer wears comfortably the rags of the politically disadvantaged and the establishment outsider. In the vernacular of Washington, D.C., environmentalists are now "major players"—so major that a closer look at organized environmentalism and its impact on public opinion is essential to understand the fundamental driving forces of environmental policy making.

Organized Environmentalism

Organization is the bedrock on which the politics of successful environmental policy making is built. About 5 percent of Americans report membership in an environmental organization, but in 2003 about 14 percent reported they were "participants" in the environmental movement.[29] Hundreds of organized national, state, and local groups, collectively enrolling several hundred thousand active members, arm the movement with absolutely essential political resources that only organized groups provide: dependable, active, informed, and experienced advocacy.[30] Organized groups create the kind of constant pressure on policy makers and the continual, aggressive surveillance of policy administration required for effective policy influence in government.

The many groups marching under the environmental banner continue to grow in number, sophistication, and political aggressiveness. To the media and public surprised by Earth Day 1970, the environmental movement seemed to materialize from a political vacuum. In fact, between 1960 and 1970 the national groups sponsoring the event had already grown from 123,000 to almost 820,000 members.[31] As always, behind the public politics of environmentalism was the driving force of calculated organizational action and adroit media manipulation—the evidence of skilled political advocacy.

The environmental movement is also changing. Membership growth has enlarged the political clout of environmental interests at the state and local levels. The proliferation of organizations manifests an increasingly divisive pluralism within the movement as well—ideologically, organizationally, and tactically. The ideological cleavages between moderates and radicals, and between the national leaders and local grassroots constituencies, has widened and solidified. After two decades of sometimes spectacular growth following Earth Day 1970, membership enrollment in the mainstream national environmental organizations has slackened in recent years and in some instances declined moderately. Nonetheless, the organizational base of environmentalism remains potent politically.

Ideological Consensus and Cleavage

Environmentalism has never been a church of one creed. The reformist politics of the 1990s exacerbated ideological, programmatic, and tactical disagreements that have always existed among the faithful. Although pluralism, and conflicts born of it, are inherent to environmentalism, this pluralism is still bounded by general values, attitudes, and beliefs—a way of looking at nature, humanity, and U.S. society—widely shared with many nuances by environmental leaders and activists. Although this pluralism lacks the coherence of an ideology, it sets environmentalists apart from mainstream American culture.

Essential Principles

Reduced to essentials, environmentalism springs from an attitude toward nature that assumes that humanity is part of the created order, ethically responsible for the preservation of the world's ecological integrity and ultimately vulnerable, as are all earth's other creatures, to the good or ill humans inflict on nature. In the environmentalist perspective, humans live in a world of limited resources and potential scarcities; like the good stewards of an inheritance, they must use their scientific genius to manage global resources. An enlightened approach to managing nature, the environmentalists argue, should stress the interdependency of all natural systems (the ecosystem concept), the importance of ecological stability and resource sustainability, and the enormously long time span across which the impact of ecological change occurs. In its approach to nature, environmentalism emphasizes the sanctity of the created order as a warning against the human assumption that we stand above and apart from the created order by virtue of our intelligence and scientific achievements. All this is summed up for many ecologists in the metaphor of "spaceship earth," the image of a unique and vulnerable ecosystem traveling through space and time, dependent on its crew for survival.

In its cultural stance, environmentalism sharply criticizes marketplace economics generally and capitalism particularly, and denigrates the growth ethic, unrestrained technological optimism, and the political structures supporting these cultural phenomena. Such an attitude places environmentalists on a collision course with dominant American values. Environmentalism challenges U.S. confidence in market mechanisms to allocate scarce resources for several reasons. Environmentalists assert that market economics esteem economic growth and material consumption above concern for ecological balance and integrity. Therefore, the market cannot be relied on to signal resource scarcity efficiently enough to prevent possibly catastrophic resource exhaustion. Many, like environmental philosopher William Ophuls, believe marketplace economies are ecologically reckless:

> An unregulated market economy inevitably fosters accelerated ecological degradation and resource depletion through ever higher levels of production and consumption. Indeed, given the cornucopian assumptions upon which a market system is based, it could hardly be otherwise; both philosophically and practically, a market economy is incompatible with ecology.[32]

Environmentalism is less hostile to technology itself than to blind faith in the power of technology to cure whatever ecological ills it begets and to bland confidence in technological expertise to meet humanity's material and spiritual needs. Environmentalists regard the public's confidence in American know-how as responsible for many of the nation's most difficult environmental problems, such as the management of commercial nuclear technologies. The environmental movement's initial political agenda arose from these attitudes toward the natural world and contemporary culture. From its inception, the movement has expressed an ambivalence toward the nation's dominant social structures that frequently translates into calls for major institutional as well as policy reforms. Many environmentalists believe that the nation's dominant political institutions and processes must be reformed because they are committed to the preservation of ecological, economic, and technological values that are hostile to prudent ecological management. For some, this is summed up as suspicion of the establishment and the traditional institutions and processes associated with it. Political scientist A. Susan Leeson argued, "If American political ideology and institutions have been successful in encouraging the pursuit of happiness through material acquisition, they appear incapable of imposing the limits which are required to forestall ecological disaster."[33] Many fear the power of an interlocking economic and political structure committed to controlling technology in environmentally reckless ways.

Until the 1980s the national organizations representing the environmental movement were largely untroubled by impassioned, divisive ideological cleavages. During the 1980s, however, an emergent radicalism and ideological conflict within the movement cohered into a multitude of newly dissident organizations and opened acrimonious schisms within many older, established groups. The environmental movement has now become an uneasy alliance of numerous, often discordant, political camps spread across a widening ideological terrain.

The Ideological Mainstream

Organized environmentalism today is divided into several ideological enclaves. The movement's dominant ideological and political style has been crafted by *pragmatic reformers,* the largest, most politically active and publicly visible organizations represented by national groups such as the Sierra Club and the National Wildlife Federation. These large membership organizations emphasize political action through government; traditional styles of politics such as bargaining and coalition building; and national environmental agendas focusing on pollution, resource conservation, and land use. Their priorities are "influencing public policy in incremental steps, forging pragmatic alliances issue by issue with those with whom they could agree," explained Michael McCloskey, former executive director of the Sierra Club. McCloskey emphasized that the pragmatists do not believe "that the entire political or economic system needed to be changed and were confident that environmental protection could be achieved within the framework of existing institutions of governance."[34]

The robust ideological diversity among the pragmatists, however, makes them appear more an ecumenical movement than a denomination. One important factional conflict pits preservationist groups, such as the Sierra Club and the Wilderness Society, which emphasize the preservation of resources rather than their economic or recreational exploitation, against groups such as the Izaak Walton League or the National Wildlife Federation, which favor prudent resource development for public use and economic growth. Another significant cleavage divides the pragmatists from antiestablishment groups such as Friends of the Earth and Environmental Action, impatient at the moderation and slowness of political action among the leading national groups but still committed to traditional forms of political activity. The national leadership in almost all mainstream environmental organizations, in fact, contends with their own grassroots factions who, in the words of critic Brian Tokar, believe "the voices of 'official environmentalism' [are] hopelessly out of step with the thousands of volunteers who largely define the leading edge of locally based environmental activism."[35] To these critics, the leaders of "official environmentalism" have become just another political elite, absorbed in promoting their careers and accommodating to the corporate interests they should be opposing. When the World Wildlife Fund, for instance, selected a former executive of Weyerhaeuser Company, an international timber industry giant, for a major management position, the organization was bitterly flayed by one grassroots environmentalist publication:

> The World Wildlife Fund functions more like a corporate enterprise than public interest group. It . . . has made millions upon millions hawking its panda logo, a brand as zealously marketed as Nike's "swoosh." But, of course, it's done almost nothing to save the panda . . . except peddle pictures to trophy wives and innocent third graders. Call it Panda porn. . . . The World Wildlife Fund also rakes in millions from corporations. . . . As a result, WWF's budget has swelled to over $100 million a year. . . . Most of it goes to pay for plush offices, robust salaries, and a tireless direct mail operation to raise even more money.[36]

These critics, who agree on little else, complain about the amount of foundation money flowing into the coffers of pragmatic environmental groups. Such generous underwriting—often by large donors such as the Pew Memorial Trusts and the Heinz Foundation—has sometimes exceeded $400 million annually and, in the opinion of the critics, compels mainstream environmentalism to compromise programs and tactics to suit its foundation patrons. "It's like throwing a huge steak in among a bunch of starving lions," complained a spokesman for Oregon's Native Forest Council. "The lions will jump on it even if it is laced with arsenic."[37] Undoubtedly, foundations do prod their environmentalist clientele toward political moderation, but such influence is highly variable. The hardliners, moreover, have had their own foundation angels, such as the Turner Foundation, created by broadcast entrepreneur Ted Turner, which contributed millions of dollars annually during the 1990s to aggressive antiestablishment environmental organizations. And many "odd couple" alliances exist between relatively moderate foundation sponsors and aggressive environmental activists such as that between the Ford Foundation and Environmental Defense. Even without these other provocations, differing organizational agendas and constituencies are themselves divisive to environmentalism. Which organizational agendas shall prevail in the competition among environmental organizations for political primacy? Shall the movement's priorities be air or water pollution, land preservation, hazardous waste management, national land-use planning, species preservation, global environmental problems, recreational development, indoor air pollution, or something else?

Deep Ecologists

Another highly vocal faction within environmentalism comprises individuals and groups ideologically committed to *deep ecology* or *lifestyle transformation*. Deep ecologists believe humans are, at best, only a part of nature—and not necessarily the most significant part. They believe that all forms of life have an equal claim on existence; that social, political, and economic institutions should promote the ecological vitality of all created orders and that fundamental changes in national institutions and lifestyles are essential to preserve global ecological integrity. The fundamental political problem, from the deep ecologist's perspective, is that social institutions have become instruments for human exploitation of the created order for the primary benefit of humans, often through technologies that threaten to destroy essential aspects of the natural order. Deep ecology inherently challenges the fundamental institutional structures and social values on which governments, economies, and societies are presently constituted. Thus, between deep ecologists and what they call the shallow ecology of mainstream environmentalism there abides a profound philosophical tension, nourished by antagonistic principles and a sharply disparate political imagination.[38]

Deep ecologists, lacking the political leverage of organizational or numerical strength, are presently a vocal, aggressive, and dissenting minority within the environmental movement. Many within the movement, preferring social to political action, have adopted individual and collective lifestyles outside conventional American culture. Nonetheless, deep ecologists continue to be politically active, often to greatest effect at the state and local levels. They also constitute a persistent, opportunistic minority in many national environmental organizations with considerable potential to become a creative as well as a disruptive influence in national environmental politics.

Radical Environmentalism

Militant and alienated from the movement's organizational mainstream, *radical environmentalism* emerged in the 1980s among environmentalists disillusioned with establishment styles and accomplishments. According to environmental historian Bill Devall, the radical environmentalists

> were discouraged by the compromising attitude of mainstream groups, by the bureaucratization of the groups, by the professionalization of leaders and their detachment from the emerging concerns of grassroots supporters, and by the lack of success of mainstream organizations in countering the Reagan anti-environmental agenda.[39]

Radical environmentalists favor so-called direct-action tactics, including the street politics of civil disobedience, nonviolent demonstrations, and political obstruction. To environmental radicals, the harassment of commercial whaling vessels on the high seas by Greenpeace protest vessels, carefully orchestrated to attract media attention worldwide, was better politics than the inhibited, reformist style of the mainstream organizations.

Radical environmentalists share a common sensibility that all life is mortally threatened by an ecological degeneration created by advanced modern cultures. Thus, radicals espouse a fundamental cultural transformation that rejects the dominant political and economic institutions of most advanced societies as incompatible with global ecological vitality. This preoccupation with transformational politics usually involves a belief in "bearing witness" by lifestyle changes emphasizing harmony with nature, conservation of resources, and cooperative living in reconstructed, ecologically sensitive societies.[40]

Despite a commitment to nonviolence, radicals betray ambivalence, if not tolerance, about forms of violence—"ecotage" or "monkey-wrenching" are euphemisms—condemned from within and without the environmental movement. Shadowy groups such as the Animal Liberation Front (ALF) and the Earth Liberation Front (ELF) are suspected of violent property destruction. (The ALF's Web site has contained information on making arson devices, and the ELF claimed responsibility for a $1 million burn down of a Boise Cascade Corporation office in Oregon.)[41] The small but aggressive movement Earth First!, created by former staff members of mainstream environmental groups, epitomizes this tendency despite its many other conventional activities. For instance, Earth First! spokespersons sometimes assert that in defense of nature, and to save old-growth trees from the lumberyards, it may be permissible to spike these trees with metal rods likely to fragment viciously when shattered by commercial logging chain saws.

Other groups, such as Greenpeace and the Sea Shepherd Society, have been accused of nonviolent direct action that provokes violence, such as disabling the nets of commercial fishing vessels whose crews refuse to protect dolphins during deep-sea tuna harvesting. In light of the profound cultural alienation inherent in many radical ideologies, an ambivalence about political violence is inevitable, although radical environmentalism's political strategies still remain—sometimes barely—within the tradition of nonviolent direct action.

Organizational Structures and Strategies

The number and size of environmental organizations expanded through the mid-1990s, but membership subsequently declined, evidence of a familiar up-and-down cycle common to environmental organizations as public perceptions of environmental crises ebb and flow. Strong membership growth throughout the early 1990s was largely a response to aggressive organizational recruiting and the highly publicized confrontations between the White House and environmentalists during the Reagan–Bush period. By the end of the 1990s the largest environmental organizations had collectively lost more than a million members. Nonetheless, the major national organizations retain the numbers and resources needed to ensure their influential presence in national policy making. Moreover, to the national membership rolls should be added thousands of grassroots state and local groups. For instance, one national organization concerned with solid waste identifies seven thousand collaborating state and local groups. Altogether, the number of national, state, and local environmental organizations is estimated to exceed ten thousand.

Membership. Although social support for environmentalism is broadly based in the United States, the organizational membership is mostly middle to upper class, white, well educated, and well off.[42] Such a socially select membership exposes environmentalists to the frequent criticism that the so-called greens are too white and too well off, that they are racists or elitists indifferent to minorities and the economically disadvantaged. To support these accusations, critics argue that environmentalism fights for clean air but not for equal employment opportunity, promotes wilderness preservation for upscale recreationists but not better schools for the disadvantaged, and condemns pollution in national parks but not inner-city decay. In short, the agenda of environmentalism is largely a wish list from the book of middle-class, white lifestyles. Mainstream environmental organizations, increasingly sensitive to such criticism, have struggled to broaden their social constituencies and policy agendas. A number of national organizations have initiated joint action with labor and minority groups intended to make environmentalism relevant to the workplace and neighborhood. Most national environmental organizations, responding to initiatives from minority groups, also have supported the emerging environmental equity movement intended to end discrimination toward the economically disadvantaged in environmental policy making. The emergence of environmental racism as a mainstream environmentalist concern is discussed in Chapter 4.

The Organizational Mainstream. The environmental movement's national leadership is concentrated in a small number of highly visible, politically skilled, and influential organizations. Most of these organizations are included in the Group of Ten, an informal alliance of mainstream organizations that often collaborate on national issues. The Group of Ten includes the National Wildlife Federation, the Sierra Club, the National Audubon Society, the Wilderness Society, Friends of the Earth, Environmental Defense, the National Parks and Conservation Association, the Izaak Walton League, the Natural Resources Defense Council, and the Environmental Policy Institute. The large mainstream groups, the movement's political pragmatists, are thoroughly professionalized and sophisticated in staff and organization. They are armed with the same high-technology tools and modern techniques of policy advocacy as any other powerful national lobby. The large membership rolls of the national organizations demonstrate an aptitude for direct-mail solicitation as good as can be found in Washington, D.C.

Growing professionalization of leadership among mainstream groups continues to provoke accusations from many environmentalists that the national organizations have lost their fire and vision. The critics charge that the national leadership is more bureaucratic than charismatic, that it has lost touch with the movement's grassroots since it has become preoccupied with bargaining and compromise. "Increased professionalization," Robert Cameron Mitchell, Riley Dunlap, and Angela Mertig observed in their study of national environmental organizations, "carries with it the dangers of routinization in advocacy, careerism on the part of staff members, and passivity on the part of volunteers, all of which have been detected in the national organizations." [43]

Factional infighting may be an inevitable price for professional advocacy. Controversy within environmentalism over the political loyalty of the professionalized leadership now frequently erupts into nasty media brawls. A typical incident was the public street fight between environmental organizations over the North American Free Trade Agreement (NAFTA), supported by establishment regulars such as the National Wildlife Federation and the National Audubon Society. Groups opposing NAFTA, including the Sierra Club, Friends of the Earth, Greenpeace, Public Citizen, and the Rainforest Action Network, prepared newspaper advertisements asking, "Why are some 'green' groups so quick to sell off the North American environment? Maybe they are too cozy with corporate funders." [44] This increasing disaffection with the national leadership is one reason for the increase in state and local environmental organizations as well as for the growth of radical environmentalism. Another important reason for the growth of grassroots organizations has been Washington's continuing devolution of regulatory authority to state and local governments, a trend initiated by Ronald Reagan's administration.

The Essential Politics of Procedure. Rep. John Dingell, D-Mich., a legislator of legendary political skill, once shared a lesson gleaned from thirty years in Congress: "I'll let you write the substance on a statute and you let me write the procedures, and I'll screw you every time." [45] Dingell's axiom illuminates a law as fundamental to policy making as gravity is to physics: the decision-making rules, as much as the policy outcomes, enlarge or diminish group power. The environmental movement, always respectful of Dingell's axiom, has been as aggressive in promoting advantageous policy procedures as in creating substantive environmental laws.

The politics of procedure is always a fundamental consideration in environmentalist political agendas. Indeed, the movement's power flows, in good part, from success in procedural politics, from aggressively exploiting advantage through the intricate manipulation of policy process. Because so many environmental laws are implemented largely through bureaucracy and the courts, environmental organizations have been especially sensitive to the importance of protecting, or enhancing, decision-making procedures that work to their benefit in these institutions. The success of this strategy depends on securing these procedural advantages through law—statutory, administrative, or judicial. The public politics of environmentalism could not have succeeded so well, and perhaps not at all, had environmentalism's political power not been anchored in procedural law during the movement's rise to influence in the 1970s. "To a great extent, environmental group power . . . was legal power," observed political scientist George Hoberg, and environmentalism survived because the new legal arrangements "granted environmental groups institutional and legal foundations that to a large extent solidified their power status within the regime." [46]

Environmental groups have benefited especially from changes in law and administrative procedure that enhance their access to information and their opportunities to participate in the implementation of environmental laws. A major environmental reform was the enactment of NEPA in 1970, requiring federal agencies to prepare environmental impact statements that have become a major source of substantive information and procedural influence in federal environmental policies. Other important reforms include provisions in almost every major environmental law to greatly expand citizen participation in administrative decision making and to make it easier for citizens to sue administrative agencies for failure to implement environmental laws. Equally important has been increased activism among federal judges in reviewing critically the regulatory decisions of environmental agencies—the so-called hard-look doctrine—that often works to the environmentalists' advantage.

Environmentalism and Its Critics

The mainstream groups are now acknowledged Washington insiders, part of the interest-group establishment. Although environmentalist organizations are committed to defending the public interest and public values, they also represent a constituency with its own ideological and material interests. As environmentalism becomes increasingly organized and politicized nationally, critics assert that it has also assumed the narrow, self-interested viewpoint of every other interest group while promoting policies that often serve no public ends.

Public Interest or Self-Interest?

Critics frequently allege that environmentalism is largely the voice of a social elite hostile to U.S. capitalism, distrustful of science, and obsessed with imagined or exaggerated ecological problems. In one such indictment, the editors of the *Detroit News* complained that environmentalists were "a small band of environmental doomsayers, mostly upper middle-class whites, who are quick to forecast disaster but never see an upside to technology and economic progress."[47] To fortify such arguments, critics assert that the environmentalists' passion for controlled economic growth will deprive the economically disadvantaged domestically and internationally, that wilderness preservation usually benefits a handful of naturalists but deprives the average American of access to and enjoyment of wilderness resources, and that locking up resources costs jobs and inhibits economic progress. To such critics, environmentalism speaks not for *the* public interest but for *a* public interest that excludes millions of Americans.

The white, comfortably middle-class ambiance of most environmental organizations does nothing to diminish such criticism, as a former executive director of the Natural Resources Defense Council, John H. Adams, acknowledged: "There is much to criticize—the predominantly white staffs, the cultural barriers that have damaged and impeded joint efforts with activists of color."[48] Many environmental organizations are striving diligently for greater social diversity in membership and programs, but the stigma of social exclusivity still clings to the movement. In addition, increased professionalization and competition among environmental groups breeds a preoccupation with organizational needs. "There's tremendous competition out there for money," observed Les Line, a former editor of *Audubon Magazine*. "And we've gotten top-heavy with bureaucrats and accountants and fund-raisers who are all good professionals but I don't think you'd catch them sloshing through the marsh."[49] Critics frequently add that environmentalism's hidden agenda is antibusiness, maybe even economic revolution.[50]

Environmental leaders also resort to the rhetoric of crisis so habitually that environmentalism's mother tongue may seem to be the Apocalypse. This hyperbolic style begets the kind of misstatements on which critics often seize to demonstrate environmentalism's distorted vision. There have certainly been errors, as discussion of the controversies over the chemicals diisononyl phthalate (DINP) and dioxin demonstrate in Chapter 4. In addition, the seriousness of many ecological issues declared to be crises may be, at most, a matter of unresolved scientific controversy. Nonetheless, environmentalists have aroused an appropriate sense of urgency about numerous ecological issues such as air and water pollution, groundwater contamination, radioactive wastes, and surface mining, to cite but a few. The crisis style, however, can eventually become trite and unappealing if it is habitual.

The mainstream environmental organizations are sometimes condemned as shrewd opportunists, promoting policies that enlarge their own political power at public expense. The environmentalist attitude toward the Superfund program is often cited as a flagrant case in point. The major environmental groups generally insist on the strictest possible standards for all Superfund site cleanups, as required in the original law. Others have suggested that some relaxation of standards would enormously shrink the huge program costs and greatly facilitate site cleanups without significantly increasing risks to public health. But, the critics assert, environmentalists insist on the stringent standards because it draws to their side the waste treatment industry and the legal profession, for whom the strictest standards ensure the greatest income.

Constructive Opposition or Destructive Obstruction?

It is a political axiom of organized environmentalism that only unremitting pressure on government will ensure that environmental laws are implemented effectively. This informal ideology of countervailing power is animated by the conviction that government officials cannot be trusted to implement environmental regulations without the coercive force of pressure politics. Bureaucratic distrust runs so deeply through environmentalism that, next to saving nature for humanity, environmentalists often seem most dedicated to protecting the public from its public servants. This sour assault on environmental regulators, for instance, comes not from regulation's embittered foes but from Michael McCloskey, the former executive director of the Sierra Club:

> [Regulatory programs] need endless follow-through and can go wrong in a thousand places. The relevant bureaucracies have minds of their own and very little loyalty to the ideas of those who lobbied the programs through. Although the bureaucracies are somewhat responsive to Presidential direction, they are not very responsive to outside lobbying and are subject to no self-correcting process if they fail to be productive.[51]

The reliance by those within organized environmentalism on countervailing power is manifest in their customary resistance to the relaxation of strict pollution standards, which critics consider to be stonewalling. Countervailing power also means continual resort to litigation, administrative process, citizen involvement, and any other procedures that equate with group pressure on government. More than half of all litigation initiated against federal agencies involving compliance with NEPA and the majority of all legal challenges to EPA regulations originate with environmental organizations, often in collaboration with labor unions, consumer groups, and private interests. Environmental organizations are extremely aggressive in challenging federal, state, and local agencies over compliance with Superfund cleanup standards and over licensing of hazardous waste disposal sites and nuclear utilities, among many other issues. Citizen involvement activities at all governmental levels are exploited, if not dominated, by environmental groups and their allies, to considerable advantage.[52]

The skilled exploitation of these and other political processes has invested environmentalists with political power they probably would not otherwise have. Moreover, countervailing power often forces administrative agencies and their regulated interests to comply with laws they might prefer to ignore and frequently improves the quality of regulatory decision making. But countervailing power also has produced enormous delay in the implementation of regulations and increased significantly the cost of environmental regulation through litigation and administrative process. In addition, countervailing power at state and local levels can virtually immobilize the process of licensing hazardous facilities. Whether the use of countervailing power has become dangerously disruptive to environmental governance is a concern to many within the environmental movement as well as to its critics, for such power can be subverted into chronic obstruction of the processes it was intended to safeguard.

The continuing controversy over environmentalism, whatever its admitted merits, reveals some political realities: that environmentalist organizations have institutional dogmas and self-serving agendas that may not always be compatible with the larger interests of the movement or even with their own professed goals. Although environmental organizations frequently speak in the name of an encompassing public interest and may unselfishly pursue it, they also speak for a distinctive social and ideological constituency that often does not include the whole public and often not even a majority of the public. Environmentalism itself is increasingly divided over the goals and social constituencies to which it should be responsive. The rancorous pluralism already inspired by these conflicting convictions will continue to expand during the twenty-first century. In addition, the professionalization of national organizational leadership—inevitable if environmentalism is to survive the fiercely competitive struggle among interest groups for political resources—is also likely to breed a growing disunity between national leadership and grassroots environmentalism.

The Public and Environmentalism

Whatever its internal dissonances, the environmental movement has been largely responsible for a remarkable growth in public environmental consciousness and acceptance of environmental protection as an essential public policy. These are public assets, essential to the movement's continuing political vitality, and environmental organizations are extremely adept at arousing public concern on environmental matters and turning it into political advantage. How durable and deep this public support may be, especially in times of severe political or economic hardship, is a different matter.

A "Core Value"

"The transformation of the environment from an issue of limited concern to one of universal concern is now complete," observed opinion analyst Everett Carll Ladd in mid-1996.[53] The strength of public support for environmental protection early in the twenty-first century, as measured by public opinion polls, certainly appears vigorous and widespread. It might even appear superficially that the United States has become a nation of environmentalists. In 2005, for example, an opinion poll by Duke University's Nicholas Institute posed this question to a representative sample of American voters: "Now, let's say you heard about a proposal that would create stronger national standards to help protect our land, air and water. Not knowing any of the specifics, but just generally, does that sound like something you would favor or oppose?" Almost 80% of the respondents reported they would favor such a proposal—responses consistent with other polls regularly reporting strongly favorable public support of environmental protection.[54]

Critics sometimes assert that environmental interest groups speak for only a small portion of the public, but the polls seem to suggest otherwise. In general, opinion polls consistently report that substantial majorities in almost all major socioeconomic groups support the environmental movement and governmental programs to protect the environment and have supported them since Earth Day 1970. Environmental activists have been especially gratified that the polls offer little support to the once widespread notion that concern for environmental quality is a "white thing." In Table 2-1, for instance, sociologist Paul Mohai compared the level of concern with environmental problems among black and white Detroit respondents in 1990 and 2002 and found few significant differences.[55] Opinion analyst Ladd, like many opinion experts, concluded that environmentalism has become a "core American value," one of those issues now firmly rooted in a national political consensus.[56] Moreover, it would appear superficially that Americans will commit their wallets, as well as their hearts, to environmental protection. In 2003, for example, 42 percent of the respondents in a Gallup poll reported they had contributed money to an environmental, conservation, or wildlife preservation group.[57]

As long as environmental questions are lofty abstractions, the public's answers can easily imply that environmentalism's roots run deeply as well as broadly across the nation. Certainly when the political bedrock of environmental regulation seems threatened—when fundamental laws such as the Clean Air Act or Clean Water Act seem imperiled—public support for environmentalism has been impressive. The most politically powerful demonstration of such support occurred during the bitter confrontation between the Reagan administration and environmental organizations in the early 1980s.

Environmentalists have also accomplished what amounts to a massive raising of the public's ecological consciousness through public education about environmental issues facing the United States and the world. On the first Earth Day, ecology and the environment were issues foreign to most Americans. Today most Americans have a rudimentary understanding of many basic ecological precepts, including the importance of resource conservation and the global scale of environmental problems. The movement has educated the public and itself into embracing a progressively larger conception of the environment. Before the 1960s, most environmental groups were concerned primarily with land and wildlife management, not with air or water pollution or hazardous waste. The goals of the early

Table 2-1 Rating the Environment

	Blacks		Whites	
	1990	2002	1990	2002
Percentage rating the environmental problem as "very serious"				
Pollution Issues				
Air pollution	80	64[c]	63	49[a]
Pollution of drinking water	78	54[c]	59	42[a]
Hazardous wastes	81	85	72	69
Pesticides in food	NA	NA	68	45[c]
Average of the above	79	68[c]	68	51[c]
Nature Preservation Issues				
Oil spills	75	79	71	64
Loss of natural places for fish and wildlife	60	64	67	57
Loss of natural scenic areas	33	34	34	30
Average of the above	56	59	58	50
Global Environmental Issues				
Acid rain	49	47	44	29[a]
Depletion of ozone layer	43	68[c]	50	50
Global warming	40	44	40	40
Loss of rain forests	NA	NA	64	50[a]
Average of the above	42	53[b]	51	43
Neighborhood Environmental Problems				
Noise level	21	9[c]	13	4[b]
Abandoned houses	21	3[c]	22	1[c]
Litter and garbage	21	5[c]	18	2[c]
Rats, mice, or roaches	20	3[c]	14	0[c]
Exposure to lead	19	1[c]	NA	NA
Bad odors or smells	NA	NA	9	2[b]
Average of the above	18	4[c]	15	2[c]
Percentage rating the attribute as "poor" or "very poor"				
Neighborhood Environmental Attributes				
Number of recreation or play areas nearby	63	17[c]	37	4[c]
General upkeep of the neighborhood	27	5[c]	18	1[c]
Quality of the air	40	12	12	4
Quality of drinking water	38	7	11	3[c]
Average of the above	42	11[c]	20	3[c]

Source: Paul Mohai, "Dispelling Old Myths: African American Concern for the Environment," *Environment* 45 (June 2003): 18.

Note: Where NA appears, the question was not asked in the indicated year. The statistical significance level represents the probability that a difference found between blacks and whites occurred by chance. Statistical significance of differences is based on *t*-tests.

[a] Statistical significance level of $p < 0.05$.
[b] Statistical significance level of $p < 0.01$.
[c] Statistical significance level of $p < 0.001$.

environmentalists were nearsighted, focused mostly on domestic issues, and the supporting science was unsophisticated in its lack of sensitivity to the complex interrelationships among environmental problems. Today viewpoints are more global, ecologically informed, and expansive.

Environmental organizations also have encouraged greater public skepticism about the credibility and managerial skills of the scientists, technicians, and other spokespersons for science and technology involved in public affairs. Since the mid-1970s, environmental organizations have repeatedly challenged the competence of scientific experts and the quality of science supporting opponents in political and administrative battles. These unrelenting technical controversies over the management of commercial nuclear power, the regulation of pesticides, the setting of appropriate air- and water-quality standards, and much else have educated the public about the limits of scientific expertise. Many environmental groups have promoted local citizen involvement in decisions about the siting of real or potential environmental hazards. Critics charge that these groups are entirely too successful at grassroots activism. They blame environmentalists for the rapid spread of NIMBYism (Not In My Backyard)—the uncompromising public opposition to living next to any potentially hazardous facility. This issue is discussed more fully in Chapter 7.

But Is Public Environmentalism Deep?

Despite the public's ecological concern, environmentalism's public impact is still restricted in politically important ways. Environmentalism may now be a consensual value in U.S. politics, but it is what public opinion analyst Riley E. Dunlap calls a "passive consensus"—a situation of "widespread but not terribly intense public support for a goal [in which] government has considerable flexibility in pursuing the goal and is not carefully monitored by the public."[58] Carll Ladd is blunter: Americans, having affirmed their environmentalism, "have turned to other things."[59]

The other things to which Americans are turning do not appear to include sustained interest or reflection about environmental issues at home, at work, or at the voting booth. Thus, when the Pew Research Center asked a sample of the American public in early 2006 which issues should receive priority in Congress and the White House that year, six in ten Americans said "protecting the environment" should be a top priority yet ranked many issues much higher on their preference lists: protecting the environment scored eleventh on the public's overall priority, behind such leading issues as defending the United States from terrorist attack, improving the educational system, strengthening the economy, and seven other concerns.[60]

Even though the public consistently rates Democrats much higher than Republicans on environmental stewardship, being green doesn't appear to help Democrats get to the White House. Environmentalism, in fact, has so far had little impact on presidential voting. In none of the past five presidential elections, for instance, did more than 11 percent of voters ever state that the environment was the most important issue in casting their ballots.[61] Despite Bill Clinton's efforts in 1996 to wrap his campaign in an environmentalist mantle with the presence of self-proclaimed environmentalist Al Gore as his running mate, fewer than 1 percent of those who voted for him cited environmentalism as the most important reason and fewer than 10 percent cited environmentalism among *any* reason for supporting him.[62] Conversely, the public may have disliked Reagan's assault on environmental regulation, but it did not hurt him at the polls. Massive environmentalist criticism of George W. Bush's environmental policies following his 2000 election, moreover, did not appear to change significantly the public's evaluation of Bush as an environmental protector—indeed, in mid-2003 more than half the public polled by Gallup reported that the nation's environmental protection policies were "about the same" as when Bush was elected.[63]

It seems environmental values are linked weakly to candidate or party preference for most voters at most elections and certainly in presidential contests. Among the reasons for environmentalism's "electoral disconnect" among voters, the Nichols Institute suggests that most voters:

• Believe significant progress has been made in environmental protection;
• Perceive the environment as "long-term issues that did not warrant the same priority as more 'immediate' concerns such as jobs and health care";
• Assume that environmental policies would have negative economic impacts such as lost jobs and higher taxes.[64]

Nonetheless, major environmental organizations remain determined to mobilize the public to support green candidates and legislation, while insisting (especially to elective officials and candidates) that environmentalism is potent at the polls. After the 2000 presidential election, the most important environmentalist political campaign organization, the League of Conservation Voters, released a public opinion poll that appeared to demonstrate, among other things, that clean air and water are "top-tier concerns among voters, that environmental issues were 'central to Americans' vote decisions in November' and at least 'important' to Presidential voting."[65] Perhaps. But, on the evidence, the message seems more like preaching to the choir.

Sudden surges of public interest or apprehension about the environment predictably rise in the aftermath of widely publicized environmental disasters or emergencies, but public concern is usually evanescent unless the issue is repeatedly dramatized and personalized. At best, it appears that deep public engagement with environmental issues is a sometime thing. "While the environment has enjoyed remarkable staying power on the national political agenda over the past thirty years," concluded political scientist Deborah Lynn Guber after studying public environmental attitudes, "public commitment to those issues can be somewhat fickle, moving in cycles that visibly advance and retreat over time." [66] Large questions remain. It is not apparent, for instance, how the public might react when confronted by a choice between environmental protection and energy supply, or more cancer research, or greater defense spending, or other difficult trade-offs. Nor has environmentalism yet proved its political toughness by surviving the most brutal test of enduring public commitment: an economic depression. It may sometimes appear to environmental leaders that the environmental equivalent of a 9/11 terrorist attack on New York is required to arouse sustained public attention for environmental issues.

Perhaps another common but unstated reason that environmental policy does not engage the public more deeply is the inherent scientific complexity of the issues, which may often confound or mystify the average person. No matter, science and science disputes are unavoidable in environmental policy discourse.

The Special Place of Science in Policy Making

What often distinguishes environmental policy making from other policy domains is the extraordinary importance of science, and scientific controversy, in the policy process. The growth of environmental legislation since the 1970s is evidence of the federal government's increasing concern with science and technology after World War II. Legislation concerning atomic power, air and water pollution, workplace and consumer safety, and hazardous wastes has put before public officials and agencies the need to make determinations of public policy by depending heavily on scientific evidence and scientific judgments. Indeed, environmental issues routinely require administrative agencies, Congress, judges, the White House staff, and even the president to make these determinations.

Science as Law

The range of scientific judgments required of administrative agencies in implementing environmental programs seems to embrace the whole domain of ecological research. For instance, the Coast Guard is authorized "in order to secure effective provisions . . . for protection of the marine environment . . . to establish regulations for ships with respect to the design and construction of such vessels . . . and with respect to equipment and appliances for . . . the prevention and mitigation of damage to the marine environment."[67]

The EPA is to set effluent standards for new sources of water pollution so that each standard reflects "the greatest degree of effluent reduction . . . achievable through application of the best available demonstrated control technology, process, operating methods, or other alternatives, including, where practicable, a standard permitting no discharge of pollutants."[68]

The EPA is required to establish "standards of performance" for classes and categories of new air pollution sources "which contribute significantly to air pollution or contribute to endangerment of public health or welfare."[69]

Congress, and particularly the congressional committees writing legislation, also may have to resolve a multitude of technical issues. When regulating hazardous substances, for instance, what is a reasonable period to specify for chemical manufacturers to produce reliable data on the human effects of potentially dangerous substances? Is it necessary to regulate air emissions from diesel trucks to reduce harmful air pollutants? Is it appropriate to include heavy metals in the list of water pollutants for which standards must be created by the EPA? Eventually judges will be compelled to weigh scientific evidence and render judgment on environmental issues. For example, did the Department of the Interior have sufficient information to file a valid environmental impact statement on a proposed coal-mining lease on federal lands as required by the National Environmental Policy Act (NEPA)? Or do federal standards for nuclear reactors adequately protect public safety as required by regulations created by the Nuclear Regulatory Commission?

Science as Politics

In policy conflict, one's data become a weapon, and science a bastion against one's critics. Indeed, torturing technical data to fit some partisan position has become an art form in policy debates. Environmental issues frequently place scientists in a highly charged political atmosphere in which impartiality and objectivity, among the most highly esteemed scientific virtues, are severely tested and sometimes fail.

Scientists are consulted by public officials in good part because the scientists' presumed objectivity, as well as technical expertise, makes them trustworthy advisers. But impartiality can be an early casualty in highly partisan and polarizing policy conflict. Even if scientists maintain impartiality, they cannot prevent partisans of one or another policy from distorting technical information to gain an advantage. Scientists suspect (with justification) that their work will often be misrepresented in political debate and their credibility consequently diminished.

In any case, it is characteristic of environmental policy that scientific evidence and opinion frequently are divided for political reasons and, thus, that expert disagreements will reinforce political conflict. Especially when political conflict tends to polarize views and force division over issues, an expert can intentionally, or unwittingly, shade opinions to fit a favored position or manipulate materials until they fit a simplistic policy position. "Experts tend to behave like other people when they engage in a controversy," Allan Mazur, a sociologist and physicist, observed. "Coalitions solidify and disagreements become polarized as conflict becomes more acrimonious."[70] Mazur further observed that experts favoring nuclear power tend to support the notion that a threshold of radiation exposure exists below which human risks are negligible; experts opposing nuclear power plants, in contrast, favor a linear conception of risk that permits no such threshold.[71] When scientific disputes erupt in the course of environmental decision making, one need not assume willful deceit on any side to suggest that political and economic bias could, and probably does, play some part in convincing experts of the truth of a position. Unfortunately, few executives or legislative agencies are innocent of data manipulation, deliberate or not, at some time.

Policy Pressures and Scientific Method

Few public officials are scientists. Faced with the technical questions inherent in environmental policy, officials customarily turn to scientists and technicians for answers or at least for definitions of alternative solutions to clarify choices. As a matter of practical politics, solving issues by resorting to credible scientific evidence can also deflect from officials the criticism they might otherwise endure—sometimes science alone legitimatizes policy. But the politician and the scientist live in fundamentally different decision-making worlds.

For instance, significant differences exist in the time frames for problem solving. "In his search for truth," biologist Roger Revelle observed, "the scientist is oriented toward the future; the politician's orientation is usually here and now. He desires quick visible pay-offs for which he often seems willing to mortgage the future. For the politician in a democratic society, infinity is the election after the next one."[72] Often, public officials are compelled to act swiftly. The Clean Air Act, for example, required the EPA administrator to set standards for sulfur oxides and nitrogen oxides within two years. The Superfund Amendments and Reauthorization Act, passed in 1986, included among its 150 deadlines a requirement that the EPA issue a plan to implement the act's radon research program, produce an annual report on radon mitigation demonstration programs, and provide a report on its national assessment of the radon problem in less than two years after the legislation was passed.[73]

If a crisis erupts—a newly discovered leaking hazardous waste dump or a potentially catastrophic oil spill, for instance—information is needed immediately. But scientific information rarely appears on demand, even in urgent situations and especially when it must be sufficiently accurate to point out a clear direction for policy.

Public officials, moreover, often must craft environmental policies amid continuing disagreement between experts and the public over the degree of risk associated with various environmental problems. For instance, whereas the public rated chemical waste disposal as the highest environmental risk, the experts ranked it considerably lower. In contrast, the experts assigned much greater risk to stratospheric ozone depletion and indoor radon than did the public. Chemical plant accidents were rated a major risk by the public but not by the experts. In effect, these differences amount to two different agendas of priority for environmental regulation. Critics of current environmental regulation, pointing to these disparate views of ecological risk, often argue that public opinion has intimidated policy makers into following the wrong environmental priorities.

Still, decisions must be made, thus confronting policy makers with an unsettling choice between a scientifically risky decision and a politically risky one.[74] Consider, for example, the decision in September 1997 by officials of the National Institute of Environmental Health Sciences (NIEHS) and the Minnesota Pollution Control Agency (MPCA) to announce publicly that samples of Minnesota surface water and groundwater had produced severe abnormalities in native frogs. Asserting they did not know what compound in the water might cause the deformities or what human health effects might follow, the agencies offered bottled water to residents with drinking wells in the affected areas, a pronouncement quickly reported and amplified by state and national news media. Little more than a month later, the NIEHS and the MPCA endured withering criticism from scientific colleagues who accused the agencies of a rushed and inept decision that unduly alarmed the public without scientific justification. Researchers in the EPA's Minnesota research laboratory, as well as other research scientists, asserted that their own evidence contradicted the agencies' conclusions, that the deformities resulted from a chemical imbalance common to Minnesota water, and that the findings were not particularly worrisome. "Now federal scientists are going to look like idiots, even ones who are ultimately proven right," complained the director of another federal research lab. Nonetheless, the NIEHS and the MPCA defended their decision. "We had no intention of going public until we were further along in interpreting the data," explained an NIEHS official, but a public announcement became unavoidable. The MPCA research scientist who made the decision to alert the public insisted she would still make the same decision. Knowledge about the frog deformities was spreading among the public, she explained, and any attempt by her agency to distribute bottled water without a public explanation would incite a panic, she noted. "We felt as a public agency we needed to let people know exactly where research was at," she concluded.[75]

The Minnesota incident was especially discomfiting for scientific professionals because the scientist prefers to measure the correctness of a policy by the standards of experimentation and empiricism. The public official, in contrast, has to calculate a standard's correctness using several additional criteria. Will it satisfy enough public and private interests to be enforceable? Can it be enforced with existing governmental personnel and within the budget? Does the standard appear credible? (It must not be so controversial as to shake public confidence.) But the scientist may measure acceptability by the single standard of precision; accuracy, not acceptability, matters. Under these circumstances, it is understandable that policy makers and their scientific consultants often disagree about what data should be used, and in what manner, in policy decisions.

Conclusion

In an important sense, environmental degradation is a twenty-first century problem resolved according to eighteenth-century rules: fundamental government arrangements such as institutional checks and balances, interest-group liberalism, federalism, and much else reviewed in this chapter are explicitly created by the Constitution or are implicit in its philosophy. The explosive growth of federal environmental legislation, and the distinctive role of science in environmental policy making, add distinctly new elements to the federal policy cycle and indicate that environmental management has become a permanent new policy domain within federal and state governments with its own set of institutional and political biases.

Suggested Readings

Cohen, Richard E. *Washington at Work: Back Rooms and Clean Air.* New York: Macmillan, 1992.

Gruber, Deborah Lynn. *The Grassroots of a Green Revolution.* Cambridge, Mass.: MIT Press, 2003.

Lindblom, Charles A., and Edward J. Woodhouse. *The Policy-Making Process,* 3d ed. Englewood Cliffs, N.J.: Prentice-Hall, 1993.

Marzotto, Toni, Vicky Moshier Burnor, and Gordon Scott Bonham. *The Evolution of Public Policy: Cars and the Environment.* Boulder, Colo.: Lynne Rienner, 2000.

Notes

1. Andrew C. Revkin, "Bush vs. the Laureates: How Science Became a Partisan Issue," *New York Times*, October 19, 2004, A1.
2. Andrew C. Revkin, "Climate Scientist Says NASA Tried to Silence Him," *New York Times*, January 29, 2006, A1
3. Chuck Schoffner, "NASA Expert Says Bush Administration Stifles Evidence on Global Warming," Associated Press State and Local Wire, October 27, 2004, www.ap.org (January 5, 2007).
4. Andrew C. Revkin, January 29, 2006.
5. Ibid.
6. Andrew C. Revkin, "NASA Chief Backs Agency Openness," *New York Times,* February 4, 2006, 1.
7. Andrew C. Revkin, "Lawmaker Condemns NASA over Scientist's Accusations of Censorship," *New York Times,* January 31, 2006, A15.
8. Ibid.
9. Andrew C. Revkin, January 29, 2006.
10. Hugh Heclo, "Issue Networks and the Executive Establishment," in *The New American Political System,* ed. Anthony King (Washington, D.C.: American Enterprise Institute, 1979), 89.
11. Charles O. Jones, *An Introduction to Public Policy* (North Scituate, Mass.: Duxbury Press, 1978), chap. 2.
12. Roger W. Cobb and Charles D. Elder, *Participation in American Politics* (Baltimore: Johns Hopkins University Press, 1972), 86.
13. J. Clarence Davies III, "Environmental Regulation and Technical Change," in *Keeping Pace with Science and Engineering: Studies in Environmental Regulation,* ed. Myron F. Uman (Washington, D.C.: National Academies Press, 1993), 255.
14. Eugene Bardach, *The Implementation Game* (Cambridge, Mass.: MIT Press, 1971), 36.
15. Peter deLeon, "A Theory of Termination in the Policy Process: Rules, Rhymes and Reasons" (Paper delivered at the annual meeting of the American Political Science Association, Washington, D.C., September 1–4, 1977), 2.
16. Richard E. Neustadt, *Presidential Power* (New York: Wiley, 1960).
17. Morton Grodzins, "The Federal System," in *American Federalism in Perspective,* ed. Aaron Wildavsky (Boston: Little, Brown, 1967), 257.
18. Ibid. See also Charles E. Davis and James P. Lester, "Federalism and Environmental Policy," in *Environmental Politics and Policy: Theories and Evidence,* ed. James P. Lester (Durham, N.C.: Duke University Press, 1989), 57–86; and James P. Lester, "A New Federalism? Environmental Policy in the States," in *Environmental Policy in the 1990s,* ed. Norman J. Vig and Michael Kraft (Washington, D.C.: CQ Press, 1990), 59–80.
19. U.S. Advisory Commission on Intergovernmental Relations, *Federal Regulation of State and Local Governments: The Mixed Record of the 1980s,* Publication A-126 (Washington, D.C.: Advisory Commission on Intergovernmental Relations, July 1993), 44–45, chaps. 4, 8.
20. This mingling of private and public power is well explored in Grant McConnell, *Private Power and American Democracy* (New York: Vintage Books, 1967). See also Helen M. Ingram and Dean E. Mann, "Interest Groups and Environmental Policy," in *Environmental Politics and Policy,* ed. Lester, 135–57.
21. James V. DeLong, "How to Convince an Agency," *Regulation* (September–October 1982): 31.
22. Graham Allison, *The Essence of Decision* (Boston: Little, Brown, 1971), 163.
23. Charles A. Lindblom, "The Science of Muddling Through," *Public Administration Review* (spring 1959): 86.
24. The reasons for this departure are examined carefully in J. Clarence Davies III and Charles F. Lettow, "The Impact of Federal Institutional Arrangements," in *Federal Environmental Law,* ed. Erica L. Dolgin and Thomas G. P. Guilbert (St. Paul, Minn.: West, 1974), 26–191.

25. Theodore Lowi, "The Public Philosophy: Interest Group Liberalism," *American Political Science Review* (March 1967): 18.
26. McConnell, *Private Power and American Democracy,* 162.
27. Charles A. Lindblom, *The Policy Making Process,* 2d ed. (Englewood Cliffs, N.J.: Prentice-Hall, 1980), 73.
28. Ibid.
29. Steve Crabtree, "Surprising Stats on 'Active' Environmentalists," *Gallup Poll Tuesday Report,* April 8, 2003, www.gallup.com (February 12, 2004).
30. Riley E. Dunlap, "The State of Environmentalism in the U.S.—Diagnosis: Neither Dead Nor Rejuvenated," www.ecoamerica.typepad.com/blog/2007/04/the_state_of_en.html.
31. Robert Cameron Mitchell, Angela G. Mertig, and Riley E. Dunlap, "Twenty Years of Environmental Mobilization: Trends among National Environmental Organizations," in *American Environmentalism: The U.S. Environmental Movement, 1970–1990,* ed. Riley E. Dunlap and Angela G. Mertig (Philadelphia: Taylor and Francis, 1991), 24.
32. William Ophuls, *Ecology and the Politics of Uncertainty* (San Francisco: Freeman, 1977), 171.
33. A. Susan Leeson, "Philosophic Implications of the Ecological Crisis: The Authoritarian Challenge to Liberalism," *Polity* 11 (spring 1979): 305.
34. Michael McCloskey, "Twenty Years of Change in the Environmental Movement: An Insider's View," in *American Environmentalism,* ed. Dunlap and Mertig, 78–89.
35. Brian Tokar, "Questioning Official Environmentalism," *Z Magazine,* April 1997, 37–43.
36. Jeffrey St. Clair, "Panda Porn: The Marriage of WWF and Weyerhaeuser," *Counterpunch Magazine,* December 5, 2002.
37. Scott Allen, *Boston Globe,* October 20, 1997.
38. Bill Devall, "Deep Ecology and Radical Environmentalism," in *American Environmentalism,* ed. Dunlap and Mertig, 51–61; G. Sessions, "The Deep Ecology Movement," *Environment Review* 11 (June 1987): 105–125; Rick Scarce, *Eco-Warriors: Understanding the Radical Environmental Movement* (Chicago: Noble Press, 1992).
39. Devall, "Deep Ecology and Radical Environmentalism," 55.
40. David Foreman, *Ecodefense* (Tucson: Abbzug Press, 1988); G. Grossman, *And on the Eighth Day We Bulldozed It* (San Francisco: Rainbow Action Network, 1988); S. Obst Love and D. Obst Love, ed., *Ecotage* (New York: Bantam Books, 1972); D. Day, *The Environmental Wars: Reports from the Front Lines* (New York: St. Martin's, 1989).
41. John H. Cushman Jr. and Evelyn Nieves, "In Colorado Resort Fires, Culprits Defy Easy Labels," *New York Times,* October 24, 1998.
42. Robert Cameron Mitchell, "From Conservation to Environmental Movement: The Development of the Modern Environmental Lobbies," in *Government and Environmental Politics,* ed. Michael J. Lacey (Washington, D.C.: Wilson Center Press, 1989), 81–114; Michael deCourcy Hinds, "The Politics of Pollution," *American Demographics* (May 1, 2001): 26.
43. Robert Cameron Mitchell, "Public Opinion and the Green Lobby," in *Environmental Policy in the 1990s,* ed. Vig and Kraft, 81–102.
44. *New York Times,* September 16, 1993.
45. George Hoberg, *Pluralism by Design: Environmental Policy and the American Regulatory State* (New York: Praeger, 1992), ix.
46. Ibid., 198–199.
47. Warren T. Brookes, "Here Comes Flat Earth Day," *Detroit News,* March 8, 1990.
48. John H. Adams, "The Mainstream Environmental Movement," *EPA Journal* 18, no. 1 (1992): 25–26.
49. *New York Times,* June 9, 1993.
50. Marc K. Landy and Mary Hague, "The Coalition for Waste: Private Interests and Superfund," in *Environmental Politics: Public Costs, Private Rewards,* ed. Michael S. Greve and Fred L. Smith (New York: Praeger, 1992), 75.
51. McCloskey, "Twenty Years of Change in the Environmental Movement," 86.
52. Michael J. McCann, "Public Interest Liberalism and the Modern Regulatory State," *Polity* 21 (winter 1988): 373–400.

53. Everett Carll Ladd and Karlyn Bowman, "Public Opinion on the Environment," *Resources* 124 (summer 1996): 5.
54. Jim DiPeso, "The 2006 Midterm Elections: An Environmental Perspective," *Environmental Quality Management* (spring 2006), www.interscience.wiley.com (January 20, 2007). See also Steve Crabtree, "Environmental Activists: Extreme to Mainstream," *The Gallup Poll Tuesday Briefing,* April 29, 2002, www.gallup.com/content/default.asp?ci= 5584 (February 12, 2004); also Riley E. Dunlap, "No Environmental Backlash against Bush Administration," *Gallup News Service,* April 21, 2003, www.gallup.com/content/ default.asp?ci=8215&pg=1 (February 12, 2004).
55. Paul Mohai, "Dispelling Old Myths: African American Concern for the Environment," *Environment* 45 (June 2003): 11–20.
56. Ladd and Bowman, "Public Opinion on the Environment," 5.
57. Dunlap, "No Environmental Backlash against Bush Administration."
58. Riley E. Dunlap, "Public Opinion and Environmental Policy," in *Environmental Politics and Policy,* ed. Lester, 131.
59. Ladd and Bowman, "Public Opinion on the Environment."
60. Pew Research Center, "Broad Support for Political Compromise in Washington But Many Are Hesitant to Yield on Contentious Issues" people-press.org/reports/display. php3?ReportID=302.
61. Ladd and Bowman, "Public Opinion on the Environment."
62. Ibid., 7.
63. Dunlap, "No Environmental Backlash against Bush Administration."
64. Jim DiPeso, "The 2006 Midterm Elections."
65. League of Conservation Voters Education Fund, "Post-Election Polling Shows That American Voters Strongly Support Proactive Environmental Policies," www.lcveducation. org/Programs/Programs.cfm?ID=91&c=24.
66. Deborah Lynn Guber, *The Grassroots of a Green Revolution* (Cambridge, Mass.: MIT Press, 2003), 177.
67. Ports and Waterways Act of 1972, Pub. L. No. 92-340.
68. Federal Water Pollution Control Act Amendments of 1972, Pub. L. No. 92-500.
69. Clean Air Act, Pub. L. No. 84-159 (1955), Pub. L. No. 91-604 (1970), Pub. L. No. 101-549 (1990).
70. Allan Mazur, *The Dynamics of Technical Controversy* (Washington, D.C.: Communications Press, 1981), 29.
71. Ibid., 27.
72. Roger Revelle, "The Scientist and the Politician," in *Science, Technology, and National Policy,* ed. Thomas J. Kuehn and Alan L. Porter (Ithaca, N.Y.: Cornell University Press, 1981), 134.
73. U.S. General Accounting Office, "Superfund: Missed Statutory Deadlines Slow Progress in Environmental Programs," Report No. GAO/RCED 89-27 (November 1988), chap. 2.
74. The epitome of this decision-making problem is explored in Riley Dunlap, *DDT: Scientists, Citizens and Public Policy* (Princeton: Princeton University Press, 1981), esp. chap. 8.
75. "Colleagues Say Frog Deformity Researchers Leaped Too Soon," *Washington Post,* November 3, 1997, A3.

Chapter 3

Making Policy:
Institutions and Politics

The right to traverse the winter wonders of the world's oldest national park in a snowmobile has become one of the nation's most complicated environmental issues. . . . While court challenges continue, the question is likely to be decided by whoever wins the presidential election in November—which means the fate of snowmobiling in Yellowstone is as uncertain as the nation's political future. "We can say for sure that we will welcome winter visitors to Yellowstone next December," said Cheryl Matthews, a spokesperson for the park. "What vehicles they will come in is something we don't know. It would be a great injustice to speculate on what may happen."

"We're totally confused, and we're the people who are supposed to know all about this," said Bill Dart of the BlueRibbon Coalition, a pro-snowmobile group. . . . "The thing changes all the time. It's on. It's off. We're in the park. We're out." . . . One U.S. district judge has ordered the National Park Service to keep the machines out, and another has ordered the park to let them in.
—Washington Post, March 15, 2004

Christine Todd Whitman and Gale Norton were meeting for lunch. Because Norton was secretary of the Department of the Interior (DOI) and Whitman was administrator of the U.S. Environmental Protection Agency (EPA), the lunch was a convenient way for two of President George W. Bush's most important environmental administrators to facilitate cooperation between their departments by sharing common concerns and exchanging important information. It was early May 2003, and, for Whitman, the year so far had gone badly. There were continued public disagreements with the Bush White House and pervasive rumors in Washington, D.C., that Whitman had fallen from White House favor and might quit her job or be fired. However, lunch with Norton—a monthly arrangement—should have been unremarkable. The lunch was civil enough, but even as they ate, the EPA was publicly announcing its support for a ban on snowmobiles in Yellowstone National Park, which Norton, the DOI, and the Bush White House had all vigorously opposed since the president's inauguration.

Norton was irritated, and a "blunt conversation" followed. She telephoned the EPA administrator that same afternoon to complain: Why had Whitman failed to tell her about the announcement while they were at lunch? Whitman was surprised because *she* was not notified, either. In fact, the EPA "announcement" was just a letter written by a relatively low-level regional EPA administrator to the National Park Service (NPS) merely recommending the replacement of snowmobiles. Someone with a distaste for snowmobiles in the EPA's Denver office had released the letter to the media, thus creating public confusion about the Bush administration's controversial snowmobile policy, adding to Whitman's discomfort and annoying Norton. "All the people who should have been notified on the snowmobile issue weren't," explained an EPA media spokesperson unhelpfully. Shortly thereafter, Whitman held a conference call with agency employees across the nation to remind them that politically sensitive information like the Denver letter should be cleared with her office.[1]

The EPA letter was merely one episode along a convoluted path left by the snowmobile policy as it labored through the federal government's policy-making labyrinth. The trail began when President Bill Clinton late in his second term recommended that the DOI ban the snowmobiles and the DOI sought to comply. When the snowmobile industry and its many allied interests vigorously protested the ban, President Bush, who opposed the Clinton decision, announced on his first day in office that he would encourage the DOI to continue allowing the vehicles in Yellowstone and Grand Teton National Parks. The EPA's embarrassing letter appeared while the department was preparing to follow Bush's initiative. Opponents of the snowmobiles responded to Bush's announcement by taking their case to the federal courts and, in December 2003, the Washington, D.C., district court ordered the DOI to reinstate the Clinton ban on snowmobiles. The Republican majority in the House of Representatives then unsuccessfully attempted to counter the district court by passing a bill, ultimately unsuccessful, that would have permitted continued snowmobiles in the parks.[2]

The snowmobile issue now motored back into the federal judiciary and through the federal bureaucracy. In August 2004 the NPS proposed to permit snowmobiles in the parks for at least three years while it studied the conflicting scientific and economic data about snowmobiles. Two months later, the NPS publicly released its plan to allow limited, guided daily treks for 750 snowmobiles in Yellowstone—about twice the average entering the previous year. Environmentalists and other opponents of the snowmobiles now moved to another venue, persuading the Washington, D.C., federal district court in September 2004 to order the DOI to *restore* the Clinton administration's snowmobile ban. The snowmobile industry and its allies countered by initiating other litigation in the Wyoming federal district court, resulting in an October 2004 court injunction, in effect *forbidding* the DOI to enforce the Clinton ban on snowmobiles in Yellowstone and Grand Teton National Parks.[3]

The Bush administration seemed to have won. "A common sense solution for snowmobile use that protects resources while also allowing appropriate access for employment by the public," exalted DOI secretary Norton. To underscore her point, Norton appeared at Yellowstone Park in February 2005 "with a jaunty orange pennant waving from the back of her black snowmobile," reported the *New York Times*, "[and] tootled through a snowscape of hills, steaming rivers and indifferent bison this week giving an unusual personal endorsement to the machines that some consider a blight and others a blessing."[4] Even though many Western political leaders in both parties, and a substantial portion of the Western public, were less enthusiastic about snowmobiles—one opinion poll reported that 80 percent of the Western public favored more limits on snowmobiles in the two parks—snowmobiles seemed to have overrun the opposition.[5]

But that was not the end of the story. The Bush administration had a surprise. When Norton resigned from the DOI in mid-2006, she was succeeded by former Idaho governor Kirk Kempthorne, whose nomination was vigorously opposed by environmentalists who considered him an arch opponent and a sure partisan for more park snowmobiles. Contrary to predictions, however, the DOI's proposed new park regulations in November 2006 rejected increased use of snowmobiles in the parks, limited snowmobile access below the DOI quota originally proposed in 2003, and suspended additional snowmobile regulations for three years while a fourth environmental impact statement on the issue was created. Observers speculated that the issue might be resolved by the winner of the 2008 presidential elections.

Although the discordant progress of its snowmobile policy undoubtedly discomforted the White House, similar instances of publicly confused policy making, often ending with problematic solutions, can be found in the history of any presidency. Policy making in the federal government is inherently time consuming, frequently highly contentious, and often mined with surprises and uncertainties. This situation arises in large part because different institutions, often with conflicting missions, are involved in the policy-making process. It could hardly be otherwise in a government of checks and balances, where institutions exercise competing and shared powers concurrently. In addition, history resonates through the policy-making process.

Today's policy discussions are infused with institutional memories of past events and nuanced with expectations for the future. This chapter examines the most important of the institutions involved in this process to exemplify how competing constitutional authority, shared powers, and historical experience shape the character of policy making in Washington.

The Presidency

"Mothers all want their sons to grow up to be president," President John Kennedy once remarked, "but they don't want them to become politicians in the process."[6] The president wields vast constitutional authority and powerful leverage over public opinion enlarged by a century of growing public tolerance for presidential assertions of additional inherent powers. But to be a successful policy maker the president must still be a proficient politician. The essential politics of presidential leadership in environmental affairs, as with other policy issues, requires, among other things, the will as well as the ability to bargain and compromise with Congress, to know how to shape public opinion and when to be governed by it, to know when to respect judicial independence and when to challenge it—in short, a capacity to move a government of divided powers and competitive institutions in the direction that presidential policies require.

Occupants of the White House since Earth Day 1970 have varied greatly in their concern about environmental protection and their ability to translate environmental commitments into practical policy. So-called green presidents have often been the least successful environmental policy makers. It is a lesson repeated endlessly in Washington that even presidents committed to the politics of policy making discover they cannot always command the ends even when they summon the means for policy leadership.

Presidential Resources

The president possesses a vast array of potentially potent resources to affect the course of environmental policy making in Washington. A short list of these resources includes the following:

- Constitutional authority to propose and to veto legislation;
- Ability to propose policy priorities and initiatives to Congress and the nation simultaneously in the constitutional State of the Union message;
- Power to draft and to present to Congress the annual federal budget;
- Authority to appoint the executive leadership of most major federal environmental bureaucracies such as the DOI and the EPA;
- Authority to appoint federal judges when judicial vacancies occur;
- Authority to issue executive orders, which require no congressional approval, to all federal executive agencies;

- Capacity to create immediate public awareness of issues and to influence public perceptions about issues; and
- Ability to appoint policy advisers to the president's personal staff and to White House advisory committees required by Congress.[7]

This inventory excludes a great deal, such as the talent of creative presidents to transmute traditional authority into new modes of influence (such as President Clinton's technique for frustrating congressional Republican opposition to new federally protected forests by creating them through executive orders immune to congressional veto). Moreover, presidential power also resides in the president's decision *not* to use his or her resources of policy leadership: inaction is also a form of policy making.

From Richard Nixon to George W. Bush

In practice, presidential ability to capitalize on the presidency's political resources for environmental purposes has varied greatly. One explanation for this variability is the many ways in which the circumstances can alter the political climate about the White House—events such as economic recessions, changing congressional majorities, and other changes in the political "seasons" to be discussed shortly. Moreover, some presidents, such as Jimmy Carter, discussed later, have been less skilled than others at Washington politics. And sometimes presidential policy making is blessed or plagued by the unexpected and the unpredictable—as, for instance, when the first Earth Day arrived to the complete surprise of President Richard Nixon and his staff. All this is evident in the environmental record of presidents since 1970.

Nixon and the New Environmentalism. It is a historical irony that no president has left a more impressive legacy of environmental legislation than Nixon, who became an environmentalist in spite of himself. Nixon personally cared little about environmental matters, and his White House advisers never anticipated the rapid political ascendancy of environmentalism signaled by the first Earth Day. But Nixon quickly appreciated environmentalism's political appeal and immediately capitalized on it.[8] In reality, the policies associated with Nixon's first term resulted as much from congressional initiatives as from White House leadership. These initiatives, consisting of an unprecedented outpouring of innovative environmental legislation, were sponsored by an unusually cohesive bipartisan coalition of environmentalist legislators in both congressional chambers who joined with the Nixon administration to create virtually the entire bureaucratic and statutory foundation for modern American environmentalism. During a remarkable period between 1970 and 1974, the president and Congress collaborated in creating the EPA, the National Environmental Policy Act, the Clean Air Act, the Council on Environmental Quality (CEQ), the Clean

Water Act Amendments, the Toxic Substances Control Act, and many other fundamental environmental programs. Nixon's first term remains the most impressive demonstration since the first Earth Day of a politically skillful president capitalizing on legislative opportunity to overcome the divisive institutional tensions between Congress and the White House so often impeding environmental policy making.

The Outsider as President. Following Nixon's 1974 resignation from office and Gerald Ford's brief succession, environmentalists celebrated Democrat Carter's 1976 presidential election, anticipating another period of progressive environmental policy making by the first self-proclaimed environmentalist president.

Carter's environmental initiatives, however, faltered from his inauguration. Carter had the misfortune of arriving in Washington when the nation's so-called energy crisis compelled his administration and Congress to invest enormous attention and political capital in essential but highly unpopular energy regulatory programs. Moreover, Carter and his advisers were often politically inept at Washington politics. (It did not help that Carter's previous political experience consisted largely of being governor of Georgia.) Then, too, his electoral strategy had involved dramatizing himself as a Washington outsider, untainted by traditional Washington politics—a posture poorly received among many of Washington's most important and experienced policy makers. Thus, Carter and his staff continually struggled at crafting the political means to achieve his environmental ends, and the ambiguous results frequently disappointed environmentalists. Achievements of his administration included creating the Department of Energy (DOE), enacting the first strict national regulation of coal surface mining (Surface Mining Control and Reclamation Act of 1977), and making important revisions to the Clean Air Act and Clean Water Act. But Carter's efforts to mitigate the energy crisis were highly unpopular, however environmentally beneficial. Most of this legislation, such as reduced speed limits on national highways and mandatory improvements in automobile energy efficiency, were rapidly repealed by Congress within a few years of their creation when the energy crisis temporarily vanished. The disaffection among many in the public with Carter's presidential style and his energy policies was exploited adeptly by Republican Ronald Reagan in his successful 1980 presidential campaign against Carter. Following Reagan's inauguration, the lingering public unhappiness with Carter added momentum to the Reagan administration's fierce assault against federal environmental regulations.

Reagan and "Regulatory Relief." Among environmentalists the Reagan years have become the gold standard of presidential antagonism. Reagan and his advisers believed they were given an electoral mandate to "get government off our back" by achieving so-called regulatory relief from excessively costly and unnecessary federal regulation. His administration placed the Clean Air Act and many other fundamental environmental laws atop their widely advertised hit list of programs they pledged to repeal or to alter radically. Environmentalists commonly dismissed Reagan as an environmental know-nothing and guardian of Big Business. However, they were reluctant to recognize that Reagan often articulated the genuine dissatisfaction among the public at large, at least among numerous important publics, with the cost of many environmental regulations and disappointment with the results of these regulations.

The Reagan administration's attack on environmental regulation proceeded along many fronts.[9] Using his executive authority, Reagan selected individuals deeply committed to regulatory relief for important leadership positions in the major environmental agencies such as the EPA, the DOI, and the DOE. He mounted a legislative attack by urging Congress to weaken major environmental laws by amendment or other strategies. He effectively slowed the implementation and enforcement of many environmental laws by reducing or reallocating agency budgets. He filled federal judicial vacancies, whenever possible, with judges thought to be less sympathetic to environmentalist litigation than their predecessors. Reagan also used his formidable platform skills to preach tirelessly against the growth of environmental regulation.

In the end, much of the administration's antiregulatory strategy was self-defeating. The public turned out to be unsympathetic to Reagan's wholesale assault on environmental laws. Congress failed to rally behind most of his legislative proposals. Members of both parties often frustrated the mission of Reagan's executive appointees when these officials appeared to obstruct the implementation of congressionally mandated environmental programs. Still, the Reagan years profoundly changed the course of environmental policy making. Over Reagan's eight years in office, his executive appointees quietly and consistently slowed or delayed the implementation of numerous environmental programs, while budget reductions put many environmental agencies years behind in accomplishing important environmental missions. Environmental pressure groups were compelled to wage a largely defensive battle; consequently, new environmental laws and reform of existing ones were infrequent. Reagan's many judicial appointees would gradually diminish the federal courts' strongly sympathetic environmentalist disposition. Equally important, the Reagan years bred an anger and suspicion still infecting the discourse between environmental activists and the Republican Party.

A Slightly Greener White House. George H. W. Bush's presidency, as noted in Chapter 1, marked a mild reawakening of White House environmentalism. Bush set out in his 1988 presidential campaign to eradicate the antienvironmental image acquired by the Republican Party during the

Reagan years. Bush promised during this campaign to be "an environmental president" and genuinely hoped to restore a measure of good will among environmental activists, the White House, and the Republican Party. To affirm this intention, Bush earned considerable approval among environmentalists by appointing William Reilly, a well known and popular environmental leader, as the EPA administrator.[10] In addition, Bush attempted to rectify the EPA's damaging budgetary reductions during the Reagan years by significantly increasing the agency's funding and personnel. Perhaps most significant, Bush strongly promoted legislative passage of the Clean Air Act Amendments of 1990, a sweeping and highly constructive reform thwarted in Congress for almost a decade by bitter partisan division and White House disfavor.

Bush's presidential tenure, despite some important environmental accomplishments, nonetheless disappointed most environmental advocates. His failure to reinvigorate U.S. participation in international environmental diplomacy was a major criticism among environmentalists (Bush was conspicuous, for instance, in his absence from the important 1992 Rio Conference, a United Nations conference on the environment and development attended by most other major heads of state). Also, Reilly was almost alone among Bush's major executive appointments in outspoken environmental leadership, and Bush's legislative initiatives rarely involved environmental proposals widely supported among environmental interest groups.

Rising Expectations. Environmentalists expected a great deal of Clinton in light of his environmental credentials. He was a Democrat, Vice President Al Gore had been the Senate's leading environmental activist, and Clinton had vigorously appealed to environmentalist voters with a strongly green platform in his presidential campaign.[11] His appointments of Carol Browner as EPA administrator and Bruce Babbitt as secretary of the interior sent encouraging signals to environmental activists. But Clinton's tumultuous presidency was punctuated by events that badly impeded his environmental initiatives. The startling "Republican Revolution" of 1994 swept a Republican majority into the House of Representatives fiercely determined to resurrect Reagan's assault on major federal environmental regulations. With Republicans intermittently controlling the Senate after 1996 as well, Congress and the president created a legislative gridlock that largely stifled both White House environmental initiatives and Republican antiregulatory reforms.[12] Environmentalism also became a casualty of Clinton's bitter second-term impeachment battle; as a result, by the end of his White House tenure, Clinton could claim relatively few major environmental victories legislatively. Among his accomplishments was the revival of U.S. engagement in environmental diplomacy, most notably by signing the Kyoto Protocol creating the framework for a treaty to control global greenhouse gas (which was subsequently rejected by the Senate).

Clinton's most conspicuous environmental legacy was his decision to designate more than 3 million acres of federal land as national monuments and 58 million more acres of national forest as wilderness areas; both designations protected the lands from resource exploitation or other development. In both instances, Clinton's orders were based on inherent presidential authority and therefore immune to congressional veto or modification. From an environmentalist viewpoint, political scientist Paul Wapner suggested that perhaps Clinton's greatest accomplishment was "not what he achieved but what he staved off." Further,

> Clinton faced an aggressive and hostile Congress that worked consistently to dismantle fundamental environmental laws . . . and to frustrate the ability of agencies like the EPA to carry out their regulatory work. Clinton consistently resisted these attacks. . . . Clinton's efforts to beat back Republican attempts to emasculate U.S. environmental law and process should not be missed when assessing his environmental legacy.[13]

Conflict Renewed. "He uses a sharpie pen," observed a former advisor to President George W. Bush. "He's not a pencil with an eraser kind of guy."[14] True to his reputation for staying a course once taken, throughout most of his administration George W. Bush mobilized his executive authority firmly and consistently to promote an environmental agenda most environmentalists found unacceptable. Bush was severely criticized especially for failing to promote governmental regulation of climate-warming gases, his support for an ambitious new program of coal- and nuclear-powered utility construction, his enthusiasm for expanding energy exploration on public lands, and his alleged suppression of federal scientific research uncongenial to his policy agenda. While Bush insisted he was neither hostile to environmentalism nor intolerant of uncongenial environmental science, the Bush White House rarely seemed concerned about its sour environmentalist image or scientific critics.[15]

Bush's chilly relations with environmentalists largely distracted attention from the administration's sometimes constructive environmental initiatives. These included, among other things, the EPA's decision to force General Electric to spend hundreds of millions of dollars to remove PCBs in the Hudson River, a cleanup that [had] been delayed; legislation speeding the clean up of urban industrial sites known as brownfields; increases in financing for private land set aside for conservation of animals and their habitats; and the first limits for diesel emissions in trucks and off-road vehicles. Moreover, Bush pleasantly surprised environmentalists late in his administration by appointing Stephen F. Johnson as EPA administrator, the first scientist to head the agency and an environmentalist preference.

Until Bush's second White House term, most voters seemed indifferent to his environmental record and highly publicized clashes with environmental scientists. By 2007, the political winds had shifted. The White

House was burdened by the increasingly unpopular Iraq war and growing public disapproval of the administration's environmental record (a national poll estimated that 54 percent of the public disapproved of Bush's environmental record in mid-2006).[16] Most important, the stunning 2006 election of Democratic majorities in both congressional chambers—an election in which Bush's environmental record for the first time appeared an important issue—persuaded a reluctant White House to reassess its environmental agenda. The Bush adminstration indicated greater receptivity to new initiatives for national and international climate-warming regulation, more deference to majority scientific opinions concerning climate change, and greater support for energy conservation and alternative energy sources. Whether the Republican White House could work constructively with the new congressional Democratic majorities on a reformed environmental agenda remained a major uncertainty in the sunset years of the Bush presidency.

Congress: Too Much Check, Too Little Balance

The president may propose, but it is often Congress that ultimately disposes. In a Madisonian government of separated institutions sharing powers, presidents and environmental administrators have good reason to look warily toward Congress. The Constitution invests Congress with enormous authority over the daily conduct of the president and the executive branch. Under ordinary circumstances, few aspects of presidential and bureaucratic behavior are untouched directly or indirectly by congressional authority and politics.

Despite a panoply of party organizations, legislative leaders, and coordinating committees, Congress is still largely an institution of fragmented powers and divided geographic loyalties. Legislative power is dispersed in both chambers among a multitude of committees and subcommittees; local or regional concerns often tenaciously claim legislative loyalties. The electoral cycle intrudes imperiously on policy deliberations. The public interest and legislative objectivity compete with equally insistent legislative concerns to deliver something from Washington to the "folks back home." In environmental affairs, Congress is an assembly of scientific amateurs who must enact programs of great technical complexity to ameliorate scientifically complicated environmental ills most legislators dimly understand.

The Statutory Setting. The most fundamental congressional responsibility is to craft environmental law. Current federal environmental legislation is a patchwork of several hundred congressional enactments written since the 1950s. Legal scholar Christopher Schroeder's verdict about federal toxic substance laws—that they have "resulted not in a well-designed cabin, but in a pile of logs"—applies as well to the whole of federal environmental legislation.[17] Many controversies prominent since the 1970s result from the inconsistencies, contradictions, confusions, and inadequacies of this statutory welter. At the same time, each law memorializes the success of a major environmental coalition in waging a battle for environmental protection that may have lasted decades. Each law acquires a politically vocal and potent constituency from congressional factions, private interests, bureaucratic agencies, and program beneficiaries. A huge volume of judicial opinions girding each law with court-derived interpretations and justifications further institutionalizes the legislation. These laws are the legal edifice on which environmental policy has been erected.

The major legislative enactments currently on the federal statute books relating to just one category of environmental pollutant, toxic substances, include fifteen major laws. Cataloging just one among the many categories of environmental law is sufficient to emphasize two realities about environmental policy controversies: (1) The existing law becomes a conservative force in policy debate because it is difficult to change, and (2) the incompatibilities and omissions in current environmental legislation are a continuing cause of difficulties in policy implementation and enforcement.

Committee Decentralization. Congress has been described as a "kind of confederation of little legislatures."[18] In both chambers the committees and subcommittees—those little legislatures wielding the most consistently effective power in the legislative system—are dispersed and competitive in environmental matters. William Ruckelshaus, the EPA's first administrator, complained in the early 1970s that he had to deal with sixteen different congressional subcommittees.[19] The situation has gotten more complicated. Today, fourteen of twenty-two standing House committees share some jurisdiction over environmental policy.

In the Senate, eleven committees and several dozen subcommittees share jurisdiction over environmentally sensitive energy issues. Water policy is even more decentralized: seventy congressional committees and subcommittees share some jurisdiction. In the 108th Congress (2002–2004), twenty-four committees and subcommittees in the Senate and twenty-six in the House of Representatives exercised some authority over the EPA's programs. With authority over environmental policy fragmented among a multitude of committees in each chamber, competition and jurisdictional rivalry commonly occur as each committee attempts to assert some influence over environmental programs. The result is that, as a rule, environmental legislation evolves only through protracted bargaining and compromising among the many committees. This time-consuming process often results in legislation that is vague or inconsistent. Divided jurisdictions, however, provide different interest groups with some point of committee access during environmental policy formulation; as a consequence, these groups resist efforts to reduce the number of committees with overlapping jurisdictions and concentrate authority in a few major committees.

Localism. When the national taxpayer organization Citizens against Government Waste (CAGW) noted in its annual *Pig Book* that Mississippi ranked sixth among the fifty states in the amount of political pork (a common term for wasteful federal spending) its congressional delegation had delivered to the state, Sen. Trent Lott, R-Miss., seemed almost pleased with his state's ranking. "The definition of wasteful 'pork' is in the eye of the beholder," he responded. "In my eye, if its south of Memphis, it sure isn't pork. . . . If we must use our political acumen to get part of our money back, then so be it. In this regard, CAGW's report indicates Mississippi is doing very well."[20] Many of his Senate colleagues would have added "amen."

Senators are unapologetically loyal to the practice of voting for each other's local public works projects, the most common political pork. This loyalty is driven by a powerful tradition of localism in congressional voting. In U.S. political culture, legislators are treated by constituents—and regard themselves—as ambassadors to Washington, D.C., from their own geographic areas. They are expected to acquire skills in the practice of pork-barrel politics, capturing federal goods and services for their constituencies. They are also expected to be vigilant in promoting and protecting local interests in the national policy arena. Congressional tenure is more likely to depend on a legislator's ability to serve these local interests than on other legislative achievements. Although not the only influence on congressional voting, such politics is deeply rooted and probably the single most compelling force in shaping voting decisions.

This localism affects environmental policy in different ways. By encouraging legislators to view environmental proposals first through the lens of local interests, localism often weakens sensitivity to national needs and interests. At worst it drives legislators to judge the merits of environmental policies almost solely by their impact on frequently small and atypical constituencies.

Localism also whets the congressional appetite for federal distributive programs freighted with local benefits. An aroma of political pork can add appeal to an environmental program, especially if other important local issues are involved. This lesson is not lost on the environmental bureaucracies. For instance, when opposition by the powerful House Ways and Means Committee appeared to threaten defeat for the initial Superfund legislation, a program strongly supported by the EPA, the agency worked with sympathetic congressional staff members to create a list of prospective Superfund sites in each committee member's district. The committee members were thereby reminded of the "ticking time bombs" in their districts *and* of the potentially great financial benefits from cleanup activities—an almost irresistible double dose of localism.[21] It is not surprising that federal grants to build pollution control facilities, such as sewage treatment plants, also have instant appeal. Even the comparatively tiny federal program for such grants to the states in the mid-1960s had great appeal. "The program was immensely popular. . . . Congressmen enjoyed the publicity and credit they received every time they announced another grant for another community in their district." [22] The huge $18 billion waste treatment facilities program, first authorized in 1972, is the second largest public works program in U.S. history and even more popular than the earlier construction grants. The EPA estimated that for every $1 billion spent, about 50,900 worker years of employment would be generated in plant and sewer construction. [23]

Elections. The electoral cycle also dominates the legislative mind. The constitutionally mandated electoral cycles of the federal government—two years, four years, or six years—partition the time available for legislative deliberation into periods bound by different elections. Within these time frames, policy decisions are continually analyzed for their electoral implications and often valued largely for electoral impacts. This affects congressional policy styles in several ways. First, the short term becomes more important than the long term when evaluating programs; legislators often attribute more importance to a program's impact on the next election than to its longer term effects on unborn generations. Second, policies are tested continually against public opinion. Although a weak or badly divided public opinion often can be ignored, a coherent majority opinion related to an environmental issue usually wields significant influence on congressional voting, especially when legislators can associate the opinion with their own constituencies. Hazardous waste cleanup programs, for example, are hard to oppose whatever their actual merits because the ticking time bomb has become a durable, powerful public metaphor in practically every constituency.

Preoccupation with elections, localism, and the other aspects of congressional culture are the givens of policy making. And congressional policy making, as much as presidential leadership, has been responsible for creating and maintaining the entire foundation of federal environmental governance—one of Congress' greatest historical achievements. However, Congress has also become a rich source of delay, confusion, and waste in making and implementing environmental policy. These problems arise from excesses and exaggeration in the authority the constitutional framers prudently invested in Congress—a case of checks and balances gone awry. Many of these difficulties could be eliminated or mitigated by a self-imposed discipline of which Congress may be incapable.

"Ready, Fire, Aim": Crisis Decision Making. The congressional response to environmental problems is highly volatile, waxing and waning according to changing public moods, emerging environmental crises, economic circumstances, or today's front-page ecological disasters. Congress

easily falls into a "pollutant of the year" mentality, mandating new programs or sudden changes in existing ones according to what environmental problems currently seem most urgent or according to the public's current mood.

The Ocean Dumping Act of 1988, for example, is the very model of crisis-inspired legislation. During the summer of 1988, popular bathing beaches along New York's eastern coast frequently were fouled with medical wastes, raw sewage, and other dangerous debris apparently washed ashore from New York City sewage dumped more than 100 miles offshore. Closed beaches and public revulsion at the widely publicized pollution quickly persuaded Congress to pass, without one dissenting vote, the Ocean Dumping Act, which prohibited additional ocean disposal of urban waste within a few years. Congress was unmoved by expert testimony that held the real cause of the contamination to be the continual overflow from New York City's antique sewer system, which would be hugely expensive to repair. Nor was Congress in the mood to evaluate alternatives. "There is no question," argued the chief engineer of the regional waste management agency, "that the New York City sewer system is the greatest cause of water pollution in the region. But a sewer system isn't sexy. It's expensive to fix, and nobody wants to hear about it. So people focused on what they understand . . . and they understand that sewage and the sea don't seem nice together."[24] Local representative Thomas J. Manton, D-Queens, initially opposed to the act, soon capitulated to political realities. "Nobody wanted to discuss the relative risks or merits," he later explained. "It had been a bad summer, and we all wanted to be able to say we did something. So we passed a law. I tried to have a debate. And it was like I was trying to destroy the planet."[25] As a result of the act, the city of New York will have spent at least $2 billion on facilities to convert sewage into fertilizer and $300 million annually for a decade thereafter to dispose of its sludge, although many experts believe an equally effective and much cheaper solution would have been possible if Congress had not ordained that ocean dumping be eliminated entirely but instead had rennovated the existing sewer system to remove the harmful pollutants from the affluent before ocean release.

Environmental policies are seldom so poorly conceived, but this reactive policy making ensures an environmental agenda in which place and priority among programs depend less on scientific logic than on political circumstance. Often the losers are scientifically compelling environmental problems unblessed with political sex appeal. Moreover, once a program is legislatively attractive, it usually acquires a mandated budget that virtually ensures survival. Most environmental scientists, for instance, consider indoor air pollution a more compelling health risk than abandoned hazardous waste sites or even some currently regulated forms of air pollution, but most of the EPA's air pollution budget is mandated for ambient air regulation, and Congress lacks enthusiasm to tackle indoor air pollution in the absence of a perceived crisis.[26]

Another result of this crisis mentality is administrative overload. The EPA and other environmental agencies have often had to implement quickly a multitude of new programs, hastily enacted without sufficient time or resources provided for the required tasks. As a result, the EPA has struggled continually and unsuccessfully to find the means to carry out all the program mandates. This crisis mentality also begets constantly mandated changes in regulatory priorities and program deadlines.

Guidance: Too Much and Too Little. Behind the facade of high purpose and ambitious action of every major environmental law likely stretches a terrain mined with muddled language, troublesome silences, and inconsistent programs. Some of this is inevitable. Mistakes in statutory design occur because federal environmental regulations address problems of great scientific and administrative complexity with which legislators have had no prior experience. Moreover, members of Congress are typically lawyers, business executives, or other nonscientific professionals who depend on the expertise of administrators to clarify and interpret the law appropriately in regard to specialized environmental programs. The constant pressure of legislative affairs discourages most members of Congress from giving considerable attention to environmental issues or from developing an adequate understanding of them. "It's tough to get Congress to focus on bills with sufficient time to develop an adequate depth of understanding," observed John A. Moore, former acting deputy director for the EPA. "You've got 1 or 2 Congressmen who truly know it; there are 400 others that are going to vote on it."[27] Even conscientious legislators can be easily intimidated when they attempt to unravel the technical complexities of environmental legislation. During congressional debate over passage of the Safe Drinking Water Act (1974), for instance, proponents argued that 12,000 contaminants existed with unknown causes. Debate raged within the EPA and Congress about whether the agency needed to regulate twenty to thirty, hundreds, or even thousands of water pollutants—even the Public Health Service's traditionally undisputed standard for selenium was made suspect. Finally, Congress had to give the EPA the final responsibility for identifying most of the appropriate pollutants for regulation.[28]

Environmental legislation is often vague and contradictory because Congress cannot or will not resolve major political conflicts entailed in the law. Instead, Congress often papers over the conflict with silence or deliberate obscurity in the statutory language. This approach results in a steady flow of political hot potatoes to the bureaucracy, which must untangle and clarify this legal language—often to the accompaniment of political conflict and legislative criticism—or leave the job to the courts. The EPA becomes enmeshed in protracted litigation and political bargaining, program regulations essential to implementing the laws often become hostage to these procedures, and Congress frequently avoids a risky political blood-letting. "Congress outsources the rulemaking to the EPA," asserted regulatory critic David Schoenbrod, "so that the legislators can claim credit for protecting health while the agency bears the inevitable blame for delays, disappointments, and costs."[29] True or not, so it often appears.

Congressional frustration with the continual delay in implementing environmental laws has led to the habitual use of extravagant, extraordinarily detailed, and inflexible language in new environmental laws; to the constant mandating of precise deadlines for completing various programs; and to prescription, in excruciating detail, of how administrators are to carry out program activities—in effect, to a cure as bad as the disease. The Clean Air Act Amendments of 1990, for instance, were packed with a multitude of new programs accompanied by hundreds of mandatory deadlines seldom carefully considered. The predictable result was that the EPA missed 198 of the 247 deadlines it was required to meet by 2000 and will miss more than half the 108 deadlines that remain to be met later.[30]

"An Odd and Intricate System of Checks and Balances." Republican victories in the 1994 congressional elections only perpetuated the fractious relationship between the EPA and Congress. The new Republican majority in both legislative chambers at first enthusiastically assaulted the EPA's budget and regulatory authority in a comprehensive effort to severely diminish both. The Reagan administration had learned, at considerable political cost, that frontal assaults on the statutory bulwark of environmental regulation invite a public backlash. Congressional Republicans relearned the lesson between 1994 and 1998 and eventually abandoned their initial assault in favor of persistent, quieter, and less publicly risky campaigns aimed selectively at portions of various environmental laws and segments of EPA budgets vulnerable to antiregulatory strategies. Republican antipathy did slow appreciably the growth of the EPA's budget, the passage of new environmental legislation and the revision of older laws. By the beginning of George W. Bush's administration, it seemed by a perverse political logic that friends and critics of environmental regulation had unwittingly contrived to ensure that excessive control of the EPA, and the administrative distrust nourishing it, would be virtually institutionalized in Congress. "Pro-environment members of Congress fear that the agency will not be ardent enough in defending the environment; members more sympathetic to business concerns fear that the agency will be too ardent," concluded a comprehensive review of federal regulatory programs by Resources for the Future, an influential Washington environmental think tank. In addition,

> The pro-environment members (and the pro-business members) write detailed instructions into law; the pro-business members try to ensure that

the agency will not have enough resources to fully implement the laws and that the courts will have authority to second guess any agency decisions. EPA is thus the focus of an odd and intricate system of checks-and-balances.[31]

The Legislative Bluff. Congress writes into major environmental laws a multitude of sanctions, many ostensibly severe, intended to encourage compliance with environmental regulation and to arm regulators with the power to compel it. The Clean Air Act, for instance, authorizes the EPA to impose a moratorium on the construction and operation of any new stationary source of air pollution in any urban area that fails to attain federally required air-quality standards by the mandated deadlines; this, in effect, gives the agency the authority to stop major urban economic development. The Clean Air Act also empowers the EPA to issue documents halting all federal highway construction funds and other major federal grants to any state with urban areas failing to meet deadlines for compliance with federally required air-quality standards. Tough penalties must be used selectively. Regulators need authority and opportunity to bargain about when and how penalties will be applied to regulated interests failing to comply with the laws. But a powerful sanction merely threatened will eventually become a rusty regulatory blunderbuss.

Congress has diminished the credibility of many tough sanctions written into environmental legislation by repeatedly extending compliance deadlines for regulations, thereby sidestepping the sanction problem. Consider, for example, the deadline of the Clean Air Act for the nation's metropolitan areas to meet national air-quality standards for ozone or face a moratorium on new factory construction and loss of federal highway funds. Congress first set the deadline for 1976, then extended it to 1982, then to 1987, then to late 1988, then to 1990—extensions granted to save more than sixty metropolitan areas from sanctions. Once Congress authorized the EPA to extend the deadlines, the message was clear. According to legal scholar R. Shep Melnick,

> Congress and the EPA once again showed that they would not stand behind the standards and deadlines previously announced with great seriousness. Every major participant knows that loopholes will always appear in the nick of time, thus obviating the need to impose sanctions in areas that fail to meet air quality standards.[32]

Continuing congressional setbacks in compliance deadlines have also been made for automobile emission requirements in the Clean Air Act, in water-quality standards for municipal waste treatment systems regulated under the Federal Water Pollution Control Act Amendments of 1972, and in many other programs in other environmental laws.

There are plausible reasons for this situation. Legislators may worry about the adverse economic impact of sanctions on the local and national economies or about the alleged difficulties in developing the technologies needed to meet compliance deadlines. But the congressional bluff often betrays a lack of political will to face the consequences of the commitments Congress has made to enforce the law. In effect, the toughest sanctions in environmental legislation often amount to little more than legislative make-believe.

The Bureaucracy: Power through Implementation

Federal agencies concerned with environmental affairs and closely related matters such as energy, consumer protection, and worker health have grown explosively since 1970. More than 150 major new federal laws, most concerned with broad regulation of business and the economy in the interest of public health and safety, have been enacted since then. More than twenty new regulatory agencies have been created to implement these programs, including the EPA, the Occupational Safety and Health Administration, and the DOI's Office of Surface Mining. An understanding of such bureaucracies, and especially the more environmentally important among them, is essential to explaining the logic of federal environmental policy making.

The Power of Discretion

The significance of the environmental agencies rests less on their size and budget than on the political realities obscured by a constitutional illusion. The Constitution appears to vest the power to formulate policy primarily in Congress, while leaving to the president and the executive branch the task of seeing that the laws are "faithfully executed." Although implemented and enforced principally in the bureaucracy, public policy actually develops in both branches of the government.

Delegated authority and administrative discretion are the wellsprings of bureaucratic power. Congress routinely invests administrators with responsibility for making a multitude of decisions it cannot or will not make itself about the implementation of policy; often this becomes legislative power delegated to the executive branch. Even when delegation is not clearly intended, administrators assume the power to make public policy when they choose how to implement policies permitting different options—hence, the existence of administrative discretion.

Congress and the president, using a variety of constitutional and statutory powers, attempt to discipline the exercise of administrative discretion. Still, this oversight holds no certain rein on administrative discretion, particularly in light of the vast number and complexity of environmental programs, the elephantine size of the bureaucracy, and competing demands on presidential and congressional time.

A commonplace example can illustrate the pervasive problem of controlling administrative discretion. In 1981 President Reagan ordered all federal administrative agencies to prepare a regulatory impact analysis—a type of benefit-cost assessment—for most of their new regulatory proposals and left to his own administrative management agency, the Office of Management and Budget (OMB), the responsibility to draft guidelines for the agencies. The OMB, in turn, interpreted the president's order as requiring the responsible agencies, such as the EPA, to include in each of its assessments an evaluation of alternatives to the proposed regulation. The EPA, for its part, issued guidelines to each of its offices recommending that at least four alternatives be considered for each proposed new regulation. A review of regulatory impact analyses prepared by one EPA office in mid-1997 suggests that the intent of the original White House directive had been significantly adulterated by this trickle-down of discretionary authority from the White House to the EPA. Of the twenty-three assessments studied, six examined only one alternative to the proposed regulation. The rest compared two or more alternatives to the proposed regulation but were not always clear about how many alternatives or which types were involved. In no instance had any agency in the chain of command violated law nor was there evidence of intent to do so.[33] Still, the documents ultimately prepared by the EPA appeared to disregard in many respects the intent of the original White House directive. Whatever the interpretation, the flow of discretionary authority and its compounding influence throughout government, for good and ill, will be reality, in all seasons, for all presidents, and for all parties. The federal bureaucracy, assured of generous discretionary authority well into the future, will continue to be an independent and largely self-regulated influence in environmental policy.

Bureaucratic Competitiveness

The bureaucracy is no monolith. Its powers in environmental affairs, although collectively vast, also are dispersed and competitive. One source of this fragmentation is the federalizing of environmental administration. Many major environmental laws enacted in Washington, D.C., are administered partially or wholly through state governments; others give states an option to participate. Under the Federal Water Pollution Control Act, for instance, twenty-seven states currently administer their own water pollution permit systems; all but six states and the District of Columbia administer the Safe Drinking Water Act. The Clean Air Act permits the states to participate in several major aspects of the program, including the control of pollutants and the establishment of emission standards for stationary sources.

Another cause of fragmented administrative authority is the chronic division of and overlapping responsibility for environmental programs among federal agencies. Twenty-seven separate federal agencies share major regulatory responsibility in environmental and occupational health. Regulating even a single pollutant often necessitates what might appear to be a bureaucratic convention. Toxic substances currently are regulated under twenty different federal statutes involving five agencies. To address all the problems in human exposure to vinyl chloride, for example, would require the collaboration of all five agencies working with fifteen different laws.[34]

Dispersed authority breeds conflict and competition among agencies and their political allies over program implementation, authority, and resources—the turf wars familiar to students of bureaucracy. The story of Whitman and Norton's lunch at the beginning of this chapter affirms a bureaucratic reality: collaboration is common but never dependable. And in environmental affairs, federal agencies are notoriously fitful collaborators. In this milieu of dispersed and competitive agency authority, policy implementation often becomes a continual process of collaboration and conflict between coalitions of agencies and their allies shaping and reshaping policy as the relative strengths of the conflicting alignments change. Moreover, administrative conflict crosses the institutional divisions of the federal government, spreading downward through the federal system to state and local governments and outward from government to organized private groups. Indeed, agencies failing to enlist diverse and active allies in their policy struggles may frustrate their own missions and leave their futures hostage to more politically skilled opponents.

The Environmental Protection Agency

The EPA, created by an executive order of President Nixon in 1970, is the largest federal regulatory agency in terms of budget and personnel. Its responsibilities embrace an extraordinarily large and technically complex set of programs ranging across the whole domain of environmental management. Asked if his job had been rewarding, a former administrator for the EPA replied that it was "like beating a train across a grade crossing— if you make it, it's a great rush. If you don't, you're dead." [35] An insider's guide to Washington, D.C., ranked the job of administrator for the EPA among the 100 toughest positions in the city. Political controversy is the daily bread of the EPA's leadership. "The Administrator rarely goes to the President with good news and is more often the bearer of bad news," observed Lee Thomas, EPA administrator from 1985 to 1988. "You almost never have a decision where many people applaud it." [36] In such a politically charged setting, the EPA administrator's office has often been a revolving door through which a succession of executives pass, unwilling or unable to manage the inherited political turbulence. Such was the case during the George W. Bush administration, when Whitman, Michael O. Leavitt, and Stephan L. Johnson all occupied the administrator's office over a five-year period.

Statutory Responsibilities. The size of the EPA's regulatory burden is suggested in Box 3-1, which summarizes the EPA's current statutory responsibilities. These regulatory programs represent the major environmental legislation of the past three decades. The EPA grew steadily in staff and budget until 1981, when the Reagan administration severely reduced both budget and personnel. The agency has recovered somewhat and presently has about eighteen thousand employees and an annual budget exceeding $7 billion, of which less than half supports its administrative activities (most of the money underwrites water treatment and Superfund grants).[37] The agency, whose administrator is appointed by the president, consists of a Washington, D.C., headquarters and ten regional offices, each headed by a regional administrator. Unlike most regulatory agencies, the EPA administers both regulatory and distributive programs such as the huge federal waste treatment grants, the Superfund program, and various research activities.

Notwithstanding some significant achievements, the EPA confronts a daunting array of problems in the early years of the twenty-first century: an unmanageable burden of continually growing regulatory responsibilities, a politically toxic inheritance of congressional distrust and disruptive oversight born of bitter controversies surrounding the Reagan administration and resurrected by the 1994 Republican congressional takeover, a chronically inadequate budget, and the administrative complexities inherent in complicated environmental regulations. The growing disparity between the EPA's administrative responsibilities and its resources has reached a point at which many observers believe the agency is, or will soon be, mired in "a pathological cycle of regulatory failure." [38]

Micromanaged and Overloaded. By the mid-1980s it was already obvious, as the CEQ observed, that "the Environmental Protection Agency cannot possibly do all the things its various mandates tell it to do," and conditions have not improved.[39] More than two decades later, the agency is still years, or decades, behind in complying with important requirements in its ten major statutory programs, and new jobs are always ahead.

One reason for the agency's chronic compliance problems is the congressional penchant for packing legislation with a multitude of demanding deadlines, detailed management instructions, and hammer clauses that threaten dire consequences should the EPA fail to comply with various

Box 3-1   *Major Responsibilities of the EPA*

The following are the major regulatory tasks assigned to the EPA in each important pollution control program.

Air quality
- Establishes national air quality standards.
- Sets limits on the level of air pollutants emitted from stationary sources such as power plants, municipal incinerators, factories, and chemical plants.
- Establishes emission standards for new motor vehicles.
- Sets allowable levels for toxics such as lead, benzene, and toluene in gasoline.
- Establishes emission standards for hazardous air pollutants such as beryllium, mercury, and asbestos.
- Supervises states in their development of clean air plans.

Water quality and protection
- Issues permits for the discharge of any pollutant into navigable waters.
- Develops effluent guidelines to control discharge of specific water pollutants, including radiation.
- Develops criteria that enable states to set water quality standards.
- Administers grants program to states to subsidize the cost of building sewage treatment plants.
- Regulates disposal of waste material, including sludge and low-level radioactive discards, into the oceans.
- Cooperates with the U.S. Army Corps of Engineers to issue permits for the dredging and filling of wetlands.
- Sets national drinking water standards to ensure that drinking water is safe.
- Regulates underground injection of wastes to protect purity of groundwater.
- With the U.S. Coast Guard, coordinates cleanup of oil and chemical spills into U.S. waterways.

Hazardous waste
- Maintains inventory of existing hazardous waste dump sites.
- Tracks more than five hundred hazardous compounds from point of origin to final disposal site.
- Sets standards for generators and transporters of hazardous wastes.
- Issues permits for treatment, storage, and disposal facilities for hazardous wastes.
- Assists states in developing hazardous waste control programs.
- Maintains a multibillion-dollar fund (Superfund) from industry fees and general tax revenues to provide for emergency cleanup of hazardous dumps when no responsible party can immediately be found.
- Pursues identification of parties responsible for waste sites and eventual reimbursement of the federal government for Superfund money spent cleaning up these sites.

Chemical regulation, including pesticides and radioactive waste
- Maintains inventory of chemical substances now in commercial use.
- Regulates existing chemicals considered serious hazards to people and the environment, including fluorocarbons, polychlorinated biphenyls (PCBs), and asbestos.

- Issues procedures for the proper safety testing of chemicals and orders them tested when necessary.
- Requires the registration of insecticides, herbicides, or fungicides intended for sale in the United States.
- Requires pesticide manufacturers to provide scientific evidence that their products will not injure humans, livestock, crops, or wildlife when used as directed.
- Classifies pesticides for either general public use or restricted use by certified applicators.
- Sets standards for certification of applicators of restricted-use pesticides. (Individual states may certify applicators through their own programs based on the federal standards.)
- Cancels or suspends the registration of a product on the basis of actual or potential unreasonable risk to humans, animals, or the environment.
- Issues a "stop sale, use, and removal" order when a pesticide already in circulation is found to be in violation of the law.
- Requires registration of pesticide-producing establishments.
- Issues regulations concerning the labeling, storage, and disposal of pesticide containers.
- Issues permits for pesticide research.
- Monitors pesticide levels in the environment.
- Monitors and regulates the levels of radiation in drinking water, oceans, rainfall, and air.
- Conducts research on toxic substances, pesticides, air and water quality, hazardous wastes, radiation, and the causes and effects of acid rain.
- Provides overall guidance to other federal agencies on radiation protection matters that affect public health.
- Maintains inventory of chemical substances now in commercial use.

Other
- Sets acceptable noise levels for construction equipment, transportation equipment (except aircraft), all motors and engines, and electronic equipment.

---

statutory deadlines. The EPA continues to experience what is probably the most relentless legislative oversight of any federal agency. (So habitually does Congress investigate activities of the EPA that the U.S. General Accounting Office, the congressional watchdog agency, has a permanent branch at EPA headquarters.) Even though EPA staff grew by approximately 18 percent during the 1990s, this growth has failed to keep pace with the accumulating new responsibilities the agency has inherited.

The cumulative result of this excessive congressional attention is written in the statistics of missed deadlines, lagging research, and impossibly distant completion dates for existing program responsibilities. The doleful litany includes the following:

- The Federal Insecticide, Fungicide, and Rodenticide Act requires the EPA to evaluate more than 50,000 individual pesticide products containing more than 600 active ingredients and 900 inert ingredients. "If EPA has to prepare interim registration standards for all 600 active ingredients," the

General Accounting Office concluded in 1986, "then the Agency may finish the first round reviews in about 2004." [40] In fact, the EPA had not yet completed its first round of reviews.

• The Food Quality Protection Act (1996) required the EPA to screen all commercial pesticides for estrogenic effects that may affect human health, to develop a screening and testing program by 1998, to implement the program by 1999, and to report to Congress on the program's accomplishments by August 2000. This required the EPA to review data on 600 pesticides in active commerce, 1,800 inert ingredients in 20,000 pesticide products, and 75,000 industrial chemicals, plus consumer products. None of this, including the report, had been accomplished by the end of 2007.

The EPA frequently resorts to improvised strategies for deciding which programs and pollutants will get priority. Sometimes it depends on litigation initiated by private interests—most often environmental groups—to force its attention to specific programs. The agency was able to give priority to a Toxic Substances Control Act requirement that it act within one year on recommendations from its experts concerning whether a substance merited testing for carcinogenicity only because the Natural Resources Defense Council sued the EPA and obtained a judicial order for the agency to speed up the review process. Sometimes the agency ignores portions of the law to make its workload manageable. Political scientist Edward Woodhouse observed that to cope with the otherwise impossible task of screening sixty thousand chemicals presently in commercial use, as the Toxic Substances Control Act requires, the EPA "simply misinterpreted the law: the agency placed its focus exclusively on new uses of new chemicals. . . . EPA apparently decided (probably implicitly) that its staff and funds were inadequate to cover tens of thousands of existing chemicals." [41]

Are Integrated Programs Possible? The EPA has come to resemble a regulatory holding company, a conglomerate of offices, each focused narrowly on problems in a single environmental medium (such as air, land, or water) or on one kind of pollutant (such as toxic waste). Further, each office is responsible for numerous regulatory laws written with little attention to their compatibility. "Each program has staked out an environmental problem that it is required to 'fix,' according to the peculiar rules embodied in its statutory mandate," observed the CEQ. [42] The EPA originally was conceived very differently. The advisory council recommending the EPA's creation to President Nixon had argued that environmental policy had a unique character because there were "interactions and trade-offs inherent in controlling different types of pollution." The EPA was expected to be the means to "rationalize the organization of environmental efforts" and "give focus and coordination to them." [43] In short, the EPA was intended to synthesize approaches to specific environmental problems into an "integrated and holistic approach"—which is precisely what the EPA has not done.

Circumstances conspired against this integrated approach from the EPA's inception. Its most grievous fault was lack of political allure. Congress and the White House, under intense public pressure to do something quickly about specific pollution problems, needed to promote what seemed the quickest solution to what appeared to be the most urgent problem of the moment. Integrated management, in contrast, seemed strange and complicated, too difficult to explain and too unpredictable in results to appeal to Congress or the public.[44] Also, the program offices concerned with air, water, and land quickly dominated the EPA and defeated most efforts to create more integrated programs; these offices had powerful constituencies whereas the cross-media programs did not. Political scientist Barry Rabe noted,

> Each environmental medium and the separate programs within each medium have attracted politically potent constituencies that are likely antagonists toward any attempt to transform—or integrate—the existing system. They include environmental professionals and agencies, representatives of business and industry, and various policy-making committees and subcommittees that operate in Congress and state legislatures.[45]

Environmental groups were usually unsympathetic, perhaps because they feared that integrated management would subvert existing programs. Moreover, environmental law usually regulates the impact of specific pollutants, such as threats to public health or groundwater quality, and legislative pressure to produce results gives regulators little incentive to take the longer time necessary to develop more holistic approaches to pollution management.

The segmented approach to pollution management embodied in the EPA's organization and programs is often unsatisfactory because it does not deal effectively with major problems such as cross-media pollution. Consider the example of regulating the hazardous wastes from the nation's more than thirty-five hundred electroplating firms. If such firms are permitted to flush their wastes into municipal waste treatment systems, these wastes (including heavy metals such as cadmium, copper, and nickel) can kill the bacteria essential for municipal water treatment. If the heavy metals are removed from the wastes before they are flushed into the municipal system, a toxic sludge remains. In 1984 the EPA decided to phase out the use of landfills for the disposal of these sludges. If electroplating firms then decided to stabilize the waste sludge by mixing it with other agents such as cement kiln dust, the poisons may be secured and acceptable for landfills but the metals then cannot be recycled and the wastes create much greater bulk in landfills rapidly filling to capacity. Under present law, these toxic metals will be managed differently according to which medium is affected. Regulating these wastes by one approach creates a new form of pollution and transfers costs from one program to another. At the present time, no federal law empowers the EPA to manage these toxic sludges by calculating the costs and risks involved in their migration from one environmental medium to another and by selecting a strategy that creates the least total cost, or risk, when all the different media are considered.

Developing an integrated approach would take considerable time at best. But integrated management has much to recommend it. It would produce regulatory methods that create significant cost reduction, and perhaps quicker results, than the segmented approaches currently applied to pollution problems. For example, removing sulfur from electric power plant air emissions usually results in toxic sludges that must then be treated by land disposal, which often creates groundwater contamination. Greater control of sulfur air emissions at their source, however, might require more costly air pollution control technologies yet result in far less overall expense and greater reduction of health and ecological risks than regulating sulfur in air, soil, and groundwater separately.[46]

Needed: Clear Priorities. Like the man who mounted his horse and galloped off in all directions, the EPA lacks a constant course. With responsibility for administering ten separate statutes and parts of four others, the EPA has no clearly mandated priorities, no way of allocating scarce resources among different statutes or among programs within a single law. Nor does the EPA have a congressional charter, common to most federal departments and agencies, defining its broad organizational mission and priorities. Although the agency has had to make informal, ad hoc decisions about program priorities to survive, these are much less satisfactory legally and politically than a clear, congressionally mandated agenda.

Congress has shown little inclination to provide the EPA with a charter or mandated priorities, in good part because the debate sure to arise on the relative merit and urgency of different environmental problems is an invitation to a political bloodletting most legislators would gladly avoid. Intense controversy over which problems to emphasize would be likely among states, partisans of different ecological issues, and regulated interests; the resulting political brawl would upset existing policy coalitions that themselves were fashioned with great difficulty. Moreover, setting priorities invites a prolonged, bitter debate over an intensely emotional issue: Should the primary objective of environmental protection be to reduce public risks associated with environmental degradation as much as seems practical or—as many environmentalists fervently believe—is the goal to eliminate all significant forms of pollution altogether? Many experts inside and outside the EPA have argued that unless Congress sets priorities enabling the agency to concentrate its resources on a relatively few feasible, measurable objectives, the nation will be dissipating its environmental resources among a multitude of different programs and objectives with few significant results.

The Reform Struggle. The EPA's administrators have been acutely aware of the agency's managerial problems and initiated many programs throughout the 1990s to encourage greater administrative efficiency and effectiveness when opportunities arose. The difficulties involved in implementing these internal reforms arose, quite often, from conflicts among the agency's numerous stakeholders, both inside and outside the organization, whose buy-in to reform is frequently essential to its success. Even politically skilled administrators, armed with a vigorous reform agenda and administrative expertise, have struggled to overcome the divisive pluralism of interest often evident among the EPA's multiple constituencies. A case in point is the "Reinventing EPA" experience.

In 1995 the EPA's leadership, headed by Administrator Carol Browner, officially announced it was "Reinventing EPA" and launched a risky reform program to transform the fundamental legal and political character of its regulatory programs. The collective reform proposals, part of the Clinton administration's highly touted Reinventing Government initiative, were intended to make the EPA a regulatory showcase. The reinvention initiative was by far the most ambitious EPA reform agenda in two decades, and all sides agreed the proposals were aimed at the priority problems.[47]

Reinventing the EPA was a well-intentioned gamble against forces over which the EPA often has little control. One problem is the agency's own organizational design and culture. The EPA's major "media offices" regulating air, water, and hazardous waste especially have been the organizational and regulatory centers of power within the agency and did not readily surrender the significant amount of authority, budgetary resources, and technical expertise required to implement many of the reinvention initiatives. Moreover, many among the large, diverse constituency of outside interests deeply concerned with the EPA's work prefer to keep or mildly amend the agency's present structure. These stakeholders include state and local officials, scientists, regulated commercial and industrial facilities, trade organizations, academics, and others, frequently with strong political and professional ties to the existing programs and organizations. Many informed observers also believe that the ills to which reinvention is addressed require a major rewriting of the numerous, inconsistent environmental laws—a congressional job. Congress still prefers continually to amend existing laws, to tinker with the EPA's administrative structure, and to propose other marginal changes in existing arrangements instead of undertaking a rationally thorough, but politically forbidding, rewrite and reorganization of the agency's fundamental regulatory mission.

The Council on Environmental Quality

The National Environmental Policy Act (NEPA) of 1969 included a provision for establishing a commission to advise the president on environmental matters. To be headed by three members appointed by the president, the CEQ was to be part of the president's staff. Among the major responsibilities prescribed for the council in Section 203 of NEPA were (1) to gather for the president's consideration "timely and authoritative information concerning the conditions and trends in the quality of the environment both current and prospective," (2) "to develop and recommend to the President national policies to foster and promote the improvement of environmental quality," and (3) "to review and appraise the various programs and activities of the Federal Government" to determine the extent to which they comply, among other things, with the requirement for writing environmental impact statements.[48] The CEQ was created, like other major presidential advisory commissions, primarily to provide policy advice and evaluation from within the White House directly to the president.

By 2000, the CEQ's early political clout had vanished. The council still administers the process for writing and reviewing environmental impact statements within the federal government. The CEQ is a small agency with no regulatory responsibilities or major environmental programs beyond modest research activities, but it had assumed symbolic importance and political value to environmental interests. Its presence within the White House implied a high national priority to environmental programs, and the council's opportunities to influence the president directly meant that it might act, in the words of environmental leader Russell Peterson, as "the environmental conscience of the executive branch." Nonetheless, as with all other presidential advisory bodies, the CEQ exercises no more influence in White House decisions than the president cares to give it; it may carry on its NEPA-mandated activities, but the president is always free to ignore any of its recommendations or other initiatives.

The CEQ's rapid decline in status since the Carter administration illustrates how much its effectiveness depends on presidential favor. The council enjoyed considerable influence under President Carter, but its influence plummeted rapidly during the Reagan administration. President George H. W. Bush's pledges of environmental concern did not, to the disappointment of environmentalists, portend better days for the CEQ, nor did the arrival of the Clinton administration after the 1992 election. President Clinton's proposal to replace the CEQ with a White House environmental policy adviser appointed by the president shocked the environmental community and seemed virtually an obituary for the council. The CEQ remains, but it has long ceased to be a major player in White House politics.

The Department of the Interior

Established as a cabinet-level department in 1845, the DOI is among the oldest and most important of all federal agencies. With a current budget of approximately $10.8 billion and 72,900 employees, the department's responsibilities leave few environmental issues untouched. These responsibilities include (1) protection and management of more than 549 million acres of public land—roughly 28 percent of the total U.S. land area—set aside by Congress for national parks, wilderness areas, forests, and other restricted uses; (2) administration of Native American lands and federal Native American programs, including authority over western tribal lands containing a large proportion of the coal, petroleum, uranium, and other largely unexploited energy resources in the western United States; (3) enforcement of federal surface mining regulations through its Office of Surface Mining; (4) conservation and management of wetlands and estuarine areas; and (5) protection and preservation of wildlife, including endangered species. Headed by a cabinet secretary appointed by the president, the department's programs historically have been a primary concern to environmentalists. The secretary of the interior has traditionally been a westerner, a political concession to the western states, where most of the public lands are found. During the 1970s the department secretaries appointed by Presidents Nixon and Carter, although not necessarily outspoken environmentalists or even conservationists, were at least tolerable to the growing environmentalist movement. Since the 1980s, however, the relationship between the environmental community and DOI secretaries has often been combative.

At the beginning of the Reagan administration, the DOI, and particularly Reagan's first choice of James Watt as the department's secretary, were a source of continual controversy as a result of their efforts to make sweeping changes in personnel and programs to conform with Reagan's regulatory reforms. These controversies were rooted in strong environmentalist convictions about the nature of the department that shape their organizational response to any departmental leadership.

The department has always been a battleground between interests seeking to conserve the resources in the public domain and those seeking generous access to them. The department's mandate to ensure "balanced use" of resources between conservation and development—a mandate that continually propels the department and its secretary into a storm of controversy concerning which use shall dominate—is a certain source of trouble for every secretary. Moreover, the department's programs serve a clientele including not only environmentalists but also the timber and cattle industries, mining companies, sports enthusiasts, a multitude of private corporations, and many other interests that expect the department to be solicitous of their viewpoints. Finally, the western states historically have maintained that they have not been given sufficient voice in the administration of the federal properties that often constitute the vast majority of land within their boundaries. The desire of these states to assume greater control over the public domain within their jurisdictions and the resulting tensions with the federal government will outlive any administration.

Watt's strident conflict with environmentalists was unusually nasty, even for a public office rich in controversy, and he was forced to resign in October 1983 after becoming a political liability for the White House. Although Watt's successor was less publicly belligerent toward environmentalists, most environmental groups were convinced that only the leadership style had changed. The Bush administration did little to appease these critics by appointing former New Mexico representative Manuel Lujan Jr. as secretary. Lujan and his management team seemed to embrace essentially the same viewpoint as their Reagan-appointed predecessors. Congress generally frustrated the Bush administration's efforts to open vast tracts of public domain for oil exploration and commercial timbering, but Lujan continued to provoke environmentalist ire. The head of the Bureau of Mines did not improve the department's environmental image by declaring at a conference of miners, loggers, and other resource developers that environmentalists were "a bunch of nuts." [49]

Although environmentalists were generally delighted with President Clinton's selection of former Arizona governor Bruce Babbitt to be secretary of the interior, they were not so satisfied with many of Babbitt's early policy initiatives, including the scope of the department's efforts to restrict timbering and other resource development on public lands. The Clinton administration's agenda of slow and cautious environmental reform, especially grating on grassroots environmentalists who expected a bold display of environmental initiative, nurtured continuing controversy, albeit more temperate than in the 1980s, between the department and its environmentalist constituency. In the closing months of his administration, however, Clinton's sudden designation of vast public land tracts for national parks, refuges, wilderness, and other restricted uses enormously gratified conservationists.

Congressional Republicans were hugely annoyed by Clinton's whirlwind designations, which they considered an arrogant, unconstitutional exercise of presidential discretion, and vowed unsuccessfully to undo them during President George W. Bush's term. Further complicating the department's relations with Congress was the opposition of environmentalists, and most congressional Democrats, to Bush's appointment of Norton as the new Secretary of the Interior. Norton's political background inspired environmentalist criticism that she was "just Jim Watt in a skirt"[50] and awakened their apprehension about another Reagan-style assault on environmentalist legislation which Norton's successor, former Idaho governor Kirk Kempthorne, did little to relieve.

The Nuclear Regulatory Commission

The Nuclear Regulatory Commission (NRC) was created by Congress in 1976 to assume the regulatory responsibilities originally vested in the Atomic Energy Commission. An independent agency with five commissioners appointed by the president, the NRC regulates most nonmilitary uses of nuclear facilities and materials. The commission's major activities related to the environment include (1) regulation of the site choice, construction, operation, and security of all civilian nuclear reactors; (2) designation and supervision of all nuclear waste repositories; (3) regulation of uranium mining and milling facilities; and (4) the closing of civilian nuclear facilities after they discontinue production (called decommissioning). In 2003 the NRC employed about twenty-seven hundred individuals and had a budget of approximately $510 million.

Environmental groups have been most concerned with the NRC's supervision of nuclear power plants and repositories for radioactive wastes. Although 104 nuclear plants were operating or approved for construction by 2004, the majority of these have been criticized by environmental groups for alleged deficiencies in structural safety, control of radioactive emissions, and waste storage.[51] In addition, environmental groups have often been aggressive in seeking NRC safety reviews of operating plants and personnel training procedures. The NRC has assumed a major responsibility for the review of site selection and the supervision of waste disposal at the nation's first permanent nuclear waste repository at Yucca Flats, Nevada. Environmental groups still regard the process of site construction and disposal as an issue likely to remain important for several decades.

The NRC and environmental groups have been both adversaries and allies. The environmental movement generally has supported the NRC's stricter enforcement and review of regulations for operating nuclear facilities and its increasingly rigorous standards for new facility licensing. Yet environmentalists also have criticized the NRC for allegedly siding too often with the nuclear power industry against its critics, for bureaucratic inertia and conservatism, and for ignoring technical criticism and data from sources not associated with the nuclear power industry or the commission. As with other regulatory agencies, the NRC is bound to its own clientele—the nuclear power industry—by professional associations, common technical and economic concerns, and historical sympathies; it is also committed to regulating the industry in the public interest while maintaining sufficient objectivity and disengagement from the nuclear power movement to do that job. These often conflicting responsibilities lead the NRC into controversies with environmental interests. Nonetheless, the NRC and its mission remain among the most environmentally significant elements in the executive branch.

The Department of Energy

Despite its size and importance, the DOE has been a stepchild of the executive branch. Widely criticized and burdened with difficult, unpopular programs throughout the 1980s, the department struggled though the 1990s with immense new problems—legal, political, economic, and technical—created by disastrous mismanagement of the military nuclear weapons facilities under its jurisdiction since the late 1970s. These unprecedented difficulties constituted more high-profile bad news for an agency with a talent for collecting misfortune.

The DOE began George W. Bush's administration still mired in high-visibility controversy, struggling against the stigma of flagrant mismanagement and still saddled with responsibility for unpopular policies. The DOE's problems seem almost inevitable in light of its history. The department was created in 1976, when Congress combined a number of independent agencies with programs already operating in other departments in order to bring the federal government's sprawling energy activities within a single bureaucratic structure. Under the DOE's jurisdiction are regulatory activities and energy programs strongly affecting the environment. The more important of these include (1) promotion of civilian nuclear power activities, (2) regulation of military nuclear facilities and radioactive wastes, (3) administration of the federal government's research and development programs in energy production and conservation, (4) regulation of price controls for domestic petroleum and natural gas, and (5) administration of federal research and development grants for commercial synthetic fuels production in the United States. With approximately sixteen thousand employees and a budget of $23.4 billion in 2006, the DOE is the principal executive agency involved in the regulation and production of many different energy technologies with significant environmental impacts. Also, by design it is expected to undertake a volatile agenda of frequently contradictory and inconsistent missions destined to set it at odds with itself and with the environmental community: to promote environmentally risky energy technologies and to minimize the environmental risks, to promote energy use and energy conservation, to stimulate research and development of new energy-consuming and energy-saving technologies, to control energy prices in emergencies, and to avert energy shortages and stimulate long-range energy planning.

By far the most politically and financially costly problem confronting the DOE remains the environmental contamination of the nation's nuclear weapons facilities to be discussed in Chapter 8. More than 122 nuclear weapons manufacturing and laboratory sites in thirty states, the Marshall Islands, and Puerto Rico have to be made safe. The cleanup program will probably exceed $250 billion and take perhaps a half century or more to accomplish—if it can be accomplished, for no public or private agency has any experience in cleaning up radioactive contamination of such scale and complexity.[52] Spending for the cleanup of these nuclear weapons sites and for other related programs could involuntarily transform the DOE into the nation's largest environmental agency and launch it on the most expensive public works program in U.S. history.[53]

Neither a new century nor a new presidency improved political karma at the DOE. The department was anointed the lead agency for President George W. Bush's ambitious new national energy policy in 2001, intended to combat what the president proclaimed as a new national energy crisis— a situation that set the DOE on a collision course with almost all organized environmental groups that considered the new plan to be extravagantly expensive and environmentally reckless. To environmentalists, the DOE seemed to be promoting hugely accelerated fossil fuel extraction and electricity production when it should be promoting energy conservation, advocating more commercial nuclear power when it should be advocating less, and proclaiming an energy crisis when one doesn't exist. Moreover, the DOE was still struggling with an apparently intractable problem of creating a permanent repository for the nation's nuclear waste. And controversy continued over the DOE's management of military nuclear waste sites.

The Courts: The Role of Appraisal

Federal judges actively participate in the environmental policy process in several ways. They continually interpret environmental law, an inevitable task in light of the ambiguities and silences common to environmental legislation. This statutory interpretation often amounts to policy making by the judicial branch. Judges also attempt to ensure that agencies discharge their mandated responsibilities under environmental legislation and otherwise comply with administrative obligations. In addition, the federal courts enforce the Administrative Procedures Act (1946), the code of administrative procedures applicable to all federal agencies. Finally, the courts ensure that environmental laws and their administrative implementation comply with constitutional standards. As the volume of environmental litigation expands relentlessly, federal judges find themselves increasingly at the pulse points of environmental policy making. Although critics have argued that federal judges are not prepared by a legal education for this pivotal role in adjudicating complex scientific and economic issues, the trend seems inexorable.

The Courts and Environmental Policy. The impact of the federal courts on environmental policy has changed over the decades since Earth Day 1970. In the 1970s, federal court decisions in both substantive and procedural issues generally worked to the advantage of environmental interests. During this period, environmentalists often saw the federal judiciary as the Great Equalizer, offsetting the previously enormous advantage enjoyed by regulated interests in administrative and judicial forums. Environmental organizations, aggressively exploiting the procedural advantages they had gained during the 1970s to compel federal enforcement of new regulatory programs, achieved some of their most significant judicial victories during this period. The federal courts greatly expanded opportunities for environmental groups to bring issues before the bench by a broadened definition of "standing to sue," a legal status that authorized individuals or organizations to sue governmental agencies for failure to enforce environmental legislation. Beginning with the *Scenic Hudson* case in 1965, for instance, the federal courts broadened for more than a decade the criteria by which citizens could acquire such standing to sue federal agencies over enforcement of environmental regulations.[54]

By the late 1980s, however, the federal judiciary was no longer a predictably friendly venue for environmentalism. Business and other regulated interests began to use the federal courts far more effectively than they had previously. The increased effectiveness of business interests also exemplified the great growth in number and activity of specialized not-for-profit legal foundations representing regulated industries in environmental litigation. Reasoning that the devil should not have all the good tunes, business patterned these associations after the successful public interest legal foundations created in the 1970s to represent environmental interests. As do environmental public interest groups, these business associations maintain they are suing the government in the public interest and enjoy tax-exempt status. However, business public interest groups are financed principally by organizations, such as the Adolph Coors Company and the Scaife Foundation, that have fought vigorously against most of the major environmental regulatory programs passed since the 1970s. The tide of judicial favor began to turn more decisively against environmental litigants in the 1990s as an increasing number of federal judges appointed by Presidents Reagan and Bush came to the bench.[55] By the end of the 1990s, environmentalists' standing to sue was significantly limited, the rights of property owners in cases involving the Endangered Species Act and conservation restrictions on private land were enlarged to the disadvantage of environmentalist litigants, and state authority to restrict the scope of federal environmental regulations was enlarged. The benefit to business interests from this growing strength in environmental litigation does not depend solely on winning cases. Exhaustive and relentless challenges to federal regulation can delay enforcement of environmental laws for many years and throw environmental groups on the defensive, compelling them to invest scarce resources in protracted legal battles. Often battles are won not by the side with the best case but by the side with the most endurance.

Environmental groups anticipated that the election of George W. Bush was the prelude to another round of federal judicial appointments equally unfriendly to environmental interests. Despite its court appointments, however, the Bush administration did not fare nearly so well as predicted in the judicial arena, particularly in the lower federal courts where most environmental cases begin and end (the Supreme Court hears fewer than 100 cases a year, the circuit (or appellate) courts hear more than 40,000 appeals annually and often create most legal precedents that become the law of the land).[56] Federal judges in the Northwest, Midwest, and Far West were especially critical of the administration's efforts to open up public lands to more energy exploration, its lackluster enforcement of the Endangered Species Act, and its enthusiasm to increase timber production on federal forests.[57]

Litigation as a Political Tactic. The impact of the courts on policy, as the previous discussion suggests, arises not only from the substance of court rulings but also from the use of litigation as a tactical weapon in policy conflict—a weapon used by all sides. Most environmental litigation arises from three sources: major environmental organizations (such as the Sierra Club or the Environmental Defense Fund); business and property interests, including public interest law firms (such as the highly aggressive Western States Legal Foundation); and federal agencies (such as the EPA or the DOI) with major environmental responsibilities. Quite often the courts become another political arena in which losers in prior policy battles fought among Congress, the bureaucracy, and the White House can launch yet another campaign. It is not surprising that environmental groups specializing in litigation, such as the Environmental Defense Fund, increased their activity during the Reagan administration in an often unsuccessful effort to counteract through the courts what they alleged to be massive regulatory resistance to their interests within the administration.

Litigation is also a stall in the policy process, a frustration to the opposition. Litigation creates a bargaining chip to be bartered for concessions from the opposition. Both environmentalists and their opposition have used the obstructive capacities of litigation to their advantage.

Many critics have pegged NEPA's requirement for environmental impact statements as an especially productive source of lawsuits working to the advantage of environmentalists, but the data suggest otherwise. The number of lawsuits challenging agency actions under NEPA has been diminishing steadily in number and importance. The federal courts in the 1980s were increasingly disinclined to sustain challenges as long as the judges were convinced that agencies had prepared and reviewed environmental impact statements properly. In addition, environmental impact statements are fast becoming a bureaucratic rite, meticulously observed but then substantively ignored.

When Should Judges Become Involved? The evolution of environmental politics increasingly embroils federal judges in resolving legal issues that have important policy consequences—in effect, implicating them in environmental policy making through the courts. Moreover, many of these issues embrace highly technical or scientific disputes. Federal judges may, for instance, have to decide whether the EPA considered the proper animal tests in deciding that a chemical constituted a significant risk to human health. Judges are often reluctant participants in these affairs so heavily weighted with policy or scientific implications. They may be compelled by law to adjudicate such matters but are acutely aware of their limitations as technical experts. Equally important, as Supreme Court justice Stephen Breyer observed, when the courts must substitute their judgment for an administrator's, the result is often politically unsatisfactory:

> Regulators must make "legislative-type" decisions, the merits of which depend upon finding, or prying out important general facts about the world; they work in a politically charged environment; they may need to seek compromise solutions acceptable to warring private groups. [But judges must make decisions] the merits of which depend upon the relevant legal norm and a record . . . that need not contain all relevant facts about the world. . . . Given these differences, a compromise solution that regulatory considers reasonable, for practical administrative reasons, might not seem practical to a judge.[58]

Both critics and defenders of existing environmental policies have frequently proposed that some alternative venue to the traditional courts be created for resolving technical and scientific controversies arising from environmental regulation. One common suggestion is the creation of a "science court" in which technical experts would resolve the scientific and technical issues involved with environmental litigation, leaving the judges free to focus on the largely legal matters. Other proposals involve creating impartial technical advisers to judges when scientific issues confront the court. These and many other alternatives discussed among environmental law activists illuminate not only the evolving impact of environmentalism on U.S. legal institutions themselves but also the larger challenge entailed in integrating effectively and appropriately the judicial branch into the whole environmental policy process.

The Political Environment of Environmental Policy Making

Governmental institutions are fated to work in a political setting that is inconstant, influential, and often fickle. The opportunities to make or change policy shift continually, often unpredictably, with changing political circumstances. At any given time, there will be differences between what policy makers want and what they can accomplish, between what they are compelled to do and what they would prefer to do, between what is feasible and what is not. This ebb and flow of opportunity is created by different circumstances. The most important of these circumstances include changes in the partisan control of governmental institutions, transient shifts of public mood, major economic change, and regulatory federalism. These can be called the changing seasons of policy making.

Changing Party Majorities

The balance of party strength within Congress and between Congress and the White House powerfully shapes the substance and opportunities for environmental policy making. In theory, opportunities to make or change policy are greatest when the White House and Congress are controlled by the same party. However, since 1970, Republicans have usually occupied the White House and Democratic majorities have usually controlled both congressional chambers. The floodtide of environmental legislation originating in Washington, D.C., during the 1970s was largely the result of a broad, bipartisan environmental coalition in both chambers that strongly supported innovative environmental programs proposed or accepted by both Republican and Democratic presidents. The political climate for environmentalists darkened dramatically with Reagan's election and has remained unsettled ever since. The eight years under Reagan were marked by conflict and impasse between a president and Congress dominated by different parties and committed to radically different policy agendas.

Throughout the eight-year Reagan presidency, Republicans won, then lost, control of the Senate while Democrats retained their House majority. The result was an environmental gridlock in which the Democratic House frustrated Senate Republican efforts to pass Reagan's sweeping agenda of change in existing environmental laws.

Reagan's enormous impact on environmental policy making in the 1980s is evidence, however, that in the hands of a politically skilled president with a clear policy agenda, White House resources can be a potent policy-making instrument, with or without congressional cooperation. During the Reagan years, especially, administrators were able to obstruct and revise many environmental regulations and manipulate their agency budgets so effectively that the administration's environmental goals were at least partially achieved without any congressional cooperation.

With the exception of EPA administrator Reilly, the environmentally important appointments of George H. W. Bush's administration generally went to persons sympathetic to the Reagan-Bush regulatory reform agenda and thereby objectionable to most environmental organizations. Bush used the authority of the executive office, especially the OMB, to revise, delay, or defeat numerous environmental regulations ideologically unacceptable to the administration. The chill blowing toward the EPA from the White House was unmistakable, a continuing and effective obstacle to many environmental policy initiatives from Congress or the bureaucracy.

The Democrats' return to the White House with Clinton in 1992 turned out to be less the prelude to a bright future anticipated by environmentalists than a false dawn. The stunning Republican congressional victories of 1994 returned a Republican majority to both congressional chambers and elevated to its leadership a cadre of Republicans outspokenly unsympathetic to most of the major environmental legislation created by Congress in the previous two decades. The Republican leadership sponsored a multitude of new legislative proposals—part of what they called their Contract with America—which would have radically recast, and usually enfeebled, most of the major environmental laws written during the 1970s and 1980s.

These early Republican initiatives failed, mostly because public opinion polls convinced party leaders that radical antienvironmentalism would be politically disastrous for the party's 1996 congressional candidates. The immediate impact of the 1994 congressional elections was to force environmentalists again on the defensive.

Finally, in the last two years of his tenure, Clinton largely abandoned efforts at congressional collaboration to achieve his environmental objectives. Instead, he relied increasingly on his inherent powers as chief executive to achieve his policy goals. Using this authority, he was able to reserve more public land from economic development than any other president— a demonstration of White House authority, discussed more fully in Chapter 9, that infuriated congressional Republicans.[59]

The first six months of George W. Bush's presidency were additional confirmation that shifting congressional majorities can profoundly—and sometimes abruptly—transform the course of environmental politics. Less than six months after the 107th Congress convened, Republicans lost their tenuous Senate majority when Sen. James M. Jeffords, previously a Vermont Republican, decided to become an independent. This, in turn, delivered the Senate majority to the Democrats, whose environmental policy agenda differed substantially from that favored by President Bush and Senate Republicans. Control of the Senate's policy agenda and all its committees now belonged to the Democrats. The White House no longer had the policy initiative in the Senate, and the president's whole environmental agenda, like the rest of his legislative program, would become more difficult to promote. While Republicans temporarily recovered their Senate majority in the 2002 elections, Democrats reclaimed control of both chambers in the startling 2006 elections, much to the satisfaction of most environmentalists, who interpreted the results as a sharp public rejection of the Bush environmental record and a mandate to the Democrats for a more environmentalist agenda.

Shifting Public Moods

"When President Nixon and his staff walked in the White House on January 20, 1969, we were totally unprepared for the tidal wave of public opinion in favor of cleaning up the nation's environment that was about to engulf us," John C. Whitaker, one of Nixon's close advisers, remembered. Congress was quicker to read the political prophecy in the polls.[60] By Earth Day 1970, recalled the same adviser, "so many politicians were on the stump that Congress was forced to close down."[61] Presidents and Congress alike always feel enormous political pressure to respond when confronted by broad public majorities demonstrating a strong interest, or apprehension, about an environmental issue.

The pressure to do something, or to *look* as if something is being done, is almost irresistible when sudden spikes of public apprehension rise in the aftermath of a well-publicized environmental crisis. Many major environmental laws and regulations are direct responses to environmental disasters, real or threatened. The Three Mile Island nuclear reactor accident of 1979 begot new regulations from the NRC increasing the requirements for emergency planning at commercial nuclear power plants. The tragic 1984 chemical plant disaster at Bhopal, India, in which five thousand nearby residents and plant workers lost their lives, almost alone produced the community right-to-know provision of the Superfund Amendments and Reauthorization Act of 1986, which required industries using dangerous chemicals to disclose the type and amount of these chemicals to individuals living within an area likely to be affected by an accident on site. "The Bhopal train was leaving the station," observed one environmental lobbyist about Congress, "and we got the kind of legislation we could put on the train."[62] When California in early 2001 suddenly experienced rolling power blackouts and steeply rising electric power costs, President Bush and congressional spokespersons of both political parties quickly proclaimed an energy crisis and produced competing prescriptions for a new national energy plan, even while experts debated whether such a crisis really existed.

Washington's impetuous reaction to any publicly perceived environmental crisis is predictably nonpartisan. This hypersensitivity to public opinion is criticized frequently because it sometimes results in hastily written laws that are difficult to implement. According to economists Robert W. Crandall and Paul R. Portney, "Congress bears a large share of the responsibility for the problems of environmental regulation. Congress has passed enabling statutes containing unrealistic deadlines and an unnecessary degree of specificity with respect to the standards that [agencies] must issue."[63]

Opinion can also become an obstacle to environmental policy making when the public mood is inhospitable to action. The disappearance of gasoline and petroleum shortages in the late 1970s, and other evidence that the so-called energy crisis was passing, quickly removed energy problems from public concern and thwarted efforts by the Carter administration to pass new energy regulatory programs after mid-1978. By the time the Reagan administration finished its first term, Congress no longer felt pressure to continue mandatory plans for national fuel rationing, to require increased fuel economy standards for automobiles after 1986, or to promote solar technologies and other fuel conservation measures. Advocates of environmental issues often must wait until the opinion climate is ripe to move the White House or Congress to action. Crisis or disaster may sometimes be the only force that moves the political will.

Economic Change

In all environmental policy making, economics is the counterpoint to ecology. The impact of environmental policies on the economy is a continual preoccupation of environmental regulators and the regulated. Economic conditions, in turn, influence environmental policy making.

The economic impact of environmental regulations is continually an issue in all discussions of environmental policy. Concern most often focuses on whether environmental regulation will inhibit expansion of the gross national product, how regulations will affect business investments and the market position of firms or industries, and whether regulatory costs are inflationary. Regulated interests frequently assert that specific policies will have most, or all, of these negative effects, whereas proponents of regulation usually claim no such negative effects will occur. Data wars erupt: each side summons its economists and econometrics to vindicate its position and discredit the opposition. Although the result of these conflicts is often inconclusive, the issues are vitally important. Policies that appear (or can be made to appear) to adversely affect economic growth, market positions, or business investment are likely to command greater and more critical attention from policy makers than those appearing more economically benign. In times of economic recession or depression, the economic impact of policies can become the major determinant of their survival.

Environmental regulations, in any case, do create major public and private costs. Between 1980 and 2000, about 60 percent of the cost of national pollution control was paid by the private sector.[64] In general, studies suggest that new capital spending for pollution control by the public and private sectors has not significantly deterred growth of the gross national product or contributed much to inflation or a rise in the Consumer Price Index. For most industries, spending for pollution control has been a gradually diminishing portion of new capital investment since 1980. In 1990, business spending on pollution control was estimated at 2.8 percent of all capital investment but was expected to diminish to less than 2 percent by 2004, although final data are unavailable.[65]

Economic conditions affect environmental policy making in several ways. Most important, the mix of economic activities in the United States largely determines the character and magnitude of the nation's pollution problems and the kinds of stress placed on its resource base. As the U.S. economy moves away from heavy dependence on manufacturing, the mix of environmental stresses changes. Between 1950 and the late 1990s, employment in U.S. manufacturing declined from 50 percent of the work force to 14 percent, while employment in service and high-technology sectors climbed to about 37 percent of the labor force. This manufacturing decline reduced the air pollution emissions from U.S. industry but increased the volume of solid and hazardous waste generated nationally. Since the early 1980s the greatest stress on regional resources produced by economic growth has occurred in the South and the West.

Perhaps no technology has created more environmental stress than the automobile. In the United States there is one automobile for every two Americans, the highest density of automobiles to people in the world; each auto will be driven on average 10,000 miles annually. The U.S. transportation sector accounts for approximately 63 percent of the nation's petroleum consumption. It is a major source of air pollution emissions and contributes significantly to water pollution through groundwater contamination from leaks at refineries and service stations, it creates major solid waste problems, and it exacerbates urban blight and growth management difficulties.

Most theorists assume that a major economic recession, depression, or serious bout with inflation would profoundly affect environmental regulation. The United States has experienced no major depression and only a few short recessions since the 1970s. The serious inflation of the 1978–1983 period, intensified by rising energy prices associated with the energy crisis of the mid-1970s, did not appear to create a political climate hostile to environmental regulation. However, the economic recession beginning in 1989 and the sluggish recovery in the early 1990s affected the environmental agendas of the Bush and Clinton administrations. The economic malaise all but extinguished the Bush administration's mild enthusiasm for environmental policy innovation after 1990 and—much to the disappointment of environmentalists—inhibited the scope of environmental reforms initiated by the Clinton administration despite the president's campaign commitment to aggressive environmentalism.

In contrast to Clinton's experience, the mild downturn of the economy at the beginning of George W. Bush's administration was congenial to Bush's environmental agenda. Like Reagan, Bush and his advisers believed that even a modest economic recession called for a relaxation of environmental regulations that allegedly inhibited economic development in the industrial sector and particularly in the energy industry—a theme that resonated well with congressional Republicans. The Bush administration seized on California's highly publicized energy problems in early 2001 as further proof that massively increased energy production had to be a national economic priority. Asserting that a national energy crisis existed, the president's early legislative agenda capitalized on the sluggish economy and California's energy ills to promote a comprehensive relaxation of environmental regulations and aggressive new energy exploration on public lands.

Regulatory Federalism

Federalism disperses governmental power by fragmenting authority between national and state governments. Despite the historical enlargement of federal powers, federalism remains a sturdy constitutional buttress supporting the edifice of authority—shared, independent, and countervailing—erected for the states within the federal system. An observer has said, "It is difficult to find any government activity which does not involve all three of the so-called 'levels' of the federal system." Yet no one level monopolizes power. "There has never been a time when it was possible to put neat labels on discrete 'federal,' 'state,' and 'local' functions." [66]

Environmental programs usually are federalized, and sometimes regionalized, in their implementation, thereby introducing another political dimension to the policy process. For instance, federal air and water pollution legislation is administered through the Washington, D.C., headquarters of the EPA, its ten regional offices, and the majority of state governments, which assume the responsibility for issuing to pollution dischargers permits specifying the acceptable control technologies and emission levels. In the mid-1990s, for instance, thirty-eight states had authority to issue water permits, and forty-nine certified pesticides under federal authority. This two- and three-tiered design ensures that state and regional interests take part in the regulatory process and that, consequently, state and local governments, together with their associated interests, actively pursue their individual, often competitive objectives during program implementation. Even if the states are not formally included in the administration of federal environmental regulations, they are likely to insist on some voice in decisions affecting them. Federalism in environmental regulation guarantees voice and influence to the multitude of states involved, providing essential representation for various geographic interests affected politically and economically by federal environmental laws.

The most untiring watchdog over state environmental interests in Washington is the U.S. Senate. Anyone doubting this senatorial vigilance need only have observed the Senate committee hearing in January 2001 to approve Whitman's nomination to be the new administrator of the EPA. For almost an hour and a half, before Whitman had an opportunity to speak, she had first to attend as each committee member welcomed her, congratulated her, and not coincidentally reminded her about some important local problem the EPA ought to be addressing. Sen. George V. Voinovich, R-Ohio, informed her that Ohio needed the EPA's help to burn more coal. Sen. Christopher S. Bond, R-Mo., wanted the EPA to ease its opposition to river barge traffic. Sen. Harry Reid, D-Nev., had an environmental justice problem involving Nevada's Peyote Indian tribe, and newly elected Sen. Hillary Clinton, D-N.Y., wanted the EPA to attend to Lake Onondaga. "The Army Corps of Engineers is in charge of cleaning up the lake, and currently the plan is expected to take 15 years to complete," noted Senator Clinton. "The EPA has been extremely involved in the cleanup and . . . I'd like to not only bring this to your attention but to ask if the EPA under your leadership will continue this high level of involvement." Of course, she was assured, the EPA would look after Lake Onondaga.[67]

The status of the states has altered considerably since the 1970s. At the time of the first Earth Day, only a few progressive states such as California anticipated federal policy makers by initiating needed environmental regulations. Most states seemed unable or unwilling to attack vigorously their own environmental ills. In fact, a major provocation for the array of new federal environmental legislation flowing from Washington during this period was the conviction among federal policy makers that most states had neither the will nor the competence to attack grave environmental problems on their own. Today the states have often been well ahead of Washington in developing innovative and experimental environmental management and in attacking emerging environmental problems. Aggressive state pressure often forces the EPA's policy implementation and innovation. Thus, a coalition of northeastern states, collaborating in 2006 to sue the EPA for failure to regulate national CO_2 emissions through the Clean Air Act, eventually forced the U.S. Supreme Court to review the scientific evidence for climate warming despite the Bush administration's opposition.

Federalism can also complicate and delay program implementation. Few issues arouse state concern more than federal aid and administrative discretion for the states in program management. Federal aid comes in many forms: grants for program administration, staff training, salary supplements, program enforcement, and pollution control facilities; technical assistance in program development or enforcement; research cost sharing; and much more. In the latter 1990s the EPA provided about one in every five dollars spent by the states on major pollution control programs and an additional $2.5 billion in grants for the construction of waste treatment facilities. The states understandably favor generous federal cost-sharing in the administration of federally mandated environmental programs. Many proponents of environmental regulation believe that the amount of federal aid directly affects the quality of environmental protection, particularly in states lacking adequate staff and technical resources to implement programs on their own.

The amount of discretion permitted the states when interpreting and enforcing federal regulations within their own borders begets ceaseless controversy in U.S. environmental administration. In general, the states prefer the federal government to leave state administrators with enough discretion to adapt federal environmental regulations to unique local conditions and to be responsive to local economic and political interests. Assailing the federal government for imposing regulations on the states without respect for local interests is a political mantra among state officials, but the criticism has grown increasingly strident as the states' competence in and resources for pollution regulation improved throughout the 1990s. States now commonly complain that federal regulations force them to conform to rules that are inappropriate, economically wasteful, or politically unfair to local interests—a mood aggravated by mounting regulatory responsibilities imposed by Washington along with diminishing financial support for their implementation.

Another fertile source of controversy in regulatory federalism is the existence of many regional conflicts deeply embedded in the nation's history. Disagreements between the western states, where most of the federal public lands reside, and Washington, D.C., over the management of the public domain west of the Mississippi—almost a third of the nation's land area—repeatedly erupt in the course of federal environmental regulation.

A newer regional conflict appeared in the mid-1980s, when scientific evidence began to validate the existence of acid rain and the transport of acid rain precursors across national, regional, and state boundaries. It soon became apparent that much of the considerable acid deposition falling in northeastern states originated among the extensive smokestack industries along the Ohio River Valley. Northeastern governors soon took the initiative in demanding that the EPA compel Ohio River states to impose stricter emission controls on their smokestack industries. The offending states resisted this onslaught, thrusting the EPA into the middle of an increasingly acrimonious dispute between Ohio River Valley states, intent on defeating new EPA emission controls on the region's fossil-fuel-burning industries, and northeastern states supporting the controls to limit the airborne pollution from Ohio River sources. Nine northeastern states have repeatedly sued the EPA to compel the agency first to issue, then to enforce regulations for state air pollution control permits, which, it was assumed, would accomplish the desired emission controls.

Conclusion

In an important sense, all the nation's environmental problems can be solved. There are almost no contemporary environmental problems for which a technical or scientific solution does not exist or cannot readily be found. Even when ensuring environmental quality might require social action—perhaps a major shift of consumer spending away from gas-guzzler vehicles to highly fuel-efficient cars to reduce urban smog—*what* could solve the problem is usually much easier to imagine than *how* to accomplish it. With this perspective, perhaps the greatest challenge to environmental policy making is finding the governmental, economic, and cultural arrangements—the institutional means—to achieve the environmental ends. To most Americans, the nation's environmental challenges are epitomized by polluted air, fouled water, dangerously unregulated hazardous and toxic wastes, and a multitude of other ecological derangements. This chapter illuminates the less obvious dimension of the nation's environmental difficulties: the institutional and economic obstacles to implementing environmental policy effectively. Despite the numerous improvements in environmental quality since 1970, in many critical respects the governmental institutions the nation now depends on to reverse its ecological degradation are struggling, and often failing, at the task.

Difficulties with environmental policy making often originate in the fundamental constitutional design of the political system or in deeply rooted political traditions. Among these problems are excessive congressional control of the agencies implementing environmental policy, legislative reluctance to create clear mandates and priorities within regulatory programs, the extreme fragmentation of committee control over environmental policy, and the resistance of entrenched bureaucracies to structural and policy reform. Although federalism is essential to the political architecture of any environmental regulatory program in the United States, it also complicates policy implementation by introducing competitive, pluralistic interests. The institutions, moreover, must function in a volatile political climate of shifting party majorities, economic cycles, fluctuating public opinion, and contentious issues of policy implementation arising from tensions deeply embedded in a federalized regulatory process.

In essence, the quality of the nation's environmental policy making is grounded in an institutional design that shapes and limits outcomes. To understand what policies are made, one inevitably must appreciate how they were created.

Suggested Readings

Epstein, Lee, and Jeffrey A. Segal, Advice and Consent: The Politics of Judicial Appointments. New York: Oxford University Press, 2005.

Graham, Mary. *The Morning after Earth Day: Practical Environmental Politics.* Washington, D.C: Brookings Institution, 1999.

Lindstrom, Matthew J., and Zachary A. Smith. *The National Environmental Policy Act: Judicial Misconstruction, Legislative Indifference, and Executive Neglect.* College Station: Texas A & M Press, 2001.

National Academy of Public Administration. *Setting Priorities, Getting Results: A New Direction for the Environmental Protection Agency.* Washington, D.C.: National Academy of Public Administration, 1995.

Notes

1. For this EPA story, see Katherine Q. Seelye, "EPA Surprises Its Leader and Interior Chief on Snowmobiles," *New York Times,* May 2, 2003, A5.
2. T. R. Reid, "For Snowmobiles, An Uncertain Fate; Future in Parks May Hinge on Election," *Washington Post,* March 15, 2004, A23.
3. Felicity Barringa, "Judge's Ruling on Yellowstone Keeps it open to Snowmobiles," *New York Times,* October 16, 2004, A9.
4. Felicity Barringa, "Secretary Tours Yellowstone on Snowmobile," *New York Times,* February 17, 2005, A18.
5. Bettina Boxall, "Bush's Grade on Environment Falls," Los Angeles Times, August 4, 2006, A1.
6. Quoted by Nancy Pelosi, Speaker of the House of Representatives, in Ken Root, "Agriculture Still Has Clout With Politicians," High Plains Journal, March 21, 2007, B12.
7. Useful illustrations of presidential activism in environmental policy making are found in Dennis L. Soden, ed., *The Environmental Presidency* (Albany: State University of New York Press, 1999) and Norman J. Vig, "Presidential Leadership and the Environment," in *Environmental Policy: New Directions for the Twenty-First Century,* ed. Norman J. Vig and Michael E. Kraft (Washington, D.C.: CQ Press, 2003), 103–25.
8. Nixon's environmental record is discussed in John C. Whitaker, *Striking a Balance: Environmental and Natural Resources Policy in the Nixon-Ford Years* (Washington, D.C.: American Enterprise Institute, 1976); and Jonathan Aitken, *Nixon: A Life* (Washington, D.C.: Regnery, 1993).
9. On Reagan's environmental record, see Barry D. Freedman, *Regulation in the Reagan-Bush Era: The Eruption of Presidential Influence* (Pittsburgh: University of Pittsburgh Press, 1995); Charles O. Jones, ed., *The Reagan Legacy: Promise and Performance* (Chatham, N.J.: Chatham House, 1988); and Richard A. Harris and Sidney M. Milkis, *The Politics of Regulatory Change: A Tale of Two Agendas* (New York: Oxford University Press, 1989).
10. John Holusha, "Bush Pledges Aid for Environmentalists," *New York Times,* September 1, 1988, 1A; Bill Peterson, "Bush Vows to Fight Pollution, Install Conservation Ethic," *Washington Post,* September 1, 1988, 1.
11. Colin Campbell and Bert A. Rockman, eds., *The Clinton Presidency: First Appraisals* (Chatham, N.J.: Chatham House, 1995).

12. "GOP Sets 104th Congress on New Regulatory Course," *Congressional Quarterly Weekly Report,* December 10, 1994, 1693–1710.
13. Paul Wapner, "Clinton's Environmental Legacy, *Tikkun,* March/April 2001, www.tikkun.org./magazine/index.cfm/action/tikkun/issue/tik0103/article/010312b.html, February 17, 2002.
14. Drew C. Revkin, "Bush vs. the Laureates: How Science Became a Partisan Issue," *New York Times,* October 19, 2004, 1A.
15. On the Bush administration and science, see Robert F. Kennedy, Jr., "The Junk Science of George W. Bush," *The Nation,* March 8, 2004, 11–18; and Union of Concerned Scientists, "Scientific Integrity," www.ucsusa.org/scientific_integrity/, February 15, 2007.
16. Boxall, "Bush's Grade on Environment Falls."
17. Christopher Schroeder, "The Evolution of Federal Regulation of Toxic Substances," in *Government and Environmental Politics: Essays on Historical Development since World War II,* ed. Michael J. Lacey (Lanham, Md.: University Press of America, 1990), 114–40.
18. Ralph Huitt, "Political Feasibility," in *Policy Analysis in Political Science,* ed. Ira Sharkansky (Chicago: Markham, 1970), 414.
19. Barry G. Rabe, *Fragmentation and Integration in State Environmental Management* (Washington, D.C.: Conservation Foundation, 1986), 16–17. See also Michael E. Kraft, "Congress and Environmental Policy," in *Environmental Politics and Policy: Theories and Evidence,* ed. James P. Lester (Durham, N.C.: Duke University Press, 1989), 179–211.
20. "Mississippi 'Pork' Ranking," Official Trent Lott Press Release, May 2, 2002, www.lott.senate.gov/news/2000/502.pork.html, February 8, 2004.
21. Mark J. Landy and Mary Hague, "The Coalition for Waste: Private Interests and Superfund," in *Environmental Politics: Public Costs, Private Rewards,* ed. Michael S. Grave (New York: Praeger, 1992), 72.
22. R. Douglas Arnold, *Congress and the Bureaucracy* (New Haven: Yale University Press, 1979), 133.
23. Lawrence Mosher, "Clean Water Requirements Will Remain Even if the Federal Spigot Is Closed," *National Journal,* May 16, 1981, 874–78.
24. Quoted in *New York Times,* March 22, 1993, B8.
25. Ibid.
26. U.S. General Accounting Office, "Indoor Air Pollution: Federal Efforts Are Not Effectively Addressing a Growing Problem," Report No. GAO/RCED 92-8 (October 1991), 6.
27. Quoted in Margaret E. Kriz, "Pesticidal Pressures," *National Journal,* December 12, 1988, 3, 125–26.
28. Jared N. Day, "Safe Drinking Water-Safe Sites: Interaction between the Safe Drinking Water Act and Superfund, 1968–1995," in *Improving Regulation: Cases in Environment, Health, and Safety,* ed. Paul S. Fischbeck and R. Scott Farrow (Washington, D.C.: Resources for the Future, 2000).
29. David Schoenbrod, "The EPA's Faustian Bargain," *Regulation* (Fall 2006): 41.
30. U.S. General Accounting Office, *Implementation of the Clean Air Act Amendments of 1990: Statement of David G. Wood, Associate Director, Environmental Protection Issues,* Document No. GAO/T-RCED-00-183 (Feb. 10, 1990), 9.
31. Clarence Davies and Jan Mazurek, *Regulating Pollution: Does the U.S. System Work?* (Washington, D.C.: Resources for the Future, 1997), 6–7.
32. R. Shep Melnick, "Pollution Deadlines and the Coalition of Failure," *Public Interest,* 75 (spring 1984): 125.
33. U.S. General Accounting Office, "Improving EPA's Regulatory Impact Analysis," Report No. GAO/RCED 97-38 (April 1997).
34. David D. Doniger, *The Law and Policy of Toxic Substances Control* (Baltimore: Johns Hopkins University Press, 1978), 3.
35. Quoted in John H. Trattner, *The Prune Book: The 100 Toughest Management and Policy-Making Jobs in Washington* (Lanham, Md.: Madison Books, 1988), 250.
36. Ibid., 249.
37. United States Environmental Protection Agency, Office of the Chief Financial Officer, FY 2008: Budget in Brief, Publication No. EPA-205-S-07-001 (Feb. 2007), v.

38. Richard J. Lazarus, "The Tragedy of Distrust in the Implementation of Federal Environmental Law," *Law and Contemporary Problems*, 54 (autumn 1991): 334. See also Marc K. Landy, Marc J. Roberts, and Stephen R. Thomas, *The Environmental Protection Agency: Asking the Wrong Questions* (New York: Oxford University Press, 1990); and Paul R. Portney, ed., *Public Policies for Environmental Protection* (Washington, D.C.: Resources for the Future, 1990), chaps. 1, 8.

39. Council on Environmental Quality, *Environmental Quality, 1985* (Washington, D.C.: Council on Environmental Quality, 1986), 14. See also Walter A. Rosenbaum, "Into the Nineties at EPA: Searching for the Clenched Fist and the Open Hand," in *Environmental Policy in the 1990s*, 2d ed., ed. Norman J. Vig and Michael E. Kraft (Washington, D.C.: CQ Press, 1994), 121–43.

40. U.S. General Accounting Office, "Pesticides: EPA's Formidable Task to Assess and Regulate Their Risks," Report No. GAO/RCED 86–125 (April 1986), 35.

41. Edward J. Woodhouse, "External Influences on Productivity: EPA's Implementation of TSCA," *Policy Studies Review* 4 (February 1985): 500.

42. Council on Environmental Quality, *Environmental Quality, 1985*, 12–13.

43. Harris and Milkis, *The Politics of Regulatory Change*, 228.

44. Peter W. House and Roger D. Shull, *Regulatory Reform: Politics and the Environment* (Lanham, Md.: University Press of America, 1985), 106ff.

45. Rabe, *Fragmentation and Integration*, 126.

46. Conservation Foundation, *State of the Environment: An Assessment at Mid-Decade* (Washington, D.C.: Conservation Foundation, 1984), chap. 9.

47. Walter A. Rosenbaum, "Still Reforming after All These Years," in *Environmental Policy: New Directions for the Twenty-First Century*, ed. Norman J. Vig and Michael E. Kraft (Washington, D.C.: CQ Press, 2003), 175–200.

48. National Environmental Policy Act, Title II, 42 U.S.C. § 4321 et seq. (1970).

49. Quoted in *New York Times*, March 23, 1991, 6.

50. Zachary Coile, "Interior Chief Gale Norton to Step Down," San Francisco Chronicle, March 11, 2006, A1.

51. Michelle Adato, James Mackenzie, Robert Pollard, and Ellyn Weiss, *Safety Second: The NRC and America's Nuclear Power Plants* (Bloomington: Indiana University Press, 1987), esp. chaps. 1, 5.

52. U.S. General Accounting Office, "Department of Energy: Cleaning up Inactive Facilities Will Be Difficult," Report No. GAO/RCED 92–149 (June 1993); see also U.S. General Accounting Office, "Much Work Remains to Accelerate Facility Cleanups," Report No. GAO/RCED 93-15 (January 1993).

53. See Christopher Madison, "The Energy Department at Three—Still Trying to Establish Itself," *National Journal*, October 4, 1980, 16–19.

54. *Scenic Hudson Preservation Conference v. Federal Power Commission*, 354 F.2d 608 (2d Cir. 1965).

55. Lettie M. Wenner, "Environmental Policy in the Courts," in *Environmental Policy in the 1990s*, 2d ed., ed. Norman J. Vig and Michael E. Kraft (Washington, D.C.: CQ Press, 1994), 156.

56. Werner J. Grunbaum, *Judicial Policy Making: The Supreme Court and Environmental Quality* (Morristown, N.J.: General Learning Press, 1976), 31. See also Lettie McSpadden Wenner, "The Courts and Environmental Policy," in *Environmental Politics and Policy: Theories and Evidence*, ed. James P. Lester (Durham, N.C.: Duke University Press, 1989), ed. James P. Lester, 261–288.

57. Barton H. Thompson, Jr., "Conservative Environmental Thought: The Bush Administration and Environmental Policy," *Ecology Law Quarterly*, 37 (2005), 307–48; John D. Graham, Paul R. Noe, and Elizabeth L. Branch, "Managing the Regulatory State: The Experience of the Bush Administration," *Fordam Urban Law Journal*, 33 (2006), 903–53. Blaine Harden, "Bush Policy Irks Judges in West; Rulings Criticize Agencies for Not Protecting the Environment," *Washington Post*, October 6, 2006, A3.

58. Stephen Breyer, *Breaking the Vicious Circle: Toward Effective Risk Regulation* (Cambridge: Harvard University Press, 1993), 59.

59. See Douglas Jehl, "Road Ban Set for One-Third of U.S. Forests," *New York Times,* January 5, 2001, A5; and Eric Pianin, "Ban Protects 58.5 Million Acres," *Washington Post,* January 5, 2001, 1.

60. John C. Whitaker, "Earth Day Recollections: What It Was Like When the Movement Took Off," *EPA Journal* 14 (July–August 1988): 14.

61. Ibid.

62. Quoted in Margaret Kriz, "Fuming over Fumes," *National Journal,* November 26, 1988, 3008.

63. Robert W. Crandall and Paul R. Portney, "Environmental Policy," in *Natural Resources and the Environment: The Reagan Approach,* ed. Paul Portney (Washington, D.C.: Urban Institute Press, 1984), 14.

64. U.S. Department of Commerce, Bureau of the Census, *Statistical Abstract of the United States, 1992* (Washington, D.C.: Government Printing Office, 1993), 217. Figures are given in dollar values of 1982, corrected for inflation.

65. U.S. Environmental Protection Agency, *Environmental Investments: The Cost of a Clean Environment: A Summary* (Washington, D.C.: U.S. Environmental Protection Agency, 1990), vi.

66. Morton Grodzins, "The Federal System," in *American Federalism in Perspective,* ed. Aaron Wildavsky (Boston: Little, Brown, 1967), 257.

67. U.S. Congress, Senate Committee on Environment and Public Works, *Confirmation Hearing for Administrator of the Environmental Protection Agency,* January 17, 2001, 107th Cong., 1st sess., 27.

Chapter 4

Common Policy Challenges: Risk Assessment and Environmental Justice

[The EPA] will need to ensure that it allocates resources to needed research on emerging issues, such as the relative toxicity of particulate matter components, and to assessing which sources of uncertainty have the greatest influence on benefit estimates. While EPA officials said they expect to reduce the uncertainties associated with the health benefit estimates in the final particulate matter analysis, a robust uncertainty analysis of the remaining uncertainties will nonetheless be important for decision makers and the public to understand the likelihood of attaining the estimated health benefits.

U.S. Government Accountability Office, 2006[1]

Risk assessment means never having to say you're certain.

—Humor among professional risk assessors

Until 1998 few Americans knew about phthlates nor cared about them. In November 1998, however, the environmental organization Greenpeace International released the first of its many reports demanding that the toy industry worldwide immediately abandon the use of the chemical DINP (diisononyl phthalate), an ingredient in vinyl, the material widely used throughout the industry in producing thousands of children's products as varied as pacifiers, rubber ducks, teddy bears, dolls, rattles, and teething rings. The report was another sortie in the organization's militant campaign against a large class of chemicals called phthalates, or plasticizers, which bond with vinyl molecules to make plastic products more flexible. In the United States the announcement unleashed a publicly alarming, escalating controversy that quickly assumed a pattern familiar in the politics of environmental risk assessment.

114

A Toxic Nightmare from Toyland?

First came a dramatic public condemnation of an important industrial chemical. Greenpeace International asserted that the Aristech Chemical Corporation of Pittsburgh, Pennsylvania, a subsidiary of the Mitsubishi Corporation, used the chemical DINP to manufacture products that children might chew, such as pacifiers and rattles, even though a similar compound caused liver damage in laboratory rats.[2] The accusation and accompanying information, quickly disseminated worldwide by the media, was alarming not only to the chemical producers and to parents whose children might be exposed to the products but also to the hundreds of manufacturers and consumers of other products using plasticizers—products such as medical equipment, food containers, consumer goods, packaging material, and much more, for plasticizers are a global commodity. Within weeks, two major U.S. medical advocacy groups, Health Care Without Harm and the American Nursing Association, issued a "health alert" warning that intravenous bags and tubing made of vinyl chloride contained a chemical, very similar to DINP, previously removed from toy products because of suspected toxicity. A story on the popular ABC news program *20/20* in early 1998 repeated many of the Greenpeace International allegations, thus ensuring a huge domestic audience for the controversy. Within a few weeks, the plasticizer debate was a media event.[3]

Next, an acrimonious, highly technical dispute erupted in the public media, abetted by technical publications and professional spokespersons caught up in the controversy, over the extent of the health risks resulting from exposure to the plasticizers. At the same time, the controversy was quickly politicized. Organized groups representing environmentalists, consumers, public health interests, the chemical and toy manufacturers, governmental agencies, parents, political think tanks, and many others rapidly aligned on disputing sides of the issue. Conflict approached the surreal, as exquisitely technical and publicly confounding arguments raged over baby bottle nipples, animal fetuses, Teletubbies, squeeze toys, liver biopsies, monkey testicles, and other exotica. Even Barbie and Dr. C. Everett Koop, the former U.S. surgeon general, appeared. At stake were possibly a billion dollars in worldwide product sales, the ethical and economic stature of the chlorine chemical industry, markets for hundreds of manufacturers using the embattled chemicals, and perhaps the health of uncounted children worldwide.

The Political Front

Within a week of the Greenpeace International announcement, twelve consumer, environmental, and religious groups demanded that the U.S.

Consumer Product Safety Commission (CPSC), the federal regulatory agency responsible for ensuring the safety of children's products sold in the United States, ban vinyl toys for small children. Shortly thereafter, twenty-eight members of Congress addressed President Bill Clinton with a letter urging him to ensure that the Department of Commerce was not pressuring European countries to keep their markets open to children's vinyl products. The National Environmental Trust, a coalition of environmental organizations, urged the U.S. government to ban all vinyl baby products. In November 1998 the CPSC also stated that it was uncertain about the risks to babies from DINP but nonetheless advised parents to throw away nipples and pacifiers made with vinyl and asked manufacturers not to use DINP in products children might put in their mouths.

Meanwhile, the manufacturer of DINP and many industrial consumers were rising to DINP's defense. Major toy manufacturers such as Mattel; large toy retailers including Toys R Us; and the industry's trade association, the Toy Manufacturers of America, all publicly defended the safety of the plasticizers used for decades in children's products. Defenders of DINP were enormously gratified when a nonprofit organization of distinguished scientific experts represented by Dr. Koop asserted that it stood "firmly behind the conclusions drawn from the weight of the scientific evidence [that] consumers can be confident that vinyl medical devices and toys are safe."[4]

A Scientific Enigma

The actual risk to children from exposure to plasticizers was anything but clear. In many respects, however, the array of problems illuminated by the technical controversy over plasticizers exemplified difficulties—the focus of this chapter—commonly embedded in the risk assessment required for environmental regulation.

One problem was the absence of a standard procedure to determine how much of the suspect chemical a child could realistically be expected to absorb. For example, how much DINP could a child be expected to consume by chewing a toy? In addition, toy components vary considerably in their plasticizer content. For example, high levels of DINP were found in the arms of the Rugrats Tommy Pickles Ice Cream Face doll and in the shoes of the Cabbage Patch Kids Starr Rosie doll but not elsewhere on either doll.

Another major problem involved the reliability of the animal tests indicating that DINP and its predecessor could cause liver damage in humans. Critics of these tests noted that similar damage did not occur in other experimental animals including guinea pigs, hamsters, and monkeys. Also, the age of the test animals might matter. Other disagreements arose over the relative importance to be given to toxic effects observed in different organs of experimental animals. Nonhuman primates, for example, were likely to be resistant to the testicular cancers that might appear in other kinds of animals exposed to the plasticizers, and critics argued that such primate experiments should be ignored in certain kinds of risk assessment.[5]

Finally, there was the unsettling enigma about how long it could take before health problems might appear among children exposed to plasticizers. Health professionals noted that the damaging effects of such exposure might be latent for many years and that, as a consequence, the current incidence of any suspected damage might greatly underestimate the long-term damage to humans. Thus, it might seem prudent to ban the plasticizers even in the absence of convincing current evidence of their danger.

Barbie Gets a Green Makeover

With the controversy public, the Toy Manufacturers of America reluctantly advised its members to voluntarily eliminate DINP-based vinyl products even while it maintained their safety. "Greenpeace has a clear agenda," the association asserted. "It's not looking for a compromise. It's looking for the elimination of a chlorine-based product."[6] Aristech, the Chlorine Chemistry Council, representing the users of all chlorine-based products, and toy manufacturers continued to defend DINP. The industry's capitulation was ensured when Mattel, the world's largest toy manufacturer, announced in December 1999 that it would substitute plant- and vegetable-based plastics for chlorine-based vinyls. Barbie was destined for a complete chemical makeover, along with a multitude of other familiar toys and products from other manufacturers, among them Teletubbies, Pony Luv, and Clear and Soft pacifiers and nipples.

And the Winner Is . . .

In 2003, to the considerable satisfaction of the Chlorine Chemistry Council and toy manufacturers, the CPSC voted unanimously to deny the petition to ban phthalates from products for children under five years old because there appeared to be "no demonstrable health risk."[7] The CPSC also knew how to defend itself. This decision, it noted, was supported by numerous scientific studies including a meticulous inquiry concerning "mouthing habits" among infants. The "average daily mouthing time" of soft plastic toys for children 12–24 months of age was 1.9 minutes, considerably less than the 75 minutes per day determined to be the risk threshold.[8] Average daily mouthing time, however, was not the science that satisfied most public health and environmental advocates who continued to advocate the elimination of phthalates from toys.

By 2006, phthalate opponents were rearmed with a new wave of highly publicized scientific studies once again implying that phthalates *might* be a human toxic. One university study suggested that mothers exposed during pregnancy to high levels of phthalates found in cosmetics, plastics, and detergents might have "less masculine" boys; another investigation noted that plastic food containers might "contribute" to breast cancer.[9] The Cosmetic, Toiletry and Fragrance Association protested that "an extensive body of science research" proved the safety of cosmetics but public health and environmental advocates persisted, determined to skewer high-profile industries, such as nail polish manufacturers, with apparently damning scientific research.

Public health and environmental organizations also exploited opportunities to bring pressure on the federal government from other political venues. Early in 2006, an unsuccessful campaign was waged in the California legislature for a law prohibiting baby toys containing phthalates. In December 2006, San Francisco became the first U.S. city to prohibit sale, manufacture, or distribution of products with high phthalate concentrations.[10] Perhaps the most powerful political blow against phthalates, however, was struck by the European Union (EU), which passed in late 2006 a law regulating the manufacture and use of 30,000 toxic substances, including phthalates, thus creating enormous pressure on U.S. industry to do the same. Still, parents and other consumers of phthalate-containing products were still left to decide which side—if any—should be trusted.

Variations on a Theme

The political and scientific issues exposed in the plasticizer controversy are not unique to the chemical DINP or other phthalates. They appear in various guises, usually less dramatic and acrimonious, whenever decisions are made to regulate a substance known or suspected to be toxic or hazardous. The DINP controversy is one episode in a continuing conflict over the proper means for measuring the risks and costs from exposure to a wide range of substances suspected of being environmentally hazardous. This chapter explores the reasons why these conflicts arise and persist.

Risk Assessment and the Limits of Science

Risk assessment in different guises has become a common component of environmental policy making. In recent years the U.S. Environmental Protection Agency (EPA) alone has written more than seventy-five hundred risk assessments annually in various forms to carry out its regulatory responsibilities.[11] In 1993, President Clinton further elevated the importance of risk assessment by requiring in Executive Order 12866 that all regulatory agencies, not only environmental ones, "consider, to the extent reasonable, the degree and nature of risks posed by various substances or activities within its jurisdiction" and mandating that each proposed regulatory action explain how the action will reduce risks "as well as how the magnitude of risk addressed by the action relates to other risks within the jurisdiction of the agency." [12]

Yet risk assessment grows increasingly controversial even as its influence expands, until it now incites the impassioned conflicts once confined to such holy wars as the benefit-cost debate. A major reason for the controversy is that risk assessment lies in the treacherous zone between science and politics, where practically all environmental policies reside and where collaboration between public officials and scientists is both essential and difficult. What public officials and scientists involved in policy making want from each other is often unobtainable. Public officials seek from scientists information accurate enough to indicate precisely where to establish environmental standards and credible enough to defend in the inevitable conflicts to follow. Scientists want government to act quickly and forcefully on ecological issues they believe to be critical.[13] Yet science often cannot produce technical information in the form and within the time desired by public officials. Indeed, science often cannot provide the information at all, leaving officials to make crucial decisions from fragmentary and disputable information.

In short, risk assessment frequently compels public officials to make scientific judgments and scientists to resolve policy issues for which neither may be trained. The almost inevitable need to resolve scientific questions through the political process and the problems that arise in making scientific and political judgments compatible are two of the most troublesome characteristics of environmental politics.

Derelict Data and Embattled Expertise

Controversy among experts commonly arises in environmental policy making. Contending battalions of experts—garlanded with degrees and publications and primed to dispute each other's judgment—populate congressional and administrative hearings about risk assessment. Policy makers are often left to judge not only the wisdom of policies but also the quality of the science supporting the policies.

Missing Data. Why is controversy so predictable? Frequently there is a void of useful data about the distribution and severity of environmental problems or possible pollutants. Many problems are so recent that public and private agencies have only just begun to study them. Many pollutants—hazardous chemicals, for instance—have existed for only a few decades; their ecological impacts cannot yet be measured reliably. The EPA alone receives about fifteen hundred petitions annually requesting approval of new chemicals or new uses of existing chemicals for which tests may be required.[14] Quite often the result is that nobody has the information "somebody should have." For instance, the EPA and the U.S. Department of Health and Human Services together have data reporting the degree of exposure among the general population for less than 7 percent of more than fourteen hundred chemicals considered to pose a threat to human health.[15] Lacking high-quality data, experts often extrapolate answers from fragmentary information, and plausible disputes over the reliability of such procedures are inevitable.

Late and Latent Effects. Disagreement over the severity of environmental problems also arises because the effects of many substances thought to be hazardous to humans or the environment may not become evident for decades or generations. The latency and diffusion of these impacts also may make it difficult to establish causality between the suspected substances, or events, and the consequences. Asbestos, a hazardous chemical whose malignancy has been documented since 1979, illustrates these problems.[16] Since World War II approximately eight million to eleven million U.S. workers have been exposed to asbestos, a mineral fiber with more than two thousand uses; its heat resistance, electrical properties, immunity to chemical deterioration, and other characteristics made it appear ideal to a multitude of major industries. In the past it was used widely to manufacture brake and clutch linings, plastics, plumbing, roofing tile, wall insulation, paint, paper, and much else. Asbestos is highly carcinogenic. Among those exposed to significant levels of asbestos, 20 to 25 percent died of lung cancer, 7 to 10 percent perished from mesothelioma (cancer of the chest lining or stomach), and another 8 to 9 percent died from gastrointestinal cancer.[17] The toxicity of asbestos became apparent only decades after worker exposure because cancers associated with it do not become clinically evident until fifteen to forty years after exposure and severe illness may appear two to fifty years after cancers first appear in humans. Added to the incalculable cost of human suffering is the immense economic impact of these delayed effects. More than two thousand new cases of incurable asbestos-related cancer now appear each year in the United States. Presently, 300,000 lawsuits arising from human exposure to asbestos are pending in the nation's courts, and 20,000 to 50,000 lawsuits are predicted annually for several decades. U.S. corporations and insurers have spent more than $30 billion to defend and settle asbestos lawsuits. The total cost of these suits, according to several professional estimates, may exceed $200 billion.[18]

Many other substances used in U.S. commerce, science, and domestic life are suspected of producing adverse impacts on humans or the environment. Yet conclusive evidence might not appear for decades, whereas government officials must decide whether to regulate these substances now. Difficult as such decisions are, a failure to act, as in the case of asbestos, eventually may prove so costly in human suffering and economic loss that many scientists may be reluctant to wait for conclusive data whereas others may argue the evidence is inconclusive. These issues are illustrated vividly by the federal government's continuing problems with the chemical dioxin.

The Case of Dioxin. The controversy over dioxin illuminates the major problems—political, scientific, and economic—common to regulatory science. Early in the 1990s the EPA was persuaded by growing scientific evidence to initiate a searching reevaluation of its twenty-year-old exposure standards for the chemical dioxin, which it had characterized earlier as one of the most lethal substances on earth.[19] The most dangerous among the seventy-five varieties of dioxin was thought to be 2,3,7,8-tetrachlorodibenzodioxin, known as TCDD, considered so harmful that the EPA's maximum exposure standards had limited human ingestion of TCDD to 0.006 trillionth of a gram per day for every kilogram (2.2 pounds) of body weight over an average lifetime—in other words, an average-sized man was limited daily to an amount equal to a grain of sand sliced one billion times.

The EPA's original exposure standard for dioxin, as with most risk assessments made by federal agencies, was extrapolated largely from animal experiments. In the late 1970s the EPA ordered an end to production of the weed killer 2,4,5-T, also a dioxin, on the basis of its own earlier studies and additional, if circumstantial, evidence of great harm to individuals exposed to high concentrations of the herbicide. When concentrations of dioxin far exceeding levels considered safe were discovered during 1981 in the soil of Times Beach, Missouri—the result of illegal toxic waste disposals—the EPA decided that public safety required the permanent evacuation of the entire Missouri community. All 2,240 residents were removed to new residences and reimbursed for their property at a cost exceeding $37 million, while an additional $100 million was spent to clean up other nearby contaminated sites. During the 1980s, hundreds of lawsuits were filed against the federal government by Vietnam War veterans for alleged health impairment from exposure to dioxin in the defoliant Agent Orange. Meanwhile, the EPA's strict standards were expected to cost the paper and pulp industry about $2 billion for pollution control.

But a growing number of scientific experts questioned not only the EPA's exposure standards for dioxin but also the reliability of all animal studies for determining safe levels of human exposure to hazardous substances.[20] A particularly damning public indictment of the EPA's own standard appeared in 1991, when the federal scientist who had ordered the evacuation of Times Beach admitted to a congressional committee that he made the wrong decision. "Given what we know now about this chemical's toxicity," then–assistant surgeon general Vernon N. Houk stated, "it looks as if the evacuation was unnecessary."[21] In 1991 the World Health Organization delivered another assault on the EPA's dioxin assessment when it declared its support for a new standard increasing the permissible human exposure by 1,600 percent above the EPA's limits.

Additional complications arose in 1992 when a panel of experts convened by the EPA concluded that although dioxin was a significant cancer threat only to people exposed to unusually high levels in chemical factories, it also wreaked biological havoc among fish, birds, and other wild animals even in minute doses.[22] In early 1993 another blow against dioxin regulation was delivered by the director of the National Institute of Environmental Health Sciences, the agency supervising all federal animal studies used in toxics regulation. The agency's director released portions of a report from a panel of leading toxicologists that concluded that many of the assumptions driving the animal research "did not appear to be valid."[23] Animal studies alone, concluded most of the experts, were not reliable means for judging the exposure risks to human beings in toxics research. Alternative approaches to animal testing that avoid the errors criticized by the panel existed, the report noted, but these tests took two to eight years to conduct and therefore seemed an impractical remedy.

Environmental organizations resisted any relaxation of the EPA's current dioxin standard. Scientific experts speaking for these organizations asserted that the new evidence created no compelling case for a new standard. "Nothing that has been learned about dioxin since 1985 when EPA first published its risk assessment findings on dioxin . . . supports a revision of science-based policy or action," Ellen K. Silbergeld, a pathologist and expert witness for environmental organizations, argued.[24] Nonetheless, the Clinton administration and EPA officials were extremely uneasy with the existing exposure standards, and a thorough restudy of the issue was ordered.

In mid-2000 the EPA released the results of its long-awaited restudy. To the surprise of the White House and most EPA officials, the agency for the first time concluded that dioxin TCCD *was* a "human carcinogen" and one hundred related chemicals were "likely" human carcinogens. The result was all the more startling because domestic emissions of dioxin had declined by 87 percent since 1984. However, TCCDs can accumulate in human body fat from repeated exposures and thus, the report asserted, dioxin was a significant health risk to humans who ingested it through a normal diet.[25] For the small proportion of the population with extremely high-fat diets, the odds of developing cancer were estimated as high as 1 in 100, or ten times the EPA's previous estimate. Low-grade exposure could create other health problems, the report concluded, including hormonal and developmental defects in babies and children. Some environmental organizations then deduced from the EPA's risk estimates that about 100 of the 1,400 cancer deaths occurring in the United States daily were attributable to dioxin. The EPA knew full well what to expect, warning its senior officials to anticipate that when the report became public "many stakeholders [will] take dramatic action" and "pressure from other interests" would grow. Predictably, the EPA's decision was assailed from both sides of the controversy. The Chlorine Chemistry Council, which represented the major chemical producers involved, asserted the EPA was "out of sync" with dioxin regulation in the rest of the world and the report was "counterintuitive to what the facts are." The U.S. Chamber of Commerce suggested the decision wasn't based on "sound science." Greenpeace International, like some other environmental groups, lacerated the EPA for failing to control aggressively the remaining dioxin emissions: "That suggests that [EPA] can't walk and chew gum at the same time," it sniffed.[26]

Still the dioxin controversy will not go away. After another review continuing until mid-2003, the EPA sent its dioxin assessment to an Interagency Working Group to be reviewed by other relevant federal agencies. Congress then passed legislation requiring the working group to request that the National Research Council (NRC), a part of the National Academy of Sciences, perform a complete review of the assessment document—a cascade of reviews that environmentalists claimed was a tactic by George W. Bush's administration to stall implementation of new dioxin regulations indefinitely.[27] In July 2006 the NAS review concluded that the agency "did not sufficiently quantify the uncertainties and variables associated with risks [of dioxin exposure]" and recommended that the EPA reassess the risks of dioxin exposure—especially exposure to very low dioxin doses—and issue a revised risk assessment explaining more clearly "how it selects both the data upon which the reassessment is based and the methods used to analyse them."[28] Meanwhile, the existing EPA risk standards would be enforced.

Animal and Epidemiological Experiments. As the dioxin controversy illustrates, estimates of health risks from suspected toxics are a source of much controversy. But, having rejected most controlled human studies as ethically repugnant, scientists are left with no certain alternatives in arriving at risk estimates. They may attempt to characterize a substance's danger based on existing knowledge of how chemical carcinogens affect human cells, but little knowledge exists about the precise way in which these chemicals alter the structure and chemistry of cells. The common alternative is the controlled animal experiments in which test animals are exposed to substances, the effects monitored, and the risks to human beings extrapolated from the findings.

These animal studies are particularly controversial when estimating the effects of low levels of chemical exposure on humans—for instance, a dose of a few parts per million or billion of a pesticide or heavy metal in drinking water over thirty years. The human risks of cancer or other serious illnesses will be small, but how small?[29] And how reliable is the estimate? Animal studies do not and cannot use enough animals to eliminate possibilities of error in estimating the effects of low-level exposure on humans. To demonstrate conclusively with 95 percent confidence that a certain low-level dose of one substance causes fewer than one case of cancer per million individuals would require a "megamouse" experiment involving six million animals.[30] Instead, researchers use high doses of a substance with relatively few animals and then extrapolate through statistical models the effect on humans from low-level exposure to the tested substance. But these models can differ by a factor of as much as 100,000 in estimating the size of the dose that could produce one cancer per million individuals. A litany of other problems are associated with small animal studies. Failure to observe any response to a substance among a small group of animals does not imply a substance is safe. Animals, moreover, differ greatly in their sensitivity to substances; dioxin is five thousand times more toxic to guinea pigs than to hamsters, for example.[31]

Epidemiological studies depend on surveys recording the relationship between known human exposure to suspected hazardous substances and the known effects; the investigator does not deliberately expose humans to possibly dangerous substances but attempts to capitalize on exposure when it occurs. Such after-the-fact studies have been used to establish the cancer risks of exposure to cigarette smoke and asbestos, for example. The lack of scientific controls is a serious deficiency in almost all epidemiological studies. As economist David Doniger observed,

> Humans are exposed to too many different substances at unknown doses for unknown periods to permit statistically reliable conclusions to be drawn. Moreover, there are synergistic and antagonistic interactions between chemicals that drastically complicate drawing conclusions about the effects of each chemical.[32]

The Limited Neutrality of Scientific Judgment

Perhaps fifty opportunities exist in a normal risk assessment procedure for scientists to make discretionary judgments. Although scientists are presumed to bring to this task an expertise untainted by social values to bias their judgments, they are not immune to social prejudice, especially when their expertise is embroiled in a public controversy. According to physicist Harvey Brooks, a veteran of many public controversies,

> The more an issue is in the public eye, the more expert judgments are likely to be influenced unconsciously by pre-existing policy preferences or by supposedly unrelated factors such as media presentations, the opinions of col-

leagues or friends, or even the emotional overtones of certain words used in the debate.[33]

Scientific judgment on environmental issues can be influenced by one's beliefs about how government should regulate the economy, by one's institutional affiliation, or by other social and political attributes. For example, a study of 136 occupational physicians and industrial hygienists working in government, industry, and academia examined the link between their political and social backgrounds and their opinions about a proposed standard for carcinogens by the Occupational Safety and Health Administration. Scientists employed in industry were more politically and socially conservative than those employed by universities or government. The industry scientists were more likely to favor scientific assumptions about identifying carcinogens that would decrease the probability that a substance would be deemed a risk to human health—in effect, they favored scientific premises that made regulation of a substance less likely.[34] Another study of several hundred risk professionals involved in federal environmental policy making suggested that once risk professionals became involved in policy making there was "a weakening of disciplinary perspectives and a strengthening of viewpoints based on politics and ideology."[35] In general, the study concluded that risk professionals working for corporations or trade associations differed from those working for government or academic institutions in their technical judgments about how risk should be determined and when substances should be regulated, as well as in broader attitudes about governmental regulation.

Social or political bias can be particularly pernicious when not recognized or admitted by the experts. It is now evident that many technical controversies in policy making may not be resolvable by resort to scientific evidence and argument because scientific solutions will be permeated with social, political, or economic bias. Indeed, political controversy often subverts scientific integrity. Experts can be readily, even unintentionally, caught up in the emotionally and politically polarizing atmosphere of such disputes, their judgment compromised so badly that, as political scientist Dorothy Nelkin remarked, their expertise "is reduced to one more weapon in a political arsenal."[36] Yet no barrier can be contrived to wholly insulate science from the contagion of social or economic bias. This is a strong argument for keeping scientific and technical determinations open to examination and challenge by other experts and laypersons.

What Risks Are Acceptable?

Risk assessment for environmental policy making is also difficult because no clear and consistent definition of acceptable risk exists in federal law. Acceptable risk is usually defined in environmental regulation by statutory criteria—that is, by standards written into law to guide regulators in determining when to regulate a substance. The EPA, like several other federal agencies, wrestles daily and inconclusively with the problem of defining acceptable risk. Despite repeated congressional efforts at clarification, the only consistency in these statutory standards is their inconsistency.[37]

The EPA, uneasy with the enormous scientific uncertainties inherent in determining acceptable risk, frequently has shrouded its discretionary decisions in a fog of verbal mystification. Nonetheless, determining acceptable risk remains an intensely discretionary—and often political—affair, however much the language of the law may try to conceal it.

A Multitude of Risk Criteria

A multitude of different congressional standards guide regulatory agencies in making determinations of acceptable risk. Different substances often are regulated according to different standards. The same agency may have to use as many as six or seven standards depending on which substances, or which laws, are involved. The same substance may be subject to one regulatory standard when dumped into a river and another when mixed into processed food. Statutory risk standards are commonly vague and sometimes confusing; congressional intent may be muddled, often deliberately.

In general, regulatory agencies encounter one or more of the following statutory formulas in determining the permissible exposure levels to various substances.[38] The examples are drawn from existing legislation.

• *Health-Based Criteria.* Regulatory agencies are to set standards based on risks to human health from exposure to a hazard. These standards are usually "cost oblivious" because they seldom permit agencies to use the cost of regulation as a consideration in standard setting. Health-based criteria, however, can involve different levels of acceptable health risk. The Clean Air Act mandates that national primary ambient air quality standards "shall be . . . in the judgment of the Administrator, based on [air quality] criteria and allowing an adequate margin of safety . . . requisite to protect human health" (Clean Air Act [1970]). The EPA is also left to determine the magnitude of this "margin of safety," and to whom it applies. In contrast, the Food Quality Protection Act (1996) requires, very precisely, that the EPA must set the standard to protect infants and children from allowable pesticide residues in food at ten times the safety factor for adults unless reliable data show that a different factor would be safe.

• *Technology-Based Criteria.* The EPA is instructed to ensure that pollution sources will use the best available or the maximum achievable technology, or some other specified technology criteria, to control their hazardous emissions. The Safe Drinking Water Act (1974) and the Federal Water Pollution Control Act (1956) use technology-based standards. In effect, acceptable risks are defined by whatever residual risks to public health may exist after the prescribed control technologies are applied to a pollution source. From the EPA's perspective, the regulatory task is eased somewhat because the agency does not have to assess the actual public health risks from exposure to a specific pollutant. Instead, it has to ensure that the prescribed technology is applied to the pollution source.

• *Balancing Criteria.* Congress mandates that an agency consider, to varying extents, the costs of regulation, or the magnitude of threat to human health, alongside the benefits in setting a standard for human or environmental exposure. Or Congress may permit cost considerations to be among other criteria an agency may consider. These statutes define how various considerations, such as cost and risk, are to be balanced in determining acceptable risk. For instance, a law may *permit* an agency to balance the benefits for a given regulatory standard (which may include health as well as monetary benefits) against the costs of its enforcement. In contrast, another law may *require* agencies to balance the benefits against the economic costs in setting standards for exposure to a substance.

A close reading of these guidelines reveals the enormous discretion customarily left to regulatory agencies in determining how to balance the various statutory criteria. It is often difficult to separate scientific from non-scientific issues; scientists usually become activists in standard setting as well as in determining the magnitude of risks on which the standards should be based. Limited by its lack of scientific expertise yet reluctant to leave agencies with too much discretion in determining acceptable risk, Congress often packs regulatory laws with so many criteria for risk determination— lest any important consideration be ignored—that regulatory decisions become enormously complicated. Consider, for instance, the criteria the EPA was ordered to use under the Toxic Substances Control Act (TSCA) of 1976 when deciding whether the risks from exposure to a substance are unreasonable:

> The type of effect (chronic or acute, reversible or irreversible); degree of risk; characteristics and number of humans, plants and animals, or ecosystems, at risk; amount of knowledge about the effects; available or alternative substances and their expected effects; magnitude of the social and economic costs and benefits of possible control actions; and appropriateness and effectiveness of TSCA as the legal instrument for controlling the risk.[39]

Agencies spend considerable time working out detailed internal regulations to translate these complexities into workable procedures. They may attempt to reach understandings concerning how criteria will be balanced, with interest groups active in the regulatory process. But agencies often face imperious deadlines for making regulatory decisions, fragmentary information relevant to many criteria for standard setting, and disputes between interest groups concerning the validity of information and the priorities for criteria in policy making. In the first years of a new regulatory program, an agency can expect virtually every major decision to be challenged through litigation, usually by an interest alleging the agency has failed to interpret properly its statutory responsibilities. An agency sometimes invites such litigation because it can work to its advantage. By interpreting the manner in which risk determinations should be made by agencies, judges often dissipate the fog of uncertainty about congressional intent and provide agencies with firm guidelines for future determinations.

Missing data and muddled laws often promote waffling when agencies struggle to define acceptable risk. This is why the EPA's encounter with TSCA's murky risk criteria seems like an adventure in regulatory wonderland. In 1991 the U.S. General Accounting Office asked the EPA why it had never used its authority under TSCA to require the testing of several chemicals whose toxicity was strongly suspected. The responsible EPA office replied that the chemicals did not pose the "significant risk to human health or the environment" that TSCA required for regulation. "In explaining why EPA has never used [its] authorities in the chemical testing program," commented the investigators, the agency stated that it "uses a 'high threshold' of risk in assessing whether a chemical imposes significant or unreasonable risks." However, noted the General Accounting Office, "the EPA has never defined the meaning of 'significant' or 'unreasonable' for the purpose of implementing TSCA."[40] In light of TSCA's confounding definitions of acceptable risk, the EPA's behavior might be considered preordained.

The Disappearing Threshold

One of the most politically controversial aspects of determining acceptable risk remains the problem of the "disappearing threshold," a largely unanticipated result of three tendencies among Congress and agencies concerned with environmental regulation. First, in writing and enforcing most environmental legislation during the 1970s, officials remained risk averse in dealing with potential hazards; risk reduction was preferred to risk tolerance. Second, Congress generally assumed that with many, or most, regulated substances, some threshold of exposure would exist below which the risks to humans or the ecosystem were negligible. Congress certainly did not anticipate removing *all* traces of human or ecological hazards. Third, legislators, who were largely indifferent to regulatory costs compared with health criteria in setting regulatory standards, discouraged agencies from using cost-benefit analyses when determining acceptable risks.

Economics and technology now present regulation writers with some difficult decisions as a result of these circumstances. Extremely sophisticated technologies enable scientists to detect hazardous substances in increasingly small concentrations, currently as small as parts per billion or trillion. It is usually impossible to assert scientifically that such low concentrations are wholly innocent of adverse risk, however slight, to humans or the environment. In addition, the cost of controlling hazardous substances often rises steeply as progressively higher standards are enforced; for instance, after reducing 85 percent of a substance in a waterway, it may cost half as much or more to remove an additional 5 to 10 percent. In effect, the risk threshold once presumed by policy makers vanished; no measurable concentration of a substance apparently could be assumed innocent of potential harm to humans or the environment. To eliminate conclusively *any* probable risks from such substances, regulators would have to require the total elimination of the substance—an extraordinarily expensive undertaking. The threshold problem thus was created. Should a trade-off be made between the costs and benefits of risk prevention, and, if so, what criteria should govern the choice?

Critics assert that regulators should err in this trade-off by insisting on extremely high standards for controlling risks out of all proportion to the benefits to society or the environment and without sensitivity to the economic burden imposed on regulated interests.[41] In critic Paul Johnson's terms, this is the "Custer Syndrome." Regulators "take action at any cost, do it as quickly as possible, and leave the thinking to afterwards."[42] This leaves the public with "unrealistic expectations" about the benefits, which in most cases will be extremely small if not undiscoverable when regulators insist on eliminating even minuscule risks from hazardous substances.[43] Advocates of strict risk management, however, usually respond that the full extent of risk is unknown or may be greater than currently estimated; they may dispute the accuracy of opposing data. Often they are indignant at the suggestion that human lives may be endangered if the cost of protection is deemed excessive—an assertion, skillfully delivered, that implies officials are venal or inhumane for imperiling lives to save money for a regulated interest.

Elected officials are understandably wary in dealing with these publicly sensitive issues, especially when advocates of strict regulation may cast them as the villains. It is easy to make tolerance for even small risks appear to be cruel gambling with the destinies of innocent people, even though risk assessment deals in probabilities, not certainties, of accident, death, or disease. And environmental groups are typically unyielding in opposition to any relaxation of existing health standards. The successful efforts by the Clinton administration to weaken the Delaney Clause in the Food and Drug Act illustrate the problem. The EPA, at the initiative of administrator

Carol Browner, proposed relaxing the Delaney Clause's strict prohibition against any carcinogenic pesticide residue on food. The EPA proposed a new but still rigorous standard allowing pesticide residues whose health risks did not exceed the probability of one extra cancer death for every million persons—a proposal seemingly in accord with a 1989 recommendation by the National Academy of Sciences that the Delaney Clause's total ban on any pesticide residues was too rigid.[44] Nonetheless, environmental groups vigorously opposed any modification of the Delaney Clause. Congress, however, accepted the EPA's proposed new standard when it approved the Food Quality Protection Act.

Searching for Solutions: The "Bright Line"

In a belated effort to eliminate some of the difficulties involved in determining acceptable risk, Congress took an apparently sensible step by writing into the Clean Air Act Amendments of 1990 what has been called a "residual-risk bright line" for determining acceptable public exposure to air toxics. Essentially, the law required the EPA to ensure that the increased lifetime cancer risk from exposure to an air toxic must not exceed one in a million (10^{-6}) for the affected population. Such a "bright line," apparently giving the EPA a precise statutory definition of acceptable risk, seemed to add needed clarity to federal risk assessment and to provide a precedent for future regulation. Moreover, it satisfied the congressional urge to tighten control over the EPA by limiting its discretion in risk management. However, it soon was obvious that the bright line left enormous discretion to the EPA's risk assessors without simplifying their job very much. "A politically motivated risk assessor could, in many situations, easily manipulate his or her analysis to produce a desired outcome on either side of the line," observed an evaluation of the EPA by the National Academy of Public Administration. "Even a more conscientious risk assessor with no interest in the impact of his or her results would make numerous decisions in the process that could change the final answers by several orders of magnitude," the evaluation concluded.[45]

The Value of Science in Environmental Policy Making

Despite the scientific disputes attending environmental policy making, it remains important to recognize how often science provides useful and highly reliable guidance to policy makers. Often the scientific data relevant to an issue clearly point to the adverse affects of substances and define the magnitude of their risks. This was certainly evident in the data leading to the federal government's decision to ban most domestic agriculture uses of the pesticides DDT, aldrin, and dieldrin, for instance. Furthermore, even when one set of data does not alone provide definitive evidence of human risks from exposure to chemicals, numerous studies pointing to the same conclusion together can provide almost irrefutable evidence; such was the case in the epidemiological evidence indicting asbestos as a human carcinogen. Often the reliability of data will be routinely challenged by those opposed to the regulation of some substance regardless of the ultimate merit—or lack thereof—of their case. In the end, public officials must make decisions on the basis of the best evidence available. For all their limitations, scientific data often enable officials to define more carefully and clearly the range of options, risks, and benefits involved in regulating a substance even when the data cannot answer all risk questions conclusively.

Even if indisputable data were available on the risks from human exposure to all levels of a substance, controversy over the acceptable level would continue. It is asserted sometimes that science should be responsible for determining the magnitudes of risk from exposure to chemicals and that government should define the acceptability. In other words, defining acceptable risk is largely a political matter. Such a division of labor is rarely possible. Scientists, too, are often drawn into the nettlesome problem of determining what levels of exposure to substances ultimately will be acceptable.

Risk and Discrimination:
The Problem of Environmental Justice

In October 1997 a jury in New Orleans in a landmark decision awarded $3.4 billion in damages to eight thousand people who had been evacuated a decade previously from their community near a major train route after a tank car filled with the chemical butadiene had caught fire. This award was the largest liability ever assessed in federal court on the basis of environmental discrimination. The fact that most of the plaintiffs lived in a poor, underprivileged neighborhood, and thus were exposed to "environmental racism," appeared to have been a major consideration in the jury's generous damage award, even though their attorneys had only alluded to such racism during the trial. "No one said this is racism," explained one of the lawyers for the neighborhood, "but the facts were such that any commonsense appraisal would tell you that the poorer, underprivileged neighborhood was discriminated against."[46] It is testimony to the political potency of the environmental justice movement in the United States that a decade previously the idea of environmental racism was virtually unknown in public discourse or in the language of the courts, let alone as a cause for civil damage claims. Now, issues of environmental justice—or environmental equity—are raised in so many different political and judicial venues that the language has become almost a staple in political discussions involving minorities and health risk.

What Is Environmental Justice?

No consensus exists in law or political debate about the meaning of *environmental justice* or about *environmental equity* and *environmental racism*—two terms often used interchangeably with *environmental justice*. After considerable difficulty, the EPA in 1994 decided that *environmental justice* should be taken to mean "the fair treatment and meaningful involvement of all people regardless of race, color, national origin, or income with respect to the development, implementation or enforcement of environmental laws, regulations, and policies."[47] In contrast, Robert D. Bullard, an environmental justice scholar and leading national advocate for the environmental justice movement, equated environmental justice with the elimination of environmental inequity, which he suggested has at least three implications:[48]

• *Procedural Inequity.* The extent to which governing rules, regulations, and evaluation criteria are applied uniformly. Examples of procedural inequity are holding hearings in remote locations to minimize public participation, stacking boards and commissions with probusiness interests, and using English-only material to communicate to non-English-speaking communities.

• *Geographical Inequity.* A situation in which some neighborhoods, communities, and regions receive direct benefits, such as jobs and tax revenues, from industrial production whereas the costs, such as the burdens of waste disposal, are fixed elsewhere. For example, communities hosting waste-disposal facilities receive fewer economic benefits than communities generating waste.

• *Social Inequity.* When environmental decisions mirror the power arrangements of the larger society and reflect the still-existing racial bias in the United States. Institutional racism, for instance, influences the siting of noxious facilities, leaving many black communities in so-called sacrifice zones.

Whether or not it is also linked with equity, or racism, the concept of environmental justice is commonly used in situations in which identifiable minorities have been exposed, deliberately or not, to disproportionate health or safety risks from a known hazard such as a chemical waste dump or an environment-polluting industrial site. Still, practically every definition of *environmental justice* or related terms abounds in ambiguities—what, for instance, is a "disproportionate health risk" and how is a "minority" defined?

As these definitions demonstrate, advocates of environmental justice now use the term, or its close relations, to embrace an enormous diversity of political and economic practices far surpassing the human health and safety issues traditionally associated with environmental risk. It has been left to the courts, legislators, advocacy groups, and scholars to render order from this definitional confusion as they struggle to translate such abstractions into law and political practice. More important than its precise definition, however, is the impact of environmental justice as social movement. From an inauspicious beginning in the mid-1980s, the movement has gradually emerged as a potent political presence that has transformed environmental politics and law. Its most important impacts have been to compel government attention at all levels to issues of environmental discrimination, to motivate grassroots political movements nationwide that mobilize minorities against apparent environmental discrimination, and to bring environmental discrimination within the scope of judicial concern and remedy.

A Growing Movement

The environmental justice movement achieved major national attention in 1991 when 600 delegates met in Washington, D.C., at the first National People of Color Environmental Leadership Summit. From its inception, the movement's relationship to mainstream environmental advocacy groups has been ambivalent. "For the most part," observed historian Martin V. Melosi, "the movement found strength at the grassroots, especially among low-income people of color who faced serious environmental threats from toxics and hazardous wastes."[49] Thus the movement assumes a very different social and economic aspect from the predominantly middle-class, white, and relatively affluent organizations dominating U.S. environmental politics. Moreover, the movement's agenda focuses primarily on local communities, toxic and hazardous waste sites, and new organizational identities. At the same time, environmental justice also generates a political gravity drawing minority advocates into a closer political orbit with organized environmentalism. Mainstream environmental organizations have been quick to recognize that environmental justice offers an opportunity to attract economic and racial minorities to the environmental movement and to overcome persistent criticism that environmentalism is, or appears to be, a "white thing." Environmental justice organizations, for their part, often create strategic partnerships with mainstream environmental advocacy groups when it works to political advantage, yet the movement insists on maintaining an identity apart from mainstream environmentalism.

The environmental justice movement continues to grow in size, organizational skill, and political influence. Its fundamental conviction that cultural, racial, and ethnic minorities have been exposed disproportionately to health and safety risks throughout the United States has inspired an aggressive campaign to identify and mobilize these minorities, to demand various forms of compensation for those afflicted by such discrimination, and to demand that governmental policy making be redesigned to weigh issues of environmental equity in environmental policy making. The movement has been aided powerfully by active support from numerous social action organizations affiliated with many of the nation's major religious denominations.

The impact of the environmental justice movement has been magnified enormously in recent years as the result of an enlarging, increasingly skillful network of collaborating local, state, and national organizations. Legal advocacy has been an especially important resource. These organizations include academically based groups such as the Clark Atlanta University's Environmental Justice Resource Center and Harvard University's Working Group on Environmental Justice, newly created advocacy specialists in the American Bar Association, the Environmental Law Institute and other professional legal associations, and a multitude of independent legal and paralegal entities at all government levels. To these are often joined numerous locally based environmental justice groups such as New York's Environmental Justice Alliance. In addition, specialized environmental justice media are increasing, such as the Inner City Press' *Environmental Justice Reporter* and the University of Michigan's "Environmental Justice Information Page" on the Internet. The Internet itself has provided a highly congenial, and virtually costless, venue for network development. The movement's leadership now embraces virtually all people of color and all the economically disadvantaged within its mission, so that Native Americans, Latinos, and Asians, among other important domestic minorities, are being recruited. Finally, the movement is crafting political alliances with the rapidly growing network of regional and international advocacy organizations promoting racial and economic justice.

This growing coalition committed to social equity in environmental regulation illustrates why the creation and solution of environmental risks is often inherently a political issue. In early 1994, President Clinton issued Executive Order 12898 instructing all federal agencies to develop strategies to ensure that their programs "do not unfairly inflict environmental harm on the poor and minorities." The executive order, applicable to all federal agencies and to any program "that substantially affects human health or the environment," was the first comprehensive effort by the federal government to address a problem long implicit in environmental policy making and only reluctantly acknowledged by past administrations.[50] The EPA became one of the first federal agencies to recognize the importance of the environmental justice movement by creating its own Office of

Environmental Justice as early as 1992. Since then, numerous state and local governments have also declared a commitment to environmental justice by law or executive order. In early 2004, for example, New Jersey's governor issued an executive order that mandated the state's departments of Environmental Protection and Transportation to develop a strategy to reduce pollution exposure in minority and low-income neighborhoods.

Administrative Challenges

Admininstering laws that mandate environmental justice has been labored and controversial from its inception. Stakeholders may agree on its necessity, yet translating "environmental justice" into public policy—like implementing other public laws—can manufacture formidable obstacles between the word and the deed.

One major obstacle has been the frequent lack of resources and (sometimes) resolve among federal agencies to implement aggressively their environmental justice mandates. The EPA, in particular, has constantly struggled with impediments—not all of its own creation—in enforcing its own environmental justice regulations and Executive Order 12898. For example, after reviewing the EPA's drafting of three major air quality regulations between 2001 to 2004, the congressional General Accounting Office (now known as Government Accountability Office) (GAO) tartly concluded,

> Even when the workgroups stated that they had considered environmental Justice . . . all three workgroup chairs told us that they received no guidance in how to analyze environmental justice concerns in rulemaking. Second, workgroup members had received little, if any, training on environmental justice. . . . Finally, the Air Office's environmental justice coordinators, whose full-time responsibility is promoting environmental justice, were not involved in drafting any of the three rules.[51]

Some of these problems arise from White House failures to fund generously the agency's environmental justice activists and from the meager data sometimes available to characterize environmental justice conditions. Often, however, pressure by environmental justice organizations is required to compel careful attention to these matters from the EPA and other federal agencies.

Scientific data relevant to environmental justice problems has been improving significantly since the mid-1990s but almost all discourse about environmental justice—whatever the venue—is still likely to ignite controversy over the scientific basis of claims to environmental injustice.[52] Fragmentary evidence accumulating for decades, and more deliberate studies in recent years, often seem to demonstrate that minorities and poor individuals are disproportionately exposed to health risks from environmental pollutants.[53] The economically disadvantaged may also be more likely than others to have a hazardous waste site for a neighbor. Several studies have suggested as much, such as one Detroit, Michigan, survey, cited by sociologists Paul Mohai and Bunyan Bryant, indicating that "minority residents in the metropolitan area are four times more likely than white residents to live within a mile of a commercial hazardous waste facility."[54]

For environmental justice advocates, the evidence seems convincing if not overwhelming. "Although communities of color, tribes and indigenous peoples, and the poor have been heavily and disproportionately affected by noxious risk producing environmental practices for decades," began a policy paper by one major advocacy group, as if stating common knowledge.[55] At the other extreme, Christopher H. Foreman Jr. of the Brookings Institution completed an extensive study of claims made by environmental justice advocates and concluded,

> [W]hen you clear away all the smoke blown over risk and racism in recent years, there turns out to be remarkably little good evidence indicating that low-income and minority citizens regularly bear a disproportionate share of society's environmental risk, much less that they develop pollution-related illnesses more often than other citizens.[56]

The controversy feeds on several refractory problems. One problem is the frequent difficulty of obtaining information about population exposures to environmental risks sufficiently rich in detail and duration to satisfy the requirements of common risk assessment methods. "Health or toxicity data for particular chemicals can be unavailable or inadequate," explained Rebecca A. Head, an environmental justice advocate and public health official:

> Current health assessment models may also fail to be capable of using all the possible variables, and therefore can be unreliable in predicting and proving potential disease or injury due to environmental contamination. Risks or dangers associated with exposures to chemicals are especially problematic in communities housing multiple facilities that may be, albeit legally, emitting various chemicals into the air, water or soil. The chances are increased that residents will be exposed to many different chemicals simultaneously.[57]

Especially when there is a possibility of population exposure to multiple environmental hazards—a situation quite common in minority communities—the appropriate scientific protocols for estimating individual or population exposure have seldom existed, and almost never existed before 2000 for regulatory decision making by government. Another difficulty is that, with the exception of lead exposure, little reliable evidence exists about the specific relationship of race or class to environmental health measures. Until recently, census information and other comprehensive social data seldom permitted comparisons between economic or social groups and exposure to various environmental hazards. In addition, any estimates of selective exposure to environmental risk must take into account complex genetic, racial, and hereditary differences among populations.

An additional obstacle is demonstrating that economic or racial minorities have been exposed deliberately to disproportionate environmental risks or that risk exposures were assumed involuntarily. For example, it may be demonstrated convincingly that populations living for decades near a known environmental hazard (such as a petrochemical plant) are largely poor racial minorities and that they are more heavily exposed to environmental pollutants than non–racial minorities in the same community. Yet it may be argued in political debate and courtrooms that such individuals often move to their residences deliberately and with knowledge of the environmental risks, so that the environmental exposures were voluntary.

Finally, difficulties arise over the appropriate strategies for identifying how risks may be distributed unfairly in environmental regulation and how this inequity can be solved. Over what period of time, for example, should risk estimates be made? Which populations qualify as disadvantaged? To what extent should the ability of individuals to protect themselves from such risk be taken into account? What sort of environmental risks should be included? How can such issues be introduced early enough in the regulatory decision-making process to influence the outcomes?

Surveying these difficulties, critics have argued that the environmental justice agenda is ultimately a means to much broader political ends. The movement's political potency, so the argument runs, is grounded less on scientific credibility than on the capacity of its grassroots organizers to mobilize minorities and to articulate deeply rooted historical social grievances for which environmental issues are often symbolic. "It effectively speaks to the fear and anger among local communities feeling overwhelmed by forces beyond their control, and outraged by what they perceive to be assaults on their collective quality of life," Foreman concluded.[58] To the movement's leadership, such assertions are likely to appear an effort to deflect attention from the evidence of environmental justice by implicitly attacking the integrity of its leadership.

In any case, the environmental justice movement now claims a salience on the agenda of national environmental policy that is unlikely to decline in the near future. For the nation's governments, one of the most daunting challenges is to find a way to effectively translate lofty goals such as environmental equity or environmental justice into specific policy procedures and specific governmental actions. How does one bring environmental justice to the desktop and conference table of routine governmental regulation? It seems evident that a successful policy translation will require, at the least, the rapid development of a science base, which means acquiring and disseminating information about exposure of minority populations to specific environmental hazards and developing reliable methodologies for estimating individual and population risks from such exposure. Administrative law and procedure must be modified in detail and depth so that considerations of inequitable environmental risk can be considered in a timely and explicit manner in regulatory decision making. All this, in turn, will require resolute legislative and executive leadership and, eventually, active participation by the nation's judicial structures. Converting prescription into practice will be arduous, however, in light of the current disagreement on appropriate metrics for measuring discrimination and equity and on the degree of difference among populations that constitutes inequity.

Conclusion

The complex new problems of risk assessment in environmental regulation confirm that we live in an historically unique era of technocratic power. U.S. science and industry, in common with those of other advanced industrial nations, now possess the capacity to alter in profound but often unpredictable ways the biochemical basis of future human life and thus to change future ecosystems radically. In its extreme form, represented by nuclear weapons, modern technology has the power to eradicate human society, if not humanity itself. But modern technologies also can alter the future ecosphere in a multitude of less dramatic but significant ways: through the deliberate redesign of genetic materials in human reproduction, through the depletion of irreplaceable energy resources such as petroleum or natural gas, through the multiplication of long-lived hazardous substances whose biological impacts on humans and the ecosystem may magnify through hundreds of years, and much more. We are practically the first generation in the world's history with the certain technical capacity to alter and even to destroy the fundamental biochemical and geophysical conditions for societies living centuries after ours. It is, as one social prophet noted, a power that people of the Middle Ages did not even credit to devils.

With this new technocratic power comes the ability to develop technologies, to manufacture new substances, and to deplete finite resources so that the benefits are largely distributed in the present and the risks for the most part displaced to the future. Future societies may inherit most of the burden to create the social, economic, and political institutions necessary for managing the risks inherent in this generational cost transfer. Such technical capacity can become an exercise of power undisciplined by responsibility for the consequences.

The status of nuclear wastes in many ways provides a paradigm for this problem. Because the wastes from civilian nuclear reactors currently cannot be recycled, as was assumed when the nuclear power industry began in the United States during the 1950s, the federal government now must find a safe and reliable way to dispose of the growing amount of nuclear wastes from these facilities.

Among the most dangerous of these substances are high-level wastes—those highly toxic to humans for long periods—found in the spent fuel rods from civilian reactors. Strontium-90 and cesium-137, for instance, must be isolated from human exposure for at least six hundred years; other high-level wastes must be isolated for perhaps a thousand years. Equally dangerous and much more persistent are the transuranic wastes forming over long periods from the decay of the original materials in the spent fuel rods after they are removed from the reactors. Plutonium-239 remains dangerous to most species for at least 24,000 years, perhaps for as much as 500,000 years. This plutonium, noted one commentator generally sympathetic to the nuclear power industry, "will remain a source of radioactive emissions as far in the future as one can meaningfully contemplate." [59] Other transuranics include americum-241 (dangerous for more than 400 years) and iodine-129 (dangerous for perhaps 210,000 years).

Practically speaking, such figures mean that hazardous wastes must be prevented from invading the ecosystem for periods ranging from centuries to hundreds of millennia. Not only must they be securely isolated physically, but also human institutions must survive with sufficient continuity to ensure their responsible administration throughout these eons. Many other chemicals created in the past few decades, including widely used pesticides such as DDT, 2,3,5-T, and dieldrin are not biodegradable and may persist throughout the world ecosystem indefinitely. Though less dangerous than nuclear wastes, these and other substances also represent a displacement of risks to human health and to the ecosystem well into the future.

This transfer of risk raises fundamental ethical and social questions for government. Should public institutions be compelled in some formal and explicit way to exercise regard for the future impact of decisions concerning environmental management today? And if so, how much regard? When deciding whether to develop dangerous technologies, should government be forced, if necessary, to consider not only the future ecological implications of these technologies but also the ability of future societies to create institutions capable of controlling them?

This issue is significant because government and economic institutions have a tendency to discount the future impacts of new technologies or newly developed chemicals when compared with the immediate impacts. In economic terms this is done in formal cost-benefit analysis by discounting future benefits and costs rather substantially. In political terms it amounts to adopting a strategy that favors taking environmental actions on the basis of short-term political advantage rather than long-term consequences. (Elected officials, especially, often treat as gospel the legendary advice of a former House speaker to a new colleague: "Remember that when it comes time to vote, most folks want to know 'what have you done for me lately?'") It is particularly difficult for public officials to develop a sensitive regard for the distant future when there are no apparent political rewards for doing so. At some time the political cynic in practically all public officials whispers, "What has posterity done for you lately?"

Suggested Readings

Bryant, Bunyan. *Environmental Justice: Issues, Policies, and Solutions.* Washington, D.C.: Island Press, 1995.

Davies, J. Clarence, ed. *Comparing Environmental Risks: Tools for Setting Governmental Priorities.* Washington, D.C.: Resources for the Future, 1996.

Foreman, Christopher H. *The Promise and Peril of Environmental Justice.* Washington, D.C.: Brookings Institution Press, 1998.

Kasperson, Jeanne X., and Roger E. Kasperson, eds. *Global Environmental Risk.* Washington, D.C.: Brookings Institution Press, 2001.

Lichter, S. Robert, and Stanley Rothman. *Environmental Cancer—A Political Disease?* New Haven: Yale University Press, 1999.

Margolis, Howard. *Dealing with Risk: Why the Public and the Experts Disagree on Environmental Issues.* Chicago: University of Chicago Press, 1997.

National Research Council. *Science and Judgment in Risk Assessment.* Washington, D.C.: National Academies Press, 1994.

Notes

1. U.S. Government Accountability Office, *Particulate Matter: EPA Needs to Make More Progress in Addressing the National Academies' Recommendations on Estimating Health Benefits,* Report No. GAO-06-992T (July 19, 2006), 8.

2. Matthew L. Wald, "Chemical Element of Vinyl Toys Causes Liver Damage in Lab Rats," *New York Times,* November 13, 1998, A20.

3. Matthew L. Wald, "Citing Possible Dangers, Groups Seek Ban on Vinyl Toys," *New York Times,* November 20, 1998, A24; Scott Allen, "IV Bag Hazards Are Alleged; Trace Toxins Found, Interest Groups Say," *Boston Globe,* February 22, 1999, A3.

4. Holcomb B. Noble, "A Debate over Safety of Softeners for Plastic," *New York Times,* September 28, 1999, B10.

5. Andrea Foster and Peter Fairley, "Phthalates Pay the Price for Uncertainty," *Chemical Week,* February 17, 1999, 54.

6. Ibid.

7. David Kohn, "New Questions about Common Chemicals," *Newsday,* March 3, 2003, www.ourstolenfuture.org/Commentary/News/2003/2003-0304-Newsday-phthalates.htm.

8. Steven Milloy, "A Toy Story," *Tech Central Station,* February 25, 2003, www.techcentralstation.com/022503C.html, February 28, 2004.

9. Seth Borenstein, "Study Links Chemical to Changes in the Womb," *Albany Times-Union,* May 27, 2005, A1; "Plastics," *Houston Chronicle,* June 3, 2005, B10.

10. Jane Kay, "San Francisco Prepares to Ban Certain Chemicals in Products for Tots, But Enforcement Will Be Tough—and Toymakers Question Necessity," *San Francisco Examiner,* November 19, 2006, A1.

11. National Academy of Public Administration, *Setting Priorities, Getting Results: A New Direction for EPA* (Washington, D.C.: National Academy of Public Administration, 1995), chap. 3.

12. Executive Order 12866—Regulatory Planning and Review, *Federal Register,* October 4, 1993.

13. For a general discussion of the political and administrative setting of risk assessment, see Committee on Risk Assessment of Hazardous Air Pollutants, National Research Council, *Science and Judgment in Risk Assessment* (Washington, D.C.: National Academies Press, 1994), chap. 2.

14. U.S. General Accounting Office, *Chemical Risk Assessment: Selected Federal Agencies' Procedures, Assumptions and Policies.* Report No. GAO-01-810 (August 2001), 14.
15. Ibid.
16. See Council on Environmental Quality, *Environmental Quality, 1979* (Washington, D.C.: Council on Environmental Quality, 1980), 194ff.
17. Ibid.
18. Gregory Zuckerman, "Specter of Costly Asbestos Litigation Haunts Old Economy Companies," *Wall Street Journal,* December 27, 2000, A3; Alex Berenson, "A Surge of Asbestos Suits, Many by Healthy Plaintiffs," *New York Times,* April 10, 2002, A1.
19. On the history of the controversy over dioxin, see John A. Moore, Renate D. Kimbrough, and Michael Gough, "The Dioxin TCDD: A Selective Study of Science and Policy Interaction," in *Keeping Pace with Science and Engineering: Case Studies in Environmental Regulation,* ed. Myron F. Ulman (Washington, D.C.: National Academies Press, 1993), 221–42.
20. Ibid.
21. Keith Schneider, "Times Beach Warning: Regrets a Decade Later," *New York Times,* August 15, 1991, D23.
22. Keith Schneider, "Panel of Scientists Finds Dioxin Does Not Pose Widespread Cancer Threat," *New York Times,* September 26, 1992, D20.
23. Joel Brinkley, "Many Say Lab-Animal Tests Fail to Measure Human Risk," *New York Times,* March 23, 1993, D20.
24. Ibid.
25. Cindy Skrzycki and Joby Warrick, "EPA Links Dioxin to Cancer; Risk Estimate Raised Tenfold," *Washington Post,* May 17, 2000, A1.
26. Ibid.
27. U.S. Environmental Protection Agency, National Center for Environmental Assessment, *Draft Dioxin Assessment,* http://cfpub.epa.gov/ncea/cfm, March 4, 2004.
28. National Research Council, *Health Risks from Dioxin and Related Compounds: Evaluation of the EPA Assessment* (Washington, D.C.: National Academies Press, 2006). See also "EPA Assessment of Dioxin Understates Uncertainty About Health Risks and May Overstate Human Cancer Risk," *The National Academies News,* www.national academies.org/onpinews/newsitem.aspx?RecordID=11688, February 20, 2007.
29. On the general problems of animal experiments, see David D. Doniger, *The Law and Policy of Toxic Substances Control* (Baltimore: Johns Hopkins University Press, 1978), pt. I.
30. Animal data are cited in Philip M. Boffey, "The Debate Over Dioxin,"*New York Times,* June 25, 1983, A10.
31. Ibid.
32. Doniger, *The Law and Policy of Toxic Substances Control,* 12.
33. Harvey Brooks, "The Resolution of Technically Intensive Public Policy Disputes," *Science, Technology and Human Values* 9 (winter 1984): 40. For estimates of discretionary judgments in risk assessment, see National Research Council, Commission on Life Sciences, Committee on the Institutional Means for Assessment of Risks to Public Health, *Risk Assessment in the Federal Government: Managing the Process* (Washington, D.C.: National Academies Press, 1983), chap. 1.
34. Frances M. Lynn, "The Interplay of Science and Values in Assessing and Regulating Environmental Risks," *Science, Technology, and Human Values* 11 (spring 1986): 40–50.
35. Thomas M. Dietz and Robert W. Rycroft, *The Risk Professionals* (New York: Russell Sage, 1987), 111.
36. Dorothy Nelkin, ed., *Controversy: The Politics of Technical Decisions* (Beverly Hills, Calif.: Sage, 1984), 17.
37. A comprehensive review of the various statutory standards for risk in federal law is found in John J. Cohrssen and Vincent T. Covello, *Risk Analysis: A Guide to Principles and Methods for Analyzing Health and Environmental Risks* (Washington, D.C.: Council on Environmental Quality, 1989), 14–15; see also Walter A. Rosenbaum, "Regulation at Risk: The Controversial Politics and Science of Comparative Risk Assessment,"

in *Flashpoints in Environmental Policymaking: Controversies in Achieving Sustainability,* ed. Sheldon Kamieniecki, George A. Gonzalez, and Robert O. Vos (Albany: State University of New York Press, 1997), 31–62.

38. This analysis is based on National Academy of Public Administration, *Setting Priorities, Getting Results,* chap. 3.
39. Council on Environmental Quality, *Environmental Quality, 1979,* 218.
40. U.S. General Accounting Office, "EPA's Chemical Testing Program Has Not Resolved Safety Concerns," Report No. GAO/RCED 91-136 (June 1991), 14.
41. A sampling of this literature may be found in the collection of articles by Peter Lewin, Gerald L. Sauer, Bernard L. Cohen, Richard N. Langlois, and Aaron Wildavsky in "Symposium on Pollution," *Cato Journal* (spring 1982): 205ff.
42. Paul Johnson, "The Perils of Risk Avoidance," *Regulation* (May–June 1980): 17.
43. Ibid.
44. Philip J. Hilts, "White House Moves on Easing Food-Pesticide Law," *New York Times,* August 20, 1993, A12.
45. National Academy of Public Administration, *Setting Priorities, Getting Results,* 54.
46. *Wall Street Journal,* October 29, 1997, B3.
47. U.S Environmental Protection Agency. "Environmental Justice," February 10, 2004, www.epa.gov/compliance/environmentaljustice, March 4, 2004.
48. Robert D. Bullard, "Waste and Racism: A Stacked Deck?," *Forum for Applied Research and Public Policy* 8 (spring 1993): 29–35; on the general problems of defining environmental justice, see Evan J. Rinquist, "Environmental Justice: Normative Concerns and Empirical Evidence," in Norman J. Vig and Michael E. Kraft, eds., *Environmental Policy in the 1990s,* 3d ed. (Washington, D.C.: CQ Press, 1997), 231–54; and U.S. Environmental Protection Agency, Office of Policy, Planning, and Evaluation, *Environmental Equity: Reducing Risk for All Communities, Vol. 1: Workgroup Report to the Administrator* (Washington, D.C.: U.S. Environmental Protection Agency, June 1992), 1.
49. Martin V. Melosi, "Environmental Justice, Political Agenda Setting, and the Myths of History," *Journal of Policy History* (January 2002): 44.
50. From Executive Order 12898—Federal Actions to Address Environmental Justice in Minority Populations and Low-Income Populations, *Federal Register,* February 11, 1994.
51. U.S. Government Accounting Office, "Environmental Justice: EPA Should Devote More Attention to Environmental Justice When Developing Clean Air Rules, Report No. GAO-05-289 (July 5, 2005), 10.
52. See, for example, Anita Milman, "Environmental Justice Analyses: Geographic Pollution Mapping of Power Plant Emissions to Inform ex-ante," *Journal of Environmental Planning and Management,* July 2006; and Paul Mohai and Robin Saha, "Reassessing Racial and Socioeconomic Disparities in Environmental Justice Research," *Demography,* May 2006, 383–99.
53. Ivette Perfecto and Baldemar Valazquez, "Farm Workers: Among the Least Protected," *EPA Journal* 18 (March–April 1992): 13–14; and D. R. Wernette and L. A. Nieves, "Breathing Polluted Air," *EPA Journal* 18 (March–April 1992): 16–17.
54. Paul Mohai and Bunyan Bryant, "Race, Poverty, and the Environment," *EPA Journal* 18 (March–April 1992): 8.
55. Center for Progressive Regulation, "Environmental Justice," *Perspectives,* www.progressiveregulation.org/perspectives/environjustice.cfm, March 3, 2004.
56. Christopher H. Foreman Jr., "The Clash of Purposes: Environmental Justice and Risk Assessment," *The Brookings Institution: Social Policy,* March 20, 1988, www.brookings.edu/views/articles/foreman/1998RPP.htm, March 5, 2004.
57. Rebecca A. Head, "Health-Based Standards: What Role in Environmental Justice?" in *Environmental Justice: Issues, Policies, and Solutions,* ed. Bunyan Bryant (Washington, D.C.: Island Press, 1995), 29.
58. Foreman, "The Clash of Purposes: Environmental Justice and Risk Assessment."
59. Phil Gailey, "Evacuation Issue Threatening Nuclear Plants," *New York Times,* May 12, 1983, A1.

Chapter 5

More Choice:
The Battle over Regulatory Economics

Benefit-cost analysis has a solid methodological footing and provides a valuable performance measure for an important governmental function, improving the well-being of society. However, benefit-cost analysis requires analytical judgments which, if done poorly, can obfuscate an issue or worse, provide a refuge for scoundrels in the policy debate.

—Scott Farrow and Michael Toman,
Using Environmental Benefit-Cost Analysis to
Improve Governmental Performance, 1998

GAO's recent reviews of four Corps civil works projects and actions found that the planning studies conducted by the Corps to support these activities were fraught with errors, mistakes, and miscalculations, and used invalid assumptions and outdated data. Generally, GAO found that the Corps' studies understated costs and overstated benefits, and therefore did not provide a reasonable basis for decision-making.

—Government Accountability Office,
Corps of Engineers: Observations on Planning and Project
Management Processes for the Civil Works Program, March 2006

Controversy over the economic rationality of environmental regulation has not ceased since the first Earth Day. Critics assert that both the process and the objectives of environmental regulation are flawed by economic inefficiency, irrationality, and contradiction. Spokespersons for the business sector, state and local governments, and other regulated interests often join many economists in advocating fundamental changes in the criteria used in formulating environmental regulations and in the methods used to secure compliance with them. Environmentalists and many economists, among others, believe that economic arguments are often inappropriate, if not deliberately deceptive, when used by critics to evaluate environmental policies.

Although some environmental regulatory programs are very costly, the total public and private cost of regulation to the United States appears reasonable. Currently the United States invests an estimated 1.5 to 2.5 percent of its gross domestic product in environmental protection—what most economists consider an acceptable amount and comparable with that of other industrialized nations. Spending for environmental regulation represents about 1.5 percent of recent federal budgets, a modest figure when compared with other social programs such as Medicare or Social Security, which account, respectively, for about 12 percent and 22 percent of recent spending.[1] Moreover, the collective benefit from all this spending, by most estimates, far exceeds the costs. The U.S. Environmental Protection Agency (EPA) has calculated, for instance, that the economic benefits from the Clean Air Act (CAA) alone are four times greater than the cost.[2]

Still, troubling problems arise. Could the same or better results—perhaps far better—be achieved much less expensively? Could regulated business also save considerable money and invest it in more socially productive activities? Might better results be had by switching to a different form of regulation? Is the average consumer paying too much for environmental protection? As regulatory costs and dissatisfaction over regulatory achievements mount, even the environmental movement, traditionally hostile to proposals for economic reform, has felt compelled to examine critically the economic basis of current environmental laws. The debate can whirl into mind-numbing complexity only an economist could love, but the answers may powerfully shape future environmental regulation, and the major issues, at least, are clear.

Controversy has traditionally focused on two issues: the use of benefit-cost analysis (BCA) as a major criterion in writing environmental regulations and the effectiveness of marketplace incentives rather than the current command-and-control methods for securing compliance with environmental standards. This chapter looks at these issues, beginning with a discussion of the BCA controversy, followed by a brief description of the command-and-control approach to regulation and a comparison with some proposed alternatives.

The Benefit-Cost Debate

In theory, BCA seems simple and straightforward. Essentially, it is a process by which federal agencies (usually regulators such as the EPA) compare the net benefits and costs of a proposed action—usually a regulatory law—to determine whether the benefits exceed the costs. Using this procedure, they can also compare alternative proposals to determine which is the more economically desirable. BCA is a constant issue in environmental regulation because a common complaint about almost all environmental regulations written since 1970 is that the congressionally mandated procedures for setting environmental standards are too often insensitive to costs. "Cost-oblivious" laws, such as the CAA or the Occupational Safety and Health Act, in which benefit-cost considerations are explicitly forbidden as regulatory criteria, are cited as examples of legislatively ordained disregard for the economic consequences of regulation. Other laws, such as the Resource Conservation and Recovery Act, have been criticized for failing to require specifically that regulatory agencies consider costs among other factors in setting environmental standards. In the view of critics, this mandated indifference toward BCA breeds a carelessness about costs among regulators that inflicts economic penalties on regulated interests. Even when Congress has permitted or required some kind of BCA in regulatory decision making, critics assert that too often agencies can ignore the results or treat them as a formality.[3]

A Long and Contentious History

The conflict over BCA resonates throughout U.S. regulatory history. Every administration since John F. Kennedy's has attempted to use some institutional arrangement to promote sensitivity to economic costs and benefits in regulatory policy making by federal agencies. Toward the end of the 1970s the White House and Congress began to pressure federal agencies through executive action and legislative mandates to give economic considerations greater attention in environmental regulation. Jimmy Carter, the most avowed environmentalist of all recent presidents, nonetheless established a White House review entity with the pugnacious acronym RARG (Regulatory Analysis Review Group) whose mission included reducing the cost of federal environmental regulations. The mildly controversial RARG annoyed environmentalists; what replaced it infuriated them.[4]

The Battle over Regulatory Impact Analyses. Ronald Reagan, whose administration was viewed by environmentalists with nearly unanimous disfavor, initiated the most aggressive effort to promote BCA in environmental policy making with Executive Order 12291. The executive order, issued practically the day Reagan was inaugurated, required all federal agencies to prepare a type of BCA, called a regulatory impact analysis (RIA), for any major new regulatory proposals and to demonstrate that the benefit of such proposals would exceed the anticipated costs. Reagan's order unleashed a prolonged, bitter conflict among ideological supporters of Reagan's so-called regulatory reform in Congress, the executive agencies, and the business community on one side and environmentalists, most congressional members, and other White House critics on the other. Proponents of the executive order believed it was long overdue, a sensible remedy to excessively numerous and expensive federal regulatory laws, and a blow to increasingly costly governmental interference in economic life. Critics were convinced that Reagan's order was a covert attack on environmental regulation, virtually a subversion of congressionally mandated environmental programs, and the enforcement of it by the Office of Management and Budget (OMB) an illegal, if not unconstitutional, presidential encroachment on the regulatory process. Contention over Executive Order 12291 became a running theme during the Reagan years, dissipating only when George H. W. Bush's administration found the contention too politically costly and quietly backed away from Reagan's aggressive enforcement policies.

Bill Clinton's administration appeared to put the BCA controversy to rest, at least temporarily, when Clinton issued Executive Order 12866 in September 1993, significantly relaxing requirements for the preparation and review of RIAs in federal agencies and greatly diminishing the OMB's role in the process, much to the satisfaction of environmentalists. Nonetheless, the new order still required federal agencies to prepare and review BCAs frequently, insisting that they remain a formal part of regulatory procedure. Thus, debate over the role of BCA in regulatory proposals continued.

The Second Generation of Benefit-Cost Analysis. When George W. Bush entered the White House in 2001, Congress had already attempted to push BCA well beyond what Clinton or even Reagan had accomplished. Greater congressional interest in BCA was evident as early as 1990 when a Democratic-controlled Congress wrote into the Clean Air Act Amendments a requirement that the EPA conduct an analysis of the costs and benefits of the CAA from 1970 to 2000.[5] The startling and overwhelming Republican victory in the 1994 congressional elections produced a Republican-controlled 104th Congress and a fusillade of new Republican legislative proposals requiring not only that BCA be compulsory for all new federal regulations but also that only proposed regulations with favorable BCAs be promulgated. Although these measures were (sometimes barely) defeated, the legislative mood was obvious to federal agencies: a Republican Congress would vigorously press BCA on regulatory agencies whenever possible and make economics a major consideration in regulatory policy debate.[6]

Apparently BCA in some form had come to stay in environmental regulation, and by the time of George W. Bush's inauguration, Washington was beginning what economist Cass R. Sunstein called "the second generation of debate" over BCA. The White House and Congress now accept the idea that BCA should be considered frequently, if not routinely, when the EPA or other regulatory agencies propose new environmental regulations. The second-generation debate, Sunstein noted, raises

> difficult questions about how (not whether) to engage in cost-benefit analysis—how to value life and health, how to deal with the interests of future generations, how to generate rules of thumb to simplify complex inquiries . . . how and when to diverge from the conclusion recommended by cost-benefit analysis. . . .[7]

In short, if calculate they must, what *kind* of BCA should environmental agencies use?

Many Varieties of Benefit-Cost Analysis. Every federal environmental law currently requires, or permits, a somewhat different approach to BCA. The one certainty is that no current federal law *compels* the EPA or any other environmental regulator to adopt or reject a proposed regulation solely on the basis of a benefit-cost calculation (although such proposals now routinely appear in Congress). One federal law, the CAA, *prohibits* the EPA from basing any regulation on a consideration of cost. Some federal laws, such as the Safe Drinking Water Act (1974), require the EPA to "consider" benefits and costs when contemplating new regulations; other statutes, such as the Occupational Safety and Health Act, may instruct regulators to consider only regulations that are "economically feasible"; and still others may allow the regulatory agency to consider benefits and costs among other factors when writing regulations, without specifying how much importance the economic considerations ought to assume.[8] Presidential requirements that agencies create an RIA apply only when an agency is not instructed to perform an economic analysis in some other manner by a particular law. It is hardly surprising, then, that environmental regulatory agencies approach BCA in different ways. Sometimes the same agency must use a different approach to BCA depending on which law it is enforcing. Most economists and other regulatory experts believe that, at the very least, the current jumble of procedures for BCA requires radical simplification.

Despite all the differences, a few common, important issues arise in virtually all approaches to BCA. These issues concern the general merits of BCA and the procedures by which benefits and costs are calculated.

The Case for Benefit-Cost Analysis

A number of advantages are claimed for BCA. Many regulatory experts believe BCA can greatly assist Congress and regulatory agencies in setting priorities for pollution control by identifying which regulations are the most economically desirable. "By drawing attention to costs and benefits," argued Sunstein, "it should be possible to spur the most obviously desirable regulations, to deter the most obviously undesirable ones, to encourage a broader view of consequences, and to promote a search for least-cost methods of achieving regulatory goals."[9]

Economists point to transparency as another advantage of BCA in the sense that "the results of a well-executed BCA analysis can be clearly linked to the assumptions, theory, methods and procedures used in it. This transparency can add to the accountability of public decisions by indicating where the decisions are at variance with the analysis."[10] Thus, an argument over the economic impact of a proposed environmental regulation would presumably be clarified considerably because a competent BCA would enable all sides to understand what went into the economic evaluation and to examine the validity of the components of that valuation. In addition, proponents believe that competent BCA can reveal where important information is lacking about costs and benefits from a policy— what has been called ignorance revelation. Moreover, it is also argued, BCA gives policy makers a common metric for comparing policies and choosing among them.[11]

Proponents of BCA argue that at the very least it can point decision makers to the most economically desirable, or cost-effective, policies for achieving a regulatory goal. "Even if one objects . . . to basing environmental policy on benefit-cost analysis," argued economist A. Myrick Freeman III, "it still makes good sense to be in favor of cost-effective environmental policies. Cost-effectiveness means controlling pollution to achieve the stated environmental quality standards at the lowest possible total cost."[12] Moreover, proponents add, critics of BCA are really objecting to *incompetent* analysis, especially when created deliberately to produce a desired outcome. Competent BCA sometimes can identify policies that are both economically and environmentally wiser than those currently implemented. According to Freeman, a well-conceived BCA would probably have revealed better alternatives to many federally financed water resource developments such as dams, stream channelization, and flood control projects that were justified originally by questionable BCAs. Freeman noted that these analyses used techniques that systematically overstated the benefits of water resource development, understated the economic costs, and ignored environmental costs. The result was construction of a number of economically wasteful and environmentally damaging projects as well as serious consideration of misguided proposals such as the one to build a dam in the Grand Canyon.[13]

When all the regulated sectors of the U.S. economy are considered, the critics reason, a huge inflationary diversion of capital from more economically desirable uses results. Critics frequently allege that excessive regulatory costs will drive some firms out of business or out of the country.

Spokespersons for major national business associations, such as the Business Roundtable and the U.S. Chamber of Commerce, have alleged that excessive regulatory costs have depressed significantly the growth rate of the gross national product.

Few proponents of BCA argue, however, that it should be the sole criterion for regulatory strategies. Still, they believe that the routine use of the procedure would make regulators more sensitive to the costs of their regulatory decisions and more likely to select regulatory procedures with net benefits, or with the least cost among alternatives. Many supporters also believe that BCA leads to a better quality of decision making. As economist Paul Johnson observed, "The value is that it injects rational calculation into a highly emotional subject. . . . It offers you a range of alternatives. Without stringent analysis, nobody knows whether costs imposed by regulatory programs are money well spent."[14] And, though seldom admitted, many advocates hope the publicity given to regulatory costs, especially when net benefits are lacking, will deter agencies from choosing such regulations.

The Case against Benefit-Cost Analysis

Environmentalists traditionally have opposed the routine use of BCA in setting environmental standards. Some still regard it a categorical evil, wholly inappropriate for the selection of environmental regulations. Others recognize that economic considerations may sometimes merit attention in writing environmental laws but believe benefit-cost calculations are easily distorted to the advantage of regulated interests. Most environmentalists regard BCA as nothing less than a covert assault on environmental regulation whenever it is used. Environmentalists assert that BCA often distorts economic reality by exaggerating regulatory costs and underestimating benefits. Regulated interests, the argument continues, often deliberately magnify their compliance costs; it is difficult, in any case, to obtain accurate economic data from them. In addition, regulated interests give little attention to the economic "learning curve," which often yields a substantial savings over the full period of regulation as they gain experience and expertise in controlling their pollutants. Benefits from regulation, in contrast, are often underestimated because they are not easily calculated. For instance, how are the health benefits from significantly cleaner air over the next several decades to be calculated? What value is to be placed on rivers, streams, and lakes made fishable and swimmable again? What is the dollars-and-cents value of an irreplaceable old-growth forest conserved for another generation?

Some benefits almost defy monetizing. For instance, an agency may consider regulatory alternatives involving different levels of risk to populations from exposure to hazardous or toxic substances. What is the appropriate value to be placed on a life saved? A variation of BCA sometimes advocated in such a situation is to compare the costs of regulation with estimates of the lives saved from the different strategies. Such a comparison implicitly requires regulators to decide how much an individual human life is worth.

As a practical example, in 2006 a BCA study conducted by the EPA examined the impact of reducing its recommended air quality threshold for soot from 15 micrograms per cubic meter to 14 micrograms. This apparently minor reduction would create an estimated $1.9 billion in additional annual control costs among the regulated industries but would also prevent an estimated 24,000 premature deaths. "It's pretty darn obvious," asserted the president of the environmental advocacy group Clean Air Watch, "that better standards would mean fewer premature deaths."[15] Not all experts would agree with this regulatory arithmetic. But a metric that measures lives against dollars spent on pollution controls appears to confront decision makers with a choice that will seem arbitrary, if not morally repugnant: saving dollars or lives. In effect, decision makers will be estimating, if only implicitly, the dollar value to each life saved—an act sure to arouse the ire of some constituency.

Critics note, moreover, that BCA traditionally ignores equity considerations—an increasingly potent argument as the environmental justice movement expands (see Chapter 4). In a sense this is correct; common BCA lacks a social conscience because it is unconcerned with the social distribution of benefits and costs—that is, with which groups are winners and losers in the distribution.[16] "It is often argued," explained economists Raymond J. Kopp, Alan J. Krupnick, and Michael A. Toman, "that [BCA] takes the existing distribution of income as given and does not consider the equity implications of the policies it seeks to evaluate. This criticism points to the anonymous manner in which the welfare changes of individuals are aggregated."[17] It is possible, however, to factor at least some equity considerations into BCA, but such an exercise is uncommon and fraught with difficulties for regulatory agencies that must decide whose equities are to be considered and how to compare equity among different groups.

Perhaps the most persuasive reason for resisting BCA, in the environmentalist's view, is that reducing an environmental value such as clean air or water to a monetary figure makes it appear to be just another commodity that can be priced, bought, and sold. According to Stephen Kelman,

> Many environmentalists fear that subjecting decisions about clean air or water to the cost-benefit tests that determine the general run of decisions removes those matters from the realm of specially valued things. . . . The very statement that something is not for sale enhances and protects the thing's value in a number of ways. . . . [It] is a way of showing that a thing is valued for its own sake, whereas selling a thing for money demonstrates that it was valued only instrumentally.[18]

Environmentalists often believe they stand apart from regulated business through a profound ethical disagreement over the intrinsic worth of wild places, uncontaminated air and water, and other environmental amenities. This conviction of moral purpose imparts to the movement much of its passion and persistence. It also elevates arguments over BCA to the level of ethical principles, making compromise especially difficult.

Reality and Rhetoric

In practice, BCA has often proven to be more paper tiger than bulldog in regulatory affairs. Reagan's BCA initiative never achieved the epic impact its proponents wished because its implementation was badly flawed. Several major environmental programs, such as the CAA and the Occupational Safety and Health Act, prohibited BCA or severely limited its application in regulations implementing them (although the EPA spent $2 million preparing an unused BCA for an air-quality standard anyway).[19] Many other regulatory proposals escaped Executive Order 12291 because their impacts did not exceed $100 million. Agencies often prepared BCAs but, lacking confidence in the results, turned to other criteria in writing regulations. And agencies showed little consistency in how they prepared their analyses, notwithstanding OMB guidelines. Experience demonstrated at the EPA, as in many other agencies, the severe limitations and inherent bias implicit in data deficiencies.[20] In some instances, however, the White House has used—or has attempted to use—BCA to stifle environmental regulations objectionable to the president. Controversy over this style of bureaucratic obstruction flared continually during the Reagan years and reignited during George W. Bush's administration.

The Reagan RIAs. During Reagan's two presidential terms, the OMB processed more than two thousand RIAs annually, accepting most RIAs accompanying regulatory proposals and, when possible, using them in arguments for revision or rejection of environmental regulations. It was here that Executive Order 12291 had its major impact on environmental laws. The OMB, together with Reagan-appointed officials in environmental regulatory agencies, exercised administrative discretion to apply these BCAs selectively to some proposals but not to others. BCA was seldom used when proposals were made to *deregulate* some aspect of the environment or some relevant private firm.[21] The Reagan administration's use of BCA, in the end, created a pervasive bias against environmental regulation that embittered environmentalists against RIAs and engendered deep suspicion of the OMB's role in regulatory review. The OMB's review of regulatory agency BCAs, however, was far less aggressive under Reagan's successor, George H. W. Bush. Although environmentalist criticism of the OMB's role in regulatory BCA subsided sharply during the Clinton years, the controversy revived with George W. Bush's presidency.

George W. Bush Adds Something New. Shortly after George W. Bush's inauguration, the OMB once more began to review aggressively and critically the BCAs produced by the EPA and other regulatory agencies—with a new twist. The office within OMB responsible for reviewing these BCAs, the Office of Information and Regulatory Affairs (OIRA), not only reviewed the BCAs produced by the EPA and related agencies but also examined critically the scientific studies used to justify environmental regulations and their related BCAs. "Once staffed mainly by economists and policy analysts," wrote science policy specialist Charles W. Schmidt, "OIRA now also employs a variety of health and environmental scientists," which has provoked criticism from environmentalists and others that "OIRA is overstepping its legislative mandate because health and environmental expertise should be concentrated in the agencies that draft legislation." [22] Critics have suspected the OIRA will use its newly acquired scientific resources to delay or reject regulatory proposals by challenging the scientific accuracy or credibility of the data supporting the regulations instead of confining itself to examining the relevant BCAs. For example, they assert, OIRA sometimes attempts to discredit proposed regulations by questioning the qualifications of peer reviewers for the science studies used by the EPA to justify the regulations. Proponents of OIRA's new approach, however, assert that scientific reviews will improve the quality of science on which environmental regulations are based and that science studies often must be reviewed to determine how BCAs were constructed. Evidence supporting the contending sides remains scarce, but environmentalists nonetheless regard the OIRA's new approach as additional evidence of a pervasive effort by the Bush administration to interfere with the conduct of science to produce findings politically acceptable to the White House.

BCA's Continuing Problems. By now, thousands of regulatory economic analyses have been prepared by federal administrators—more than twelve thousand by the EPA alone. Yet federal agencies continue to struggle when attempting to estimate realistically the benefits or costs of the regulatory programs they implement. Whatever the reason—incompetence, inexperience, creative bookkeeping, or something else—regulatory cost estimates frequently prove inaccurate. For example, the EPA's Superfund cost estimates have been unreliably low, and the situation is no better for hazardous waste site remediation required by the Resource Conservation and Recovery Act. [23] Often, EPA officials, like other regulatory officials, appear nonchalant about guidelines—or perhaps confounded by them—even when guidance is explicit. For instance, the Clean Air Act Amendments of 1990 required the EPA to produce a BCA for any proposed regulations to implement the amendments. Congress specifically required that the EPA describe the key economic assumptions, the extent to which benefits and costs were quantified, and the extent to which alternatives were considered in the BCA procedure. When the U.S. General Accounting Office evaluated twenty-three RIAs written under these guidelines, it discovered considerable disparities. Eight RIAs did not identify key economic assumptions such as the value placed on human life. Analyses explicit about economic assumptions were often silent about the reasons for those chosen. All the RIAs assigned dollar values to the estimated costs of proposed regulations, but only eleven assigned dollar values to the benefits.[24]

Regulatory officials, environmental or otherwise, still frequently discount their own agency analyses when making regulatory decisions. This is not necessarily administrative malfeasance—federal agencies are usually required only to consider the benefits and costs in the course of policy making—but the situation bespeaks the considerable practical difficulty in using BCAs and the substantial official uneasiness about the situation. Nonetheless, estimates about policy benefits and costs, some perhaps grievously flawed, continue to pack policy debates.[25]

At least one agency, the U.S. Army Corps of Engineers, seems almost incapable of conquering a historical addiction to "cooked" BCAs. Environmentalists are especially critical of these dubious BCAs because of the Corps' enormous impact on the nation's environmental management: the Corp budget annually exceeds $4 billion for "civil works"—local public works such as levees, dams, and drainage canals, dear to all congressional members even though these projects often become environmental disasters. For almost a century, these projects have frequently been justified by dubious BCAs, which Congress uncritically accepts because it works to the advantage of local constituencies. Every president from Jimmy Carter to George W. Bush has vigorously opposed these questionable projects, with mixed success. "On Capitol Hill," wrote a veteran political reporter, "it is still considered almost bad form to oppose a water project in another member's district. . . . Corps authorizations have long been viewed as congressional prerogatives, nearly as automatic as the franking privilege or special license plates."[26] Despite repeated promises to swear off "cooked" economics, the Corps still invites suspicion of its BCA math. Few verdicts about the Corps' BCA process have been as blistering as the Government Accountability Office (GAO) evaluation, toward the end of George W. Bush's administration, which had virtually nothing good to conclude. "The cost and benefit analyses performed by the Corps to support decisions on Civil Works projects or actions were generally inadequate to provide a reasonable basis for deciding whether to proceed with the project or action" stated the GAO, and offered proof:

• For the Delaware Deepening Project, GAO found credible support for only about $13.3 million a year in project benefits compared with the $40.1 million a year claimed in the Corps' analysis.

• For the Oregon Inlet Jetty Project, GAO's analysis determined that if the Corps had incorporated more current data into its analysis, benefits would have been reduced by about 90 percent.

• Similarly, for the Sacramento Flood Control Project, GAO determined that the Corps overstated the number of properties protected by about 20 percent and used an inappropriate methodology to calculate the value of these protected properties.[27]

Despite the Corps of Engineers, BCA has not necessarily been an administrative charade. Impressive examples of improved economic efficiency and substantial savings from BCA at the EPA, for instance, exist. Nonetheless, and despite confidence among many economists that BCA quality and influence is improving among regulatory agencies, the evidence still is not convincing. More persuasive is the conclusion from a meticulous study of forty-eight major federal health, safety, and environmental regulations between 1996 and 1999: "We find that economic analyses prepared by regulatory agencies do not provide enough information to make decisions that will maximize the efficiency and effectiveness of a rule," it concluded. Moreover, the findings "strongly suggest that agencies failed to comply with the executive order and adhere to the OMB guidelines."[28]

Some Lessons

Much can yet be learned from the experience since 1980. The blizzard of econometric data normally accompanying arguments over the cost of regulation should be at least initially suspect—on all sides. Willfully or not, regulated business will often overestimate the costs of regulation and proponents of regulation will often underestimate them. Also, as experience with the Reagan and George W. Bush administrations illustrates, BCA is so vulnerable to partisan manipulation that it is often discounted by officials even when they are *allowed* to consider the economics of regulation. A former adviser to President Richard Nixon recalled, "In executive branch meetings, the EPA staff repeatedly seemed to minimize pollution costs, while other agencies weighed in with high costs to meet the identical pollution standard. Often, we halved the difference. . . ."[29] Many regulatory decisions made on the basis of political, administrative, or other considerations are sanctified later by economics for the sake of credibility. Sometimes, costs are inflated grossly not so much by individual regulations as by the multiplicity and unpredictability of regulatory procedures.

This discussion should clarify at least a few aspects of the benefit-cost controversy. First, there is no substantial evidence that regulatory costs have become so excessive that BCA must be routinely imposed on *all* environmental regulation programs. Second, there are doubtless instances, perhaps a substantial number of them, in which BCA might suggest better solutions to environmental regulation than would otherwise be selected. For this reason, such analysis should not be excluded categorically from consideration unless Congress specifically mandates an exclusion. Third, it matters a great deal who does the calculating. All BCAs should be open to review and challenge during administrative deliberations. Fourth, Congress should indicate explicitly in the text of environmental legislation or in the accompanying legislative history how it expects regulatory agencies to weight economic criteria alongside other statutory guidelines to be observed in writing regulations to implement such legislation. Fifth, regulatory costs might be diminished significantly not by using BCA but by using economic incentives in securing compliance of regulated interests with environmental programs.

The Emerging Problem of Environmental Valuation

The BCA controversy illuminates an especially vexing problem inherent to most debates about environmental policy: how can environmental amenities be valued accurately if some metric must be devised? This issue is at the core of traditional economic theory because it raises profound questions about the assumptions implicit in placing value on nonmarket goods, such as clean air or pristine wilderness. In recent years this problem has stimulated considerable debate among economists and others concerned with environmental valuation, which has led to several significant proposals for a radical change in the way environmental amenities are evaluated and, as a consequence, in how environmental policy making transpires.

Environmental Accounting. Many economists, recognizing that the continuing development of environmental policy making increasingly confronts policy makers with problems of environmental valuation not addressed by traditional economics, propose the development of environmental accounting as an alternative. In effect, environmental accounting attempts to broaden enormously the scope of environmental amenities to which society attaches significant value and to devise a metric appropriate for comparing these values with other, usually monetary, values involved in policy evaluation. In this perspective, environmental amenities with obvious and immediate human benefit would be valued—clean air and water, for instance—but so would habitats essential to the preservation or proliferation of species, ecological sites essential for biosphere preservation or improvement, environments of unusual beauty, flora and fauna of biological significance, or other aspects of the human environment important for ecological reasons. Identifying these distinctively valued ecological elements will be difficult and challenging but no less so than assigning an appropriate value to them.

Environmental accounting is especially difficult because it requires both economists and ecologists to work at the intellectual margins of their disciplines where theory and evidence are often tenuous. Ecologists, for instance, may strongly suspect that the eradication of certain species will create economically long-term disruption of human environments— without being able to prove it or to estimate the scope of the disturbance. Because many environmental amenities are neither bought nor sold in markets, economists would have to construct shadow prices—best estimates of real market value—by a tortuous, inevitably contentious logic. "Demand and supply curves must be constructed," explained economist Roefie Hueting:

> The supply curve can, in principle, be constructed by estimating the costs of the measures necessary to prevent environmental damage. . . . However, constructing a complete demand curve is difficult because the intensity of individual preferences for environmental functions cannot be expressed in market behavior or translated into market terms. This is further complicated by the fact that the consequences of today's actions will often only be manifest in future damage.[30]

Many economists assert, in rebuttal, that a procedure called revealed preferences is a reasonable substitute for a market in valuing environmental amenities. Economists Kopp, Krupnick, and Toman offered an example:

> It would be wrong . . . to think of economic values as dollar-denominated values in one's brain to be downloaded when a person is asked the worth of a beautiful sunset; rather, such a value might be inferred from the things that one gives up to see the sunset (e.g., the cost of travel to the ocean). . . . To economists . . . the importance of things (tangible or intangible) is revealed by what a person will give to obtain them. . . . If the thing given up was money, the value can be expressed in monetary units; otherwise, it is expressed in the natural units of the thing given.[31]

Contingent Valuation. One profound consequence of environmentalism's political ascendancy in the United States has been to compel a sustained rethinking of traditional economic and ecological theories in order to come to terms with the problems of environmental valuation implicit in contemporary environmental regulation. One approach to environmental valuation currently proposed for federal policy makers is a methodology called contingent valuation, meaning that a monetary value is to be assigned to an environmental amenity whose use or destruction would deprive others of its future availability. Contingent valuation could be used, for example, to estimate the monetary cost to the public created by haze over the

Grand Canyon, by widespread pollution of Alaskan waters caused by oil tanker spills, or by any other event that deprives the public of the passive value in an environmental amenity. In a typical case, a representative segment of the relevant public would be asked how much it would be willing to pay to prevent haze over a national park, to avoid an oil spill, or to preclude some other environmental problem. Through statistical procedures, a monetary value would then be assigned to an environmental amenity based on these public valuations. Alaska's state government used contingent valuation in the early 1990s to discover what value Americans who might never visit Prince William Sound would assign to preventing a catastrophic oil spill there—a strategy used to estimate the monetary damages for which the Exxon Corporation would be held liable for the devastating oil spill by the tanker *Exxon Valdez* in 1989. Based on an average response of $30 per person, Alaskan officials estimated that Americans would collectively pay $2.8 billion to avoid such a disaster.[32] In 1989 the federal courts, apparently influenced by an endorsement of contingent valuation by a panel of distinguished U.S. economists, ordered the Department of the Interior to take into account the losses to people not directly affected by environmental problems when estimating the cost of CAA and Superfund violations in facilities under its jurisdiction. The first proposed guidelines for the use of contingent valuation in federal policy making, however, emerged from the National Oceanic and Atmospheric Administration in mid-1993.

Contingent valuation remains controversial among economists and other policy makers, as the Clinton administration's crabwise approach to the matter suggests. Many economists dismiss the methodology as "junk economics" because, they assert, the public cannot accurately assess the value in the passive use of an environmental amenity. Critics argue that the public is overly generous with hypothetical statements about personal outlays, tends to exaggerate the value of an amenity, and is often influenced by the wording of questions. To support these contentions, critics cite studies showing enormous variability in public environmental valuations: saving an old-growth forest in the Pacific Northwest was valued between $119 billion and $359 billion; sparing the whooping crane from extinction, between $51 billion and $715 billion.[33] Understandably, some of the most aggressive opponents of contingent valuation in federal policy making are corporations, such as Exxon, which feel at considerable financial risk. The Clinton administration proposed that contingent valuation be discretionary in federal policy making and that, in any event, agencies using the procedure discount any contingent valuation by 50 percent for policy-making purposes. Because neither Clinton nor his successor, George W. Bush, has been willing to issue an executive order explicitly permitting, or encouraging, contingent valuation, the legal status of the procedure remains unclear. Whatever federal agency may adopt the methodology on its own can expect to defend it before a federal judge because it is certain to be challenged legally and, thus, unlikely to be implemented for several years at least.

Environmental Risk. An alternative approach to environmental valuation might be to substitute risk for dollars, thereby avoiding the problem of monetizing environmental amenities. Such an approach might, for instance, compare the risks of losing an environmental amenity with those of preserving it, assuming that a satisfactory risk metric can be created. Or, in another variation, the monetary benefits in altering an amenity might be compared with the risks in losing it. Suppose, for example, that federal regulators must decide whether to open a large portion of wilderness area, the habitat of a rare or endangered species, to oil and gas exploration. The benefits of exploration could be calculated in terms of the potential governmental royalties, new employment, regional economic development, corporate taxes, or other monetized considerations. These might be compared with the expected number of species endangered or lost, the extent of land made unusable for other purposes, the amount of air and water pollution generated, and the special resources affected (such as historic sites, national parks, recreation areas, and the like). These strategies require a comparison of dollars to risks, or risks to risks, each with its own difficulties. Nonetheless, environmental officials often do make such comparisons implicitly or informally in arriving at regulatory decisions, and formalizing the procedure would at least force the comparisons to become explicit and reviewable. Moreover, proponents of BCA or some variation in regulatory decision making argue that defensible, rational approaches can be created for ecological valuation with sufficient time and effort. Until that day arrives, however, all existing approaches to BCA in environmental decision making are likely to be contentious and, at best, greeted with profound suspicion among environmental interests.

Regulation Strategies: Command and Control vs. the Marketplace

The CAA was the first in a long succession of federal environmental laws based on the command-and-control approach to environmental regulation (see next section). Chapters 6 and 7 illustrate well how this approach has been translated into specific statutes to control air and water pollution, toxic and abandoned waste, drinking water quality, and practically every other environmental hazard currently regulated by Washington, D.C. Many economists, regulatory scholars, and policy practitioners, including some environmental leaders, now consider command-and-control regulations to be a statutory antique, too economically flawed and administratively clumsy to cope effectively with many current environmental problems. At the very least, they suggest, command-and-control laws often require refitting with newer economic approaches. The most commonly proposed reform for the command-and-control approach is to substitute or add market-based approaches that rely fundamentally on economic incentives and markets to accomplish the environmental improvements intended.

Market-based regulation, in fact, has become a fundamental standard by which critics judge almost all aspects of command-and-control regulation. Thus, it is helpful to compare briefly the philosophy of command-and-control with market-based regulation before discussing current environmental regulations in greater detail.

Command-and-Control Regulation

The foundation of federal pollution regulation is the command-and-control approach, also called standards and enforcement. The structure and philosophy of this approach create many of the characteristic processes and problems familiar from current governmental management of the environment. Regulatory horror stories abound, convincing believers that a better approach lies in less direct governmental involvement and more economic incentives to encourage pollution abatement. In fact, both approaches have virtues and liabilities, and a combination of both approaches often seems more effective than one alone.[34] The command-and-control approach can best be understood as a set of five phases through which pollution policy evolves: goals, criteria, quality standards, emission standards, and enforcement.

Goals. In theory, the first step in pollution abatement begins with a determination by Congress of the ultimate objectives to be accomplished through pollution regulation. In practice, these goals are often broadly and vaguely worded. Sometimes, as when Congress decides to "press technology" by setting pollution standards that it hopes will force industry to develop control technologies not currently available, the goals are deliberately made extremely ambitious as an incentive for vigorous regulatory measures by regulated interests. The principal goals of the CAA are, for example, to protect public health and safety. Vague goals are not as important in defining the operational character of a regulatory program as are the more detailed specifications for the setting of pollution standards, emission controls, and enforcement—the real cutting edges of regulation. Statements of goals, however, may be politically significant as signals to the interests involved in regulation concerning which pollutants and sources will be given priority and how vigorously Congress intends to implement programs. The CAA goal of establishing national air-quality standards for major pollutants, for instance, was an unmistakable signal that Congress would tolerate no longer the continual delays in controlling air pollution caused by past legislative willingness to let the states create their own air-quality standards. It was also evidence that regulated interests had lost their once dominant position in the formation of air pollution policy.

Criteria. Criteria are the technical data, commonly provided by research scientists, indicating what pollutants are associated with environmental damage and how such pollutants, in varying combinations, affect the environment. Criteria are essential to give public officials some idea of what pollutant levels they must achieve to ensure various standards of air and water quality. If regulators intend to protect public health from the effects of air pollution, they must know what levels of pollution—sulfur oxides, for instance—create public health risks. In a similar vein, restoring game fish to a dying lake requires information about the levels of organic waste such fish can tolerate. Criteria must be established for each regulated pollutant and sometimes for combinations of pollutants.

Obtaining criteria frequently is difficult because data on the environmental effects of many pollutants still may be fragmentary or absent. Even when data are available, there is often as much art as science in specifying relationships between specific levels of a pollutant and its environmental effects because precise correlations may not be obtainable from the information. The reliability of criteria data also may vary depending on whether they are obtained from animal studies, epidemiological statistics, or human studies. Criteria are likely to be controversial, especially to those convinced that a set of data works to their disadvantage. Given the limitations in criteria data, regulatory agencies often have had to set pollution standards with information that was open to scientific criticism but was still the best available.

Quality Standards. Goals and criteria are preludes to the critical business of establishing air-quality and water-quality standards—the maximum levels of various pollutants to be permitted in air, soil, workplaces, or other locations. As a practical matter, defining standards is equivalent to declaring what the public, acting through governmental regulators, will consider to be "pollution." An adequate set of quality standards should specify what contaminants will be regulated and what variation in levels and combinations will be accepted in different pollutant categories.

Creating quality standards—in effect, another way of defining acceptable risk—is ultimately a political decision. Criteria documents rarely provide public officials with a single number that defines unambiguously what specific concentration of a pollutant produces precisely what effects. A rather broad range of possible figures associated more or less closely with predictable effects is available; which one is accepted may be the result of prolonged struggle and negotiation among interests involved in regulation. This battle over numbers is a matter of economics as much as science or philosophy. The difference between two possible pollution standards, only

Table 5-1 National Ambient Air Quality Standards

Pollutant	Standard value[a]		Standard type[b]
Carbon Monoxide (CO)			
8-hour average	9 ppm	10 mg/m^3	Primary
1-hour average	35 ppm	40 mg/m^3	Primary
Nitrogen Dioxide (NO^2)			
Annual arithmetic mean	0.053 ppm	100 μg/m^3	Primary and secondary
Ozone (O^3)			
1-hour average	0.12 ppm	235 μg/m^3	Primary and secondary
8-hour average[b]	0.08 ppm	157 μg/m^3	Primary and secondary
Lead (Pb)			
Quarterly average		1.5 μg/m^3	Primary and secondary
Particulate (PM$_{10}$) *Particles with diameters of 10 microns or less*			
Annual arithmetic mean		50 μg/m^3	Primary and secondary
24-hour average		150 μg/m^3	Primary and secondary
Particulate (PM$_{2.5}$) *Particles with diameters of 2.5 microns or less*			
Annual arithmetic mean[b]		15 μg/m^3	Primary and secondary
24-hour average[b]		65 μg/m^3	Primary and secondary
Sulfur Dioxide (SO^2)			
Annual arithmetic mean	0.03 ppm	80 μg/m^3	Primary
24-hour average	0.14 ppm	365 μg/m^3	Primary
3-hour average	0.50 ppm	1,300 μg/m^3	Secondary

Source: U.S. Environmental Protection Agency, Office of Air Quality Planning and Standards, *www.epa.gov/airs/criteria.html.*

[a] Two values are approximately equivalent concentrations.
[b] The ozone 8-hour standard and the PM$_{2.5}$ standards are included for information only. A 1999 federal court ruling blocked implementation of these standards, which the EPA proposed in 1997.

a few units apart, may seem trivial to a layperson. But the higher standard may involve millions or billions of additional dollars in pollution control technologies for the regulated interests and possibly many additional years before standards are achieved. Sometimes Congress establishes a standard based on a number's political "sex appeal." The original requirements in the CAA that automobile emissions of hydrocarbons and carbon monoxide be reduced by 90 percent of the 1970 levels by no later than 1975 were accepted largely because the 90 percent figure sounded strict and spurred the auto industry into action. In practical terms the figure might have been set at 88 percent or 85 percent, or some other number in this range, with about the same results. Air-quality standards created by the EPA for the major criteria pollutants—that is, pollutants that the CAA specifically designates for regulation because of their well-known, pervasive threat to public health—are identified in Table 5-1.

Emission Standards Standards for clean air or water are only aspirations unless emission standards exist to prescribe the acceptable pollutant discharges from important sources of air or water contamination. If emission standards are to be effective, they must indicate clearly the acceptable emission levels from all important pollution sources and should be related to the pollution control standards established by policy makers.

Congress has used two different methods of determining how emission standards should be set. In regulating existing air pollution sources under the CAA, Congress requires that emissions be limited to the extent necessary to meet the relevant air-quality standards; determining what emission controls are necessary depends on where the quality standards are set. In controlling new air pollution sources, and most water polluters, the emission controls are based on the available technologies. This technology-based approach sets the emission levels largely according to the performance of available technologies. A direct and critical relationship exists between air-quality standards and emission controls. For example, once the EPA declares national ambient air-quality standards, each state is required in its State Implementation Plan to calculate the total emissions of that pollutant within an airshed and then to assign emission controls to each source of that pollutant sufficient to ensure that total emissions will meet air-quality standards. In effect, this approach calls for the states to decide how much of the total pollution "load" within an airshed is the responsibility of each polluter and how much emission control the polluter must achieve. This process has become bitterly controversial. Experts often have difficulty in determining precisely how much of a pollution load within a given body of water or air can be attributed to a specific source; this difficulty compounds the problem of assigning responsibility for pollution abatement equitably among a large number of polluters.[35]

Regulated interests, aware of the relationship between air-quality standards and emission controls, will attack both standards and controls in an effort to avoid or relax their assigned emission controls. Regulated industries also chronically complain that insufficient attention is given to the cost of emission controls when government regulators prescribe the acceptable technology. Polluters often balk at installing specific control technologies prescribed by governmental regulators. The scrubber wars between electric utilities and regulatory authorities, for instance, continued for more than two decades. Alleging that the scrubbers—complex and expensive technologies that remove toxic gases from power plant air emissions—prescribed by the government are inefficient and unreliable, coal-fired utilities fiercely resisted installing the scrubbers until compelled to do so. The battle ended only when the 1990 amendments to the CAA permitted other control alternatives.

The backlash against emission controls often falls on state government officials who, under existing federal law, usually are responsible for setting specific emission levels, prescribing the proper technologies, and enforcing emission restraints on specific sources. Enforcing emission controls is accomplished largely through issuing a permit to individual dischargers specifying the permissible emission levels and technological controls for their facilities. Despite several decades of experience and substantial financial assistance from the federal government, some state regulatory authorities remain understaffed and undertrained. In the latter 1990s, however, most state regulatory agencies had become highly professional to the point where failures in state environmental regulation could no longer be routinely attributed to incompetence. The political and economic influence of regulated interests, nonetheless, is often far more formidable in state capitals than in Washington, D.C., and state regulators often feel especially vulnerable to these local pressures.

Enforcement. A great diversity of enforcement procedures might be used to ensure that pollution standards are achieved; adequate enforcement must carry enough force to command the respect of those subject to regulation. Satisfactory enforcement schemes have several characteristics: They enable public officials to act with reasonable speed—very rapidly in the case of emergencies—to curb pollution; they carry sufficient penalties to encourage compliance; and they do not enable officials to evade a responsibility to act against violations when action is essential. It is desirable that officials have a range of enforcement options that might extend from gentle prodding to secure compliance at one end all the way to litigation and criminal penalties for severe, chronic, or reckless violations at the other. In reality, when it comes to enforcement, administrative authority is often the power to "make a deal." Armed with a flexible variety of enforcement options, administrators are in a position to bargain with polluters not in compliance with the law, selecting those enforcement options they believe will best achieve their purposes. This bargaining, a common occurrence in environmental regulation, illustrates how political pressure and administrative discretion concurrently shape environmental policy; enforcement is examined in greater detail in the next section. In the end, an effective pollution abatement program depends largely on voluntary compliance by regulated interests. No regulatory agency has enough personnel, money, and time to engage in continual litigation or other actions to force compliance with pollution standards. Furthermore, litigation usually remains among the slowest, most inflexible, and inefficient means of achieving environmental protection. Administrative agencies prefer to negotiate and maneuver to avoid litigation as a primary regulatory device whenever possible.

What's Wrong with the Command-and-Control Approach? Economists have been the most outspoken critics of command-and-control regulation. However, they are now joined by an increasing number of other critics, including some leading environmental organizations such as

Environmental Defense, whose experience with command-and-control regulation since 1970 has demonstrated some severe deficiencies. First, they assert, it offers regulated interests few economic incentives to comply rapidly and efficiently with mandated pollution standards. In the economist's perspective, the standards-and-enforcement approach lacks an appeal to the economic self-interest of the regulated. Even severe penalties for noncompliance with the law often fail to motivate polluters to meet required pollution control deadlines. Penalties are often not assessed or are severely weakened by negotiation with regulatory agencies. Some firms find it more profitable to pay penalties and to continue polluting in violation of the law than to assume the often far steeper costs of compliance. In addition, polluters have no economic incentive to reduce their emissions below the regulatory requirements.

Second, traditional regulatory approaches require the federal government to specify the appropriate technologies and methods for their use in practically every instance in which pollutants are technologically controlled. Highly complicated, exquisitely detailed specifications that make poor scientific or economic sense for particular industries or firms can result. One reason for this situation is that neither Congress nor administrators may have sufficient scientific training or experience to make correct judgments about the appropriate technologies for pollution abatement in a specific firm or industry. Also, regulators sometimes lack sufficient information about the economics of firms or industries to know what technologies are economically efficient—that is, which achieve the desired control standards the least expensively. In general, according to economists Allen V. Kneese and Charles L. Schultze,

> Problems such as environmental control . . . involve extremely complicated economic and social relationships. Policies that may appear straightforward—for example, requiring everyone to reduce pollution by the technologically feasible limit—will often have ramifications or side effects that are quite different from those intended. Second, given the complexity of these relationships, relying on a central regulatory bureaucracy to carry out social policy simply will not work: there are too many actors, too much technical knowledge, too many different circumstances to be grasped by a regulatory agency.[36]

Examples of costly mistakes in specifying technological controls are not hard to find. Instances occurred in the writing of regulations to implement the Surface Mining Control and Reclamation Act of 1977. For example, International Inc., a General Electric subsidiary, complained that the EPA and the Office of Surface Mining in the Department of the Interior required that all runoff from areas disturbed by surface mining must pass through a sedimentation pond, although other management practices, such as the use of straw dikes and vegetative cover, would achieve substantially the same results. The company had to build at its Trapper Mine near Craig, Colorado, a $335,000 sedimentation pond when alternative methods could have achieved the same results at 10 percent of the cost.[37]

As another example, the Conoco Company complained that Consolidated Coal, its subsidiary, unnecessarily spent $160 million annually to meet engineering standards imposed on surface mines by the federal government. The National Academy of Sciences, speaking through its National Research Council, had recommended a different, less expensive, and apparently equally effective approach.[38]

Third, proponents assert that incentive approaches can be simply and economically administered. "Incentive-based systems are administratively simple," noted a National Academy of Public Administration report,

> because . . . they require much of the regulatory energy to be expended up front in the design state of the regulatory program. If the design is correct, less burdensome administration may be facilitated. Further, once the program is in place, regulators can rely on the energies of the private sector to drive pollution downward.[39]

The alternative seems to require bureaucratic legions toiling endlessly in the regulatory vineyards. "Command-and-control regulation," continued the report, "may impose a never-ending requirement on regulators to develop new and more stringent industry-specific regulations on smaller and smaller discharge points."[40]

Fourth, proponents point out that a market incentive approach is easier for the public to understand and presumably easier to approve. Economic incentives focus on a pollution reduction goal that the public would presumably find much more comprehensible—hence, easier for government to defend politically—than technology specifications with all the mystifying technical disputation about their appropriateness and efficiency.

Regulation Goes to the Market

Economic incentives are not new to U.S. environmental management. Many familiar forms of environmental control, such as sewage treatment charges, taxes on leaded gasoline, and deposit-refund systems for disposable beer and soft drink containers, use the pulling power of economic incentives to encourage pollution control. Table 5-2 provides a brief summary of the different methods used in the United States.

Not until a decade after Earth Day 1970 did the EPA first experiment warily with economic regulatory incentives. This set in motion a succession of additional economic innovations at the EPA, culminating in the current emissions trading program in the CAA.

Table 5-2 Economic Incentives Used in Environmental Regulation

Incentives	Examples	Pros and cons
Pollution charges and taxes	Emission charges Effluent charges Solid waste charges Sewage charges	*Pros:* stimulates new technology; useful when damage per unit of pollution varies little with the quantity of pollution *Cons:* potentially large distributional effects; uncertain environmental effects; generally requires monitoring data
Input or output taxes and charges	Leaded gasoline tax Carbon tax Fertilizer tax Pesticide tax Virgin material tax Water user charges Chlorofluorocarbon taxes	*Pros:* administratively simple; does not require monitoring data; raises revenue; effective when sources are numerous and damage per unit of pollution varies little with the quantity of pollution *Cons:* often weak link to pollution; uncertain environmental effects
Subsidies	Municipal sewage plants Land use by farmers Industrial pollution	*Pros:* politically popular; targets specific activities *Cons:* financial impact on government budgets; may stimulate too much activity; uncertain effects
Deposit-refund systems	Lead-acid batteries Beverage containers Automobile bodies	*Pros:* deters littering; stimulates recycling *Cons:* potentially high transaction costs; product must be reusable or recyclable
Marketable permits	Emissions Effluents Fisheries access	*Pros:* provides limits to pollution; effective when damage per unit of pollution varies with the amount of pollution; provides stimulus to technological change *Cons:* potentially high transaction costs; requires variation in marginal control costs
Reporting requirements	Proposition 65 Superfund Amendments and Reauthorization Act	*Pros:* flexible, low cost *Cons:* impacts may be hard to predict; applicable only when damage per unit of pollution does not depend on the quantity of pollution
Liability	Natural resource damage assessment Nuisance, trespass	*Pros:* provides strong incentive *Cons:* assessment and litigation costs can be high; burden of proof large; few applications
Voluntary programs	Project XL 33/50 Energy Star	*Pros:* low cost; flexible; many possible applications; way to test new approaches *Cons:* uncertain participation

Source: U.S. Environmental Protection Agency, Office of Policy, Economics, and Innovation, "The United States Experience with Economic Incentives for Protecting the Environment," Document No. EPA-240-R-01-001 (January 2001), ix.

Bubbles, Nets, and Offsets. In 1979 the EPA moved away from the traditional standards-and-enforcement approach to air pollution by introducing its "bubble policy" for controlling emissions from existing air pollution sources. This policy assumed "that an imaginary enclosure, or bubble, is placed over an industrial plant. From this enclosure, or bubble, a maximum allowable level of emissions is permitted. A firm in this bubble would be free to use more cost-effective pollution controls than are usually allowed."[41] For example, a firm with three smokestacks emitting pollution might find it least costly to cut back severely on the emissions from one stack while leaving the others only slightly controlled. If the total emissions leaving the imaginary bubble over the plant did not violate air-quality standards, the firm would be free to decide how best to comply with the law. Advocates of the approach assumed that the result would be a substantial cost savings for the firm and quicker compliance with pollution standards because the firm would be free to choose the solution best suiting its economic self-interest. With bubbling, the EPA also allowed emissions banking, which permitted a regulated firm to earn credits for keeping pollutants below the required level. Firms could apply these credits against their own future emission-control requirements, sell them to other firms, or save them.

The results have been inconclusive since air pollutants have been netted, offset, bubbled, and banked. Estimates suggest that the aggregate cost savings for firms have been modest. By the mid-1980s the 132 federal and state sanctioned "bubbles" had saved firms an estimated $435 million, netting about $4 billion, both relatively small sums when compared with the total compliance costs for firms regulated by the CAA.[42] Some experts believe that the savings from emissions trading have been exaggerated by the private sector. Others argue that the rules have not been vigorously enforced. In any case, few firms seized the opportunity to start emissions trading. Then came Title IV of the 1990 amendments to the CAA, initially permitting many of the nation's biggest fossil-fuel-burning electric utilities to create what could potentially be a huge market for emissions trading. Title IV also allows smaller utilities to join the "big dirties"—the most polluting industries—within a few additional years, thereby expanding the prospective marketplace in emissions. Title IV creates by far the most significant test of market-based regulation since the inception of the environmental era in 1970. Title IV's acceptance by influential spokespersons for mainstream environmentalism—albeit with fingers crossed—betrays a recognition that market-based reform is probably inevitable and perhaps overdue.

Cap and Trade: The Gamble on Sulfur Dioxide Emissions Trading. The most innovative provision of the 1990 amendments to the CAA is the emissions trading scheme created by Title IV. These provisions, sometimes called the Acid Rain Program, aim specifically at emissions of sulfur oxides associated with human health risks, environmental degradation, and especially acid precipitation. The regulatory approach, known as cap and trade, is intended to reduce by the year 2010 the nation's total emissions of sulfur dioxide to 8.5 million tons below the level of 1980 emissions. To accomplish this overall goal, a mandatory cap is established on the total sulfur dioxide emissions annually from the nation's utilities. The program is implemented in two phases:

Phase I: Began in 1995 and regulated 110 of the nation's electric utilities with the largest sulfur dioxide emissions, primarily coal-burning facilities, and 182 smaller units, all in the East and Midwest.

• A mandatory cap is set on the total sulfur dioxide emissions permitted annually from these sources.
• Each source is granted by the EPA an annual allowance—each allowance equals one ton of sulfur dioxide emissions—based on its current emission levels and the overall emission cap.
• At the end of each year, each source must have allowances equal to its emissions for that year.
• Each utility is permitted to bank, sell, or carry over to the following year any emission allowances in excess of its actual emissions.
• Each utility must carefully measure and report its annual emissions and submit to an annual EPA emission audit.
• Each utility is free to select whatever method it chooses to control its emissions and to meet its annual emission cap.

Phase II: Began in 2000 and regulated electric utilities and other sources of sulfur dioxide emissions nationally. Altogether, more than two thousand units were affected by this phase by the beginning of 2001. All units are regulated in the same manner as in Phase I.

The early results of cap and trade were keenly scrutinized. The critical tests: would a market in tradable emission permits develop among the regulated utilities, and would it produce the economic and environmental benefits predicted by its proponents?

By early 1994 the Chicago Board of Trade had created a national emissions trading market for Title IV, and modest trading had occurred there, and in California (which has its own version of emissions trading), between some utilities. Several important issues were evident immediately. First, environmental groups in the Northeast expressed a concern that midwestern utilities would purchase permits from other areas and stockpile them, thus permitting themselves to continue emissions at unacceptably high levels. Proponents of Title IV, however, believe that other utilities will not have emission permits enough to sell to the advantage of the midwestern facilities. A second concern among environmentalists is that some of the big dirties will abandon plans to replace existing plants with new, less polluting facilities and will, instead, stockpile emission permits for older, dirtier facilities. Midwestern utilities and their supporters, in contrast, have been concerned that the emission limits will inhibit economic growth in the economically depressed Ohio River Valley and adjacent areas. Utilities elsewhere have been concerned also with the effect of emission levels on economic growth. Most utilities remain apprehensive about the impact of the new scheme on their own market share and economic future.

Most economists believe it is too early for confident judgments about the impact of emissions trading, but early evidence suggests what the EPA has called "impressive environmental and economic results." During the first four years of Phase I, "power plants reduced their sulfur dioxide emissions far below the level that was legally allowable under all the provisions of the program," the EPA concluded.

> Furthermore, in response to the economic dynamics created . . . these plants released substantially less pollution relative to the more stringent level of "base" allowable emissions established by Congress. At the same time, the [sulfur dioxide] emissions trading market has done what markets do best: drive down costs.[43]

Other studies have indicated that the pollution control costs experienced by the electric utilities were substantially less than had been anticipated at the outset of the program.[44] These economic benefits have also been associated with substantial reductions in ambient sulfur dioxide originating from utility emissions.[45]

Economist Robert N. Stavins, an expert on emissions trading and Title IV, believes there have been other, less tangible but equally important benefits as well. The Title IV experience has demonstrated to both sides of the debate that emissions trading can be implemented without a multitude of lawsuits, argued Stavins, and proves as well that the system can be administered with relative simplicity. Stavins suggested that environmentalists should take the credit for a valuable lesson learned from experience with Title IV. The program, he noted,

> has brought home the importance of monitoring and enforcement provisions. In 1990, as their "price" for supporting an allowance trading system, environmental advocates insisted on continuous emissions monitoring . . . a feature that some analysts now consider to be a major achievement of the act.[46]

Moreover, the big dirties were not buying up additional permits to increase their allowable sulfur dioxide emissions, as many environmentalists had feared would happen. "While in their youth," wrote economic historians Hugh Gorman and Barry D. Solomon about emissions trading programs, they are "now a legitimate policy tool, and a regulatory infrastructure and culture is emerging that allows regulators to use this tool."[47]

But important questions remain. Many of the largest utilities have yet to initiate major plant expansions long planned for the future. Once expansion begins, will they begin to buy additional permits to increase their allowable emissions, as critics have predicted? As Phase II begins, thousands of additional emission sources of all kinds will become regulated. Will the system work as well in this very different emissions market? Will regulated utilities and other sulfur dioxide emission sources find permit trading as attractive if they must also bear additional costs from anticipated new controls on other air emissions, such as nitrogen oxides? Many economists and other experts on emissions trading have also warned against using the limited experience with Title IV as a justification for prescribing a similar approach to controlling global greenhouse gases. Although Congress may be tempted to take this one-size-fits-all approach to controlling air pollution emissions internationally, most experts feel much more domestic experience with emissions trading is still necessary.

Conclusion

To most Americans, the nation's environmental troubles are epitomized by polluted air, fouled water, dangerously unregulated hazardous and toxic wastes, and a multitude of other ecological derangements. This chapter illuminates a less obvious dimension of the environmental crisis that is equally dangerous in its ecological implications: the economic problems in implementing environmental policy effectively. In many critical respects, the institutions and policies the nation now depends on to reverse its ecological degradation are failing, sometimes badly. Equally as imperative as new technological solutions to ecological ills are new economic and institutional solutions. Finding these solutions will require critical, difficult debate within the environmental movement and among public policy makers at all governmental levels concerned with ecological restoration.

These problems are especially refractory because they often originate in the fundamental constitutional design of the political system or in deeply rooted political traditions. Among these is a historical dependence on traditional policy approaches to environmental problems, particularly the command-and-control method of regulation and the single-media approach to controlling specific pollutants. Although other approaches often seem more appropriate, and in some cases have been tried experimentally, they are strongly resisted by a multitude of institutional, professional, and economic interests with a stake in the status quo. Often the environmental movement itself has been excessively conservative in resisting policy innovation.

Among the significant economic problems arising from environmental regulation, none is debated more often than the high cost of environmental regulation. As costs continually rise well above expectations, the need to find cost-effective, cost-saving approaches to policy making grows more apparent. Although BCA is sometimes a useful strategy for reducing regulatory costs, its serious political and economic deficiencies suggest that other approaches, involving more economic incentives for pollution abatement in the private sector, are likely to be more broadly effective. None of the problems now associated with regulatory incapacity are likely to be solved easily or quickly.

Suggested Readings

Anderson, Terry, and Donald Leal. *Free Market Environmentalism*. Rev. ed. New York: Palgrave Macmillan, 2001.

Hackett, Steven C. *Environmental and Natural Resource Economics: Theory, Policy, and Sustainable Society*. 2d ed. Armonk, N.Y.: M. E. Sharpe, 2001.

Harrington, Winston, Richard D. Morgenstern, and Thomas Terner, eds. *Choosing Environmental Policy: Comparing Instruments and Outcomes in the United States and Europe*. Washington, D.C.: Resources for the Future Press, 2004.

Heal, Geoffrey. *Nature and the Marketplace: Capturing the Value of Ecosystem Services*. Washington, D.C.: Island Press, 2001.

Portney, Paul R., and Robert N. Stavins, eds. *Public Policies for Environmental Protection*. 2d ed. Washington, D.C.: Resources for the Future Press, 2000.

Notes

1. U.S. Environmental Protection Agency, National Center for Environmental Economics, "Environmental Protection: Is It Bad for the Economy?," February 13, 2001, www.epa.gov/economics.

2. U.S. Environmental Protection Agency, Office of Policy and Office of Air and Radiation, "The Benefits and Costs of the Clean Air Act, 1990 to 2010: EPA Report to Congress," Document No. EPA-410-R-99-01 (November 1999).

3. The arguments for considering costs in environmental regulation are usefully summarized in Allen V. Kneese and Charles L. Schultze, *Pollution, Prices and Public Policy* (Washington, D.C.: Brookings Institution Press, 1975). See also A. Myrick Freeman III, "Economics, Incentives, and Environmental Regulation," in *Environmental Policy in the 1990s,* 2d ed., ed. Norman J. Vig and Michael E. Kraft (Washington, D.C.: CQ Press, 1997), 189–208.

4. On the history of BCA, see Richard A. Liroff, "Cost-Benefit Analysis in Federal Environmental Programs," in *Cost-Benefit Analysis and Environmental Regulations: Politics, Ethics and Methods,* ed. Daniel Swartzman, Richard A. Liroff, and Kevin G. Croke (Washington, D.C.: Conservation Foundation, 1982), 35–52; Richard N. L. Andrews, "Cost-Benefit Analysis as Regulatory Reform," in *Cost-Benefit Analysis and Environmental Regulations: Politics, Ethics and Methods,* ed. Daniel Swartzman, Richard A. Liroff, and Kevin G. Croke (Washington, D.C.: Conservation Foundation, 1982), 107–36; and Norman J. Vig, "Presidential Leadership and the Environment: From Reagan to Clinton," in *Environmental Policy in the 1990s,* 2d ed., ed. Norman J. Vig and Michael E. Kraft (Washington, D.C.: CQ Press, 1997), 98–118.

5. On the history of congressional and presidential mandates for regulatory BCA at the EPA and other federal environmental agencies, see Scott Farrow and Michael Toman, "Using Environmental Benefit-Cost Analysis to Improve Government Performance,"

Discussion Paper 99-11 (Washington, D.C.: Resources for the Future, December 1998); and Cass R. Sunstein, "Cost-Benefit Default Principles," Working Paper 00-7 (Washington, D.C.: AEI–Brookings Joint Center for Regulatory Studies, October 2000).

6. For a summary of the issues involved, see Walter A. Rosenbaum, "Regulation at Risk: The Controversial Politics and Science of Comparative Risk Assessment," in *Flashpoints in Environmental Policymaking: Controversies in Achieving Sustainability*, ed. Sheldon Kamieniecki, George A. Gonzalez, and Robert O. Vos (Albany: State University of New York Press, 1997), 31–62.

7. Sunstein, "Cost-Benefit Default Principles," 7; see also John D. Graham, Paul R. Noe, and Elizabeth L. Branch, "Managing the Regulatory State: The Experience of the Bush administration, *Fordham Urban Law Journal*, May 1, 2006, 953–1001.

8. Ibid., 10–14.

9. Ibid., 10.

10. Raymond J. Kopp, Alan J. Krupnick, and Michael A. Toman, "Cost-Benefit Analysis and Regulatory Reform: An Assessment of the Science and Art," Discussion Paper No. 97-19 (Washington, D.C.: Resources for the Future, 1997), 14.

11. Ibid.

12. Freeman, "Economics, Incentives, and Environmental Regulation," 150, 153.

13. Ibid.

14. Paul Johnson, "The Perils of Risk Avoidance," *Regulation* (May–June 1980): 17.

15. Brian Hansen, "New Soot Rules to Cost Power Sector $400 Million Annually, EPA Reckons," *Inside Energy,* Oct. 16, 2006, 6.

16. Kopp, Krupnick, and Toman, "Cost-Benefit Analysis and Regulatory Reform."

17. Ibid.

18. Stephen Kelman, "Cost-Benefit Analysis: An Ethical Critique," *Regulation* (January–February 1981): 39.

19. U.S. General Accounting Office, "Cost-Benefit Analysis Can Be Useful in Assessing Regulations, Despite Limitations," Report No. GAO/RCED 84-62 (April 1984), iii.

20. Ibid.

21. On the history of the OMB's use of BCA under the Reagan administration, see W. Norton Grubb, Dale Whittington, and Michael Humphries, "The Ambiguities of Cost-Benefit Analysis: An Evaluation of Regulatory Impact Analysis under Executive Order 12,291," in *Environmental Policy under Reagan's Executive Order,* ed. V. Kerry Smith (Chapel Hill: University of North Carolina Press, 1984), 121–66; U.S. General Accounting Office, "Cost-Benefit Analysis Can Be Useful in Assessing Regulations, Despite Limitations," 7; Edward Paul Fuchs, *Presidents, Managers and Regulation* (Englewood Cliffs, N.J.: Prentice-Hall, 1988), 124ff; and Joseph Cooper and William F. West, "Presidential Power and Republican Government: The Theory and Practice of OMB Review," *Journal of Politics* 50 (November 1988): 864–95.

22. Charles W. Schmidt, "Subjective Science: Environmental Cost-Benefit Analysis," *Environmental Health Perspectives* (August 2003): A530.

23. U.S. General Accounting Office, "Much Work Remains to Accelerate Facility Cleanups," Report No. GAO/RCED 93-15 (January 1993), 17.

24. U.S. General Accounting Office, "Improving EPA's Regulatory Impact Analyses," Report No. GAO/RCED 97-38 (1997), 2.

25. Traci Watson, "Clean Air: EPA Report Hails Law as Success," *USA Today,* October 21, 1997.

26. Michael Grunwald, "An Agency of Unchecked Clout: Water Projects Roll Past Economics, Environmental Concerns," *Washington Post,* September 10, 2000.

27. U.S. Government Accountability Office, "Corps of Engineers: Observations on Planning and Project Management Processes for the Civil Works Program, Report No. GAO-06-529T, March 15, 2006, 1.

28. Robert W. Hahn, Jason K. Burnett, and Yee-Ho I. Chan, "Assessing the Quality of Regulatory Impact Analyses," Working Paper 001 (Washington, D.C.: AEI–Brookings Joint Center for Regulatory Studies, January 2000), executive summary. For similar conclusions, see also Winston Harrington, Richard D. Morgenstern, and Peter Nelson, "On

the Accuracy of Regulatory Cost Estimates," Working Paper 99-18 (Washington, D.C.: Resources for the Future, January 1999).

29. John C. Whitaker, "Earth Day Recollections: What It Was Like When the Movement Took Off," *EPA Journal* 14 (July–August 1988): 11.

30. Roefie Hueting, "Correcting National Income for Environmental Losses: A Practical Solution for a Theoretical Dilemma," in *A Survey of Ecological Economics*, ed. Rajaram Krishnan, Jonathan M. Harris, and Neva R. Goodwin (Washington, D.C.: Island Press, 1995), 248.

31. Kopp, Krupnick, and Toman, "Cost-Benefit Analysis and Regulatory Reform," 30.

32. *New York Times*, September 6, 1993.

33. Ibid.

34. Winston Harrington, Richard D. Morgenstern, and Thomas Sterner, eds. "Overview," in *Choosing Environmental Policy: Comparing Instruments and Outcomes in the United States and Europe* (Washington, D.C.: Resouces for the Future, 2004), 1–22; National Academy of Public Administration, *The Environment Goes to Market* (Washington, D.C.: National Academy of Public Administration, 1994), chap. 1; Paul R. Portney, ed., *Current Issues in U.S. Environmental Policy* (Baltimore: Johns Hopkins University Press, 1978), esp. chap. 1; Erica L. Dolgin and Thomas G. P. Guilbert, eds., *Federal Environmental Law* (St. Paul, Minn.: West Publishing, 1974), esp. Robert Zener, "The Federal Law of Water Pollution Control," 682–791, and Thomas Jorling, "The Federal Law of Air Pollution Control," 1058–1148.

35. On the problem generally, see Kneese and Schulze, *Pollution, Prices and Public Policy*, chap. 2.

36. Ibid., 116.

37. *National Journal*, May 30, 1981, 971–73.

38. Ibid.

39. National Academy of Public Administration, *The Environment Goes to Market*, 12.

40. Ibid.

41. Robert W. Hahn and Gordon L. Hester, "EPA's Market for Bads," *Regulation* (December 1987): 48–53.

42. Ibid.

43. U.S. Environmental Protection Agency, Office of Air and Radiation, "Progress Report on the EPA Acid Rain Program," Document No. EPA-430-R-99-011 (November 1999). See also U.S. Environmental Protection Agency, Office of Policy, Economics and Innovation, Office of the Administrator, "The United States Experience with Economic Incentives for Protecting the Environment," Document No. EPA-240-R-01-001 (January 2001).

44. Ibid.

45. Douglas R. Bohi and Dallas Burtraw, "SO_2 Allowance Trading: How Experience and Expectations Measure Up," Discussion Paper 97-24 (Washington, D.C.: Resources for the Future, February 1997).

46. Robert N. Stavins, "What Can We Learn from the Grand Policy Experiment?: Positive and Normative Lessons from SO_2 Allowance Trading," *Journal of Economic Perspectives* 12 (1998), 69–88.

47. Hugh Gorman and Barry D. Solomon, "The Origins and Practice of Emissions Trading," *Journal of Policy History* (September 2000): 315.

Chapter 6

Command and Control in Action:
Air and Water Pollution Regulation

In environmental history, the twentieth century qualifies as a peculiar century because of the screeching acceleration of so many of the processes that bring ecological change.

—J. R. McNeill
Something New Under the Sun (2000)

Despite substantial progress in improving air quality, the problems posed by pollutant emissions in the United States are by no means solved. Future economic and population expansions and the concomitant increased needs, for example, for electricity and transportation, will undoubtedly increase the potential for emissions. Consequently, additional effort will almost certainly be needed to maintain current air quality; even more effort will be needed to make further improvements.

—National Academies of Science,
Air Quality Management in the United States, 2004

Clean air and clean water are powerful public images. Leaders of the environmental movement regard the Clean Air Act (CAA) of 1970 and the Federal Water Pollution Control Act Amendments (FWPCAA) of 1972 as foundations of the environmental era. Public opinion polls show that Americans universally recognize the nation's degraded air and waters as major ecological problems. This means that clean air and water acquire political chic. Politicians so routinely assure constituents of their unceasing regard for clean air and clean water that both have become clichés instead of realities.

After more than thirty years of sustained effort by federal, state, and local governments to eliminate air and water pollution and an estimated

174

public expenditure during the 1990s of more than $210 billion annually, the nation's air and water remain seriously polluted. Some dramatic achievements, many lesser but impressive gains, and a multitude of marginal improvements make up the veneer that brightens reports about implementation of the CAA and the FWPCAA with a cosmetic success. But air and water quality remain seriously degraded throughout much of the United States. At the turn of the twenty-first century, the U.S. Environmental Protection Agency (EPA) estimated that more than 122 million Americans, mostly urbanites, lived in counties where pollution levels exceed at least one national air-quality standard.[1] The water quality in almost two-thirds of the nation's river miles has never been assessed because of deficient state monitoring resources.[2] The water quality in approximately one-third of the nation's surveyed lakes, estuaries, and streams is still considered by the EPA to be significantly impaired.[3]

Why not truly impressive results from so massive a national investment? Many difficulties arise from inexperience in implementing wholly new regulatory programs. To many observers, as noted in the discussion of market approaches to regulation in Chapter 5, the problem is the policy itself, the command-and-control logic so firmly embedded in the two earliest, and most important, national pollution laws of the first environmental era. Other difficulties result from new or unexpected scientific discoveries that complicate pollution control. But all these difficulties are compounded by a failure of political will: a reluctance to invest the enormous resources, and to make the politically difficult decisions needed to deal effectively with air and water pollution on a national scale. These and other significant influences shaping current air and water pollution regulation will become apparent as this chapter examines the implementation of the CAA and the FWPCAA during the 1980s and 1990s.

The Political Anatomy of Command-and-Control Regulation

The language and logic of command-and-control regulation is politically innocent. Formally, as observed in Chapter 5, environmental regulators are supposed to follow a legislatively prescribed pathway to pollution control by now built in to virtually every federal environmental law: (1) Regulate toward the *goals* identified by Congress, (2) identify the *criteria* for setting pollution standards, (3) set the *quality standards* for each regulated pollutant, (4) create the *emission standards* for regulated pollutants, and (5) see to *enforcement* of quality and emission standards. In reality, each command-and-control element is a distinctive decision-making arena rich with political implications—often unintended—lurking behind the statutory language and shaping the impact of regulation as much as the formal language of the law.

The technicality of pollution regulation, however, frequently creates a language and style of action that conceals, sometimes deliberately, the extent to which these political forces are operating behind the facade of prescribed regulatory procedures. Nonetheless, regulation is fundamentally a political enterprise. A number of characteristic political processes and issues arise regardless of the specific pollution program involved. Basically, political pressure and conflict flow to wherever administrative discretion exists in the regulatory process. Such administrative discretion ordinarily is found at several characteristic points in pollution regulation:

- *When Words, Phrases, or Policy Objectives Are Unclear.* Congress may deliberately shift responsibility to administrators for settling disputes between interests in conflict over how a law should be phrased. Tossing this political hot potato to administrators ensures that partisans on all sides of an issue with something to gain or lose by the law's interpretation will scramble to influence whatever officials or bureaucracies resolve such obscurities. Sometimes this lack of legislative clarity results less from deliberation than from congressional confusion or ignorance. In any case, regulators usually find themselves caught between competing group pressures to interpret statutes or regulations in different ways. Such pressures, in fact, should be considered routine in the regulatory process.

- *When Technical Standards Must Be Created or Revised.* Existing legislation regulating air pollution, water pollution, and hazardous substances ordinarily requires the EPA to define the standards and prescribe the appropriate control technologies necessary to meet mandated standards. Often regulatory agencies also are required by such legislation to review periodically and, if appropriate, revise such standards or technology requirements. Legitimate disagreement often exists, as noted in Chapter 5, over the technical and economic justification for most regulatory standards. In the presence of expert dissension about such issues, a large measure of discretion rests with regulatory agencies for resolving such disputes. This discretion, and the conflict it invites, will reappear whenever agencies review regulatory standards. In fact, virtually all major technical determinations by regulatory agencies are politicized by the activity of pressure groups, Congress, competing governmental agencies, and other interests seeking to shape discretionary decisions to their respective advantage.

- *When Compliance Deadlines Are Flexible.* Pollution legislation may bristle with explicit compliance deadlines, but administrators almost always have authority to extend them. Legislation is particularly generous in granting administrators authority to extend compliance deadlines when, in their opinion, economic hardship or other inequities may result from strict enforcement. Thus the CAA instructs the EPA to set emission standards for new air pollution sources by considering, among other things, "the degree of emission limitation achievable through the application of the best system of emission reduction which (taking into account the cost of achieving such reduction) the administrator determines has been adequately demonstrated." Such a fistful of discretionary authority in effect permits the EPA to extend compliance deadlines for specific air pollution sources by increasing the time allowed to search for pollution controls meeting these multiple criteria. In many cases a compliance deadline also may be relaxed if an agency determines that it is beyond the technical ability of a polluter to install the proper controls in the required time. Agencies sometimes can achieve backdoor extension of compliance deadlines by deliberately delaying the establishment of a standard long enough to permit the regulated interests to make adjustments to the anticipated standard. The EPA, for instance, waited until 1976—more than two and a half years after vinyl chloride was identified as a human carcinogen—before setting an exposure standard for that substance. The reason, the agency explained, was to avoid creating "unacceptably severe economic consequences" for the vinyl chloride manufacturers and users through an earlier standard establishing a more rapid deadline for controlling the chemical's emissions.[4]

Beyond Public View

Implementation of most environmental regulatory programs does not routinely involve the public, or public opinion, in the process. Unlike the White House and Congress, the federal bureaucracy is neither highly visible nor readily understood by the public; regulation operates, in the words of political scientist Francis E. Rourke, behind an "opaque exterior"[5] that the public seldom cares to penetrate. This dearth of dependable public interest means that the constellation of political forces and actors involved in regulatory politics ordinarily is confined to organized interests, governmental officials, scientists, technicians, and other insiders. Given the complexity and technicality of environmental issues, this situation is not surprising. But it emphasizes the extent to which regulatory politics tends to involve a process highly specialized and commonly closed to public involvement.

When Enforcement Is Discretionary

Few provisions in current pollution legislation compel federal officials to stop a polluting activity. Most often enforcement actions are discretionary, as in section 111 of the CAA, which instructs the EPA administrator to regulate any pollutant from a stationary source when, in the judgment of the administrator, it may cause or contribute to "air pollution which may reasonably be anticipated to endanger public health or welfare." Even when enforcement action is initiated, officials are usually given optional methods for securing compliance.

Typically, air and water pollution laws are enforced through state or local agencies with considerable discretion to decide what level of emission controls will be required of an air or water polluter and when emission controls must be achieved. These become conditions for the permit that all air- and water-polluting firms must obtain from state, federal, and local authorities to operate. In air pollution regulation, for instance, this discretion can arise from the regulator's authority under the CAA to decide which emission controls are technically and economically feasible and to issue variances that temporarily waive emission control deadlines or technology specifications.[6] Regulators seek voluntary compliance. They want to avoid penalties as a means of ensuring compliance if possible because they know that resort to administrative or judicial tribunals likely will involve a protracted, inflexible process with no assurances that the polluter will be compelled to control emissions speedily and efficiently at the conclusion. In fact, polluters often provoke such action, hoping to avoid emission controls indefinitely by exploiting the complexities of the administrative or judicial procedures involved.

Regulated firms often balk at a regulatory agency's initial specification of acceptable control technologies and deadline dates for compliance with emission standards. The usual solution is bargaining between regulator and regulated, particularly when regulatory agencies confront an economically and politically influential firm, or group of firms, capable of creating political pressures on the regulatory agency to reach some accommodation over required control technologies or compliance deadlines. Regulatory agencies typically will make some concession to firms concerning required control technologies or compliance deadlines. One form of these concessions is the frequently used variance that allows a firm some delay in achieving emission controls otherwise required under the law. A firm often is able to negotiate a variance permitting it to discharge on an interim basis at its existing emission levels and to obtain several additional variances that can delay significantly the achievement of required emission controls.

Agencies also depend heavily on firms to monitor and to report their own pollution emissions, in part because of the sheer volume of regulated entities. Under the CAA, for instance, more than 3,400 major sources and 45,600 minor sources of waste-water discharge must be controlled. The 1990 amendments to the CAA increased the regulated sources to more than 35,000 major and 350,000 minor facilities.[7]

Most regulatory agencies still lack the personnel and other resources to inspect routinely and to monitor all emission controls within their jurisdictions. Voluntary compliance is almost a necessity in regulation. Quite often, regulatory agencies monitor only the larger sources of pollution emissions within their jurisdiction, leaving smaller sources to report their own compliance with permit conditions under all but exceptional circumstances. Even monitoring the largest pollution sources does not necessarily ensure their compliance with pollution permits. For example, the EPA reported in 1999 that the agency and the states had conducted routine inspections on the nation's largest air pollution sources and found more than 88 percent complied with their pollution permits. However, the EPA subsequently became concerned that these inspections were insufficiently rigorous and conducted an extensive review of permit compliance in four of the most important regulated industries: electric utilities, petroleum refining, pulp and paper mills, and wood products. Among many enforcement deficiencies, the investigations "found widespread noncompliance with certain air pollution control requirements," according to the subsequent report. "EPA found that 76 percent of wood products facilities that it investigated had made operational changes without revising their permits. Moreover," it concluded, "EPA's investigations in the refining industry found widespread underreporting of emissions from leaking valves and other equipment."[8]

Although administrative discretion and political pressure clearly limit the vigor and strictness in enforcement of environmental regulations, these constraints are sometimes inevitable and may even be prudent. Often the use of administrative discretion to "make a deal" over pollution allows a regulatory agency to achieve more pollution abatement than would be the case if it insisted on extremely stringent emission standards in full and immediate compliance with the law. This is true particularly when the regulated firm either is unable to comply fully and immediately with a strict interpretation of the law or is willing to fight indefinitely in the courts or administrative hearing rooms to prevent any regulation. Many regulatory agencies, limited by staff and funding inadequate for their mandated responsibilities, have no practical alternative to relying on voluntary compliance and accommodation. Finally, regulatory agencies often confront regulated interests—including other governmental agencies subject to pollution control—too politically or economically powerful to be compelled to comply fully and immediately with the law. Although this should be no excuse for exemption from full compliance with environmental regulation, it is often an immutable political reality with which regulatory agencies must make peace. In such circumstances, agencies may logically conclude that it is better to bargain with the regulated interests in the hope of achieving some limited goals than to adopt what may well become an ultimately futile strategy of insisting on stringent compliance with the law in spite of massive resistance from the polluter.

Discretion in the enforcement of pollution regulation, however inevitable, also means that discretion at times will be abused. Discretion sometimes leads agencies to yield needlessly and negligently to political pressures that prevent enforcement of essential pollution controls. It is unfortunate that these are among the unavoidable risks inherent in the exercise of discretionary authority without which environmental administration would be impossible.

Regulating Air Quality

Since Earth Day 1970 the federal government has continually monitored a variety of environmental indicators and has published current assessments of environmental quality using these indicators. These data provide a useful baseline for observing change in national environmental quality since major federal environmental programs began in the early 1970s. They are also an essential standard for judging the impact of the CAA and other federal legislation. The CAA, together with its important 1977 and 1990 amendments, constitutes one of the longest, most complex, and most technically detailed regulatory programs ever enacted on a federal level. The CAA creates a standards-and-enforcement program in which the federal government establishes national ambient air-quality standards for major pollutants, the states and local government agencies assume primary responsibility for implementing the program within federal guidelines, and the various levels of government share enforcement responsibilities. However, the states may enact more stringent standards for airsheds in their jurisdictions.

Overall, national air quality has undoubtedly improved—in a few instances, dramatically—since the CAA's enactment in 1970. By 2006 the EPA was regulating more than two hundred air pollutants—most of them toxic air pollutants identified by Congress in 1990. However, the most important of these pollutants in terms of public health and political significance are the so-called criteria pollutants—carbon monoxide, nitrogen oxides, ozone, particulate matter, sulfur dioxide, and lead—whose regulation was mandated in 1970 by the original CAA and whose health effects are summarized in Box 6-1. After 2006, the EPA regulated only so-called small particulates (those smaller than 2.5 microns). As Table 6-1 illustrates, the improvement in both air quality and pollution emissions associated with these six pollutants between 1983 and 2005 has been, in most cases, significant and, in the case of lead, dramatic. Airborne lead, especially hazardous to children, has been virtually eliminated through the abolition of leaded automobile fuels. Since 1980, sulfur dioxide emissions decreased by more than 63 percent and carbon monoxide emissions by almost 70 percent. America's urban environment has improved significantly. The data

---

Box 6–1 *Human Health and Environmental Effects of Common Air Pollutants*

Ozone (ground-level ozone is the principal component of smog)
- *Source.* Ozone is produced by a chemical reaction involving volatile organic compounds and nitrogen oxides.
- *Health Effects.* Ozone causes breathing problems, reduced lung function, asthma, irritated eyes, stuffy nose, and reduced resistance to colds and other infections and may speed up aging of lung tissue.
- *Environmental Effects.* Ozone can damage plants and trees; smog can cause reduced visibility.
- *Property Damage.* Ozone damages rubber, fabrics, etc.

Volatile organic compounds (VOCs; smog-formers)[a]
- *Source.* VOCs are released from burning fuel (e.g., gasoline, oil, wood, coal, natural gas) and from solvents, paints, glues, and other products used at work or at home. Cars are a common source of VOCs. VOCs include chemicals such as benzene, toluene, methylene chloride, and methyl chloroform.
- *Health Effects.* In addition to ozone (smog) effects, many VOCs can cause serious health problems such as cancer and other effects.
- *Environmental Effects.* In addition to ozone (smog) effects, some VOCs such as formaldehyde and ethylene may harm plants.

Nitrogen dioxide (one of the nitrogen oxides; smog-forming chemical)
- *Source.* Nitrogen dioxide is produced in the burning of gasoline, natural gas, coal, oil, etc. Cars are a common source of nitrogen dioxide.
- *Health Effects.* Nitrogen dioxide causes lung damage and illnesses of breathing passages and lungs (i.e., respiratory system).
- *Environmental Effects.* Nitrogen dioxide is an ingredient of acid rain (acid aerosols), which can damage trees and lakes. Acid aerosols reduce visibility.
- *Property Damage.* Acid aerosols can eat away stone used in buildings, statues, monuments, etc.

Carbon monoxide
- *Source.* Carbon monoxide is produced in the burning of gasoline, natural gas, coal, oil, etc.
- *Health Effects.* Carbon monoxide reduces the ability of blood to bring oxygen to body cells and tissues; cells and tissues need oxygen to work. Carbon monoxide may be particularly hazardous to people who have heart or circulatory (i.e., blood vessel) problems and to people who have damaged lungs or breathing passages.

Particulate matter (dust, smoke, soot)
- *Source.* Particulate matter is produced in the burning of wood, diesel, and other fuels; by industrial plants; through agriculture (i.e., plowing, burning off fields); and from driving on unpaved roads.

---

[a] All VOCs contain carbon, the basic chemical element found in living things. Carbon-containing chemicals are called organic. Volatile chemicals escape into the air easily. Many VOCs, such as the chemicals listed in the preceding description, are also hazardous air pollutants, which can cause serious illnesses. The EPA does not list VOCs as criteria air pollutants, but they are included here because efforts to control smog also target VOCs for reduction.

(Box continues on next page)

Box 6–1 Continued

- *Health Effects.* Particulate matter causes nose and throat irritation, lung damage, bronchitis, and early death.
- *Environmental Effects.* Particulate matter is the main source of haze that reduces visibility.
- *Property Damage.* Ash, soot, smoke, and dust can dirty and discolor structures and other property, including clothes and furniture.

Sulfur dioxide
- *Source.* Sulfur dioxide is produced in the burning of coal and oil, especially high-sulfur coal from the eastern United States and through industrial processes (e.g., paper, metal).
- *Health Effects.* Sulfur dioxide causes breathing problems and may cause permanent damage to lungs.
- *Environmental Effects.* Sulfur dioxide is an ingredient in acid rain (acid aerosols), which can damage trees and lakes. Acid aerosols reduce visibility.
- *Property Damage.* Acid aerosols can eat away stone used in buildings, statues, monuments, etc.

Lead
- *Source.* Lead is found in leaded gasoline (being phased out), paint (e.g., houses, cars), and smelters (i.e., metal refineries) and is used in the manufacture of lead storage batteries.
- *Health Effects.* Lead causes brain and other nervous system damage; children are at especial risk. Some lead-containing chemicals cause cancer in animals. Lead causes digestive and other health problems.
- *Environmental Effects.* Lead can harm wildlife.

Source: Adapted from Environmental Protection Agency, Office of Air Quality Planning and Standards, *The Plain English Guide to the Clean Air Act.* www.epa.gov/oar/oaqps/peg_caa/pegcaa11.html (March 6, 2001).

---

understate the significance of these achievements because they do not estimate what pollution emissions would have been in the absence of regulation, during a period (1970–2005) when the U.S. population increased by 42 percent and vehicle miles traveled increased by 178 percent. Improvements in air quality have been especially significant since the mid-1980s as the cumulative effect of earlier regulation began to appear. Additional improvement is predicted as new regulatory programs are implemented. For example:

- New EPA diesel regulations for trucks are expected to remove 90 percent of the soot from present diesel motor emissions;
- The new EPA 2006 Clean Air Mercury Rule is expected to significantly reduce mercury emissions from coal-fired power plants—the largest remaining sources of mercury emissions in the country—from 48 tons a year to 15 tons, a reduction of nearly 70 percent.

Despite improvement, the nation's air remains seriously degraded in several respects. First, ground-level ozone, a primary component of urban smog, remains a pervasive problem. This low-level ozone poses significant

Table 6-1 Changes in Air Quality and Emissions of Seven Principal Pollutants
Regulated by the Clean Air Act, 1980–2005

	Percent Change in Air Quality	
	1980–2005	*1990–2005*
Nitrogen Dioxide (NO$_2$)	−37	−25
Ozone (O$_3$) (1-hr)	−28	−12
(8-hr)	−20	−8
Sulfur Dioxide (SO$_2$)	−63	−48
Large Particulates (PM$_{10}$)	—	−25
Small Particulates (PM$_{2.5}$)	—	−7[a]
Carbon Monoxide (CO)	−74	−60
Lead (Pb)	−96	−38

	Percent Change in Emissions	
	1980–2005	*1990–2005*
Nitrogen Oxides (NO$_x$)	−30	−25
Volatile organic compounds (VOCs)	−47	−31
Sulfur Dioxide (SO$_2$)	−42	−35
Large Particulates (PM$_{10}$)[b]	−68[c]	−38
Small Particulates (PM$_{2.5}$)	—	−13
Carbon Monoxide (CO)	−50	−38
Lead (Pb)	−96	−40

Source: http://www.epa.gov/air/airtrends/sixpoll.html, April 14, 2007.

— Trend data not available.

[a] Based on percentage change from 1999.
[b] Includes only directly emitted particles.
[c] Based on percentage change from 1985. Emission estimates prior to 1985 are uncertain.

human health risks and produces more than $1 billion in agricultural
crop damage annually. Currently, more than 127 million Americans, mostly
urbanites, live in areas not in compliance with the ozone standard. Second,
emissions of nitrogen oxides, a precursor of acid precipitation and a greenhouse gas contributing to urban smog, have increased since 1970. Third,
U.S. releases of greenhouse gases, especially carbon dioxide (CO^2), is predicted to increase by more than 42 percent between 2000–2020 under present U.S. air quality policies—a surge in climate warming emissions considered highly undesirable by most climate scientists, unacceptable by
environmentalists, and internationally threatening (as discussed fully in
Chapter 10).[9] In addition, control of small particulates, identified as an
important public health problem in the early 1990s, has just begun. Fourth,
air toxics have yet to be adequately regulated. The 1990 amendments to
the CAA required the EPA to regulate 188 air toxics, including well-known
health threats such as dioxins, benzene, arsenic, beryllium, mercury, and

vinyl chloride. To date, the EPA has established emission standards for only ninety-nine of these pollutants.

Improved air quality, like other environmental gains in recent decades, is fragile and highly vulnerable to technological change, economic cycles, and other social impacts. A case in point is the rapidly growing consumer demand for light trucks, minivans, pickups, and other sports vehicles. The EPA estimates that light trucks will be the fastest growing source of greenhouse gases in the first decade of the twenty-first century, exceeding the combined emissions of all domestic industrial sources. Sport utility vehicles (SUVs), essentially a passenger vehicle mounted on a light truck platform, have the fastest growing segment of the domestic automotive market. Environmentally they have little to recommend them. SUVs emit 30 to 70 percent more smog-producing pollutants than standard passenger cars. And they are much less fuel efficient. But consumers love them: Americans now buy almost two million SUVs annually, accounting for almost 19 percent of annual passenger vehicle sales.[10]

Equally important, SUVs paralyze the political will. Federal officials, aware of the vehicles' popularity, have been loath to propose more stringent emission controls for this environmentally hazardous technology. Light truck regulation, especially, has become a "third rail" political issue. "Detroit is giving people what they want," noted one observer. "Americans—even ones who fancy themselves as environmentalists—have fallen in love with trucks."[11]

The Clean Air Act and the 1977 Amendments

In broad outline, the CAA, including the 1977 amendments, mandates the following programs:

1. *National Air-Quality Standards.* The act directed the EPA to determine the maximum permissible ambient air concentrations for pollutants it found to be harmful to human health or the environment. The EPA was instructed to establish such standards for at least seven pollutants: carbon monoxide, hydrocarbons, lead, nitrogen oxide, particulates, ozone, and sulfur oxides. The agency was to set two types of national ambient air-quality standards without considering the cost of compliance:

a. *Primary Standards.* These standards were supposed to protect human health with an adequate margin of safety for particularly vulnerable segments of the population, such as the elderly and infants. Originally all air-quality control regions in the United States were required to meet primary standards by 1982; this deadline was extended several times and still remains unenforced.

b. *Secondary Standards.* These standards were intended to maintain visibility and to protect buildings, crops, and water. No deadline was mandated for compliance with secondary standards. The EPA is required by the 1977 amendments to the CAA to review all criteria for ambient air quality every five years after 1981.

2. *Stationary Source Regulations.* The EPA was to set maximum emission standards for new stationary sources, called new source performance standards. The following procedures were to be followed:

a. Standards were to be set on an industry-by-industry basis; the states then were to enforce the standards.

b. In setting new source performance standards, the EPA was required to take into account the costs, energy requirements, and environmental effects of its guidelines.

c. For existing sources (those dischargers active at the time the act was passed), the EPA was to issue control-technique guidelines for the states' use.

3. *State Implementation Plans.* Each state was required to create a plan indicating how it would achieve federal standards and guidelines to implement the act fully by 1982. The state implementation plans, which the EPA was to approve no later than 1979, were to contain information relating to several important elements:

a. The nation was divided into 247 air-quality control regions for which states were made responsible. The regions were classified as either attainment or nonattainment regions for each of the regulated pollutants.

b. States were also made responsible for enforcing special air-quality standards in areas with especially clean air. These regions were called prevention of significant deterioration, or PSD, regions.

c. States were required to order existing factories in nonattainment areas to retrofit their plants with control technologies representing "reasonably available control technology." Companies wanting to expand or build new plants in nonattainment areas had to install control equipment that limited pollutants to the least amount emitted by any similar factory anywhere in the United States. This technology was to be specified by the states without regard to cost.

d. New factories in nonattainment areas also were required to purchase offsets from existing air polluters. This involved purchasing new pollution equipment for an existing polluter or paying an existing polluter to eliminate some of its pollution to the extent that the offset equaled the pollution the new source was expected to emit after it installed its own control technology.

e. States in nonattainment areas were given until 1987 to meet carbon monoxide and ozone standards if the states required an annual automobile inspection and maintenance on catalytic converters on newer automobiles. In 1987 Congress extended the deadline for compliance in nonattainment areas to 1988.

f. In PSD areas, all new stationary emission sources were required to install the best available control technology.

4. *Mobile Source Emission Standards (for automobiles and trucks).* Title II of the CAA created a detailed but flexible timetable for achieving auto and truck emission controls.

a. For autos there was to be a 90 percent reduction in hydrocarbon and carbon monoxide emissions by 1975 and a 90 percent reduction in nitrogen oxide emissions by 1976, when measured against 1970 emission levels.

b. The administrator of the EPA was authorized to grant extensions of these deadlines for approximately one year. Considerable extensions were granted by the EPA and others authorized by Congress:

i. In 1973 the EPA granted a one-year extension of the 1975 deadline for hydrocarbons and carbon monoxide emissions and a one-year extension of the nitrogen oxide deadline.

ii. In 1974 Congress granted an additional one-year extension for all emission deadlines.

iii. In 1975 the EPA granted another one-year deadline extension for enforcement of hydrocarbon and carbon monoxide standards.

iv. In 1977 compliance deadlines for all emissions were extended for two more years, to be followed by stricter standards for hydrocarbons and carbon monoxide in 1980 and further tightening of the hydrocarbon standard in 1981, together with higher nitrogen oxide standards.

v. Beginning in 1982 Congress repeatedly waived compliance deadlines for auto emission controls until 1990. The Clean Air Act Amendments of 1990 set new, and greatly reduced, tailpipe standards for cars. Emission standards for hydrocarbons, carbon monoxide, and nitrogen oxides were greatly reduced, and all new cars were required to comply with the standards by 1996.

By 1990 the original CAA and its massive 1977 amendments apparently had achieved significant reductions in several ambient air pollutants, particularly suspended large particulates, lead, and carbon monoxide, as Table 6-1 indicates. With the exception of lead, however, reductions in other pollutants still seemed unsatisfactorily slow, and urban air pollution—especially concentrations of nitrogen oxide, ozone, and volatile organic compounds—continued to be a major concern. After almost a decade of bitter impasse arising from the Ronald Reagan administration's opposition to amending the CAA, George H. W. Bush's administration cooperated with environmentalists and a congressional majority to rewrite comprehensively the 1970 legislation by passing the Clean Air Act Amendments of 1990, the most important, and imaginative, regulatory reform in more than a decade.

The Clean Air Act Amendments of 1990

The new amendments are a curious melange of hammer clauses, multitudinous deadlines, and other tread-worn approaches combined with a timely sensitivity to emerging problems and an aggressive new approach to global climate protection based on an innovative market-inspired scheme for emissions trading. This mix of tradition, invention, and desperation represents what may be the last, best hope for fortifying the original CAA sufficiently to achieve its purpose. The 1990 amendments added to the original act two titles concerning acid precipitation and ozone protection and substantially amended most of the remaining provisions while keeping the basic command-and-control approach of the original legislation. The major features are outlined in the sections that follow:[12]

Title I: Nonattainment Areas. The amendments established a new classification of areas failing to meet national air-quality standards for ozone, carbon monoxide, and particulates and created deadlines from three to twenty years for attaining these standards. They also created a graded set of regulatory requirements for each area, depending on the severity of the pollution. An example of the new regulatory regime is the requirement that urban areas meet two regulatory standards depending on their degree of ozone and carbon monoxide pollution. Unlike the original act, which required only that cities make "reasonable further progress" in meeting air-quality standards, the new amendments set specific air quality goals and deadlines.

Title II: Mobile Sources. The new amendments set more than ninety new emission standards for autos and trucks. The most important emission requirements were as follows:

• Tailpipe emissions of hydrocarbons were to be reduced by 35 percent, and nitrogen oxides were to be reduced by 60 percent for all new cars by the 1996 model year.

• Beginning in 1998, all new cars were required to have pollution control devices with a ten-year, 100,000-mile warranty.

• Auto manufacturers were required to produce by 1996 a fleet of experimental cars available in Southern California that met emission standards more stringent than the 1996 levels already required by the amendments.

• Petroleum companies were required to produce cleaner-burning fuel to be used in the most polluted areas by 1992 and in all areas with ozone problems by 1996.

Title III: Hazardous Air Pollutants. The amendments required the EPA to create national emission standards for hazardous air pollutants for all major sources of hazardous or toxic air pollutants and specified 189 chemicals to be regulated immediately. They established a multitude of specific deadlines by which the EPA was ordered to list categories of industrial processes that emit dangerous air pollutants, to establish health-based standards for each hazardous chemical emission, and to ensure that sources of hazardous emission have established safety controls at their facilities.

Title IV: Control of Acid Deposition. The amendments created a new emissions trading program for sulfur oxides, a major precursor of acid precipitation. Under this new approach, the EPA was "to allocate to each major coal-fired power plant an allowance for each ton of emission permitted; sources cannot release emissions beyond the number of allowances they are given. Allowances may be traded, bought, or sold among allowance holders. . . . The EPA [was] required to create an additional pool of allowances to permit construction of new sources or expansion of existing ones."[13] Title IV required that national sulfur oxide emissions be reduced by half by the year 2000—a reduction of ten million tons annually from the 1980 levels. The 110 largest sulfur oxide sources in the utility industry were required to meet stricter emission standards. In addition, emissions of nitrogen oxides were to be reduced by two million tons annually, compared with 1980 levels, through more traditional regulatory methods.

Title VI: Stratospheric Ozone Protection. Title VI listed specific ozone-depleting chemicals and created a schedule for phasing out their production or use. It also pledged the United States to an accelerated phaseout of ozone-depleting chemicals that exceeded the schedule to which the United States agreed in the 1989 Montreal Protocol on Substances that Deplete the Ozone Layer.

Current Controversies in Air Quality Regulation

The CAA is the nation's longest, most complex regulatory law. Its legal and technical intricacy seems to ensure employment for a generation of lawyers and judges unborn and unrelenting partisan debate about its wisdom and implications among politicians and economists. At the same time, it is among the most revolutionary and ambitious environmental laws in U.S. history, the foundation of U.S. environmental regulation. Thus the issues and their embedded controversies have profound implications for the future of the U.S. environment. One of these important matters, discussed in Chapter 5, is emissions trading. Other major issues involved with the CAA concern the impact of federalism, regulatory science, and partisan change in the presidency. Current controversies over urban smog, small particulate regulation, and controls for new air pollution sources illustrate these issues.

Combative Federalism: The Smog Wars. Regulating urban smog has been difficult because so many varied sources contribute to its creation.

Large stationary sources, such as fossil-fuel-burning utilities, factories, mineral smelters, and chemical manufacturers, are major contributors. But thousands of small sources, most previously unregulated and many until recently unrecognized—including paint manufacturers, dry cleaners, and gasoline stations—collectively make a major contribution. The automobile stubbornly remains a chronic polluter despite the advent of efficient emission-control technologies. One reason is that pre-1970 vehicles, the worst auto polluters because they lack emission controls, are not being replaced as quickly as predicted. And at least one-fourth of the pollution-control devices on new cars are "disabled" (in the EPA's illusive phrase)—that is, deliberately destroyed.[14] In addition, as noted earlier, the ever-growing fleet of new, highly polluting light trucks and other sports vehicles continues to capture a large proportion of the domestic new vehicle market. Many state and local governments also have failed to enforce their own implementation plans, especially requirements for annual auto emission inspections, proposals to limit auto access to urban areas, and other arrangements publicly annoying and costly to business. Even the best available technologies may be insufficient to control adequately all important emissions. The newest Detroit emission controls now remove 96 percent of the pollutants emitted before controls were instituted in 1972.[15] Many experts believe existing auto emission controls have reached "the knife edge of technological feasibility" and that additional emission reductions are unlikely unless a great many states require motorists to switch from conventional to new, more expensive reformulated fuels or hybrid motor vehicles.

In a forceful, politically risky move to reduce urban air pollution further, the EPA in 1997 promulgated new ambient air-quality standards for ozone and particulates, two primary causes of smog, but only after a ferocious political fight that laid bare the tensions between state and federal governments inherent in regulatory federalism. The EPA's review of these standards had been long overdue, according to the requirements of the CAA, and was compelled only through a lawsuit sponsored by the American Lung Association. The new standards, finally proposed in early 1996, were considerably tougher than the existing ones. Experts predicted that the new regulations would increase the number of counties (virtually all urban) out of compliance with particulate standards from 41 to 150 and those violating the ozone standard from 189 to 332—in short, a huge increase in the population and political weight of the counties affected. Massive opposition from organized business developed quickly. "Industry and business interests, led by the National Association of Manufacturers and the American Petroleum Institute, have urged that the . . . standards not be tightened," observed the Congressional Research Service, "claiming excessive costs, lack of significant demonstrable benefits, loss of competitiveness, and technical infeasibility. An industry-business Air Quality

Standards Coalition has been formed to contest the stronger rules, and has picked up support from the small business community, farm groups, and the U.S. Conference of Mayors. At the same time, health and environmental stakeholders have either supported the proposals or proposed tightening them further."[16] The EPA defended its decision by citing the strong support from its own scientific advisory panels and by asserting that the new rules would avert 15,000 premature deaths, 350,000 cases of aggravated asthma, and 1 million cases of decreased lung function in children.

Congress—the second front in all political battles between the states—was immediately embroiled in the affair. Eleven different congressional committees collectively held more than a month of hearings on the revised standards. More than 250 senators and representatives wrote to the EPA and congressional committees about the matter. Congressional alignments generally reflected the ongoing battle over smog between the northeastern and midwestern states. Northeastern states believed the new regulations would diminish cross-border air pollution originating in the Midwest and would compel midwestern utilities to assume more responsibility for reducing those emissions. The midwestern states, generally in compliance with existing air-quality standards, anticipated having to enact economically costly, politically distasteful new air emission controls, especially on utilities, some of which would have to reduce existing emissions by 85 percent. Bill Clinton's administration wavered for months in the political heat despite outspoken support for the proposals by EPA administrator Carol Browner; the president's own congressional party was divided deeply on the matter. Finally, in July 1997, President Clinton approved the regulations, to the surprise of many environmentalists convinced the president would never accept the political risks. Several months later, even as the EPA proposed stringent new emission controls on utilities to implement the new air-quality standards, the northeastern states renewed the geographic struggle. Asserting that the EPA's newly proposed emission controls would take too long to implement, they sued the EPA for failing to order emission reductions in forty midwestern power plants in accordance with other provisions of the CAA. Although the federal courts refused to mandate that the EPA issue such orders, the agency indicated that it might revise its proposed emission standards anyway and, in any case, that it intended to issue its final version sometime in 2001. When this final version was issued, the regulated utilities promptly, and unsuccessfully, sued the agency in an effort to prevent implementation of the new standards.

The advent of the George W. Bush administration provoked additional confrontations between the EPA and the northeastern states. Complaining that mideastern air pollution made the northeast "the tailpipe of America," nine northeastern states sued the EPA in 2002 to prevent the enactment of new rules delaying the installation of new pollution control technologies on older Midwestern utilities (see the section "New Source Review" that follows) and in 2005 initiated additional suits against the Bush administration's proposed new standards for power plant mercury emissions. The Northeast's sustained legal and political pressure on EPA produced a truce of sorts by 2007. The battle over New Source Review had stalled in the courts, and the Bush administration announced in 2005 a new Clean Air Interstate Rule (CAIR) that was intended to reduce power plant emissions of nitrogen and sulfur oxides by more than 60 percent within a decade.

Litigation, however, is unlikely to end such a tooth-and-claw sectional brawl because the conflict feeds on deeply nested political tensions in the federalist system: sectional competition for political and economic power, conflicts over interpretation of the Constitution's federalist language, corporate conflicts over state market regulation, and more. Still, the contention is a virtual primer on U.S. environmental regulation. It involves both separated federal institutions and state governments, pluralistic private and public interests, congressional advocacy of state and regional viewpoints, scientific contention about environmental standards, judicial intervention in regulation, the resort to litigation as a political weapon, and much more that is fundamental to U.S. environmental policy making. In broadest perspective, it is politics American-style.

Science and Regulatory Change: Small Particulates. Regulation strives for predictability, consistency in interpreting and applying the law, and stability in established norms for decision making. Science breeds discovery, embraces change, promotes experimentation, and challenges tradition. Science is troublesome to regulatory order. Since 1970 the CAA has regulated airborne particulates as one of the original criteria pollutants. But the continuing enrichment of the scientific base for regulation since 1970 is forcing a change in understanding which substances should be regulated and what levels can be tolerated. New scientific evidence poses for the EPA difficult and disruptive new choices about particulate regulation.

In 1971 the EPA issued air-quality standards for particulates without distinction regarding size. Particulates—extremely small solid particles of matter found in the air and produced by dust, smoke, fuel combustion, agriculture, and forest cultivation, among other sources—have been known for many decades to pose health hazards. Initially, however, the EPA's standards on particulates assumed that size was not a significant factor in the health risks posed. By 1987 accumulating scientific research had demonstrated conclusively that small particulates, those smaller than 10 microns (one micron equals 1/25,000 inch), are especially hazardous to humans because they can be inhaled into lung tissue, unlike larger particulates that are caught in the air passages to the lungs.[17] These smaller particulates are commonly found in cigarette smoke, diesel engine emissions, windblown dust, and many other sources. They are also dangerous because they can carry carcinogenic chemicals into the lungs. In 1987 the EPA issued new air-quality standards for small particulates. However, existing emission controls for particulates were not designed specifically to control small particulates, and many sources of small particulates were not regulated at all.

About 250 air-quality control regions failed the new ambient air-quality standards for fine particulates. In the West, a major problem was wind-blown dust not easily controlled by any existing technology. The EPA established tailpipe standards for emissions from diesel trucks and buses, beginning with the 1988 model year, which became increasingly stringent for models beginning in 1991. But monitoring data about the origin and distribution of fine particulates were inadequate, and states were slow to identify the magnitude of their problems and the sources to be regulated. Control technologies for stationary sources of small particulates were not well tested, and the control costs were not accurately known. In effect, small particulates had become a separate emission-control problem, and the states spent much of the 1990s acquiring a capability to regulate them. The EPA's most recent particulate standards, enacted concurrently with the 1997 revised smog rules, created new regulations specifically for particulates smaller than 2.5 microns because scientific research had demonstrated that these posed a distinct human health risk. Automobile manufacturers, fossil-fuel-burning facilities, and the trucking industry were predictably concerned about the additional compliance costs to meet the proposed standards. And they were angered by this regulatory ratcheting—the appearance of progressively more stringent new regulatory rules with which they must comply—creating the third different particulate standard in a decade. Proponents of the new standards argued that they were protecting the elderly, children, and people with chronic lung disease from a new, scientifically verified health risk. For regulated interests, the real problem seemed to be the potent, economically disruptive impact of regulatory science on environmental management.

Predictably, the disaffected truckers, utilities, and other regulated industries took their case to court—all the way to the Supreme Court, in fact—by challenging the EPA's authority to promulgate the new regulatory rules in what turned out to be perhaps the most significant environmental regulatory cases since the 1970s. Essentially, the dissidents challenged the EPA's discretionary authority, granted by Congress in the CAA, to set ambient air-quality standards solely on the basis of public health considerations. The EPA, they argued, had interpreted this authority too broadly, and Congress had been negligent in permitting the agency too much discretion in interpreting such authority. Had the Supreme Court agreed with this argument, the logic could well have overturned a huge array of other environmental regulations across the whole domain of federal environmental regulation and left a chaos of regulatory confusion. The Supreme Court, however, rejected the assault on the EPA's congressionally delegated authority and in a landmark ruling (*Whitman v. American Trucking Association, 99-1257*) affirmed in 2001 both the delegated authority and the EPA's latitude in interpreting that authority.

What followed was a consummate example of EPA decision making driven by the judicial lash. With Supreme Court approval, the EPA began to issue regulations in 2002 to implement its small particulate standards. But the agency was sued again in 2002, this time by environmental groups, for failing to review its standards for small and large particulates by a 2002 deadline set by the CAA (which required an EPA review of all air-quality standards every five years). After further negotiation, the EPA reached a settlement with the environmental groups in which it agreed to review again its particulate standards. In 2006, EPA decided to implement its new small particulate standard and also to abandon its earlier standard for large particulates—an instance of "regulatory ratcheting" driven by ongoing scientific research. Meanwhile, the EPA estimated in 2005 that at least 129 counties with more than 68 million people appeared to exceed the standard for small particulates established in 1997 and almost 400 additional counties with a population exceeding 91 million people had insufficient data to even determine whether they had met particulate standards.[18] Thus a substantial proportion of the national population, most of them urban dwellers, appeared to be living in areas that might be subjected in the near future to increasingly stringent air pollution controls that could significantly affect economic development.

Politics and Regulatory Change: New Source Review. In mid-2002 the EPA brought to a full boil a controversy simmering since the CAA's creation in 1970. By then the conflict had escalated into a major confrontation between the George W. Bush administration and environmentalists. All this resulted from a volatile combination of circumstances that repeatedly transformed environmental rule making into partisan political warfare: large regulatory costs and environmental risks, a major economic sector, vague legislation, and (especially in this instance) a new presidency. The outcome, moreover, was likely to profoundly affect air quality for a generation or more.

The controversy began with an arcane section of the CAA concerned with "new source performance standards." The original CAA of 1970 required all major stationary sources of air pollution built after 1975 to install pollution control technologies but exempted existing pollution sources. Many of these existing operations, especially major pollution sources, such as coal-burning electric power plants, continued to operate older facilities with occasional modification instead of building new plants with the required, expensive pollution control technologies. This situation, in effect, perpetuated thousands of major air-polluting facilities well beyond their normal lifetime and prompted Congress to amend the law.

The Clean Air Act Amendments of 1977 added to the original legislation a new source review (NSR) provision that required older air-polluting facilities to install the best available control technologies whenever they underwent "major modification"—a strategy meant to discourage the continued existence of the older pollution sources. At the same time, however, the act still permitted companies to carry out "routine maintenance" of existing facilities without replacing them. Thus, a crucial issue arose: when did "routine maintenance" become a "major modification?" As one legal analyst explained,

> The wording of the NSR was vague enough to allow companies to fight regulators over the definition of major modification. . . . [The companies] could try to define almost all construction on existing plants as minor or routine. The grandfather clause exempting old plants, combined with uncertainty about what, exactly, was routine maintenance, permitted companies not only to keep old, heavily polluting plants running, but to use those plants to boost output in a way that escaped Clean Air Act emission requirements.[19]

Companies—especially the electric utilities—fought the EPA over the NSR standards. Throughout the 1980s and most of the 1990s the federal and state governments struggled with the definition of "major modification," and few companies were compelled to upgrade their existing facilities by the NSR provisions.

This stalemate ended in the late 1990s. New York, on behalf of other northeastern states downwind of air pollution originating from midwestern power plants, sued several large midwestern utilities in 1999 for failure to comply with the NSR standards that required new pollution controls. The Clinton administration also sued fifty-one large coal-fired electric utilities for similar reasons. The stakes were enormous. The court rulings would affect seventeen thousand power plants nationally, involve several billion dollars in potential new pollution control costs for the utilities, and possibly determine the breadth and quality of national air pollution control for decades. The new litigation was vigorously opposed by the coal-fired electric power utilities and their trade associations, the petroleum and mining industries, major manufacturing corporations, and virtually every other economic interest at risk if the NSR provisions were aggressively enforced as interpreted by the Clinton administration's EPA. Corporations with facilities at risk argued that EPA's standards for defining a "major modification" were unclear and that, in any case, there were more economically and technically efficient ways of achieving the purposes of the

NSR besides an inflexible requirement that new facilities must install the best new pollution controls.

This litigation was still before the courts when the 2000 presidential elections brought a sea change to environmental regulation in Washington. The new Bush administration strongly identified with the nation's energy producers and their regulatory viewpoint while opposing the EPA's general command-and-control approach to air pollution regulation during the Clinton era. In addition, the first National Energy Plan proposed by the Bush administration tilted heavily in the direction of new energy production and called, among other increased production measures, for the building of 1,300 to 1,900 new electric power plants by 2020. Bush preferred to terminate the Clinton administration's lawsuits against the electric utilities and, instead, to encourage expansion of the electric power industry by relaxing the NSR standards and creating a market for emissions trading as an alternative to technological controls for all new electric power plants. Congressional Democrats generally regarded the Bush proposals as a reincarnation of Reagan's antienvironmentalism, and debate over reforming the NSR tended to divide along party lines. In late 2003 the EPA proposed to revise the NSR regulations by generously increasing the opportunities for companies to enlarge their existing pollution sources without installing the pollution control technologies the NSR seemed to require.[20] A coalition of environmental, public health, and state regulatory agencies promptly initiated a lawsuit challenging the EPA's new proposal. The coalition charged that the proposal would drastically increase the volume of future air pollution and further discourage the replacement of older, polluting facilities with newer, environmentally cleaner ones, and a federal court agreed.[21]

The EPA was now under court order to rewrite its NSR standard again. In late 2005, the EPA proposed—to the satisfaction of most environmental groups—a new NSR standard creating nationwide consistency in how states implemented the program for electric generating units. The proposed changes would standardize the emissions tests used in NSR to determine if a physical or operational change at a power plant would cause emission increase that would require the plant to install additional pollution controls. By the end of 2006, a series of additional federal court decisions had largely eliminated the NSR standards supported by the Bush administration. The new, tougher NSR standards were, for the moment, in place and, if implemented, would affect 800 electric power plants and 17,000 factories nationally.

Urban smog, airborne toxics, and small particulates are a few among many ambient air problems challenging the nation's ability to realize the ambitious goals set by the CAA in 1970. These problems test the nation's technological skill and economic resiliency. They will challenge the political determination of its officials and the public's commitment to the environmental protection the majority professes to support. These problems are also reminders of how incrementally slow the implementation has been and also how modest the achievements of the CAA have been. The nation's experience with water pollution has been much the same.

Regulating Water Quality

The nation's aquatic inheritance is not just water but different water systems, each essential to modern U.S. society and each currently threatened, or already severely polluted, by different combinations of pollutants.

Surface Water

The nation's surface waters—streams, rivers, lakes, wetlands, and coastal areas—are the nation's most visible water resource. Almost 99 percent of the population lives within fifty miles of a publicly owned lake. Streams, rivers, and lakes account for a high proportion of all recreational activities, commercial fishing grounds, and industrial water resources. Because surface waters are so intensively used and so highly visible, their rapidly accelerating degradation became the most immediate cause for congressional action in the 1960s and 1970s; arresting water pollution and restoring the nation's once high water quality became a focal point for environmental legislation. Most of the fragmentary data available on national water quality since 1970 come from monitoring surface-water conditions. But surprisingly little reliable information exists about the quality of most U.S. surface waters.

Even after the turn of the twenty-first century, estimates of surface-water quality continue to be ambiguous and uncertain, largely because comprehensive, reliable monitoring data remain unavailable. Federal agencies such as the EPA and the Council on Environmental Quality have traditionally based their surface-water-quality indexes on only six pollutants, excluding common sources of water degradation such as heavy metals, synthetic organic compounds, and dissolved solids. In general, surface-water quality seems, despite some spectacular achievements, to have remained in about the same condition since the late 1980s. It is often difficult, in any case, to know what significance to impute to available statistics because EPA assessments cover only about one-third of all U.S. surface-water area. This translates into an assessment of approximately 19 percent of river miles, 43 percent of lake acres, and 36 percent of estuary square miles. Wetlands are still largely terra incognita; only 8 percent of wetlands acreage has been evaluated for water quality.

The states' haphazard water-quality monitoring creates massive information deficiencies that frustrate accurate national assessment. Just how problematic is state monitoring is suggested by a U.S. General Accounting Office (GAO) description of the evaluated data used by many states. "Evaluated data," explained the GAO, "include site-specific monitoring data more than 5 years old and information that serves as an indicator of water quality conditions, such as anecdotal evidence or reports on wildlife or habitat conditions"—in short, sophisticated guesswork.[22]

The leading causes of surface-water pollution, summarized in Figure 6-1, can be identified readily. By far the largest contributors to this pollution are agricultural runoff, urban runoff, and other sources of so-called nonpoint pollution—that is, pollution arising from diffuse, multiple sources rather than from a pipe or other point source—the most technologically and politically formidable pollutants yet to be controlled.

The Federal Water Pollution Control Amendments. The federal government's major water pollution regulatory program is embodied in the FWPCAA of 1972, which concerns primarily surface-water quality. The 1972 legislation amended the Water Pollution Control Act of 1948. The 1972 amendments completely changed the substance of the earlier legislation and established the regulatory framework prevailing ever since. The 1972 legislation was strengthened greatly by new amendments passed in 1987 as the Water Quality Act. In more than 120 pages of fine print, the FWPCAA mandates the following regulatory program for the nation's surface waters:

1. *Goals.* The amendments established two broad goals whose achievement, if possible, assumed an unprecedented regulatory structure and unusually rapid technological innovation:

a. "the discharge of pollutants into navigable waters of the United States be eliminated by 1985";

b. "wherever attainable, an interim goal of water quality which provides for the protection and propagation of fish, shellfish and wildlife and provides for recreation in and on the water be achieved by 1 July 1983."

2. *Regulatory Provisions for Existing Dischargers.* The legislation required that all direct dischargers into navigable waterways satisfy two different standards, one relating to water quality, the other to effluent limits. The water-quality standards, established by the states according to guidelines issued by the EPA, were to identify the use for a body of water into which a polluter was discharging (such as recreation, fishing, boating, waste disposal, irrigation, and so forth) and to establish limits on discharges in order to ensure that use. Effluent standards, established by the EPA, were to identify what technologies any discharger had to use to

Figure 6-1   Leading Sources of River and Stream Impairment[a]

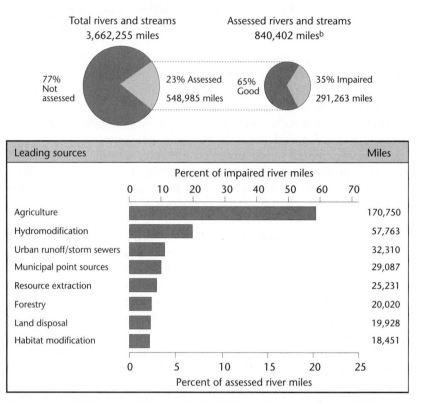

States assessed 23 percent of the total miles of rivers and streams for the 1998 report. The larger pie chart on the left illustrates that proportion. The smaller pie chart on the right shows that, for the subset of assessed waters, 65 percent are rated as good and 35 percent as impaired. When states identify waters that are impaired, they also describe the sources of pollutants associated with the impairment. The bar chart presents the leading sources and the number of river and stream miles they impact. The percent scales on the upper and lower x-axis of the bar chart provide different perspectives on the magnitude of the impact of these sources. The lower axis compares the miles impacted by the source to the total assessed miles. The upper axis compares the miles impacted by the source to the total impaired miles.

Source: Environmental Protection Agency, Office of Water, "The Quality of the Nation's Waters: A Summary of the National Water Quality Inventory: 1998 Report to Congress," EPA Document No. EPA 841-S-00-001 (June 2000), 62.

Note: Percentages do not add up to 100 percent because more than one pollutant or source may impair a river segment.

[a] Excluding unknown and natural sources.

[b] Includes miles assessed as not attainable.

control its effluents. In meeting these dual requirements, the polluter was required to achieve whichever standard was stricter. A different set of standards was established for municipal waste-water treatment facilities.

a. *Effluent limits for existing nonmunicipal sources.* Except for city waste treatment plants, all existing dischargers were required to have technological controls, prescribed by the EPA, which were to meet the following criteria:

i. the "best practicable control technology currently available" by July 1, 1979;

ii. the "best available technology economically achievable" by July 1983.

b. *Effluent limits for municipal treatment plants.* All treatment plants in existence on July 1, 1977, were required to have "secondary-treatment" levels. All facilities, regardless of age, were required to have "the best practicable treatment technology" by July 1, 1983.

c. *Effluent limits for new nonmunicipal sources.* All new sources of discharge, except municipal treatment plants, were required to use control technologies based on "the best available demonstrated control technology, operating methods or other alternatives."

d. *Toxic effluent standards.* The EPA was required to establish special standards for any discharge determined to be toxic.

3. *Regulatory Provisions for Indirect Dischargers.* Many pollutants, including chemical toxics, are released into municipal waste-water systems by industrial and commercial sources and later enter waterways through city sewage treatment plants unable to eliminate them. The law required the EPA to establish pretreatment standards, which were to prevent the discharge of any pollutant through a public sewer that "interferes with, passes through or otherwise is incompatible with such works." The purpose of this provision was to compel such indirect dischargers to treat their effluent before it reached the city system.

4. *Federal and State Enforcement.* The EPA was authorized to delegate responsibility for enforcing most regulatory provisions to qualified states that would issue permits to all polluters specifying the conditions for their effluent discharges.

5. *Waste Treatment Grants.* The act authorized the expenditure of $18 billion between 1973 and 1975 to assist local communities in building necessary waste-water treatment facilities. The federal government assumed 75 percent of the capital cost for constructing the facilities.

6. *Nonpoint Pollution Regulation.* Amendments added in 1987 require each state to have a plan approved by the EPA for controlling pollution from nonpoint sources. Such plans must include "best management practices," but states are permitted to decide whether to require owners and managers to use such practices or to make them voluntary.

The 1972 legislation was written by a Congress unchastened by the political, economic, and technological obstacles to pressing technology in pollution regulation. The legislation, as originally written, was the purest example of "technology forcing" in the federal regulatory code. The use of effluent standards in addition to water-quality standards for dischargers was based on the premise that "all pollution was undesirable and should be reduced to the maximum extent that technology will permit."[23] Compliance deadlines were almost imperiously ordained for the total elimination of water pollution in a decade. Nonetheless, the administrative and technical complexities of making the legislation work seemed surmountable. The original legislation serves as an enduring monument to the U.S. politician's belief in the possibilities of social engineering and to the political muscle of the environmental movement in the early 1970s.

Even the most ardent advocates of the legislation, however, recognized that the rigorous compliance deadlines for effluent treatment and wastewater facility construction would not be attained. They were convinced that pressing technology ultimately worked—eliminating all pollutants from the nation's waters hardly seemed impossible to a people who would launch a satellite carrying their language a billion light-years into space. Acknowledging the likelihood of short-term failures, advocates of the legislation were nonetheless convinced that only by pressing technology relentlessly for rapid compliance with regulations could they sustain the sense of urgency and bring sufficient weight of federal authority to bear on polluters to obtain their long-term objectives.

The Political Setting. The political struggle over implementation of the FWPCAA has been shaped by several factors. First, the implementation of the legislation is federalized. The 1972 amendments made concessions to the states that Congress had been unwilling to make in the CAA of 1970 and that environmentalists generally opposed. The 1972 amendments permitted the states to decide on the designated use for a body of water. In general, state regulatory agencies are more vulnerable than Washington, D.C., to pressure from local water polluters to designate uses for bodies of water that will permit moderate to heavy pollution. This propensity of local regulatory agencies to accommodate regulated interests also extends to enforcement of designated water uses and the associated emission controls. Regulated interests often are likely to press vigorously for a major state role in the administration and enforcement of water-quality standards, believing that this works to their advantage more than implementation through the EPA's regional and national offices. State enforcement of pollution controls on major dischargers improved significantly in the 1990s, but many violators still go undetected or unpunished. In the mid-1990s the GAO calculated that as many as one in every six of the nation's major dischargers regularly violated their permits, but the EPA estimated the number might be twice that amount.

Thirty-five states have assumed major implementation responsibilities, such as issuing and enforcing permits for effluent dischargers, initiating requests for federal grants to build new local waste treatment facilities, and supervising the administration of the grant programs in their jurisdictions. The states thus exercise considerable influence on program implementation directly through their own participation—and the pursuit of their own interests in the program—and through their congressional delegations, which remain ever vigilant in protecting the interests of the folks back home. Moreover, conflict arising from differing state and federal viewpoints on program implementation becomes interjected immediately into the daily administrative implementation of the law. Control standards vary greatly among the states for the same pollutant, often provoking states with strict standards to complain that more lenient states enjoy an unfair advantage in the competition for new business. Among six major states, for instance, the same five toxic pollutants were treated very differently:

> In some states, the permitting authorities consistently established numeric limits on the discharges, while in other states, the authorities consistently required monitoring. In some states, no controls were imposed. In addition, the numeric discharge limits for specific pollutants differed from state to state and even within the same state for facilities of similar capacity.[24]

The political character of the program also depends on the enormous administrative discretion left to the EPA in prescribing the multitude of technologies that must be used by effluent dischargers to meet the many different standards established in the law. At the time the Clean Water Act was amended in 1972, for instance, about 20,000 industrial dischargers were pouring pollutants into more than 2,500 municipal waste treatment facilities. The EPA was charged with identifying the pretreatment standards to be used by each major class of industrial discharger. This might eventually require standards for several hundred different classes and modified standards for subclasses. The final standards issued by the EPA in 1976 for industries producing "canned and preserved fruits and vegetables" alone contained specifications for fifty-one subcategories. Administrators also are limited by the state of the art in treatment technologies and by dependence on the regulated interests for information concerning the character of the discharger's production processes and technical capacities. We already have noted that administrative discretion invites political pressure and conflict. The technical determinations required in setting effluent standards also invite controversy and litigation.

Finally, the program's implementation has been affected continually by the active, if not always welcome, intervention of the White House, Congress, and the federal courts in the program's development. Federal and state regulatory agencies have had to conduct the program in a highly political environment, in which all major actions have been subject to continual scrutiny, debate, and assessment by elective public officials and judges. This is hardly surprising for a program involving so many billions of dollars and so many politically and economically sensitive interests. But, as we shall observe later in this chapter, the economic and environmental costs of such politicized administration are high.

A Stubborn Problem: Nonpoint Pollution. The most common source of surface-water pollution has remained virtually uncontrolled in every state since the 1972 passage of the FWPCAA. Nonpoint pollution is estimated to be the major cause of pollution in 65 percent of the stream miles not meeting state standards for their designated use.[25] Overall, more than one-third of the stream miles in the United States appear to be affected by nonpoint pollution. Nonpoint pollution also affects ground-water quality. Earlier we noted that nonpoint pollution is the leading cause of water-quality impairment. Figure 6-2, which portrays the proportion of nitrogen in major streams across the United States originating from nonpoint sources, illustrates the geographic breadth of nonpoint pollution.

This pollution is especially troublesome for several reasons. Its origin is often elusive. Almost all states lack enough information to identify most of the nonpoint sources polluting their surface waters.[26] It is not easily controlled technically or economically. Many different sources require many different control strategies. The largest source of nonpoint pollution is agriculture: crop lands, pasture, and range lands together pollute about one-third of the nation's stream miles with metabolic wastes from animals, sediment, fertilizers, pesticides, dissolved solids, and other materials.

Agricultural runoff and urban storm water runoff are the major causes for the eutrophication of lakes, whereby dissolved organic substances create such a high level of oxygen demand in the waters that higher forms of plants and animals die from oxygen deprivation. Eutrophication eventually leaves most lakes lifeless.

Reducing agricultural pollution requires a number of difficult strategies because technological solutions are rarely available. Most often, production practices must be altered. Farmers might be encouraged, or required, to reduce the volume of fertilizer, pesticides, and other chemicals used in crop production. Animal populations might be limited or dispersed. New crop and land management techniques might reduce soil runoff. In many instances, land-use planning might be used to prevent, or reduce, agricultural activities. But powerful agricultural groups and members of Congress for whom they are a major constituency believe such strategies will have adverse economic impacts and have opposed most measures intended to reduce agricultural runoff by most of these methods. Many state governments, fearful of damaging a major component of the state economy, are reluctant to do more than encourage farmers to voluntarily seek ways to limit their pollution runoff.

Figure 6-2 Point and Nonpoint Sources of Nitrogen in Watersheds of Continental United States

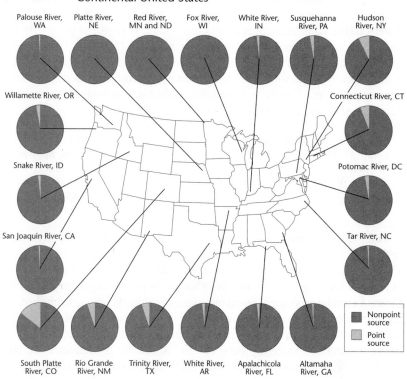

Proportions of nonpoint and point sources of nitrogen vary in watersheds across the continental United States. Commercial fertilizer and manure typically constitute the major sources of nitrogen to the first NAWQA study units. Atmospheric nitrogen is significant in most study units except in the far West and the Northern Great Plains. Point sources are an important source of nutrients to watersheds near large urban areas, such as Denver in the South Platte River Basin and Hartford in the Connecticut, Housatonic, and Thames River Basins.

Source: U.S. Department of the Interior, U.S. Geological Survey, "The Quality of Our Nation's Water—Nutrients and Pesticides," Circular No. 1225 (November 2000), 29.

The current strategy for controlling nonpoint pollution has set regulators on a collision course not only with agricultural organizations but also with the commercial timber industry, the commercial and residential construction industry, meat packers and shippers, coal mining firms, and a multitude of trades and professions associated with each. Since the early

1990s the EPA has required states to identify all their waters that fail water-quality standards and, for each impaired water, to identify the amount by which each nonpoint pollutant must be reduced to meet these water-quality standards. Specifically, each state is required to specify for each nonpoint pollutant a total maximum daily load (TMDL)—that is, the maximum amount of each pollutant permitted in each water body over a twenty-four-hour period. This calculation has proved enormously difficult and controversial. The scale of the undertaking is staggering. The National Academy of Sciences reported in 2000:

> Given the most recent lists of impaired waters submitted by EPA, there are about 21,000 polluted river segments, lakes, and estuaries making up over 300,000 river and shore miles and 5 million lake acres. The number of TMDLs required for these impaired waters is greater than 40,000 [and] most states are required to meet an 8- to 13-year deadline for completion of the TMDLs.[27]

Nonetheless, most states have created some TMDLs or have attempted to do so. Perhaps the most nationally visible conflict over these calculations has arisen from efforts by the state of Florida and the federal government to create TMDLs for dissolved phosphorous in runoff degrading the Everglades from the vast sugar-growing region north of Lake Okachobee. In this instance, as in most others involving the creation of TMDLs, scientific and legal controversy abounds and litigation proliferates. The TMDL calculation remains inherently problematic, and state regulators complain that the process is so adversarial that TMDL should mean "too many damn lawyers."

"This State's Gone Hog Wild": The Battle over Concentrated Animal Farms. In mid-1997, corporate animal farms for the first time made national news, and in the worst possible way. In eastern North Carolina, one corporate hog farm, home to twelve thousand pigs, was flooded by runoff from heavy rain. The swirling runoff flushed twenty-five million gallons of feces and urine from the farm's eight-acre waste lagoon into a knee-deep tide that inundated surrounding cotton and tobacco fields and then poured into the New River. The spill killed ten million fish along a seventeen-mile stretch of the river between Richlands and Jacksonville, closed 364,000 acres of wetlands to shellfishing for months, and prompted Rep. Charlie Rose, D-N.C., to demand that the EPA declare a moratorium on new factory farms until their environmental contamination could be controlled. The following year, North Carolina's largely corporate hog farms produced more than sixteen million hogs—the nation's second largest state hog production. "This state's gone hog wild," Rose complained. "We have a wonderful quality of life here, but a greedy, unregulated hog industry will ruin it overnight if we're not careful."[28]

The North Carolina spectacle was among the first of an increasing number of highly publicized incidents to thrust the problem of concentrated animal farming into national visibility and frame an ongoing political struggle in almost every agricultural state. Concentrated animal feeding operations (CAFOs) are a collision point between the rapidly accelerating vertical integration in U.S. food production and the tired pace of regulatory reform—another instance of regulation racing to catch up with economic and technological innovation. Moreover, the issue is a tangle of surface water, groundwater, and drinking water regulatory problems falling between the margins of state and federal water pollution laws and provoking the jurisdictional problems common to regulatory federalism.

Large corporate animal feeding operations (AFOs) are quickly transforming virtually all sectors of major animal production in the United States—cattle, hogs, poultry, turkey, dairies. The EPA describes these farms as

> facilities that confine animal feeding activities, thereby concentrating animal populations, animal manure, and animal mortality. AFO activities can cause a range of environmental and public health problems, including oxygen depletion and disease transmission in surface water, pathogens and nutrient contamination in surface and ground water, methane emissions to the air, and excessive buildup of toxins, metals, and nutrients in soil.[29]

The production of small, family-owned AFOs is diminishing rapidly in the wake of increasing CAFOs. For example:

- "The structure of the pork industry has also changed dramatically during the past three decades. The number of hog producers in the United States was more than 1 million in the 1960s but fell to about 67,000 by 2005. . . . Although the total inventory of hogs has changed little over the years, the structural shift toward concentration has been dramatic with the 110 largest hog operations in the country, each of which has over 50,000 hogs, now constituting 55% of the total national inventory (USDA 2005)."[30]
- "The number of farms in Iowa raising hogs decreased from 64,000 in 1980 to 10,500 in 2000—an 84% decrease—while the average number of hogs per farm increased from 250 to 1,430 over this same period. . . . Farms with more than 500 hogs now account for 65% of the statewide inventory and 75% of the U.S. inventory."[31]

About seven thousand very large CAFOs currently operate in the United States, most owned by large food production corporations and housing from 1,000 to more than 100,000 animals each. Currently, ten corporations produce 92 percent of all domestic poultry and fifty pork farms account for almost half the nation's pork production.

In Oklahoma, North Carolina, Missouri, Georgia, Colorado, Texas, and Utah—to cite but a few examples—corporate animal production has become a major agricultural industry and the provocation for bitter political conflict. The EPA estimates that groundwater in seventeen states has been impaired by fecal streptococci and fecal coliform bacteria originating on animal feedlots. In these states, CAFOs are more than an environmentalist matter: they set smaller family farmers against corporate farms, rural legislators against urban ones, and economic boomers against proponents of slow growth.

The EPA has found it difficult to regulate very large CAFOs under existing provisions of the Clean Water Act, the Safe Drinking Water Act (SDWA), and various groundwater control measures. Essentially, it has relied on voluntary cooperation from CAFOs and state regulators to manage the problem. The states vary enormously in the extent to which their existing water pollution laws control CAFOs. Intense disputes have become common concerning how strictly CAFOs should be regulated and whether their continued proliferation should be encouraged. Congressional members from every state experiencing a growth surge in large CAFOs have introduced legislation calling for a comprehensive federal regulatory program affecting all states and thereby eliminating the possibility that some states might create so-called pollution havens for large CAFOs. Although President Clinton called for newer, more stringent regulations in his 1998 Clean Water Action Plan, neither Congress nor the responsible federal regulatory agencies initiated tougher comprehensive measures, an impasse due largely to conflicts between Washington and the states over their respective roles in a new regulatory regime and to disagreement among major corporate animal producers over acceptable regulations.

Results: Is "Significant" Really Significant. The nation did not eliminate all pollution discharges into its waters by 1985, nor did it make even most waterways "fishable and swimmable" by mid-1983, as the FWPCAA intended. The combined impacts of the multi-billion-dollar construction grants program and the national permit system for pollution dischargers have prevented the additional degradation of many surface waters, reduced pollution in others, and undoubtedly saved some high-quality waters from degradation. But evidence of a major, long-term improvement in the overall quality of the nation's surface waters is, as noted earlier, quite elusive. Considering the nation's population growth and economic expansion since 1980, the stability of water quality must be considered an achievement of sorts—it could have been much worse. But the quality of the nation's surface water apparently is not greatly improved, and the goals of the FWPCAA still seem decades from achievement.

There is no convincing evidence that massive governmental spending on municipal waste-water treatment plants has significantly improved the nation's surface waters. Since 1960 the federal and state governments have spent more than $113 billion to construct or upgrade these facilities.[32] This governmental largess has certainly produced high-quality treatment plants in abundance. Since 1970 more than eight thousand projects in five thousand municipalities have been undertaken. Today almost three-quarters of all municipal facilities achieve at least secondary treatment for their wastes, and the proportion of the nation served by these high-quality plants has risen from 42 to 56 percent.[33] But more high-technology treatment plants do not necessarily mean better water quality. The amount of pollutants dumped into the nation's surface waters from municipalities has decreased, but how much this decrease has improved water quality is unclear.[34] Monitoring data and other information essential to assessing the impact of the construction grants on surface-water quality are inadequate. Existing information is often inconsistent. And so things will remain as long as the dull but essential task of data collection remains politically unattractive and underfunded.

Groundwater

During the 1980s the nation's groundwater became a major concern. Lying below the earth's upper porous surface and a lower layer of impermeable rock, groundwater percolates through the upper layer and collects until it eventually saturates subsurface soil and rock. Much of this water flows slowly to the sea through permeable layers of sand or gravel called aquifers. These aquifers sustain the life and vitality of communities throughout much of the United States. Groundwater is as essential as surface water to the nation's existence and far more abundant: the annual flow of groundwater is fifty times the volume of surface flows, and most lies within one-half mile of the earth's surface. Almost 50 percent of the U.S. population and 95 percent of its rural residents depend on groundwater for domestic uses. More than 40 percent of all agricultural irrigation originates from groundwater. Because groundwater filters slowly through many levels of fine soil as it percolates downward and flows onward through the aquifers, it traditionally has been virtually free of harmful pollutants. Today, however, groundwater is seriously degraded in many areas of the United States.

Almost every state has one or more sources of serious groundwater contamination. The U.S. Office of Technology Assessment first reported the good news in 1984 that only 1 to 2 percent of the nation's available groundwater was known to be contaminated and then delivered the bad news that "this may be an underestimate because monitoring for contamination has focused on public water supplies . . . while the release of substances known to contaminate ground water is undoubtedly widespread."[35]

Although groundwater monitoring has improved since then, the complexity of groundwater systems and the expense of monitoring have convinced the EPA that "we may never have a complete picture of the nature and extent of the problem."[36] But the EPA has identified an enormous number of actual or potential sources of groundwater contamination:

• About 13,000 hazardous waste sites that are now potential candidates for the Superfund National Priority List (an inventory of the most dangerous sites)
• Millions of septic systems
• More than 180,000 surface impoundments, such as pits, ponds, and lagoons
• An estimated 500 hazardous waste land disposal facilities and about 16,000 municipal and other landfills
• Millions of underground storage tanks
• Thousands of underground injection wells, used to dispose of hazardous and solid wastes by flushing them into deep aquifers
• Millions of tons of pesticides and fertilizers spread on the ground, mostly in rural areas

Many Programs, Many Governments, Many Agencies. The 1977 discovery of massive groundwater contamination caused by the abandoned hazardous waste site at New York's Love Canal became the nation's first groundwater crisis. Groundwater contamination has been a crisis-driven issue, thrust on governmental agendas by waves of public apprehension following revelations of widespread groundwater contamination from hazardous waste dumps, agricultural chemicals, and industrial and governmental chemical accidents. Improved monitoring also has added urgency to the groundwater issue by revealing previously unknown chemical contamination (although often in only trace amounts). But monitoring has just begun, and the quality of most underground waters remains unknown.

Traditionally, groundwater management has been considered a state and local governmental responsibility. Although the federal government has no comprehensive groundwater management program, approximately forty-five different federal programs affect groundwater in some manner.[37] The primary federal responsibility for implementing many of the major programs affecting groundwater rests with the EPA. In addition to the FWPCAA, other important legislation affecting groundwater quality includes the Marine Protection, Research and Sanctuaries Act (1972); the SDWA (1974) and its 1986 amendments; the Resource Conservation and Recovery Act (1976); and the Superfund legislation (1980) together with its 1984 amendments. However, many other agencies and programs are also involved. The melange of federal agencies and programs involved in groundwater management ensures incoherence, inconsistency, and competing authority in the federal government's approach to groundwater problems.

The states' considerable responsibility for groundwater management has been acquired through federal legislation and their own initiative. Forty-one states currently have their own groundwater-quality standards, although little consistency exists among them. The number of groundwater contaminants regulated varies from 14 in one state to 190 in another. In addition, almost all states have assumed responsibility for implementing federal drinking water standards established under the SDWA.

Controlling subsurface pollution is troublesome because groundwater filters very slowly as it flows. An aquifer may move no more than ten to one hundred feet annually. In any case, many toxic contaminants are not captured or neutralized by filtering. Moreover, the extent of groundwater pollution may be impossible to estimate adequately because the pollution plume radiating outward through an aquifer from a pollution source can take a number of unpredictable directions. Often, plumes will contaminate millions or billions of gallons of water.

Many sources of groundwater contamination, however, are still being identified. The nation's estimated 1.2 million abandoned oil and gas wells, of which perhaps 200,000 are not properly plugged, are examples. Abandoned wells, often drilled to a depth of more than one mile, can contaminate groundwater with brine, which is four times more saline than seawater and contains heavy metals, radioactivity, and other possible toxics. In Texas, perhaps 40,000 to 50,000 abandoned wells may pose pollution problems, and an estimated 386,000 wells have never been registered. Said one Texas health official, "We've found leaking wells from the old days that were rock-plugged, bucket-plugged, tree-stump plugged and even one plugged with nothing more than a glass jug." In Louisiana, almost fifteen hundred unplugged wells are uncontrolled because money is lacking.[38]

Continuing Chemical Contamination. The many substances known or suspected to contaminate groundwater defy concise enumeration. One survey indicated that the states collectively have set standards for approximately 35 inorganic compounds, 39 volatile organic compounds, 125 nonvolatile organic compounds, and 56 pesticides, among other substances.[39] These chemicals represent only a small portion of those used in the U.S. economy and found in groundwater. These contaminants originate from many sources. The states are just beginning to regulate many of these sources, such as underground storage tanks, underground injection wells, and abandoned waste sites. Although most states have at least some standards for groundwater quality, it is unclear how well the standards are enforced. Among groundwater contaminants, synthetic chemicals and nutrients, particularly nitrates and phosphates, remain especially difficult to regulate because of their great number and wide diffusion in the ecosystem.

Most states set standards for and monitor only a fraction of the chemicals likely to be present in groundwater. Almost all states identify toxics as a major source of water-quality problems. These toxics can originate in thousands of abandoned and poorly regulated hazardous waste sites or from agricultural activity, injection wells, municipal landfills, and sludges. Sludges—the semisolid wastes produced in many air and water pollution control activities—often contain many hazardous or toxic chemicals. Municipal waste treatment plants in the United States annually produce more than 7.7 million dry metric tons of hazardous sludge, and this figure more than doubled by the year 2000. The dangerous chemicals removed from water as sludge frequently infiltrate the ecosystem again when they migrate to surface and underground water. Many states as yet have no regulatory program to manage this cross-media pollution migration.[40]

During the 1990s federal and state regulators made three chemical groundwater contaminants a priority: nutrients, pesticides, and underground storage tanks (USTs). Nutrients, such as nitrates, are found most often in groundwater affected by agricultural production, including both crops and livestock. Recent estimates indicate that nitrate concentrations exceeding federal standards are found in about 12 percent of domestic water supply wells; trace amounts, not considered dangerous, are more often found in wells near agriculture activity.[41] Nitrate infiltration is not now considered a major national problem, but pesticides and USTs are more troublesome. In the 1990s at least 143 pesticides and 21 of their transformation products were detected in the groundwater of forty-three states. These pesticide concentrations usually do not exceed state water-quality standards for agricultural areas. However, pesticides may be a more serious problem in nonagricultural areas, particularly around golf courses, commercial and residential areas, rights-of-way, timber production and processing areas, and public gardens. In any case, pesticides are ubiquitous in all U.S. waters. The U.S. Geological Survey reported that more than 90 percent of the water and fish samples from all streams contained one or several pesticides, and half the wells sampled contained pesticides—all evidence that pesticides have seriously infiltrated groundwater.

A major concern is the limited information available about the health effects associated with exposure to most pesticides, even in trace amounts. Federal groundwater standards, called maximum contaminant limits (MCLs), have yet to be established for most of these pesticides. Existing MCLs are often based on incomplete information. The U.S. Geological Survey cautioned,

> Existing criteria may be revised as more is learned about the toxicity of these compounds. . . . MCLs and other criteria are currently based on individual pesticides and do not account for possible cumulative effects if several dif-

ferent pesticides are present in the same well. Finally, many pesticides and most transformation products have not been widely sampled for in ground water and very little sampling has been done in urban and suburban areas, where pesticide use is often high.[42]

Governmental concern about USTs grew steadily through the 1990s with the increasing number of discovered sites. Five to six million tanks, most used for retail gasoline or petroleum storage, are buried throughout the United States. Of the 1.7 million tanks currently regulated, at least 300,000 are known to be leaking.[43] These leaks contaminate the groundwater, damage sewer lines and buried cables, poison crops, and ignite fires and explosions. More than 80 percent of the tanks in use were constructed of bare steel, are easily corroded, and had to be replaced or severely modified to meet new federal standards mandated in the mid-1990s. Unfortunately, many of these tanks have been abandoned and long forgotten. Often located under active or abandoned gasoline stations, airports, large trucking firms, farms, golf courses, and manufacturing plants, many leaking sites may never be discovered.

Federal law required all known USTs to comply with stringent new control standards by December 1998. As a result, 1.3 million substandard USTs have been closed, and about 760,500 are registered under the new standards with regulators. However, discovering and controlling the remaining USTs will be a formidable matter. Among those yet to be controlled, half of the abandoned USTs known to regulators have been orphaned (that is, no identifiable owner can be found), and perhaps as many as half of the remaining abandoned USTs (an estimated 76,000) may never be located.[44]

Drinking Water

One need look no further than the kitchen tap for an emerging groundwater concern. All ecosystems are intricately and subtly interrelated. The negligent dumping of contaminants into surface water and groundwater eventually follows a circle of causality, delivering the danger back to its source. So it is in the United States.

The average American uses one hundred gallons of water daily (most of it to water lawns and wash motor vehicles). More than 80 percent of the nation's community water systems depend on groundwater for domestic use, and the remainder use surface water to provide Americans with the one billion glasses of drinking water consumed daily. Recognizing that community drinking water was threatened by the rising volume of pollutants entering surface and groundwater, Congress passed in 1974 the SDWA to ensure that public water supplies achieved minimum health standards. In

1977 the EPA, following the SDWA's mandate, began to set national primary drinking water standards that established maximum levels in drinking water for microbiological contaminants, turbidity, and chemical agents, and by 1985, standards existed for approximately thirty substances. Standard-setting lagged badly at the EPA, however, and in another demonstration of excessive congressional control, the 1986 amendments to the SDWA required the EPA to adopt standards for sixty-one more contaminants by mid-1989, create twenty-five more standards from a new list by 1991, and set standards for twenty-five additional chemicals every three years thereafter. Once standards are established, the states are given primary responsibility for enforcing them, and other provisions of the act, on more than seventy-nine thousand public water systems. Since the 1986 amendments were written, the number of regulated contaminants has expanded to 72 and is expected to reach 120 by 2010.

By 1996 it was apparent that this excursion into legislative micromanagement was ill conceived, and in an enlightened moment rare to its oversight of the EPA, Congress relaxed its grip on the EPA's regulatory process with the 1996 amendments to the SDWA. The amendments instructed the EPA to focus its efforts on the highest-risk drinking water contaminants with special attention to those particularly dangerous to the elderly and children—a more manageable and productive task. Equally important, the 1996 amendments contained right-to-know provisions requiring all community drinking water systems to provide consumers with periodic information about the quality of their drinking water, about compliance with existing federal and state quality controls, and about opportunities for public involvement in local drinking water regulation. The states welcomed other provisions of the amendments offering federal financial assistance to upgrade local water systems because a great many states lacked the financial, technical, and staff resources to enforce even the SDWA's minimum standards and many small and large water systems were virtually ignored.

In many respects, the SDWA has been a success. By the end of the 1990s about 90 percent of the U.S. population was served by community water systems with no reported violations of existing health-based standards, and almost one hundred contaminants were regulated under the act.[45] Unfortunately, many water systems, including some of the largest, are still infiltrated by dangerous concentrations of chemical and biological contaminants, many for which no standards exist and, as a consequence, no regulatory controls exist. In many cases, existing treatment technologies cannot fully remove many microbial and chemical contaminants, including synthetic organic compounds and pesticides.

Injection wells appear to be a major source of drinking water contamination. More than 253,000 active or abandoned injection wells exist in the

United States. About half of the liquid hazardous waste generated in the United States is pumped into these injection wells, the largest portion from oil and gas production and refining facilities. Although liquid hazardous wastes are subject to federal regulation, no detailed national standards exist for solid waste eliminated through injection wells. Rural water supplies seem especially vulnerable to contamination from injection wells and abandoned hazardous waste sites. A 1984 EPA assessment of rural water quality reported unsafe levels of cadmium in about one-sixth of the nation's rural wells, mercury concentrations above safe levels in about one-quarter of the wells, and lead at dangerous levels in one-tenth of these wells.

Conclusion

Air and water are the primary issues on the environmental agenda. They are the first, most essential, most politically visible, and most important tasks of environmental restoration and regulation. The condition of the nation's air and water has been examined in considerable detail in this chapter to emphasize the daunting scope and complexity of the challenge of ecological restoration and to illustrate how short a distance the United States has traveled toward that goal since environmentalism emerged as a major political force in the country in the 1970s.

This chapter illustrates that difficulties in cleaning up the nation's air and water cannot be blamed solely on political incompetence, policy deficiencies, administrative failures, or scientific bungling. Rather, scientific and technological development continually poses new challenges to regulation by creating new chemicals, and new technologies, with unanticipated environmental effects. In addition, scientific research continually redefines and elaborates the nature of environmental degradation and its consequences— as shown in the study of airborne particulates and toxics, for instance— forcing continual rethinking and change in regulatory strategies. And even so unexciting and obscure an activity as environmental monitoring leads to new definitions of environmental degradation, as the study of groundwater contamination reveals. The United States, as with all other nations now committed to environmental restoration, must suffer a learning curve: it must acquire experience in a policy domain with which no government on earth was involved a scant few decades ago. Those who govern can learn, but it takes time.

This review of the nation's current air and water pollution control programs is a sobering reminder that it will take a very long time, and require an enormous amount of money, scientific resources, and administrative skill, to give us back the healthful air and water we once had and hope to have again. So formidable a goal will not be easily realized. It may not happen in the lifetime of any American living today.

Suggested Readings

Bryner, Gary C. *Blue Skies, Green Politics: The Clean Air Act and Its Implementation,* 2nd ed. Washington, D.C.: CQ Press, 1995.

Cohen, Richard E. *Washington at Work: Back Rooms and Clean Air.* New York: Macmillian, 1992.

Morag-Levine, Noga. *Chasing the Wind: Regulating Air Pollution in the Common Law State.* Princeton, N.J.: Princeton University Press, 2003.

Rogers, Peter. *America's Water: Federal Role and Responsibilities.* Cambridge, Mass.: MIT Press, 1999.

Thornton, Joe. *Pandora's Poison: Chlorine, Health, and a New Environmental Strategy.* Cambridge, Mass.: MIT Press, 2000.

Notes

1. Environmental Protection Agency, "Air Trends," www.epa.gov/air/airtrends/sixpoll. html, March 1, 2007.

2. U.S. General Accounting Office, "EPA: Major Performance and Accountability Challenges," Report No. GAO-01-257 (January 2001), 16.

3. U.S. Environmental Protection Agency, Office of Water, "Water Quality Conditions in the United States: A Profile from the 1998 National Water Quality Inventory Report to Congress," EPA Document No. EPA-841-F-00-006 (June 2000), 1.

4. David D. Doniger, *The Law and Policy of Toxic Substances Control* (Baltimore: Johns Hopkins University Press, 1978), 67.

5. Francis E. Rourke, *Bureaucracy, Politics, and Public Policy* (Boston: Little, Brown, 1969), 103.

6. Paul B. Downing and James N. Kimball, "Enforcing Pollution Laws in the U.S.," *Policy Studies Journal* 11 (September 1982): 55–65.

7. U.S. General Accounting Office, "EPA Cannot Ensure the Accuracy of Self-Reported Compliance Monitoring Data," Report No. GAO/RCED 93-21 (March 1993), 4; and U.S. General Accounting Office, "Air Pollution: Difficulties in Implementing a National Air Permit Program," Report No. GAO/RCED 93-59 (February 1993), 2.

8. U.S. General Accounting Office, "Air Pollution: EPA Should Improve Oversight of Emissions Reporting by Large Facilities," Report No. GAO 01-46 (April 2001), 2.

9. Environmental Protection Agency, "Climate Change-Greenhouse Gas Emissions," www.epa.gov/climatechange/emissions/index.html#proj, March 12, 2007, based on data from U.S. Department of State, *U.S. Climate Action Report-2002* (Washington, D.C.: U.S. Department of State, 2002); for other U.S. projections, see Environmental Protection Agency, *Inventory of U.S. Greenhouse Gas Emissions and Sinks: 1990–2004,* Document No. USEPA #430-R-06-002 (April 2006); and Juliet Eilperin, "Ex-EPA Chiefs Agree on Greenhouse Gas Lid," *Washington Post,* January 19, 2006, A04.

10. Brent D. Yacobucci, "Sport Utility Vehicles, Mini-Vans, and Light Trucks: An Overview of Fuel Economy and Emissions Standards," Congressional Reference Service, Report No. RS 20298 (January 16, 2001).

11. Keith Bradsher, "Study Says Height Makes S.U.V.'s Dangerous in Collisions," Top of Form *New York Times,* May 16, 2001, C4.

12. These summaries are adapted from Gary C. Bryner, *Blue Skies, Green Politics: The Clean Air Act of 1990 and Its Implementation,* 2d ed. (Washington, D.C.: CQ Press, 1995), chap. 4.

13. Ibid., 126.

14. *"States Faulted on Inspections," New York Times,* March 11, 1989, B6.

15. *New York Times,* March 29, 1989.

16. James E. McCarthy, "Clean Air Act Issues," Issue Brief 97007 (Washington, D.C.: Congressional Research Service, October 8, 1997).

17. U.S. Environmental Protection Agency, Office of Air and Radiation, *1995 National Air Quality Trends Brochure: Particulate Matter (PM-10)* (Washington, D.C.: Environmental Protection Agency, 1997).

18. Environmental Protection Agency, "Air Trends" at www.epa.gov/air/airtrends/sixpoll. html, March 1, 2007.

19. The Environmental Literacy Council, *New Clean Air Regulations,* May 5, 2003, www.enviroliteracy.org/article.php/537.html, March 20, 2004.

20. The details of this controversy are described by Katherine Q. Seelye, "Regulators Urge Easing U.S. Rules on Air Pollution," *New York Times,* January 8, 2002, A10; and Christopher Drew and Richard Oppel Jr., "Remaking Energy Policy: How Power Lobby Won Battle of Pollution Control at E.P.A.," *New York Times,* March 6, 2004, A10.

21. For details, see Earth Justice, *Lawsuit Challenges Gutting of Crucial Clean Air Act Program,* October 27, 2003, www.earthjustice.org/news/print.html?ID=705, March 20, 2004.

22. U.S. General Accounting Office, "Water Quality: Identification and Remediation of Polluted Waters Impeded by Data Gaps," Report No. GAO/T-RCED 00-88 (February 2000), 5; see also U.S. General Accounting Office, "The Nation's Waters: Key Unanswered Questions about the Quality of Rivers and Streams," Report No. GAO/PEMD 86-6 (September 1986), 3.

23. Robert Zener, "The Federal Law of Water Pollution Control," in *Federal Environmental Law,* ed. Erica L. Dolgin and Thomas G. P. Guilbert (St. Paul, Minn.: West, 1974), 694.

24. U.S. General Accounting Office, "Drinking Water Quality," Report No. GAO/RCED 97-123 (July 29, 1997), 3–4.

25. U.S. Environmental Protection Agency, *Environmental Progress and Challenges: EPA's Update* (Washington, D.C.: U.S. Environmental Protection Agency, 1996), 49.

26. U.S. General Accounting Office, "National Water Quality Inventory Does not Accurately Represent Water Quality Conditions Nationwide," Report No. GAO/RCED 00-54, March 22, 27.

27. National Academy of Sciences, Commission on Geosciences, Environment and Resources, *Assessing the TMDL Approach to Water Quality Management: Executive Summary* (Washington, D.C.: National Academies Press, 2000), 2.

28. Michael Satchell, "Hog Heaven—and Hell," *U.S. News & World Report,* January 22, 1996, 55, 57–59. See also Natural Resources Defense Council, *America's Animal Factories: How States Fail to Prevent Pollution from Livestock Waste,* December 1998, www.nrdc.org/water/pollution/factor/aafinx.asp, March 30, 2004.

29. U.S. Environmental Protection Agency, "Corporate Animal Feeding Operations (CAFO)-Final Rule," http://cfpub.epa.gov/npdes/afo/cafofinalrule. cfm?program_id=7, February 6, 2007.

30. Kelley J. Donham, Steven Wing, David Osterberg, Jan L. Flora, Carol Hodne, Kendall M. Thul, and Peter S. Thorn, "Community Health and Socioeconomic Issues Surrounding Concentrated Animal Feeding Operations," *Environmental Health Perspectives,* February 2007, 1.

31. Peter S. Thorne, "Environmental Health Impacts of Concentrated Animal Feeding Operations: Anticipating Hazards—Searching for Solutions," *Environmental Health Perspectives* (February 2007): 1.

32. U.S. General Accounting Office, "The Nation's Waters," 87.

33. U.S. Environmental Protection Agency, *Environmental Progress and Challenges,* 46.

34. Conservation Foundation, *State of the Environment: A View toward the Nineties* (Washington, D.C.: Conservation Foundation, 1987), 105.

35. U.S. Office of Technology Assessment, *Protecting the Nation's Groundwater from Contamination: Volume I* (Washington, D.C.: U.S. Office of Technology Assessment, 1984).

36. U.S. Environmental Protection Agency, *Environmental Progress and Challenges,* 52.

37. U.S. General Accounting Office, "Groundwater Quality: State Activities to Guard against Contaminants," Report No. GAO/PEMD 88-5 (February 1988), 13.

38. Thomas C.Hayes, "Making a Difference; Taking On Big Oil," *New York Times,* Top of Form April 12, 1992, 3(14).
39. U.S. General Accounting Office, "Groundwater Quality," 38–39.
40. U.S. General Accounting Office, "Water Pollution: Serious Problems Confront Emerging Municipal Management Program," Report No. GAO/RCED 90-57 (March 1990), 3.
41. David K. Mueller and Donald R. Helsel, "Nutrients in the Nation's Waters—Too Much of a Good Thing?" *U.S. Geological Survey Circular 1136* (Washington, D.C.: U.S. Geological Survey, 1996).
42. U.S. Geological Survey, *Pesticides in Ground Water,* USGS Fact Sheet FS-255-95 (Washington, D.C.: U.S. Geological Survey, 1995).
43. U.S. Environmental Protection Agency, *Securing Our Legacy* (Washington, D.C.: U.S. Environmental Protection Agency, 1988); and U.S. Environmental Protection Agency, *Environmental Progress and Challenges,* 102–03.
44. U.S. Environmental Protection Agency, Office of Underground Storage Tanks, *The UST Corrective Action Program* (Washington, D.C.: U.S. Environmental Protection Agency, 1997); see also U.S. Environmental Protection Agency, Office of Underground Storage Tanks, "Report to Congress on a Compliance Plan for the Underground Storage Tank Program," Document No. EPA-510-R-00-001 (June 2000).
45. U.S. Environmental Protection Agency, Office of Water, "Drinking Water: Past, Present, and Future," Document No. EPA-816-F-00-002 (February 2000).

Chapter 7

A Regulatory Thicket:
Toxic and Hazardous Substances

As a result of their tests, the [Consumer Product Safety Commission; CPSC] issued a public statement last year reassuring consumers they had nothing to worry about: "Based on the extremely low levels of lead found in our tests, in most cases, children would have to rub their lunchbox and then lick their hands more than 600 times every day, for about 15–30 days, in order for the lunchbox to present a health hazard."

But the results were disconcerting to experts who reviewed them for the Associated Press. "They found levels that we consider very high," said Alexa Engelman, a researcher at the Oakland, California-based Center for Environmental Health, which has filed a series of legal complaints about lead in lunchboxes. Said Rep. Henry Waxman, D-California: "I am concerned that the CPSC has failed to protect children from an unnecessary hazard they have known about for some time. We should protect our children by banning lead in all children's products.

—Associated Press, "Lead-laden Lunchboxes OK'd by Government," CNN News, February 18, 2007[1]

Because of a general lack of data on new chemicals, EPA has developed methods to predict their potential exposure and toxicity levels by using scientific models to compare the new chemicals with chemicals that have similar molecular structures and for which toxicity information is available. However, the use of these models can be problematic because the models are not always accurate in predicting chemical properties and EPA's evaluation of general health effects of the chemicals is contingent upon the availability of information on chemicals with similar molecular structures. Additionally, the estimates of a chemical's production volume and anticipated uses . . . can change substantially after EPA completes its review.

—U.S. Government Accountability Office, August 2, 2006[2]

If legal historians should choose a Top Ten in Toxic Litigation, a place surely will be reserved for the small community of Glen Avon, California. There, in early 1993, a legal spectacle began that demanded superlatives. "It's got to be among the top five civil cases in the history of American jurisprudence," one defense lawyer burbled as the proceedings began. Indeed, everything seemed dramatically oversized, like a production from some Hollywood of Hazardous Waste.[3] After eight years of planning and screening of two thousand jurors, the trial began with thirty-seven hundred plaintiffs (all Glen Avon residents); thirteen defendants, including the state of California and major corporations such as Rockwell International, Northrop, McDonnell Douglas, and Montrose Chemicals; and injury claims exceeding $800 million. At issue was liability for injuries alleged to have been inflicted on Glen Avon residents from exposure to more than two hundred chemicals in thirty-four million gallons of waste dumped into the Stringfellow Canyon between 1956 and 1972.

By the time the trial began, Glen Avon residents had already received more than $50 million in damages from one hundred companies that had used the site for dumping, but $22 million had been spent to initiate the new trial. The thirty lawyers and twenty-four jurors would eventually review more than 300,000 pages of court documents and 13,000 defense and 3,600 plaintiff exhibits for the initial proceeding. By then, the Stringfellow site had graduated from top billing on the U.S. Environmental Protection Agency (EPA) National Priority List of the nation's worst abandoned waste sites to "one of the most contaminated sites on the planet."[4]

The trial has been held in installments. The first trial, involving seventeen plaintiffs, ended on September 17, 1993, when the jury found the state of California responsible for allowing toxic releases from the Stringfellow site but awarded the plaintiffs only $159,000 of the $3.1 million they had claimed in damages. The second trial, which began in September 1994, involved plaintiffs claiming much more serious injuries. In 1994 most of the plaintiffs settled out of court and the number of plaintiffs was reduced to only 763. The next year, the federal court ruled that the state of California was liable for all the site cleanup costs. After three more years of litigation, California agreed to assume the cleanup costs if seventeen private plaintiffs dropped their demands for $90 million in reimbursement for their own cleanup costs.

In early 2000 another federal judge determined that only 135 of the 763 remaining plaintiffs still had standing-to-sue status (see Chapter 3). This litigation will continue, by conservative estimate, through 2010. Estimates also suggest that the site may require four hundred years of remediation at a cost of $740 million. In 2000, California also initiated lawsuits against thirty-five of its own insurers for refusing to compensate the state for the Stringfellow cleanup costs. In early 2005, sixteen insurers finally settled with the state for $93 million in cleanup costs (which made the list of "The 100 Top Insurance Verdicts of 2005" in one legal publication).[5] Trials began in 2006 for the first of the remaining 19 insurers. Meanwhile, California is spending more than $10 million annually to clean up and monitor the waste site.

The box score: More than thirty-five years from site closure to latest litigation, $150 million spent on cleanup, $96 million in current settlement costs, seventeen acres of contaminated ground, and thirty-four million gallons of toxic waste for which to account.[6] Considering the magnitude of the site contamination and the cleanup so far accomplished, the EPA impetuously claimed Stringfellow a "success story."[7] But new pollution still appears: In 2002, plumes of the chemical perchlorate were discovered contaminating drinking water wells near the site. It may also take decades before the emotional pain associated with the Stringfellow site dissipates from Glen Avon's civic life. The local school board voted in 2003 to name a new $60 million school Glen Avon High School only by a narrow three-to-two majority and only after months of bitter contention within the community. Opponents of the new name contended that it helps to perpetuate the Stringfellow stigma and inhibits civic growth. "Glen Avon," explained one civic activist, suggests to many people a community that is "nothing but white trash, toxic waste and toothless women."[8]

The Stringfellow Canyon site is considered among the worst toxic site cleanups ever attempted. Even so, many legal experts believe that the Stringfellow litigation is a signpost along an upward road to ever more expansive and expensive future litigation as hazardous waste regulations multiply and government seeks more aggressively to satisfy public apprehension about toxic and hazardous substances.

An ironic counterpoint to this growing litigation with its burgeoning liability awards has been the mounting disagreement among scientific experts about the extent of public risk from exposure to manufactured, stored, and abandoned chemical substances. Indeed, in no other area of environmental regulation has scientific uncertainty about the extent of risk and identity of hazardous substances been greater or more public.

This chapter is about the ambitious and extraordinarily difficult task of regulating the creation, use, and disposal of the nation's hazardous and toxic wastes. It focuses on four complex federal laws. Congress once predicted that three of these laws—the Toxic Substances Control Act (1976), the Resource Conservation and Recovery Act (1976), and the Comprehensive Environmental Response, Cleanup and Liability Act (known as "Superfund")—would amount to "cradle-to-grave" regulation of toxic and hazardous substances. The fourth law, the Food Quality Protection Act (1996), is an effort to improve this regulation as a result of new concerns about public exposure to hazardous and toxic substances arising since the earlier laws were enacted. Implementing these laws has proved enormously challenging not only because the scope and expense of regulation were vastly underestimated but also because new scientific controversies arise concerning the extent to which existing hazardous and toxic substances—or others continually being created—constitute significant risks to humans or to the environment. To illustrate why these conflicts defy satisfactory resolution, the chapter describes the ongoing scientific and political controversies associated with efforts to regulate a well-known group of chemicals called "dioxins" and another class of chemicals, called "endocrine disruptors," which many critics argue are more political fiction than scientific reality.

In short, cradle-to-grave regulation is no reality, although progress has been made. After many decades of massive public investment in a multitude of regulatory programs aimed at almost every aspect of toxic and hazardous substances, accomplishments seldom satisfy either program proponents or critics—even though (or maybe because) altogether the EPA enforces thirteen major laws affecting hazardous substance use and disposal in the United States. Most of these laws are burdened by the daunting variety of materials to be regulated, by inadequate data on the distribution and effect of these substances on humans and the environment, by political and administrative impediments to implementation, and by widespread public criticism and distrust. These chronic problems gravely debilitate the nation's waste management laws.

An Ambiguous Inheritance

The environmentalist's hell is a firmament of compacted pesticide awash in toxic sludge. Environmentalists are not alone in attributing to chemicals a special malevolence. Most Americans apparently believe that the air, water, and earth are suffused with real or potential toxic menaces. The Gallup Organization polled a sample of Americans in mid-2000 concerning what environmental risks they "personally worry about" and discovered that Americans worried most about (1) drinking-water pollution; (2) river, lake, and reservoir pollution; (3) contamination of soil and water by toxic waste; and (4) air pollution—all more or less associated with chemical substances.[9]

Americans are often misinformed about the extent of environmental risks and frequently exaggerate the danger from environmental pollutants they most fear. But widespread media coverage of hazardous chemical spills, newly discovered abandoned toxic waste sites, and other real or alleged crises involving dangerous substances have forced attention on toxic and hazardous substances and imparted a sense of urgency to resolving the problems. Moreover, mounting evidence about the pervasiveness of potentially dangerous chemicals throughout the United States and uncertainty about the risks they pose to society and the environment increase public apprehension and provoke demands that the government do something to control public exposure to these substances. Toxic and hazardous substances have progressed rapidly from secondary importance in the environmental agenda in the early 1970s to primary concern in the early years of the twenty-first century.

Chemicals

Most toxic and hazardous substances are an inheritance of the worldwide chemical revolution following World War II. The creation of synthetic chemicals continued at such a prolific pace after 1945 that by the mid-1960s the American Chemical Society had registered more than four million chemicals, an increasing proportion of which were synthetics created by U.S. chemists since 1945. Today, about thirty-five thousand chemicals are used daily in U.S. industry. Between five hundred and one thousand new chemicals are created annually. Currently the EPA has more than ten thousand new chemicals pending review, as required by the Toxic Substances Control Act (TSCA) of 1976.[10]

About 98 percent of chemical substances used commercially in the United States (most of them polymers) are considered harmless to humans and the ecosystem. Less than 7 percent of approximately one thousand new chemicals proposed for manufacture and reviewed by the EPA have aroused concern among the agency's scientific review panels.[11] However, about 120,000 establishments in the United States create and distribute chemicals, and the industry's capacity to produce and distribute still more new substances is growing. As new chemicals proliferate and the long-term risks associated with older chemicals are better understood, the need to protect humans and the environment from the relatively small but enormously diverse set of toxic and hazardous substances grows more imperative.

Toxic and Hazardous Chemicals

Although many chemicals have been tested to determine their hazardousness—it is often relatively easy to decide if a chemical is corrosive, ignitable, or otherwise clearly dangerous when handled or abandoned in the environment—few have been tested rigorously to determine their toxicity or risk to human or environmental health. Testing is particularly difficult and expensive when the long-term effects of a chemical are being investigated. Studies may require decades. The lack of data about the human health effects of possibly dangerous chemicals is illustrated in Table 7-1, based on a U.S. General Accounting Office (GAO) survey of potentially harmful chemicals identified by several federal agencies.

Table 7–1   *Availability of Human Exposure Data for Potentially Harmful Chemicals through the EPA and the Department of Health and Human Services*

Priority Chemicals	Chemicals Measured or Being Measured		
Description of list	Number in list	N	%
Chemicals found most often at the national Superfund sites and of most potential threat to human health	275	62	23
EPA's list of toxics of concern in air	168	27	16
Chemicals harmful because of their persistence in the environment, tendency to bioaccumulate in plant or animal tissues, and toxicity	368	52	14
Pesticides of potential concern as listed by EPA's Office of Pesticide Programs and the U.S. Department of Agriculture's Pesticide Data Program	243	32	13
Chemicals that are reported in the Toxic Release Inventory; are considered toxic; and are used, manufactured, treated, transported, or released into the environment	579	50	9
Chemicals most in need of testing under the Toxic Substances Control Act (Master Testing List)	476	10	2

Source: U.S General Accounting Office, "Major Challenges and Program Risks: EPA," Report No. GAO-01-257 (October 2000), 4.

Cancer is the gravest and most widely feared of all toxic impacts from hazardous substances. By 2007, perhaps 1,500 to 2,000 of all chemical substances, a small proportion of all suspected carcinogenic chemicals produced in the United States, had been tested sufficiently to determine their carcinogenicity. Among those tested, more than three hundred showed substantial evidence of carcinogenicity.[12]

The list of chemicals convincingly associated with acute or chronic human cancer is growing slowly. However, persuasive scientific evidence that *environmental* pollutants are causing widespread cancer is still largely unavailable. For example, the National Cancer Institute and the Centers for Disease Control and Prevention reported a lack of confirmed evidence that such pollutants were associated with cancer epidemics. The National Cancer Institute estimated that perhaps 1 to 3 percent of all annual U.S. cancer deaths resulted from exposure to environmental pollution.[13] The elusiveness of data, in turn, seems to the critics of current regulation like a confirmation that existing toxics legislation is scientifically, as well as economically, flawed.

Currently, more than twenty-four federal laws and a dozen federal agencies are concerned with regulating the manufacture, distribution, and disposal of carcinogenic substances. Their work is impeded seriously not only by disagreement over the health risks posed by the many chemicals under their jurisdiction but also by a lack of accurate, current information about the variety and composition of those chemicals.

Pesticides are a large component of toxic and hazardous waste. More than 20,700 pesticides are currently used in the United States. The United States produces more than 1.2 billion pounds of pesticides annually, with more than 890 active ingredients.[14] Pesticides are so widely and routinely used in U.S. agriculture that many farmers believe productivity cannot be sustained without them.

Common foods are treated with dozens of possible carcinogens used widely in commercial agriculture; for example, twenty-five are used for corn, twenty-four for apples, twenty-three for tomatoes, and twenty-one for peaches.[15] Consider the chemical bath in which the dinner table onion was likely raised:

- *Fungicides:* chlorothalonil (Bravo), 2 pints per acre, seven to ten times a year; maneb (Manex), 1 to 3 pounds per acre, seven to ten times a year; metalaxyl (Ridomil), 1.5 to 2 pounds per acre, once a year
- *Insecticides:* Parathion, 0.5 pint per acre, or azinphos methyl (Guthion), 1 to 1.5 pounds per acre, two or three times a season; chlorpyrifos (Lorsban), placed in furrow at planting and sprayed twice to control onion maggots
- *Herbicide:* Oxyfluorfen (Goal), 0.25 ounces per acre, one application a season
- *Sprout inhibitor:* Maleic hydrazide, 2 pounds per acre before harvest to prevent onions from sprouting before they reach market[16]

The EPA has prohibited or restricted the manufacture of more than five hundred commercial chemicals, including many proven carcinogens such as dioxin, asbestos, polychlorinated biphenyls (PCBs), and the pesticide DDT. Even if a substance is restricted or prohibited, the EPA often lacks the resources to implement controls quickly. For example, although the EPA estimates that more than half a million office buildings, apartment houses, stores, and other public or commercial buildings presently contain potentially dangerous loose asbestos, the agency decided as early as 1988 to take no action because the federal government, the states, and the private sector lacked the money and personnel to remove safely the deteriorating asbestos.[17]

Chemical Testing

Chemical testing of any sort is time consuming and costly, but when the long-term effects of a chemical are investigated, studies may require decades. Moreover, substances currently suspected of having toxic effects often have not existed long enough for long-term impacts to be apparent. Today's middle-aged, American blue-collar workers may be the first generation of U.S. laborers to reveal the chronic effects of workplace exposure to chemicals introduced in U.S. industry during World War II. If testing deals with chronic effects of exposure to small quantities of chemicals—doses as small as parts per billion or trillion—difficulties in identifying the presence of the substance and the rate of exposure among affected populations may be formidable. Thus, a major problem in regulating dangerous substances has been to obtain the essential test data on which determinations of risk depend.

Pesticides illustrate the test burden confronting the EPA. Most of the fifty thousand pesticide products used in the United States since 1947 were registered before their long-term effects were understood. Amendments in 1972 to the Federal Insecticide, Fungicide, and Rodenticide Act required the EPA to reevaluate all existing pesticides in light of new information about their effects on humans and the environment. In addition, more than three billion pounds of pesticides are used annually in the United States. These pesticides contain about six hundred active ingredients that must be reviewed by the EPA. The EPA has prohibited, or limited severely, the use of many pesticides, including DDT, aldrin, dieldrin, toxaphene, and ethylene dibromide, and, as a result, levels of persistent pesticides in human fatty tissue had declined from about eight parts per million in 1970 to slightly more than two parts per million by the mid-1980s. However, the EPA is decades behind in reviewing all the active ingredients and the pesticide compounds made from these ingredients.

Toxics

In the 1990s airborne toxics received major federal attention for the first time, adding another large category of substances to the EPA's regulatory responsibilities. The Superfund Amendments and Reauthorization Act (SARA) of 1986 required the EPA to create the first national inventory of toxic releases into the environment from industries in the United States. Almost all these chemicals are among the 188 specifically destined for regulation under the Clean Air Act Amendments of 1990. In broader perspective, the latest Toxic Release Inventory (TRI), issued by the EPA in mid-2006, disclosed that discharges of 650 toxic wastes from all reporting sources totaled about 4.2 billion pounds in 2004, a decrease of 45 percent since the TRI was created.[18] These 2004 discharges included

- 1.549 billion pounds of air emissions;
- 242 million pounds of surface water emissions to streams, rivers, and lakes;

Figure 7-1   TRI Total Disposal or Other Releases, 1988–2004

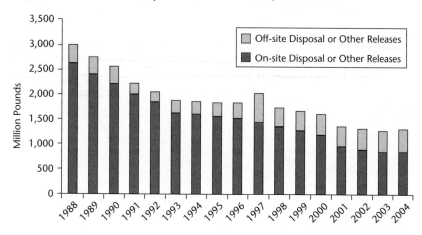

Source: U.S. EPA, *2004 TRI Public Data Release eReport: Data Tables and Charts, Section Charts* (April 2006), A-3.

Note: This information does not indicate whether (or to what degree) the public has been exposed to toxic chemicals. Therefore, no conclusions on the potential risks can be made based solely on this information (including any ranking information). For more detailed information on this subject refer to The Toxics Release Inventory (TRI) and Factors to Consider When using TRI Data document at www.epa.gov/tri/tridata/tri04. Data are from TRI Form, Section 5 (all parts) and Section 6.1 (metals and metal compounds only) and Section 6.2 (disposal codes only and metals and metal compounds reported under codes M40 and M61). Does not include delisted chemicals, chemicals added in 1990, 1994 and 1996, aluminum oxide, ammonia, hydrochloric acid, PBT chemicals, sulfuric acid, vanadium and vanadium compounds. For the year 1998 and after, does not include industries, other than manufacturing industries, that are required to report for 1998 and later years only. Data as of April 2006.

- 238 million pounds of underground waste injections;
- 1.6 billion pounds of direct land releases.

One significant aspect of the 2004 TRI data is the decrease in the total volume of toxic releases by industries consistently reporting since the TRI's creation: Between 1988 (the first reporting year) and 2004, the volume decreased by 57 percent.[19] (See Figure 7-1) However, data from specific industries can be highly variable (for example, toxic metal discharges from mining and underground disposal of toxics increased between 2001–2004). Thus, TRI figures for specific industries and toxics may reveal important trends hidden by aggregate data. What the TRI clearly demonstrates is the scale on which the toxic release problem affects every state and territory (Table 7-2). The TRI has also become an especially effective psychological weapon for environmentalists because the average American now can readily identify the nature and source of toxic releases at home or work.

Table 7-2   *Hazardous Waste Sites on the National Priority List,*
              by State, 2004

State and outlying area	Total sites	Rank	Percent distribution	Federal	Non-federal
Alabama	15	25	1.2	3	12
Alaska	6	44	0.5	5	1
Arizona	9	41	0.7	2	7
Arkansas	10	40	0.8	—	10
California	95	3	7.4	23	72
Colorado	18	21	1.4	3	15
Connecticut	16	23	1.2	1	15
Delaware	14	28	1.1	1	13
District of Columbia	1	(X)	0.1	1	—
Florida	52	6	4.0	6	46
Georgia	15	26	1.2	2	13
Hawaii	3	46	0.2	2	1
Idaho	9	42	0.7	2	7
Illinois	47	7	3.7	5	42
Indiana	30	13	2.3	—	30
Iowa	13	31	1.0	1	12
Kansas	12	33	0.9	2	10
Kentucky	14	29	1.1	1	13
Louisiana	16	24	1.2	1	15
Maine	12	34	0.9	3	9
Maryland	20	19	1.6	9	11
Massachusetts	32	12	2.5	7	25
Michigan	69	5	5.4	1	68
Minnesota	24	18	1.9	2	22
Mississippi	5	45	0.4	—	5
Missouri	26	16	2.0	3	23
Montana	15	27	1.2	—	15
Nebraska	12	35	0.9	1	11
Nevada	1	49	0.1	—	1
New Hampshire	20	20	1.6	1	19
New Jersey	114	1	8.9	8	106
New Mexico	13	32	1.0	1	12
New York	91	4	7.1	4	87
North Carolina	30	14	2.3	2	28
North Dakota	—	50	0.0	—	—
Ohio	37	11	2.9	5	32
Oklahoma	11	37	0.9	1	10
Oregon	11	38	0.9	2	9
Pennsylvania	96	2	7.5	6	90
Rhode Island	12	36	0.9	2	10
South Carolina	26	17	2.0	2	24
South Dakota	2	47	0.2	1	1
Tennessee	14	30	1.1	4	10
Texas	43	9	3.3	4	39
Utah	17	22	1.3	4	13
Vermont	11	39	0.9	—	11
Virginia	30	15	2.3	11	19
Washington	47	8	3.7	14	33
West Virginia	9	43	0.7	2	7

Table 7-2 *Continued*

State and outlying area	Total sites	Rank	Percent distribution	Federal	Non-federal
Wisconsin	39	10	3.0	—	39
Wyoming	2	48	0.2	1	1
Guam	2	(X)	(X)	1	1
Puerto Rico	12	(X)	(X)	1	11
Virgin Islands	2	(X)	(X)	—	2
Total	1,302	(X)	(X)	164	1,138
United States	1,286	(X)	100.0	162	1,124

Source: U.S. Department of Commerce, Bureau of the Census, *Statistical Abstract of the United States, 2006* (Washington, D.C.: Government Printing Office, 2006), 226.

Note: —, zero; X, not applicable. As of December 31. Includes both proposed and final sites listed on the National Priority List for the Superfund program as authorized by the Comprehensive Environmental Response, Compensation, and Liability Act of 1980 and the Superfund Amendments and Reauthorization Act of 1986.

Abandoned Wastes

The discovery in 1978 of a huge abandoned toxic waste site near Niagara Falls, New York, made the site—called Love Canal—a national synonym for chemical contamination. The debacle of Love Canal escalated rapidly into a national media event dramatizing to Americans the apparent danger of abandoned toxic wastes within the United States. A flood tide of further media revelations about abandoned chemical wastes throughout the country followed, together with intense environmentalist lobbying and growing public pressure for congressional response. In the crisis-driven style characteristic of the 1970s, Congress reacted by passing in 1980 the Superfund legislation, which included an appropriation of $1.6 billion to clean up the nation's worst abandoned toxic and hazardous waste sites. By the latter 1990s, however, it was evident that the magnitude of the abandoned waste problem and the cost to clean up the worst abandoned waste sites far exceeded original expectations. Moreover, Superfund's implementation proceeds glacially. The Superfund legislation required the EPA to create a list of the nation's most dangerous hazardous waste sites, called the National Priority List (NPL); to rank the sites according to human health and environmental risk; and to initiate action to clean up sites according to their ranking. The NPL in 2002 included 1,291 sites (Table 7-2). By the year 2004, almost 900 of NPL sites had been cleaned up substantially since 1980 and removed from the NPL list. But new sites are added as others are removed.[20] Moreover, the agency estimates that there are at least fifty thousand eligible sites, and many experts believe the actual number may exceed this estimate by at least twenty thousand.[21] Thus, even though the pace of Superfund site cleanup improved significantly in the 1990s, the program still confronts a huge backlog of contaminated sites while contending with massive cost over-runs, technical complexities, political squabbles, and endless litigation. Moreover, the rate of NPL site cleanup appeared likely to diminish because the pace at which new sites have been added to the NPL list declined to approximately half between the end of Bill Clinton's administration and the end of 2004.[22] Now in its third decade, Superfund lumbers toward a future certain only in political controversy.

Despite the enormous publicity attending Superfund, most of the waste produced each year in the United States is not dangerous when it is disposed of properly. But a ton (literally) of hazardous waste is created annually for every American in the United States. Among the more than fourteen thousand regulated producers of waste, the overwhelming majority are chemical manufacturers or allied industries that produce almost 80 percent of the nation's hazardous waste. Other significant sources include mining and milling, municipal household and commercial waste, and the processing of radioactive materials. America's chemical junkyards are increasing in volume by an estimated 3 to 10 percent annually.

More than half of the nation's liquid waste is flushed into deep underground cavities, or water systems by many industries and municipalities, where it is presumed to disperse too deeply to contaminate water or soil used by humans. However, such disposal is seldom carefully monitored or regulated. Experts suspect that many hazardous materials buried in this way will migrate through subsurface water flows until they contaminate drinking water wells and aquifers used for irrigation, lakes, rivers, or soil. For these reasons, the National Academy of Sciences has recommended that the federal government promote incineration, chemical processing, or other more modern procedures for waste disposal While federal and state water quality regulators have succeeded in diminishing underground disposal, more than 12 million gallons of waste materials are still injected underground.[23]

The Rush to Regulate

Considering all the difficulties involved in regulating toxic and hazardous substances, Congress and environmentalists expected too much of science by requiring in TSCA that all new chemicals be screened before marketing to determine their toxicity. It is difficult, perhaps impossible, to know in advance how a chemical will be used, in what quantities, and where, even though manufacturers are required to provide an estimate in their "Premanufacture Notice" to the EPA.[24]

The Risk Problem

The risk assessment problems discussed in Chapter 4 abound with toxic and hazardous chemical regulation, as illustrated by the continuing controversy over the effects of toxic chemicals on the neighborhood adjacent to the Love Canal dump site. In late 1982 the EPA released the results of a massive inquiry it had made, along with the U.S. Public Health Service, into the health effects of the Love Canal site. Contrary to earlier studies by the State of New York, the EPA asserted that it had found the neighborhood near Love Canal no less safe for residents than any other part of Niagara Falls, New York. The evidence seemed formidable. More than six thousand samples of human and environmental materials near the site were collected and subjected to 150,000 analytical measurements to determine what contaminants they contained. This evidence suggested that only a ring of houses a block from the waste site or closer had been affected significantly. But the study was challenged immediately because 90 percent of the samples were free of *any* chemicals. This result, asserted experts, could mean either an absence of chemicals or insufficient sensitivity among the measuring procedures. Although the assistant secretary for health and the deputy EPA administrator for New York testified to congressional committees that they were confident the undetected chemicals could not be present in more than minute quantities, the Environmental Defense Fund's own scientific expert asserted that so much variance existed in the competence of the many laboratories conducting the tests and that so many sources of error could exist in some tests that chemicals could indeed have been present. Officials at the National Bureau of Standards also questioned the sensitivity of the test procedures. That same year, the federal Centers for Disease Control released its own study of former Love Canal area residents, indicating that they were no more likely to suffer chromosomal damage than residents elsewhere in Niagara Falls. Even if such damage were present, noted the study, it was impossible to know if it was linked to the later occurrence of illnesses.[25]

Uncertainties about risk must almost be assumed to be a constant in regulating hazardous substances, and as a consequence, errors of judgment leading to excessively strict regulation or perhaps to dangerously negligent control of chemical substances are probably inevitable. In general, Congress and the regulatory agencies implementing congressional hazardous waste programs have been risk averse, preferring to err, if err they must, in the direction of stricter control and more willingness to accept pessimistic estimates of risk from toxic substances. Beginning with the later years of Jimmy Carter's administration, however, federal agencies have moved toward greater attention to costs and regulatory complexity in setting standards of exposure and control.

Costs and Complexity

It is doubtful that either friend or foe of the federal regulatory programs enacted in the mid-1970s realistically understood the enormous expense that would be involved in the new hazardous substance legislation. New regulatory agencies would have to be created or existing ones expanded. An inventory of many thousands of chemicals would have to be created, existing literature on the health effects of chemicals searched, new research initiated, new regulations promulgated, litigation involving the legality of new regulatory standards conducted, and so forth. Only as regulatory agencies began the first tentative steps in assembling data on the human and environmental effects of chemical substances did the vast vacuum of relevant information become obvious. A major reason for the protracted delays in implementing the new laws has been the tedious but essential work of building a foundation of necessary technical data on which regulatory standards could be erected. The collective costs to the 14,000 regulated chemical manufacturers will add billions of dollars to the regulatory total.

A small sample of direct and indirect costs associated with recent hazardous substance legislation can only suggest the scale on which such regulatory programs must operate:

> The average priority abandoned waste site cleaned up by the EPA under Superfund legislation has cost $2.1 million and will cost far more in the future; the aggregate expense for eliminating all the nation's worst abandoned waste sites is expected to be many times the initial Superfund authorization of $1.6 billion.[26]

> The EPA's regulations for disposal of hazardous waste on land sites exceeded 500 pages in the *Federal Register*. EPA officials say the costs of compliance for the affected industries will exceed $1 billion yearly.[27]

When massive costs are projected against the fragmentary scientific data on the effects of many chemicals and the often tenuous evidence relating to chronic impacts from extremely low levels of exposure, arguments over the acceptability of the costs in light of the benefits inevitably arise. Critics of federal environmental programs have asserted that most impose not only unacceptable costs for the regulation of acknowledged hazards but also staggering costs for the stringent control of substances with unproven effects. Some critics, including leaders in the administrations of Ronald Reagan and George H. W. Bush, argued that costs and benefits should become a routinely important—though not necessarily the most important—factor in determining whether a substance should be regulated.

Criticism of regulatory costs often feeds on the disparity between the timing and character of the costs and the timing and character of the benefits from regulation. The costs tend to be tangible, immediate, and massive: dollars must be spent, agencies created, rules promulgated, and other expensive actions initiated. In contrast, years or decades may pass before any apparent benefits accrue. The benefits may be intangibles—deaths and illnesses prevented, public costs of future regulation avoided, or public safety enhanced—that tend to be discounted by those who must pay for regulation in the present. Examples exist that show how the future benefits of regulation can be enormous. The number of U.S. deaths from exposure to asbestos as much as forty years ago will grow to between eight and ten thousand annually. More than 200,000 claims outstanding against major asbestos manufacturers at the beginning of the twenty-first century must be settled. The current value of these future claims has been estimated conservatively at $40 billion.[28]

A Continuing Controversy: Endocrine Disruptors

The list of worrisome chemicals enlarged in the latter 1990s when scientific and governmental attention turned suddenly to a potentially huge inventory of chemicals called endocrine disruptors. Scientific research has suggested that certain externally produced chemicals, especially many human-made synthetic compounds, may sometimes mimic naturally produced hormones in humans and animals and may interfere, perhaps disastrously, with the normal functioning of the endocrine system. Many of these disruptors, according to some scientific theories, gain their potency from the bioaccumulation of extremely small doses in human and animal tissue over long periods of time. The possible human health effects could include cancers of the reproductive system, reduced sperm counts in males, abnormalities of fetal development leading to learning and behavioral disorders, and many other pathologies associated with hormonal malfunctions. Some scientists believe that disruptors have been responsible for sexual abnormalities and deformities in gulls, terns, eagles, and fish.[29]

If endocrine disruptors exist, apprehension seems prudent. "The number of substances which have been suggested as possibly contributing to perturbation of the endocrine system . . . is vast," explained one careful study of the issue.

> Man-made or generated substances include broad classes of chlorinated and non-chlorinated compounds and heavy metals widely used in industrial and household products such as paints, detergents, lubricants, cosmetics, textiles, pesticides, and plastics, as well as byproducts of sewage treatment and waste incineration and other forms of combustion. Many pharmaceutical products, including contraceptives, have hormonal activity. There are also large amounts of plant hormones (mainly phytoestrogens) commonly ingested in human (and animal) diets—especially vegetarian products. . . .[30]

In short, there is something to unnerve everybody. Yet the disruptor issue emerges from a fog of enormous uncertainty and scientific controversy. The effect of disruptors on humans and animals, the identity of truly dangerous substances, the results of long- and short-term exposures, the relative dangers to adults and fetuses, and much more are largely unknown. Scientists themselves disagree about the danger. "Even though sound scientific evidence can be found on both sides . . . simple cause and effect data are not available," explained one expert review of the evidence. "But even without certain scientific evidence, the potential health, social and economic effects are forcing government, organizations and the general public to take notice."[31]

The public history of endocrine disruptors is the very model of how environmental issues acquire political clout. Expert meetings held in the United States in 1991 and 1993 first called major scientific attention to the possible danger of endocrine disruptors. However, the issue's political momentum began to mount when the BBC broadcast in 1993 the documentary *Assault on the Male,* which suggested that human and animal reproductive problems might arise from endocrine disruptors. The issue rose to national attention with the publication in 1996 of *Our Stolen Future,* written by a team of U.S. scientific interpreters, who vividly described the menace presumably posed by disruptors:

> Hormone-disrupting chemicals are not classical poisons or typical carcinogens. They play by different rules. They defy the linear logic of current testing protocols built on the assumption that higher doses do more damage. For this reason, contrary to our long-held assumptions, screening chemicals for cancer risk has not always protected us from other kinds of harm. Some hormonally active chemicals appear to pose little if any risk of cancer . . . such chemicals are typically not poisons in the normal sense. Until we recognize this, we will be looking in the wrong places, asking the wrong questions.[32]

This aura of mystery, dread, and imminence proved to be a powerful political catalyst, creating additional media attention, provoking public concern, and compelling a response from government officials. In 1996 Congress passed the Food Quality Protection Act, which amended several major federal environmental and public health laws to require that the EPA within three years create and then implement an endocrine disruptor screening program for chemicals and—as if to prove beyond refutation its environmental vigilance—Congress further mandated the EPA to add an additional ten-fold safety factor to protect infants and children when setting standards for allowable pesticide residues in food, unless reliable data showed that a different factor would be safe. The EPA appointed a scientific advisory committee on endocrine disruptors in 1996, and two years later, it reported that although available data were insufficient to verify the magnitude of risk or the variety of chemicals associated with endocrine disruption, enough evidence existed to justify more intensive research and more public information about the potential problems arising from suspected endocrine disruption.

Although Congress mandated that the EPA craft an endocrine disruptor screening program and implement it by 1999, the administrative and scientific difficulties have frustrated both objectives—additional testimony to the impotence of congressional micromanagement. Also, preliminary estimates suggest that the necessary testing protocols will probably be extremely expensive, perhaps approaching $1 million for each chemical tested, and that tests would be required for many hundreds of chemicals and their compounds. The chemical industry believes that insufficient evidence exists to justify the imposition of such an expensive testing regimen, and scientists themselves disagree about the magnitude of the endocrine disruptor problem. "Every policy paper, every study gets embroiled in scientific disputes over the EPA's assumptions on everything from children's dietary habits to the amount of roach killer an average family is likely to use," observed one progress report.[33] Although the issue predictably attracts public attention, environmental advocates have yet to discover the political leverage to shake the program from its glacial pace.

Chemical Threat or "Chemiphobia"?

Endocrine disruptors raise anew the recurring controversy about whether the public and its governments have become "chemiphobic"— exaggerating the health risks posed by chemicals and intolerant of even reasonable risks. The controversy grows with the relentless increase in the cost and complexity of regulation. Although experts agree that the public should be concerned about health risks associated with exposure to chemical substances and chemical wastes, they cannot easily determine *which* kinds of exposure and *how much* exposure are unacceptably risky. A related issue is that the elimination of *all* risk from exposure to toxic and hazardous substances is often impossible or unacceptably expensive, yet federal regulations such as the Superfund legislation do not clearly define how much cleanup is enough. The problem, two informed critics observed, is "how clean is 'clean,'" and the solution is not apparent. According to political scientists Marc Landy and Mary Hague,

> In principle, one would want to clean until [an abandoned hazardous waste] site is called perfectly "safe." However . . . there is no scientifically identifiable point at which an "unsafe" site becomes "safe." No matter how much cleanup has been performed at a site, it can always be argued that more cleanup would reduce risk even further.[34]

A second issue involves political chemistry. When public fear about hazardous substances blends with official eagerness to appear tough on pollution, the resulting risk-averse political climate often spawns hasty, severe regulatory policies. A political synergy between public fear and governmental overreaction often results, as we observed previously, in targeting for greatest attention those pollutants exciting the greatest public apprehension rather than those posing the most scientifically documented health risks. Risk-averse regulation can result in a regulatory intolerance for even minimal health risks, mistaken environmental priorities, and excessive regulatory costs.

Finally, regulatory costs have been especially controversial in toxic and hazardous substance regulation because of the rapid and severe escalation in the number of regulations and the growing recognition that future regulations will cost enormously more. Federal regulations, for instance, require all municipal landfills to be built with plastic and clay liners, liquid collectors, and treatment systems to prevent leaking toxic waste. These regulations have drastically raised the cost of opening a new municipal landfill and forced most of the country's existing sixty-five hundred landfills to close when retrofitting became too expensive. And future landfill costs may be far greater still as the variety of waste-dump toxics and their health risks are better documented.[35]

To many critics, all these problems are proof of chemiphobia impelling governmental regulators to appease public opinion through excessively harsh chemical controls at enormous economic, scientific, and political cost to the nation. To many conservative critics, these regulations are too often "animated by a quasi-religious mind-set that combines an aversion to even minimal risks with a strong preference for governmental intervention in markets and a fierce hostility toward corporations."[36] Even the many experts who disagree with these conclusions often recognize, as subsequent discussion reveals, that toxic and hazardous substance regulation is the most difficult, least satisfactory domain of contemporary environmental policy making.

Federal Law: Regulation from the Cradle to the Grave?

Among the two dozen federal laws relating to toxic and hazardous substances, four federal laws, three passed in the 1970s, define the fundamental framework for regulating the disposal of these substances: the Toxic Substances Control Act (TSCA) of 1976, the Resource Conservation and Recovery Act (RCRA) of 1976, the Superfund legislation, and the Food Quality Protection Act (1996). These laws represent a congressional effort to create a comprehensive regulatory program for all chemical substances from initial development to final disposal—the cradle-to-grave control that seemed essential to achieving for the first time responsible public management of chemical products. Few laws, even by the standard of recent environmental legislation, mandate a more complex and technically formidable administrative process than do these programs. A brief review of their major provisions suggests the immense regulatory tasks involved.

TSCA: Regulating Chemical Manufacture and Distribution

The major purpose of TSCA and its 1986 amendments (the Asbestos Hazard Emergency Response Act) is to regulate the creation, manufacture, and distribution of chemical substances so that substances hazardous to humans and the environment can be identified early and then controlled properly before they become fugitive throughout the ecosystem. TSCA and its amendments require the EPA to achieve five broad objectives:

1. *Information Gathering.* The EPA is required to issue rules asking chemical manufacturers and processors to submit to the administrator information about their newly developed chemicals. The information is to include the chemical's name, formula, and uses; estimates of production levels; a description of byproducts; data on adverse health and environmental effects; and the number of workers exposed to the chemical. In achieving these goals the administrator also is to
    a. publish a list of all existing chemicals
    b. see that all persons manufacturing, processing, or distributing chemicals in commerce keep records on adverse health reactions, submit to the EPA required health and safety studies, and report to the EPA information suggesting that a chemical represents a previously undetected significant risk to health or the environment
2. *Screening of New Chemicals.* Manufacturers of new chemicals are to notify the EPA at least ninety days before producing the chemical commercially. Information similar to that required for existing chemicals is also required for new chemicals. The EPA is allowed to suspend temporarily the manufacture of any new chemical in the absence of adequate information as required under the law and to suspend production of a new chemical permanently if it finds a "reasonable basis to conclude that the chemical presents or will present an unreasonable risk of injury to health or the environment."[37]
3. *Chemical Testing.* The EPA is given the authority to require manufacturers or processors of potentially harmful chemicals to test them. The Interagency Testing Committee, composed of representatives from eight federal agencies, was created to recommend to the EPA priorities for chemical testing. As many as fifty chemicals can be recommended for testing within one year.

4. *Control of Chemicals.* The EPA is required to take action against chemical substances or mixtures for which a reasonable basis exists to conclude that their manufacture, processing, distribution, use, or disposal presents an unreasonable risk of injury to health or the environment. Permitted actions range from a labeling requirement to a complete ban. The control requirements are not to "place an undue burden on industry," yet at the same time they are to provide an adequate margin of protection against unreasonable risk. TSCA specifically required regulation and eventual elimination of PCBs.

5. *Control of Asbestos.* The EPA is required to develop a strategy for implementing the congressional mandate that all schools be inspected for asbestos-containing material and to develop and implement plans to control the threat of any asbestos discovered.

RCRA: Regulating Solid Waste

The major purposes of RCRA and its 1980 and 1984 amendments are to control solid waste management practices that could endanger public health or the environment and to promote resource conservation and recovery. Solid wastes are defined in the act to include waste solids, sludges, liquids, and contained gases—all forms in which discarded toxic and hazardous substances might be found. In addition to providing federal assistance to state and local governments in developing comprehensive solid waste management programs, RCRA also mandates the following:

1. *Criteria for Environmentally Safe Disposal Sites.* The EPA is required to issue regulations defining the minimum criteria for solid waste disposal sites considered environmentally safe. It is also required to publish an inventory of all U.S. facilities failing to meet these criteria.

2. *Regulation of Hazardous Waste.* The EPA is required to develop criteria for identifying hazardous waste, to publish the characteristics of hazardous wastes and lists of particular hazardous wastes, and to create a manifest system that tracks hazardous wastes from their points of origin to their final disposal sites. The EPA also is to create a permit system that would require all individuals or industries generating hazardous waste to obtain a permit before managing such waste. Permits would be issued only to waste managers meeting the safe disposal criteria created by the EPA.

3. *Resource Recovery and Waste Reduction.* The act requires the Commerce Department to promote commercialization of waste recovery, to encourage markets for recovered wastes, and to promote waste recovery technologies and research into waste conservation.

4. *State Implementation.* The act provides for state implementation of regulations affecting solid waste management and disposal if state pro-

grams meet federal standards. The EPA will enforce these provisions in states that do not, or cannot, comply with federal regulations for the program's enforcement.

5. *Mandated Deadlines and Waste-by-Waste Review.* The 1984 RCRA amendments create deadlines for the EPA to set standards for disposal of specific wastes. If the EPA fails to do so, congressionally mandated standards will be applied. The EPA is also ordered to evaluate nineteen specific substances, and deadlines are established for the agency to regulate new kinds of waste disposal activity.

The 1984 amendments—bristling with mandated deadlines and meticulously detailed instructions—bespeak a profound congressional distrust of the EPA's commitment to enforcing RCRA during the first Reagan administration. The amendments were conceived in an atmosphere strident with congressional censure of the EPA. Sen. George J. Mitchell, D-Maine, captured the mood of the majority:

> Strong congressional expression of disapproval of EPA's slow and timid implementation of the existing law is necessary, as well as a clear congressional direction mandating certain bold, preventive actions by EPA which will not be taken otherwise. . . . The Agency has missed deadlines, proposed inadequate regulations, and even exacerbated the hazardous waste problem by suspending certain regulations.[38]

Congress was determined to drive the EPA hard: It instructed the EPA in exquisite detail concerning how to implement virtually every aspect of RCRA, from the allowable permeability of liners for surface impoundments to the concentrations at which many different chemical wastes must be banned from land disposal. Twenty-nine different deadlines for specific program activities were listed: a ban on land disposal of bulk liquid in landfills within six months, new regulations for small-quantity waste generators within seventeen months, interim construction standards for underground storage tanks within four months, and so forth.[39]

Superfund

When the first Superfund legislation was enacted, the nation's abandoned and uncontrolled hazardous waste dumps were largely an uncharted wasteland. The nation's governments knew little about the location or composition of many waste sites, some abandoned longer than memory of their existence. The law seldom clearly placed financial responsibility for the management or removal of these wastes with their creators; liability for damage or injury to individuals or communities from such wastes often was difficult, or impossible, to assign or to enforce. Often, procedures for cleaning up waste sites were unknown, or local officials were ignorant of accepted procedures.. The financial burden on state and local governments to control or remove these wastes seemed overwhelming. Because a comprehensive, collaborative program among the nation's governments seemed essential, Congress attempted to address these and other major abandoned waste problems through four major Superfund programs:

1. *Information Gathering and Analysis.* Owners of hazardous waste sites were required to notify the EPA by June 1981 about the character of buried wastes. Using this information, the EPA would create a list of national sites.

2. *Federal Response to Emergencies.* The act authorized the EPA to respond to hazardous substance emergencies and to clean up leaking chemical dump sites if the responsible parties failed to take appropriate action or could not be located.

3. *The Hazardous Substance Response Fund.* The act created an initial trust fund of $1.6 billion to finance the removal, cleanup, or remedy of hazardous waste sites. About 86 percent of the fund was to be financed from a tax on manufacturers of petrochemical feedstocks and organic chemicals and on crude oil importers. The remainder was to come from general federal revenues.

4. *Liability for Cleanup.* The act placed liability for cleaning up waste sites and for other restitution on those responsible for release of the hazardous substances.

By the mid-1980s it was obvious that the number of abandoned sites needing immediate cleanup and the costs had been grossly underestimated. The 1984 chemical disaster at Bhopal, India, had drawn congressional attention to the lack of community planning for chemical emergencies in the United States. And Congress was increasingly critical of the slow pace of Superfund site cleanups. In 1986 Congress passed the Superfund amendments, known as SARA, which changed the original legislation significantly in the following ways:

1. *Greatly Increased Spending.* The new amendments authorize an additional $8.5 billion for NPL site cleanups and an additional $500 million specifically to clean up pollution created by abandoned underground liquid storage tanks.

2. *New Cleanup Standards.* The standards mandated for all sites are to be permanent remedies to the maximum extent practicable, using the best available technologies. State standards for cleanup are to be followed when they are more stringent than federal standards. People who live near the sites are to be informed about all phases of the process and are to be involved in the cleanup planning process.

3. *The Emergency Planning and Community Right-to-Know Act.* Title III of SARA authorizes communities to get detailed information about chemicals made by, stored in, and emitted from local businesses. It requires the formation of state and local planning committees to draw up chemical emergency response plans for every community in the nation.

The intent of Congress was to make the creators of hazardous waste sites bear as much financial responsibility as possible for ensuring the safety of the sites. With Superfund and SARA, Congress finished its attempt to craft, within less than a decade, the first truly comprehensive federal regulation of virtually all hazardous or toxic materials in the United States. With TSCA, RCRA, and Superfund, Congress in effect ordered the federal government, in collaboration with state and local authorities, to become the primary manager of all dangerous chemical substances currently used or planned for production.

Improved Pesticide Regulation: The Food Quality Protection Act

Somewhere on the learning curve for environmental policy making belongs the Food Quality Protection Act, a constructive congressional effort to eliminate the regulatory muddle created by fifty years of different statutory standards for pesticide residues on food. The act simplified regulatory standards for an extremely widespread, diverse, and politically contentious group of chemicals. It also represented a thoughtful congressional effort to create a consistent and reasonable risk standard to replace the multitude of standards previously existing for pesticide residues. Equally important, it abolished the zero-tolerance provisions for pesticide residues required by the Delaney clause of the Federal Food, Drug and Cosmetic Act (1949), which had become widely regarded as unreasonably stringent scientifically and economically. The most important provisions of the act include the following:

1. *A Single, Health-Based Standard.* All pesticide residues must demonstrate "a reasonable certainty of no harm" if they are to be permitted in food products.

2. *Tightened Risk Standards.* Risk calculations must consider all nonoccupational sources of exposure, including drinking water, and exposure to other pesticides with a common mechanism of toxicity when setting tolerances. This provision allows regulators to consider not only the effect of the residue itself but also the impact of other kinds of exposure to the same, or similar pesticides, outside a workplace.

3. *Provisions for Children.* This provision requires an explicit determination of safe exposures for children and, if necessary, a tenfold increase

in the adult safety standards to be used for children when the relevant children's data are uncertain.

4. *Endocrine Testing*. The EPA is required to establish a comprehensive screening program for chemical endocrine effects on humans, to implement the program, and to report on its progress to Congress.

5. *Consumer Right-to-Know*. This provision requires distribution of brochures in grocery stores on the health effects of pesticides, how to avoid risks, and which foods have tolerances for pesticide residues based on benefit considerations.

Leading national environmental advocacy groups generally accepted the new legislation warily, recognizing reluctantly that zero tolerance for pesticide residues probably had become an indefensible cancer exposure standard economically and even scientifically. Still, many environmental leaders feared the new legislation might have breached irreparably a high wall of resistance to cancer risk they had legally erected over fifty years, inviting a flood of other legislation eroding the zero-tolerance standard for other ingredients in food.

The Regulatory Thicket

TSCA, RCRA, and the Superfund regulatory programs described in the preceding sections, each a morass of administrative and technical complexity, were passed in less than four years. The EPA and other responsible governmental agencies were confronted with an avalanche of new regulatory mandates, bristling with insistent compliance deadlines, for which they were expected to be rapidly prepared. It is doubtful that the agencies could have discharged these responsibilities satisfactorily under the most benign circumstances. From their inception, the programs were afflicted in varying degrees by technical, administrative, and political problems impeding their development. By 2000 most of these programs were running years behind statutory deadlines, mandated or not. The nation is still at serious risk from the toxic and hazardous waste problems Congress intended to remedy with TSCA, RCRA, and Superfund and is still uncertain about the danger of endocrine disruptors. Serious doubt exists that these programs may ever achieve their legislative objectives without radical reformulation.

Regulatory Achievements: Few But Sometimes Significant

There have been a few conspicuous regulatory successes. Federal regulations have largely eliminated the manufacture of PCBs, chemicals used primarily in commercial electrical equipment such as capacitors and transformers. Of the billion pounds produced in the United States between 1929 and 1976 (when PCB production was halted), fewer than 300 million pounds are still used in millions of electrical devices.[40] High levels of PCBs in human tissue declined from 12 percent of the population in 1979 to virtually 0 percent in the late 1980s. Trace amounts, once found in as much as 62 percent of the U.S. population, have also declined significantly.[41]

In conjunction with the Federal Insecticide, Fungicide, and Rodenticide Act, the newer regulatory programs have largely eliminated all domestic uses of the pesticides DDT, aldrin, dieldrin, toxaphene, and ethylene dibromide and most domestic uses of chlordane and heptachlor, all known carcinogens. Asbestos is slowly being eliminated from domestic commerce and industry. U.S. production of asbestos has dropped by more than half since 1976, and practically all industrial and commercial uses are being eliminated. In 1978 the EPA banned the use of chlorofluorocarbons from domestic aerosol cans, an important first step in controlling the destruction of the atmospheric ozone layer. The elimination or reduction of these substances removes some of the most dangerous and widespread chemicals in the United States, yet these represent only a tiny portion of the chemicals known, or strongly suspected, of posing grave risks to humans or the environment.

TSCA and RCRA: Administrative Overload

TSCA and RCRA abound in delays and complications. Many of these problems arise from the volume and complexity of work thrust on the EPA within a few years. The numerous failures in program implementation also testify to the difficulty in obtaining technical data, to protracted scientific disputes over regulatory decisions, to the lack of resources and experience in program management, and to past political interference that plunged the EPA into demoralizing and acrimonious disputes with Congress.

One formidable problem is that each new law requires the EPA to assume the initiative for creating and interpreting a vast volume of integrated technical information. Obtaining the data often requires that chemical manufacturers, processors, consumers, and waste depositors provide timely, accurate information—information they previously guarded jealously. With this heavy burden of initiative, the agency would have been hard pressed to meet all its program obligations under TSCA and RCRA with even the most benevolent funding and generous personnel levels—both of which they did not enjoy.

The required testing of potentially harmful chemicals required by TSCA has been an exercise in frustration. Consider, for instance, the agency's attempt to create test rules for a whole category of chemicals. Some chemical groups are quite small, but others are voluminous: the aryl phosphates include about three hundred existing chemicals, with more being manufactured continually. The chemical industry complained that testing by broad categories would involve very high costs, would stigmatize many "innocent" chemicals along with dangerous ones in the same group, and would prevent introduction of new chemicals until all existing chemicals in a category were tested. Small wonder that the EPA explained its delay in establishing chemical testing guidelines by citing "gross underestimation of the number and complexity of the issues and time spent in resolving one-time issues."[42]

By 2000, the EPA had been able to test fewer than 200 of more than 62,000 commercial chemicals on is original TSCA agenda. In an effort to lighten its testing overload, the EPA resorted to an alternative strategy of encouraging chemical companies to voluntarily provide test data on about 2,800 chemicals produced or imported in amounts of one million pounds or more. However, the chemical industry would not agree to provide data on several hundred chemicals. Moreover, TSCA requires the EPA to determine whether a chemical about which it received data will pose an "unreasonable risk" before the EPA can regulate its production or use. "EPA officials say the act's legal standards for demonstrating unreasonable risk are so high," reported the GAO in 2006, "that they have generally discouraged EPA from using its authorities to ban or restrict the manufacture or use of existing chemicals. Since Congress enacted TSCA in 1976. EPA has issued regulations to ban or limit the production of only five existing chemicals or groups of chemicals."[43]

It is also becoming evident that the number of potential waste storage and treatment facilities in the United States requiring corrective actions under RCRA is likely to exceed vastly the initial estimates. The EPA has estimated that perhaps 3,700 waste treatment and storage facilities will require cleanup under RCRA rules.[44] Moreover, the current list of twenty thousand facilities subject to RCRA inspections is likely to grow as more facilities are discovered. If the estimates are accurate, the size and scope of the cleanup program would be as large as the expected Superfund cleanup and may cost more than $22.7 billion. The cleanup of all sites may not be completed until the year 2025.

The impediments to the RCRA program are common to most federal regulatory efforts: cost and complexity, foot-dragging by regulated waste managers, insufficient money for needed oversight, and wrangling about cleanup terms. "The agency, the states, and companies often disagree on how cleanup should be pursued," explained the GAO. "These disagreements prolong the cleanup process because more time is needed [to define] the cleanup terms, and companies must sometimes meet the duplicate requirements of both federal and state regulators."[45]

Superfund: "The Largest, Most Complicated, and Most Disliked"

The Superfund program has been a consensus choice as the most controversial, expensive, and problematic of all environmentalism's showcase legislation. Since Superfund's enactment in 1980, more than sixteen hundred abandoned hazardous waste dumps have been registered on the NPL of the most dangerous sites. Another 11,500 sites are considered the next potential additions. By George W. Bush's second term, EPA officials, increasingly testy at continued criticism of Superfund, were pointing to significant improvements in the speed and economy of site cleanups. The agency asserted that "recent cleanups are faster, with some sites spending 8 years in the program"; the average before had been almost eleven years.[46] That the EPA could soberly proclaim an eight-year site cleanup to be remarkably speedy betrays much of the ambiguity and disagreement still prevailing over the program's accomplishments. By 2007, EPA nonetheless claimed to be making "significant progress," and pointed to its substantial accomplishment in cleaning up a total of 1,006 NPL sites.[47]

The EPA's annual Superfund reports remain relentlessly optimistic, but the total Superfund costs cast a more pessimistic aspect. Superfund long ago exhausted its originally authorized funding of $15.4 billion and will greatly exceed the $26.4 billion that the EPA estimated in the early 1990s would be necessary to complete the entire program. Careful estimates predict Superfund costs during the decade 2000–2010 alone will be approximately $14–16.4 billion.[48] Superfund now survives by continual dependence on annual congressional appropriations averaging more than $1.4 billion with no certain termination date.

Completed cleanups have averaged about $2.1 million each, but many troublesome sites are creating enormous cost escalations. One hundred fifty-four Superfund projects costing more than $50 million—such as California's Stringfellow dump—have achieved "megasite" status because of the time, technical complexity, and legal difficulties they entail.[49] About 20 to 33 percent of each Superfund site expenditure has been absorbed in litigation and negotiation, which has become a growth industry for the legal profession. One estimate suggests that approximately twenty thousand lawyers are now engaged in Superfund litigation.[50]

The reasons for Superfund's plodding pace and bloated costs are clear. The enormous legal costs generated by Superfund are largely the result of the complexities involved in establishing liability for abandoned hazardous waste dumps and the difficulty in recovering damages from private parties. In 1984, for instance, the EPA placed the Helen Kramer Landfill in Mantua, New Jersey, high on the NPL and awarded $55.7 million for the cleanup contract. To recover these costs through liability claims, the federal government subsequently sued twenty-five private firms, and the State of New Jersey sued the same firms and twenty-five additional ones. A few of these fifty defendants sued 239 other parties who they claimed were responsible for these wastes, including the city of Philadelphia and other municipalities. And most of *these* litigants have sued their insurance companies.[51]

The litigation is still active. So far, the EPA has been able to recover only a small fraction of cleanup expenses from parties alleged to be liable for the costs.

Another inducement to delay and expense has been controversy between regulatory officials and communities affected by Superfund over the appropriate amount of cleanup required to make sites safe. Because the Superfund legislation and its implementing regulations do not clearly establish cleanup criteria, Superfund officials have been under considerable community pressure to insist on the most stringent and costly standards for site restoration. When officials and communities disagree about the matter, litigation often results even before cleanup begins. In addition, the list of prospective Superfund sites continues to grow.

Unquestionable improvements have not pacified program critics, especially congressional Republicans who seldom ever found much to like about Superfund. Less partisan experts and even many Superfund proponents, however, also believe additional reforms are imperative. Among the most important, in the opinion of a great many, is the development of a reliable method for ranking all Superfund sites according to human and environmental health risks and allocating cleanup dollars on the basis of risk priorities. Many observers believe the EPA needs to recover a much larger share of the site cleanup costs from private parties—the agency has been criticized for failing to recover more than $2 billion in cleanup costs just through careless bookkeeping.[52] Also, many observers assert that the EPA and the states need to reduce the time required to add a qualifying site to the NPL.

Congress and the White House have been under increasing pressure from insurance companies, private industry, state and local governments— indeed, practically all parties potentially liable to Superfund cleanup claims—to radically simplify the process by which liability for site cleanup is established and to create a cleanup standard that does not require total elimination of all risk from site wastes. These, and many other reforms, have been repeatedly proposed in Congress since 1996, and many observers had hoped that Congress would finally pass a major Superfund reform measure after George W. Bush's election in 2000. Congress, soon preoccupied with other urgent matters, had neither time nor enthusiasm for such a contentious matter.

The NIMBY Problem

He appears most often as a white-collar professional or executive, articulate, well educated, politically sophisticated. She is often a housewife, an executive, or a professional. They personify the members of a growing citizen resistance movement known as NIMBYism (NIMBY stands for "Not In My Backyard").[53] NIMBYism is all too familiar to federal, state, and local officials attempting to implement state programs for permitting hazardous waste sites as required by RCRA, or trying to plan for the designation or cleanup of a Superfund site. NIMBYism poses a formidable obstacle to waste site management under RCRA and Superfund. It is the environmental movement's problem, too. NIMBYism is a dissonance within the environmental ethic—a disturbing contradiction between the movement's commitment to participatory democracy and its insistence on rapid, effective environmental regulation.

NIMBYism thrives because of numerous, and still increasing, state and federal laws that empower citizen activism in the implementation of many different environmental laws and regulations. Most states now have legislation in which citizens are given some role in the writing, implementation, and enforcement of environmental laws. Seventeen states require the appropriate agencies to prepare environmental impact statements for their activities and mandate public notice and involvement in the process.[54]

Federal law provides many opportunities for citizen participation in environmental regulation. Major environmental laws, such as the Clean Air Act, the Clean Water Act, RCRA, and Superfund grant citizens the standing to sue federal agencies to compel their enforcement of environmental regulations. The Surface Mining Control and Reclamation Act (1977), the 1984 RCRA amendments, and the 1972 Clean Water Act amendments, among many others, require the responsible federal and state agencies to involve the public in writing and implementing regulations. Several federal environmental laws also permit citizens, or citizen organizations, to sue private firms for failure to comply with the terms of their pollution discharge permits and to recover the costs involved in the suits. Public notice and hearings are routinely required of environmental agencies before major regulations are promulgated or permits are issued for pollution discharges or hazardous waste sites. Behind these generous provisions for citizen participation, legal scholar Michael S. Greve noted, is congressional distrust, a "reflexive suspicion that the executive, if left to itself, would systematically under-enforce the law."[55]

These statutory provisions have set in motion political forces powerfully abetting NIMBYism. One such force is the rapid proliferation of national and state organizations specifically committed to educating Americans about hazardous waste and to helping local communities organize politically to deal with local hazardous waste problems. Among the earliest and most visible national organizations is the Citizen's Clearinghouse for Hazardous Waste, created in 1981 by Lois Gibbs, a housewife whose experiences with the Love Canal waste crisis convinced her of a need to educate other communities about hazardous waste. There also has been an explosion of ad hoc state and local groups that have organized to deal with specific hazardous waste issues, ranging from the closing of city waste dumps to state policy for hazardous waste transportation.

Many existing state and national environmental organizations now give major attention to hazardous waste issues and provide technical assistance and education for concerned citizens. These groups believe they are ultimately contributing to better implementation of RCRA and Superfund by ensuring greater citizen understanding and acceptance of waste policy decisions made by government officials. Often, however, this activism arouses or emboldens citizen opposition to permits for local hazardous waste sites. Public officials and waste producers commonly complain that organized citizen groups too often agitate rather than educate in community waste issues.

Public resistance to hazardous waste site permits and management plans under RCRA or Superfund is a serious and unsolved political problem afflicting both programs. Coupled with litigation, the many political and administrative strategies available to citizen groups determined to prevent permits for local hazardous waste dumps can delay program implementation for years or decades.

State governments are not innocent of NIMBYism. Almost any hazardous waste proposal can arouse it. Public hearings on siting hazardous facilities, as political scientist Michael E. Kraft observed, can become "a perfect forum for elected officials and the general public to give vent to fears and concerns, and to denounce decision making on the siting question. The public hearing procedure . . . facilitated the classic NIMBY response to siting unwanted facilities that impose localized costs and risks while offering diffuse national benefits."[56]

Many administrative strategies have been tried, but none seems to dispel NIMBYism. States that financially compensate local governments and citizens for risks and other problems entailed in accepting a hazardous waste site are no more successful in gaining public approval for the siting than states using only scientific criteria for site selection. Evidence suggests that most citizens who oppose a hazardous waste site will not change their minds under any circumstances.[57] Opponents may occasionally be converted if they are convinced that the local community will have continuing, accurate information about the site status and continuing control over the site's management. But converts are few. Opponents to hazardous waste sites are numerous, vocal, and unyielding. Moreover, they are apt to win their fights.

NIMBYism will continue to be tough, stubborn, and durable, its ranks crowded with well-educated, socially active, organizationally experienced people. NIMBYism is rarely routed by better information, more qualified experts, improved risk communication techniques, and other palliative actions premised on the assumption that the public will be more reasonable about hazardous facility siting if it is better educated about the issues. All this belies the widespread belief among scientific experts and risk professionals that NIMBYism is rooted in the public's scientific illiteracy.[58]

Why is better risk communication not enough? Because NIMBYs usually distrust the *source* of governmental risk information: public officials and their scientific spokespersons. In addition, critics of governmental hazardous waste management often have their *own* experts and information sources. The conflicting sides, noted Harvard physicist and science policy expert Harvey Brooks, tend to become "noncommunicating publics that each rely on different sources and talk to different experts. Thus, many public policy discussions become dialogues of the deaf. . . ."[59] Often the true wellsprings of public anxiety about waste siting are not understood by technical experts: people worry about "potentially catastrophic effects, lack of familiarity and understanding, involuntariness, scientific uncertainty, lack of personal control by the individuals exposed, risks to future generations," and more.[60]

Critics often hold environmentalists responsible for NIMBYism. They assert that the environmentalist rhetoric favored by NIMBYs is little more than deceptive but respectable packaging for middle-class selfishness. In reality, argue the critics, most NIMBYs want somebody else to bear whatever risks are associated with hazardous waste sites while they continue to benefit from the products and economic activities that produce the waste. Even if NIMBYism is well intentioned, critics also note, it fails to solve waste problems. Eventually, waste has to go someplace. It is unfortunate, the critics conclude, that the waste often ends up at whatever sites are the least well defended politically, not at the most appropriate places. Thus, many environmental justice problems, as was observed in Chapter 4, and numerous controversies between the states over high-level nuclear waste disposal (see Chapter 8) are created or intensified by NIMBYism.

Whatever its merits, the certain continuation of NIMBYism poses difficult problems for environmental regulation. Is it possible to secure informed public consent to the siting and management of hazardous waste facilities? If no public involvement techniques or risk communication procedures can produce public consensus or acquiescence to hazardous waste site planning under RCRA and Superfund, must solutions be imposed by judicial, administrative, or political means? Is there danger that continuing promotion of public involvement in making these decisions will enshrine procedural democracy at the expense of social equity—in effect, will citizen participation gradually result in selectively exposing the least economically and politically advantaged publics to the most risks from hazardous waste? How much responsibility for the worst impacts of

NIMBYism rests with the environmental movement? These questions can only grow in importance as the hazardous waste problem magnifies in the twenty-first century.

Conclusion

In no other major area of environmental policy is progress measured in such small increments as the regulation of toxic and hazardous wastes. The slow pace at which TSCA, RCRA, and Superfund have been implemented so far has produced a quality of regulation so tenuous and variable that a serious question often exists regarding whether regulation in any significant sense has been achieved. Hazardous waste in abandoned or deliberately uncontrolled landfills numbering in the thousands has yet to be controlled properly. Federal and state governments have yet to approve and implement on the appropriate scale the strategies required to ameliorate hazardous waste problems. The risks already associated with hazardous substances, and the many others to become apparent with continuing research in the twenty-first century, are unlikely to diminish without a massive and continuing federal commitment of resources to implement the programs as intended by Congress—a commitment of resources and will on a scale lacking so far.

Even with sufficient resources, the implementation of TSCA, RCRA, and Superfund is likely to be slow because these laws raise technical, legal, and political problems on an order seldom matched in other environmental policy domains. First, no other environmental programs attempt to regulate so many discrete, pervasive substances; we have observed that the hazardous substances that may lie within the scope of these laws number in the tens of thousands. Second, regulation is delayed by the need to acquire technical information never previously obtained by government, to conduct research on the hazardousness of new chemicals, or to secure from corporations highly guarded trade secrets. Third, almost every major regulatory action intended to limit the production, distribution, or disposal of chemical substances deemed toxic or hazardous by government is open to technical controversy, litigation, and other challenges concerning the degree of risk associated with such substances and their suitability for regulation under the laws. Fourth, opponents of regulatory actions under TSCA, RCRA, and Superfund have been able to use to good advantage all the opportunities provided by requirements for administrative due process and the federalized structure of regulation to challenge administrative acts politically and judicially. Fifth, in many instances the states responsible for implementing the programs have been slow to provide from their own resources the means necessary to ensure proper implementation. None of these problems is unique to hazardous substance regulation, but few other environmental policies raise all these problems persistently and acutely.

In a broader perspective, the enormous difficulties in controlling hazardous substances once they are released into the ecosystem, together with the problems of controlling their disposal, emphasize the crucial role that production controls must play in hazardous substance management. Indeed, it may be that the human and environmental risks from hazardous chemicals may never be constrained satisfactorily once these substances are let loose in the environment. American technology development has proceeded largely with an implicit confidence that whatever human or environmental risks may be engendered in the process can be contained adequately by the same genius that inspired technology's development—a faith, in effect, that science always will cure what ills it creates. The risk to humans and the environment from now pervasive chemical substances created since World War II ought to prompt thoughtful reservation about the efficacy of technological solutions to technological problems. Toxic and hazardous substances pose for the nation a formidable technological challenge: how to reckon the human and environmental costs of technology development while technologies are yet evolving and, then, how to prudently control dangerous technologies without depriving the nation of their benefits.

Suggested Readings

Foster, Kenneth R., David E. Bernstein, and Peter W. Huber. *Phantom Risk: Scientific Inference and the Law.* Cambridge, Mass.: MIT Press, 1999.

Gerrard, Michael B. *Whose Backyard, Whose Risk?* Cambridge, Mass.: MIT Press, 1999.

Rabe, Barry G. *Beyond NIMBY: Hazardous Waste Siting in Canada and the United States.* Washington, D.C.: Brookings Institution Press, 1994.

Raffensberger, Carolyn, and Joel Tickner, eds. *Protecting Public Health and the Environment.* Washington, D.C.: Island Press, 1999.

Rahm, Dianne, ed. *Toxic Waste and Environmental Policy in the 21st Century United States.* Jefferson, N.C.: McFarland, 2002.

Wilson, Duff. *Fateful Harvest: The True Story of a Small Town, a Global Industry, and a Toxic Secret.* New York: Harper Collins, 2002.

Notes

1. Associated Press, "Lead-laden Lunchboxes OK'd by Government," CNN News, February 18, 2007, www.cnn.com/2007/HEALTH/02/18/lunchbox.lead.ap, February 21, 2007.
2. U.S. Government Accountability Office, "Chemical Regulation: Actions Are Needed to Improve the Effectiveness of EPA's Chemical Review Program," Report No. GAO-06-1032T (August 2, 2006), 1.
3. Nick Madigan, "Largest-Ever Toxic Waste Suit Opens in California," *New York Times,* February 5, 1993, A17.
4. U.S. Environmental Protection Agency, "Superfund Success Stories," www.epa.gov/superfund/randomize/thumbs3.htm, March 25, 2004.

5. Verdictsearch, "Top 100 Verdicts of 2005," www.verdictsearch.com, March 10, 2007.
6. Ibid.
7. U.S. Environmental Protection Agency, "Superfund Success Stories," www.epa.gov/superfund/randomize/thumbs3.htm, March 25, 2004.
8. Will Matthews, "Stringfellow Retains Reputation: 'Glen Avon' Backlash Underscores Lasting Stigma," *Inland Valley Daily Bulletin* (Ontario, Canada), January 11, 2003, 1A.
9. The Gallup Organization, "The Environment: People's Chief Concerns" (April 2000). Cited in "The Public Agenda Online," www.publicagenda.org, March 12, 2001.
10. U.S. Environmental Protection Agency, *Environmental Progress and Challenges: EPA's Update* (Washington, D.C.: U.S. Environmental Protection Agency, August 1988), 126. See also U.S. General Accounting Office, "Toxic Substances: Status of EPA's Reviews of Chemicals under the Chemical Testing Program," Report No. GAO/RCED 92-31FS (October 1991).
11. Conservation Foundation, *State of the Environment: A View toward the Nineties* (Washington, D.C.: Conservation Foundation, 1987), 136; Council on Environmental Quality, *Environmental Quality, 1981* (Washington, D.C.: Council on Environmental Quality, 1982), 11.
12. The number of carcinogenic chemicals includes those classified as "known to be a human carcinogen" and those "reasonably anticipated to be a human carcinogen." See U.S. Department of Health and Human Services, Public Health Service, National Toxicology Program, *Report on Carcinogens,* 10th ed. (Washington, D.C.: National Toxicology Program, 2002).
13. Keith Schneider, "Second Chance on Environment," *New York Times,* March 26, 1993, B16.
14. National Research Council, Committee on the Future Role of Pesticides in U.S. Agriculture, *The Future Role of Pesticides in US Agriculture* (Washington, D.C.: National Academies Press, 2000), 33.
15. Philip Shabecoff, "Moderation Becomes Mainstream: The Nation Is Getting Ready to Cut Its Use of Pesticides," *New York Times,* April 16, 1989, 4(6).
16. Ibid.
17. Philip Shabecoff, "EPA Pulls Back on Asbestos Rules,"*New York Times,* March 9, 1985, 1(48).
18. U.S. Environmental Protection Agency, *2004 Toxics Release Inventory (TRI), Public Data Release Report,* EPA Document EPA-260-R-06-001 (April 2006), 6.
19. U.S. Environmental Protection Agency, *2004 TRI Public Data Release eReport: Summary of Key Findings,* April 2006, epa.gov/tri/tridata/tri04, March 30, 2007.
20. U.S. Environmental Protection Agency, Office of Solid Waste and Environmental Remediation, "Treatment Projects Applied to 62 Percent of Superfund Sites," www.epa.gov/superfund, March 26, 2004.
21. U.S. General Accounting Office, "Superfund: Estimates of Number of Future Sites Vary," Report No. GAO/RCED 95-18 (November 1994), 14. See also Council on Environmental Quality, *Environmental Quality, 1992* (Washington, D.C.: U.S. Government Printing Office, 1993), 127.
22. Jennifer Lee, "Drop in Budget Slows Superfund Program," *New York Times,* March 9, 2004, 8.
23. U.S. EPA, "2004 Toxics Release Inventory (TRI) Public Data Release Report," April 20, 2007.
24. Joseph G. Morone and Edward J. Woodhouse, *Averting Catastrophe* (Berkeley: University of California Press, 1986), 34–35.
25. U.S. Centers for Disease Control, "Cytogenetic Patterns in Persons Living near Love Canal—New York," ww.cdc.gov/mmwr/preview/mmwrhtml/00000084.htm.
26. U.S. General Accounting Office, "Superfund: Estimates of Number of Future Sites Vary," 1, 47.
27. Philip Shabecoff, "EPA Streamlines Cleanup Program,"*New York Times,* May 14, 1983, 1(6).
28. Estimates by Paul MacAvoy, *New York Times,* February 14, 1982, B3. See also Library of Congress, Congressional Research Service, *Six Case Studies of Compensation for*

Toxic Substances Pollution (Report to the Committee on Environment and Public Works, U.S. Senate, No. 96-13, Washington, D.C., 1980).

29. Center for Bioenvironmental Research, Tulane and Xavier Universities, *Environmental Estrogens: What Does the Evidence Mean?* (New Orleans: Center for Bioenvironmental Research, 1996); Center for the Study of Environmental Endocrine Disruptors, *Significant Government Policy Developments* (Washington, D.C.: Center for the Study of Environmental Endocrine Disruptors, 1996); Center for the Study of Environmental Endocrine Disruptors, *Effects: State of Science Paper* (Washington, D.C.: Center for the Study of Environmental Endocrine Disruptors, 1995).

30. Center for the Study of Environmental Endocrine Disruptors, *Effects*.

31. Center for the Study of Environmental Endocrine Disruptors, *Significant Government Policy Developments*.

32. T. Colborn, D. Dumanoski, and J. P. Meyers, *Our Stolen Future: Are We Threatening Our Fertility, Intelligence and Survival?* (New York: Penguin, 1996).

33. "Toughest Decisions Still to Come in Pesticide Review," *USA Today*, August 30, 1999, 1A.

34. Marc Landy and Mary Hague, "The Coalition for Waste: Private Interests and Superfund," in *Environmental Politics: Public Costs, Private Rewards*, ed. Michael S. Greve and Fred L. Smith (New York: Praeger, 1992), 70.

35. Keith Schneider, "Rule Forcing Towns to Pick Big New Dumps or Big Costs," *New York Times*, January 6, 1992, A1.

36. Michael S. Greve, "Introduction," in *Environmental Politics*, ed. Greve and Smith, 5–6.

37. Linda Schierow, "Summaries of Environmental Laws Administered by the EPA: The Toxic Substances Control Act, *Congressional Research Service Report RL30022* (Washington, D.C.: Congressional Research Service, 2006).

38. Quoted in Christopher Harris, William L. Want, and Morris A. Ward, *Hazardous Waste: Confronting the Challenge* (New York: Quorum Books, 1987), 87.

39. Ibid., 90–91.

40. Council on Environmental Quality, *Environmental Quality, 1986* (Washington, D.C.: Council on Environmental Quality, 1987), Table 9-6.

41. U.S. General Accounting Office, "Toxic Substances: EPA Has Made Limited Progress in Identifying PCB Users," Report No. GAO/RCED 88-127 (April 1988), 3; Council on Environmental Quality, *Environmental Quality, 1986*, Table 9-9.

42. Council on Environmental Quality, *Environmental Quality, 1986*, 219.

43. U.S. Government Accountability Office, "Chemical Regulation: Actions Are Needed to Improve the Effectiveness of EPA's Chemical Review Program," Report No. GAO-06-1032T (August 2, 2006), 1; see also Mary Cole, "When Superfund Expenses Go Mega," *Los Angeles Times*, January 26, 2007, 1A.

44. U.S. General Accounting Office, "RCRA Corrective Action Program," Report No. GAO/RCED 97-3 (1997); U.S. General Accounting Office, "Hazardous Waste: EPA Has Removed Some Barriers to Cleanups," Report No. GAO/RCED 00-2000 (August 2000), 10–11; see also EPA, Office of Solid Waste, Economics, Methods, and Risk Analysis Division, "A Study of the Implementation of the RCRA Corrective Action Program," www.coxcolvin.com/newsletter/CAImplemstudy.pdf, May 15, 2002.

45. U.S. General Accounting Office, "RCRA Corrective Action Program," 2.

46. Reported in U.S. General Accounting Office, "Superfund: Progress and Challenges," Statement by David G. Wood, Associate Director, Environmental Protection Issues, Resources, Community, and Economic Development Division, Before the Committee on Environment and Public Works, U.S. Senate (GAO Document No. GAO/T-RCED 99-202).

47. U.S. EPA, Region Six, "Superfund Success: EPA Continuing Cleanup Progress at Hazardous Waste Sites," at www.epa.gov/Region6/6xa/superfund-jump.htm, March 30, 2007.

48. Robert Hersh, Michael B. Batz, and Katherine D. Walker. *Superfund's Future: What Will It Cost?* (Washington, D.C.: Resources for the Future), 131.

49. U.S. Government Accountability Office, "Superfund Program: Current Superfund Program and Future Challenges," Report No. GAO-04-475R (February 18, 2004).

50. Landy and Hague, "The Coalition for Waste." On the general problems with Superfund, see, for example, Steven Cohen and Sheldon Kamieniecki, *Environmental Regulation through Strategic Planning* (Boulder: Westview Press, 1991); and Daniel Mazmanian and David Morell, *Beyond Superfailure: America's Toxics Policy for the 1990s* (Boulder: Westview Press, 1992).

51. Barnaby J. Feder, "In the Clutches of the Superfund Mess,"*New York Times,* June 16, 1991, 3(1).

52. Ibid.

53. On the sources and impact of NIMBYism generally, see Luther J. Carter, *Nuclear Imperatives and Public Trust: Dealing with Radioactive Waste* (Washington, D.C.: Resources for the Future, 1987); Clarence Davies, Vincent T. Covello, and Frederick W. Allen, eds., *Risk Communication* (Washington, D.C.: Conservation Foundation, 1987); Roger E. Kasperson, "Six Propositions on Public Participation and Their Relevance for Risk Communication," *Risk Analysis* 6 (September 1986): 275–81; and Patrick G. Marshall, "Not in My Backyard," *CQ Editorial Research Reports,* June 1989, 311.

54. Michael S. Greve, "Environmentalism and Bounty Hunting," *Public Interest* 97 (fall 1989): 15–29.

55. Ibid., 24.

56. Michael E. Kraft, "Managing Technological Risks in a Democratic Polity: Citizen Participation and Nuclear Waste Disposal" (Paper presented at the national conference of the American Society for Public Administration, Boston, 1987). See also Council on Environmental Quality, *The National Environmental Policy Act: A Study of Its Effectiveness after Twenty-Five Years* (Washington, D.C.: Council on Environmental Quality, Executive Office of the President, January 1997).

57. William Lyons, Michael R. Fitzgerald, and Amy McCabe, "Public Opinion and Hazardous Waste," *Forum for Applied Research and Public Policy* 2 (fall 1987): 89–97. See also Michael E. Kraft, "Risk Perception and the Politics of Citizen Participation: The Case of Radioactive Waste Management," in *Advances in Risk Analysis,* Vol. 9, ed. Lorraine Abbott (New York: Plenum Press, 1990).

58. Thomas M. Dietz and Robert W. Rycroft, *The Risk Professionals* (New York: Russell Sage Foundation, 1987), 60.

59. Harvey Brooks, "The Resolution of Technically Intensive Public Policy Disputes," *Science, Technology and Human Values* 9 (winter 1984): 48.

60. Kraft, "Risk Perception and the Politics of Citizen Participation," 7.

Chapter 8

Energy:
Nuclear Dreams, Black Gold, and Vanishing Crude

Vice President Dick Cheney, who headed the White House energy task force, criticized environmentalists for relying too much on renewables and conservation to solve the nation's energy problems. "Conservation may be a sign of personal virtue, but it is not a sufficient basis for a sound comprehensive energy policy," Cheney said.
—Press report following publication
of the 2001 national energy plan[1]

We don't have to take away the cars from the people. The SUVs, the Hummers and the muscle cars. No, that formula is a formula for failure. Instead, what we have to do is make those muscle cars and those SUVs and those Hummers environmentally muscular.
—California Governor Arnold Schwarzenegger
to the Council on Foreign Relations[2]

In mid-2001 George W. Bush's administration released its much anticipated national energy plan, titled *Reliable, Affordable and Environmentally Sound Energy for America's Future.* The report began with a warning from the task force preparing the plan under the leadership of Vice President Dick Cheney. "America in the year 2001 faces the most serious energy shortage since the oil embargoes of the 1970s. The effects are already being felt nationwide," it observed. "This imbalance, if allowed to continue, will inevitably undermine our economy, our standard of living, and our national security," it added. Environmentalist organizations strongly agreed with this ominous preface but found little else to commend in the report's numerous policy proposals.

Five years later, President Bush signed the Energy Policy Act of 2005 (EPAt)—the first comprehensive national energy legislation in almost three decades—ending a protracted and contentious congressional struggle to implement the recommendations of the administration's 2001 energy report. The 2005 EPAt was in many respects a different creation from the energy plan originally envisioned by the Bush administration as a result of the politically daunting struggle to gain the necessary bipartisan congressional majority to pass the measure. Nonetheless, EPAt seemed to most environmentalists little more than a cosmetic makeover of the original Bush plan. Twelve major environmental organizations delivered a verdict early and emphatically:

> After five years, the U.S. Congress has crafted an energy bill that fails to reduce America's dependence on oil, fails to address the threat of global warming, fails to make any new investments in clean energy, and by the President's own admission, fails to help consumers at the gas pump. When it comes to solving America's pressing energy problems, this bill can only be classified as a miserable failure. Instead of moving toward a new energy future, the energy bill provides tens of billions of dollars to the oil, gas, coal and nuclear industries, significantly weakens environmental protections such as the Clean Water Act and Safe Drinking Water Act, and undermines numerous consumer protections. This energy bill doesn't meet America's 21 century needs.[3]

Thus continued the bitter debate between the Bush administration and environmentalism's organized advocates that pervades almost all discussion of Bush's national energy policy.

EPAt created many new programs with evident environmental appeal. These included more than $14 billion in various tax incentives over the next three decades for increased energy conservation and efficiency, substantial support for research on biofuels such as ethanol, various research and development incentives for the creation of a "hydrogen economy" based on hydrogen fuel cells, and other proposals for increased energy efficiency.[4] EPAt temporarily put to rest the administration's controversial plan to expand energy exploration in the Arctic National Wildlife Refuge (ANWR). But the apparently implacable environmentalist opposition to the Bush energy plans fed on profoundly different visions of the energy future for nuclear power, fossil fuels, and energy conservation.

These controversies seldom escaped national media attention. They persistently aroused rancorous partisan wrangling within Congress. They preempted much of organized environmentalism's political agenda. All with good reason. The EPAt followed after two years of growing public dissatisfaction with sharply climbing domestic gasoline prices far exceeding the price run-up during the 1970s energy crisis; the continuing, massive national War on Terrorism; U.S. military invasions of Afghanistan and

Iraq; and almost weekly crises involving U.S. strategic military interests in the petroleum-rich Middle East. Events since the original 2001 energy plan seemed to invest the ongoing debate about national energy policy with urgent importance for most Americans, regardless of party or policy preferences. However, it appeared that domestic energy problems were not politically compelling for most Americans, however much they might profess concern about energy affairs.

Fossil Fuels and Public Apathy: A Perilous Combination

Early in 2006 the Pew Center reported that energy matters ranked only tenth in a public opinion poll concerning the issues to which most Americans thought the president and Congress should give priority. Opinion polls among American voters before and after the 2006 congressional elections indicate that energy issues were rarely an important consideration at the voting booth. Yet a Gallup survey in early 2007 indicated that 43 percent of the public worried "a great deal" about the availability and affordability of energy.[5] Other contemporary polls suggest that a majority of Americans believe the United States faces a serious energy shortage or an energy crisis. This fusion of apprehension and indifference about national energy conditions remains, as it has since the early 1980s, among the most durable dissonances in contemporary voting national behavior. The energy crisis of the 1970s seems, in retrospect, to have left no lasting public legacy.

Energy Consumption

The United States has a ravenous energy appetite. Collectively, Americans constitute approximately 4.6 percent of the world population and consume about 25 percent of the world's energy production; on average, one American uses more energy in a year than a European, a South American, and an Asian *combined*.[6] Many of the nation's major pollution problems are caused directly by current methods of producing and consuming this energy. Consider the environmental impact of fossil fuels. About 86 percent of all energy currently consumed in the United States comes from petroleum, natural gas, and coal.[7] The ecological consequences of this combustion are numerous:

- Transportation and other fossil fuel combustion annually produce 34 percent of the volatile organic compounds, 78 percent of the carbon monoxide, 85 percent of the sulfur oxides, and 95 percent of the nitrogen oxides emitted into the air.[8]
- The land area disturbed by coal surface mining in the United States now exceeds 5.7 million acres, an area equal in size to the state of New

Hampshire. Of this total, more than 3 million acres remains abandoned, creating an abandoned, sterile wasteland.

• During the 1990s an average of more than nine thousand large spills of hazardous substances, mostly petroleum, were reported in U.S. waters yearly. More than one million gallons of petroleum and chemicals were spilled annually during the decade.[9]

So intimate is the association between energy and environmental quality—a link revealed again by the emerging problems of global climate warming and acid precipitation—that the nation's environmental agenda for the first decade of the twenty-first century will become energy policy by another name.

Until 1990 the average American's interest in energy matters had been fading as fast as memories of the 1970s energy crisis. Then came Iraq's invasion of Kuwait in August of that year. Domestic gasoline prices climbed sharply, stock values vacillated, and rising apprehension about economic turbulence in the wake of the invasion was compounded with anxiety about U.S. security. Americans were momentarily reminded of how dependent they had become on Middle Eastern petroleum and, thus, how gravely their military and economic future could be affected by the volatile politics of the Persian Gulf. But the Gulf War passed, and energy worries faded. The 2003 U.S. invasion of Iraq and the resulting protracted military conflict equally failed to awaken a politically compelling public apprehension about U.S. energy vulnerabilities. Environmentalists joined many national security experts in warning that the United States was poised between the energy crisis it had momentarily averted in the 1970s and its certain return, hastened by the nation's failure to learn from its earlier energy troubles. Americans, however, had relapsed into a rising, and untroubled, dependence on imported petroleum.

Petroleum: Consumption or Addiction?

U.S. dependence on imported oil declined sharply in the years immediately following the second oil shock created by Iran's sudden 1978 cutback in U.S. petroleum exports, and it seemed for a few years that the United States had learned the lesson of the oil embargoes. But imports rose again, and by 2007 the nation was importing almost 62 percent of its annual petroleum consumption—far more than the 38.8 percent imported when the first Arab embargo hit.[10] Moreover, an increasing proportion of this imported oil—currently about one barrel in four consumed in the United States—originates in a Persian Gulf nation. At the same time, U.S. oil production is dwindling slowly. By2007, U.S. production was at its lowest

Figure 8-1　Projected U.S. Oil Consumption, Production, and Shortfall, 2000–2020 (Millions of Barrels per Day)

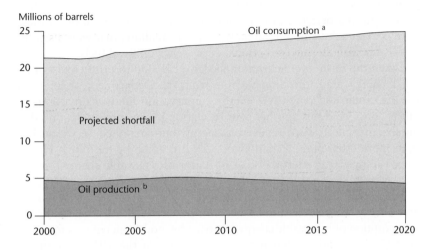

Source: Data from Energy Information Administration, *Annual Energy Outlook 2004 with Projections to 2025, Market Trends, Oil and Natural Gas,* Figures 94 and 96, www.eia.doe.gov/oiaf/aeo/gas.html (accessed June 3, 2004.)

[a] These projections are based on low growth estimates for oil consumption. Other estimates (high growth, high oil prices) would actually show a greater shortfall.

[b] These projections include the total on-shore and off-shore production for the lower 48 states.

level since 1954 and was not ever expected to increase.[11] The growing disparity between the nation's petroleum consumption and domestic production is indicated in Figure 8-1.

　　The nation's surging dependence on imported oil occurs amid considerable uncertainty about the duration of global petroleum supply and increasing international competition for access to known petroleum reserves. The International Energy Agency, for instance, predicts that mainland China's rapid economic growth will increase its dependence on imported petroleum from 22 percent in 2000 to 77 percent of its annual petroleum consumption by 2020, and, during the same period, European dependence on imported oil will rise from 52 to 79 percent of annual demand.[12] The economic and political assumptions undergirding all predictions of future world energy supply are at best informed speculation, often confounded easily by unanticipated events. Given these uncertainties, and the enormous ecological, economic, and security risks entailed in continuing heavy dependence on imported oil, the United States has reason to consider imported oil a major problem. Currently, however, few short-term alternatives exist. The most often considered of these alternatives are renewable energy (solar, thermal, wind, and hydroelectric power) and energy conservation. None of these have yet created the popular appeal, or political allure, that would significantly diminish the current national dependency on fossil fuels.

When the Bush administration needed $135,000 to print copies of its 2001 energy plan, the money came from the Department of Energy's (DOE's) solar and renewable energy conservation funds.[13] Environmentalists considered this another sour revelation of the administration's dismissive attitude toward renewable energy, but energy conservation has been more often praised than vigorously promoted by the White House since Jimmy Carter's term. Today, all forms of renewable energy provide only 6 percent of the nation's total energy consumption. Conventional hydroelectric facilities and wood fuels provide almost 80 percent of renewable energy (45 percent and 34 percent, respectively). Although national consumption of renewable energy has risen by modest increments in recent decades—particularly when the energy crisis of the 1970s prompted momentary congressional attention to alternative fuels—the White House, Congress, and the public have demonstrated a feeble and inconstant commitment to renewable energy when compared with the national investment in fossil fuels. Indeed, the federal government, without public objection, dismantled within a few years almost all the most potent incentives to energy conservation and renewable energy production created during the short-lived energy crisis of the 1970s.

A Fading Governmental Concern

Public sensitivity about energy shortages and fossil fuel dependency was hurried toward extinction by the Ronald Reagan administration's rapid elimination of the energy conservation and regulatory programs enacted in the late 1970s and by the return of ample world petroleum supplies and lower petroleum prices. Neither the George H. W. Bush nor Bill Clinton administrations seemed interested in disturbing the public reverie. Thus, George W. Bush inherited both a superheated energy economy and two decades of apathetic energy planning when he entered the White House in 2001.

By any environmental accounting, the national energy condition in the fading first decade of the twenty-first century was disturbing. The United States had barely created its first coherent, but untested, energy plan in two decades to deal with the accelerating depletion of global petroleum reserves, including its own. Whatever its merits or deficiencies, the Bush administration's 2005 Energy Policy Act at least aspired to a national energy policy and promoted a renewed, national discussion of energy issues. Bush, an oil man from an oil state, could hardly be indifferent about energy. It was evident that his administration would push hard and unapologetically to accelerate domestic petroleum, natural gas, and coal production. The new president's executive appointments were conspicuously populated with individuals associated with energy industries, beginning with Vice President Cheney, another oil man. The early selection of Gale Norton, an enthusiastic western proponent of expansive new energy production in federal lands, as secretary of the Department of the Interior (DOI) sent an unmistakable signal to the environmental community that aggressive domestic energy development would be a major battlefront again. Bush's benign regard for commercial nuclear power and tepid interest in energy conservation technologies reinforced the environmentalist suspicion that the new administration tilted heavily toward the supply side of the energy equation. To the environmentalist community, all this seemed like an unwelcome reprise of Reagan's energy politics with its heavy dependence on fossil fuels and expansive new domestic energy production.

The 2005 Energy Policy Act

The 2005 EPAt, unlike the Bush National Energy Plan of 2001, gave significant attention to energy conservation by creating numerous federal subsidies, tax incentives, and research support for the development of new energy-efficient technologies and improved energy conservation practices in the domestic economy. The important energy conservation and efficiency features included:

• $4.19 billion in tax credits for the production of renewable energy (biomass, wind, solar, thermal, hydroelectric) and increased energy efficiency in existing homes;
• New energy standards for a large variety of appliances, and tax credits for hybrid vehicle purchases;
• Increased federal funding for research, development, and demonstration of new, efficient energy technologies;
• Increased federal spending and tax incentives for production and blending of biofuels in domestic motor vehicles.

From the perspective of most environmental spokespersons, however, these conservation and efficiency proposals seemed feeble when compared to EPAt's fossil-fueled, production-driven, nuclear inspired plans for the energy future. These major provisions include:

• Numerous incentives for continued development of nuclear electric power production, including more than $6 billion in federal subsidies, tax incentives, and research grants for construction of six new nuclear power plants and development of new nuclear reactor technologies; increased federal risk insurance protection for new nuclear power plants;

• Federal loan guarantees to build at least sixteen new coal-fired power plants and federal research support, tax incentives, and subsidies for development of "clean coal" technologies;

• Up to $1.5 billion in new subsidies to the oil industry for ultradeep oil drilling and exploration;

• Mandated, rapid development of commercial oil shale/tar sands leasing programs and other incentives for accelerated production of unconventional fossil fuels.

Perhaps most important to environmentalists was that EPAt did *not* contain what they considered such essential elements as new fuel efficiency standards for motor vehicles, mandatory regulation of domestic greenhouse gas emissions, and reduced dependence on imported petroleum.

Spokespersons for the Bush administration asserted that sufficient regulations existed, or would be created, to ensure adequate environmental protection during this surge of new development. However, environmentalists were convinced that the administration was intent on promoting a new and unprecedented raid on national energy resources unrestrained by environmental sensibilities.

The intricate interdependence of energy production and environmental quality can be appreciated by examining three national energy issues in greater depth. Conventional nuclear power and coal, both important energy sectors, pose significant ecological risks likely to continue as long as the United States builds its energy future on a foundation of fossil fuel. And the sudden emergence of a new nuclear issue—the staggering financial and technical task of cleaning up the nation's military nuclear weapons facilities—threatens to create costs so massive and work so protracted that it will be the most expensive federal environmental program through most of the twenty-first century.

Nuclear Twilight or Second Dawn?

At the turn of the twenty-first century, statistics about commercial nuclear power read like the industry's obituary. Since 1980 the Nuclear Dream—the vision of almost unlimited, cheap electricity generated from nuclear reactors by the hundreds—has been dying. The commercial nuclear power industry has been failing under a burden of economic and technological misfortunes, an increasingly hostile political climate, inept public relations, persistent environmental risks, and regulatory pressures that have been mounting since the early 1970s. Predictions of the industry's imminent demise have been common.

The nuclear industry, however, now hopes to revive through what might be called the other greenhouse effect. Buoyed by a conviction that global warming and acid precipitation can dispel its gathering misfortunes, the industry initiated in the 1990s an increasingly aggressive strategy to promote itself as the most desirable economic and environmental alternative to fossil fuel for electric power generation. Environmentalists continue to reject this assertion, citing the industry's continuing ecological risks and unresolved technological difficulties. The industry was enormously encouraged when the Bush administration declared in its 2001 National Energy Plan that a "dramatic improvement in U.S. nuclear power plant performance over the last 25 years" had occurred and that the industry "has established a strong foundation for the expansion of nuclear energy in the next two decades."[14] The DOE's 2004 support for an industry proposal to build fifty new power plants and to prolong the operating life of numerous existing facilities to the year 2020 was additional encouragement. The Energy Policy Act's very substantial commitment to nuclear power development in 2005 seemed to nuclear power advocates confirmation that industry was, at last, truly reviving.[15] Still, proponents of nuclear power have massive difficulties to overcome before the technology can again be considered a plausible national energy option.

The Peaceful Atom and Its Problems

Peaceful atomic power began with the Dwight D. Eisenhower administration's determination to demonstrate to the world that the United States was concerned with more than the military uses of nuclear power and the prevention of global nuclear proliferation. The federal government offered to the electric power industry massive subsidies and other powerful incentives to create a nuclear electric power infrastructure. Once the electric power industry agreed to the bargain, the regulation and management of the new technology were invested in the Atomic Energy Commission (AEC) and in the Joint Committee on Atomic Energy, a new congressional watchdog for the commission.[16]

The industry prospered from benevolent regulation, huge infusions of federal subsidies reaching between $12 billion and $15 billion by the mid-1980s, public and political favor, and unique governmental concessions never given its competitors, such as the Price-Anderson Act (1957), which limited a nuclear utility's insurance liability to $540 million for any single reactor accident, thus ensuring that the industry would obtain the necessary insurance coverage. Until the 1970s all but a handful of scientists, economists, and public officials associated with the new technology seemed, in the words of economists Irvin C. Bupp and Jean-Claude Derian, so "intoxicated" by the enterprise that they largely ignored grave technical and economic problems already apparent to a few critical observers.[17] When problems could not be ignored, they usually were hidden from public view; when critics arose, they were discredited by Washington's aggressive defense of the industry.

The Nuclear Dream seemed most resplendent in 1975: 56 commercial reactors had been built, another 69 were under construction, and 111 more were planned. Then came the near catastrophic reactor meltdown at Three Mile Island, near Harrisburg, Pennsylvania, in March 1979, the most politically damaging episode in the program's brief history, forcing national attention on an industry already in serious trouble. Grave technical and economic problems had been evident even in the early 1970s. The accident at Three Mile Island, however, was a catalytic political event, powerfully altering public consciousness about nuclear power and strengthening the credibility of the industry's critics. Moreover, the industry's grave economic, technical, and environmental problems continued to worsen as the 1980s progressed. The May 1986 core meltdown at the Chernobyl nuclear power plant in the Soviet Ukraine was one more catastrophe in a series of baleful events hastening the extinction of the Nuclear Dream. As the twentieth century ended, the domestic industry was almost moribund.

The Nuclear Industry Today

In 2007 there were 103 operating nuclear reactors licensed to U.S. electrical utilities, down from a peak of 112 in 1990. Most reactors are located along the East Coast, in the southeast, and in the midwest (Figure 8-2). These reactors currently represent about 21 percent of U.S. net electricity-generating capacity. Under current schedules, half the present reactors will end their legal operating lives between the years 2005 and 2015; the remainder will shut down before 2075. In short, commercial nuclear power will disappear within a few generations, unless some of the present facility licenses are extended and new ones are constructed. The major reason for this threatened extinction is that U.S. utilities have not ordered a new reactor since 1979 while simultaneously cutting back sharply on planned construction.

Despite notable improvement in the industry's safety procedures, technology, and operating efficiency since Three Mile Island, its troubles remain substantial, including economic and technical difficulties, unsolved waste management problems, and a volatile regulatory climate made worse by new fears of terrorist attacks on nuclear facilities.

Economic Ills. The cost of constructing and maintaining commercial nuclear power plants climbed so steeply between 1980 and 2000 that investment capital has been scarce and costly. A new nuclear facility will

Figure 8-2   U.S. Commercial Nuclear Power Reactors

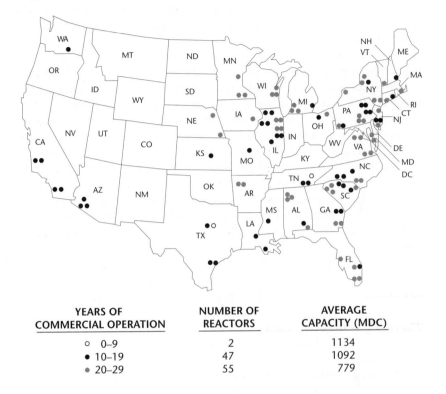

YEARS OF COMMERCIAL OPERATION	NUMBER OF REACTORS	AVERAGE CAPACITY (MDC)
○ 0–9	2	1134
● 10–19	47	1092
● 20–29	55	779

Source: U.S. Nuclear Regulatory Commission, "Map of Power Reactors Sites," at www.nrc.gov/reactors/operating/map-power-reactors.html (April 3, 2007).

Note: There are no commercial reactors in Alaska or Hawaii. Calculated data as of 12/00.

currently cost its builders between $1.5 and $2.0 billion—enough to discourage even financially secure utilities. Many operating facilities are producing power at a unit cost far exceeding original projections. Facilities completed in the late 1990s in general will be 500 to 1,000 percent over budget.[18] New Hampshire's bitterly contested Seabrook No. 1 facility, finally granted an operating license in 1990 after a fifteen-year battle with opponents, was originally expected to cost $900 million. At startup in 1990 the costs had exceeded $5.8 billion. When Detroit Edison's Enrico Fermi II plant began generation in 1988, it was $4 billion over its original budget.[19]

Among the major reasons for this cost escalation are issues concerning public safety and environmental protection. The time required to secure the many governmental licenses that ensure the facility will meet safety and environmental standards has been lengthening continually. Currently, surmounting these regulatory hurdles requires four to eight years and may involve almost a hundred different federal, state, and local governmental permits. Industry officials also complain about the costs imposed during plant construction through regulatory "ratcheting" by the Nuclear Regulatory Commission (NRC)—its habit of requiring facilities to make new safety modifications or other expensive design changes retroactively. Additional costs have been imposed on many utilities by protracted litigation involving environmental groups and others challenging various aspects of plant design and safety. These costs have reduced the market competitiveness of nuclear-generated electricity in comparison with fossil-fuel-burning plants. A portent of the future seemed to occur in 1998 when Chicago's Commonwealth Edison closed its Zion nuclear power plant permanently—the costliest commercial nuclear shutdown in U.S. history and the result of persistent technological problems, cost overruns, extended downtime, and regulatory difficulties that seemed increasingly evident in numerous other facilities well.[20]

The industry's economic ills cannot be blamed wholly on regulators and environmental critics. Operating plants acquired a lackluster efficiency image because many performed below design levels throughout the 1980s and 1990s, even though the industry's annual capacity rate reached 90 percent by 2007.[21] And serious, expensive technical problems continue to beset the industry.

Technical Problems. Proponents of nuclear power argue correctly that its safety record, notwithstanding the accident at Three Mile Island, is excellent and that critics have exaggerated its technical problems. However, continuing revelations of technical difficulties suggest serious deficiencies in the basic design and operation of the plants and frequent carelessness or incompetence in plant management. Whatever their real significance, these problems have worked against the industry politically. Continuing admissions of safety risks and technical difficulties at a time of growing public apprehension about nuclear terrorism continue to inspire the opposition.

Several technical problems have been especially damaging to the industry. Materials and design standards for many plants currently operating or under construction have failed essential safety requirements. Reactor parts, for instance, have aged much faster than anticipated. Steam generators meant to last a plant's lifetime—approximately fifty years—are wearing out much sooner than expected; this is a particularly serious problem in New York, Florida, Virginia, Wisconsin, and South Carolina.[22] Mistakes have been made in plant specifications or construction. Pipes have cracked and "wasted" (the walls becoming thinner) from extended exposure to radiation. As early as 1988 the U.S. General Accounting Office (GAO) recommended a mandatory inspection of all plants for pipe deterioration after finding that nearly a third of the plants it surveyed did indeed have pipe deterioration. The NRC betrayed its own misgivings about plant safety in 1979, when it repudiated its 1974 estimate, contained in the so-called Rassmussen report, that a potential catastrophic reactor accident would occur only once in ten million years of reactor operation—as probable as a single meteorite striking someone on earth. The NRC failed at the time to provide an alternative safety estimate.

Finally, continuing revelations of plant mismanagement, administrative bungling, and secrecy raise serious questions about the competence of plant managers and technicians. The industry must still contend with disclosures such as the NRC's announcement in early 2007 that it had downgraded the safety rating of the nation's largest nuclear plant, subjecting it to more inspectors and a level of scrutiny shared by just one other plant in the nation. "The NRC's announcement," the Associated Press reported,

> ended three years of problems in various safety systems at the Palo Verde nuclear plant west of Phoenix. Inspectors in September found that one of its emergency diesel generators had been broken for 18 days. Emergency generators are critically important at nuclear reactors, providing electricity to pumps, valves and control rooms if the main electrical supply fails. Only FirstEnergy Corp.'s Perry nuclear plant in Ohio has a safety rating as bad as Palo Verde's, NRC spokesman Victor Dricks said.[23]

Industry officials insist that critics have distorted and misrepresented the safety record of commercial nuclear utilities by seizing on these disclosures as if they characterized the entire industry. Indeed, many utilities have a virtually uninterrupted record of safe operations and skilled management. Still, after more than thirty years of operation, the industry continues to experience serious design, management, and engineering failures. The Union of Concerned Scientists' verdict seems fair:

> Is nuclear power in the United States safe enough today just because a reactor has not experienced a meltdown since 1979? The answer is a resounding no. In the 27 years since the TMI meltdown, 38 U.S. nuclear power reactors had to be shut down for at least one year while safety margins were restored to minimally acceptable levels. Seven of these reactors experienced two-year-plus outages. Though these reactors were shut down before they experienced a major accident, we cannot assume we will continue to be so lucky. The number and length of these shutdowns testifies to how serious and widespread the problem is.[24]

Moreover, the industry has not solved its grave waste disposal and emergency management problems.

The Waste Nobody Wants. No problem has proved more politically troublesome to the nuclear power industry and its federal regulators than where, and how, to dispose of the enormous, highly toxic, and mounting volume of nuclear wastes in the United States. The problem, never anticipated when commercial nuclear power was first promoted, has been especially difficult because reactor wastes incite great public fear and chronic conflict among federal, state, and local officials concerning where to put them.

This nuclear waste originates from uranium mining, civilian nuclear power plants, military nuclear weapons programs, hospitals, educational institutions, and research centers. Current controversy involves four categories of waste:

• *High-Level Wastes.* This category of waste comprises highly radioactive liquids created through the reprocessing of reactor fuels. These wastes are generated by both civilian and military reactor programs. Currently, more than 100 million gallons of high-level wastes are stored in temporary containment facilities in Idaho, New York, South Carolina, and Washington state.

• *Transuranic Wastes.* Some of the elements in these radioactive byproducts of reactor fuel and military waste processing remain dangerous for extraordinarily long periods. Plutonium-239, with a half-life of 24,000 years, and americum-243, with a 7,300-year half-life, are among the transuranics. Other more exotic transuranic elements have a half-life exceeding 200,000 years.

• *Spent Nuclear Fuel.* About 32,000 metric tons of spent fuel, mostly from civilian reactors, are stored temporarily in cooling ponds at reactor sites. By 2000 this spent fuel increased to more than 42,000 metric tons.

• *Low-Level Wastes.* Any material contaminated by radiation and emitting low levels of radioactivity itself belongs in this category. This includes workers' clothing, tools, equipment, and other items associated with nuclear reactors or nuclear materials. Low-level wastes currently are stored at repositories in Nevada, New York, and South Carolina.

Figure 8-3 shows where the wastes from commercial reactors and military activities are stored. In the early years of nuclear power promotion, it was assumed that spent fuel from civilian and military plants would be reprocessed: the fissionable materials, primarily plutonium, would be recovered for use again as reactor fuel, and the remaining high-level waste eventually would be contained and isolated at appropriate disposal sites. In the planners' early view, the high-level and transuranic wastes remaining after reprocessing posed a largely technical and readily solvable problem of finding the appropriate containment materials and geographic location for permanent storage. They did not anticipate the failure of civilian reprocessing and the resulting volume of nuclear waste. They did not foresee the necessity to store military wastes for decades longer than the con-

Figure 8-3   Current Locations of Spent Nuclear Fuel and High-Level
Radioactive Waste Destined for Geological Disposition

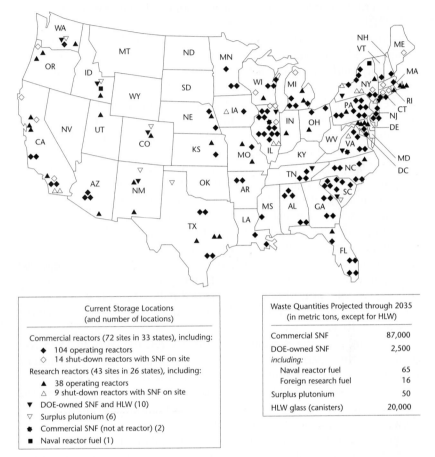

Current Storage Locations (and number of locations)	Waste Quantities Projected through 2035 (in metric tons, except for HLW)	
Commercial reactors (72 sites in 33 states), including:	Commercial SNF	87,000
◆ 104 operating reactors	DOE-owned SNF	2,500
◇ 14 shut-down reactors with SNF on site	*including:*	
Research reactors (43 sites in 26 states), including:	Naval reactor fuel	65
▲ 38 operating reactors	Foreign research fuel	16
△ 9 shut-down reactors with SNF on site	Surplus plutonium	50
▼ DOE-owned SNF and HLW (10)	HLW glass (canisters)	20,000
▽ Surplus plutonium (6)		
✦ Commercial SNF (not at reactor) (2)		
■ Naval reactor fuel (1)		

Source: U.S. Department of Energy, Office of Civilian Radioactive Waste Management, www.rw.doe.gov/wasteaccept/snflocationspic.jpg (March 27, 2001).

Note: HLW = high-level radioactive waste; SNF = spent nuclear fuel. Symbols do not reflect exact locations.

tainment structures were designed to last. They did not anticipate the political repercussions of trying to find a place to put the waste.

Existing and planned commercial facilities were designed to store temporarily no more than three years' worth of accumulated spent fuel in cooling ponds until the fuel assemblies were reprocessed. Since the early 1970s, however, virtually all spent fuel has been stored in these cooling ponds. Space and time are running out. The United States continues to reprocess its spent military fuel, thereby generating most of the high-level liquid wastes accumulating at military nuclear reservations. Until 1982 the federal government had no comprehensive plan for the permanent storage of these nuclear wastes. The federal government and the states quarreled for more than a decade over how a permanent waste depository would be designed and which states would be depository sites—nobody wanted it.[25] Idaho and South Carolina, already accommodating large volumes of high- and low-level wastes from other states, were increasingly reluctant to accept more. In 1976 California ordered a moratorium on the construction of commercial nuclear facilities until Washington, D.C., could certify that a permanent repository for their spent fuel existed. The nuclear waste issue was approaching a crisis.

The States Play Nuclear "Keep Away." In 1982 Congress finally passed the Nuclear Waste Policy Act (NWPA), which was intended to create a process for designating and constructing the first permanent repositories for nuclear waste. The act appeared to end a decade of nasty legislative infighting during which each state scrambled to write language into the law ensuring that it would not be a candidate for the repository. The legislation assigned the site-selection task to the DOE and created what appeared to be a meticulously detailed, impartial, and open process by which all possible sites would be studied thoroughly and reduced to a few from which the president would eventually select two, one east and one west of the Mississippi River.

Following procedures required by the NWPA, the DOE in 1985 recommended three permanent western sites to the president from which he was to select one: Deaf Smith County, Texas; the Hanford Nuclear Reservation in Washington State; and Yucca Mountain, Nevada (near the Nevada atomic test site). The political leadership of both parties in all three states complained vehemently that their states had been improperly designated and attempted to overturn the designation in the courts. Environmental groups in each state went to court, challenging the designations on technical and procedural grounds. Rather than abide the continuing controversy, Congress found a simpler solution to the designation problem. In December 1987 Congress suddenly renounced the procedures it had ordered in the NWPA and summarily designated Nevada to be the first permanent waste site. As a consolation, Nevada was assured of receiving up to $20 million annually to manage the job. Nevada legislators were outraged. It "will turn our state into a federal colony," accused Republican representative Barbara F. Vucanovich.[26] "Instead of leadership and principle, it's a gang-rape mentality," added a spokesperson for Richard Bryan, Nevada's governor. The man who arranged it all thought otherwise. "If I were a Nevadan living in the real world, I would be happy with this bill," asserted Sen. J. Bennett Johnston, D-La. "I would bet that in a very few years, Nevada will deem this one of their most treasured industries."[27] Throughout the 1990s, however, Nevada continued to resist development of the Yucca Mountain facility with every political resource it had available.

This trench warfare slowed the facility's construction to a crawl, but Congress in 1997 left little doubt that Nevada was still the nation's most eligible nuclear waste bin. Both the House and the Senate passed legislation, over the vehement objections of the state's leaders, that would create a temporary repository near the Yucca Mountain site for the high-level nuclear waste still awaiting the completion of the permanent Nevada site.[28] In the keep-away politics of nuclear waste, the most weakly defended constituency was still "it."

Repository Problems

"It's fair to say we've solved the nuclear waste problem with this legislation," Senator Johnston assured his colleagues with premature optimism after they awarded the waste to Nevada. But after more than two years of preliminary work and an expenditure of $500 million at the Nevada site, the DOE announced in 1989 that it was abandoning its initial repository plan because it lacked confidence in the technical quality of the proposal.[29] The DOE predicted that the repository would be delayed until at least 2010, even though it was committed to accepting high-level wastes from commercial reactors by 1998 and the commercial utilities had already paid $3 billion in taxes to use the repository. However, by 2007 it was evident that the DOE would not be ready to receive the wastes at even a temporary repository, and the availability of a permanent repository remained equally speculative. "A realistic date for having a permanent repository operational keeps receding farther into the future," concluded the GAO.[30] Frustrated by these continuing delays, the Bush administration in 2002 declared its intention to open the site by 2010, requested a large budget increase to underwrite accelerated site construction in 2003, and was promptly sued by the state of Nevada and numerous other plaintiffs, thereby relegating the Yucca Mountain facility to a judicial limbo and an uncertain future once again.

Meanwhile, reports on the DOE's other nuclear waste management projects have been unrelieved bad news since the late 1980s. In mid-1989 the DOE announced that it was delaying the opening of its Waste Isolation Pilot Project (WIPP) near Carlsbad, New Mexico. The WIPP, begun in the late 1970s, was intended to store the plutonium wastes generated at the Rocky Flats nuclear military facility near Denver, Colorado, where space for the liquid wastes was fast disappearing. The underground repository had been scheduled to receive its first shipments in 1992, but the DOE's scientific advisers urged a delay of two or three years because the DOE needed to complete technical diagrams of twenty-one systems already built into the structure, including the electrical, radiation control, and fire protection systems.[31] In fact, the WIPP did not receive its first nuclear waste until 2001.

The WIPP's delay added another chapter to the already protracted, acrimonious debate about the safety of that facility and raised doubts that the WIPP will ever be used. Thus, the nation still lacks a permanent repository for its civilian and military nuclear wastes. Waste storage capacity at civilian utility sites continues to dwindle. At the same time, military waste-containment structures are deteriorating dangerously at places such as the Hanford Nuclear Reservation, where 440,000 cubic yards of high-, low-, and extremely long-lived nuclear wastes are stored, some since 1943, awaiting permanent deposition.[32] This is not, however, the whole of the national nuclear waste problem. The controversy attending reactor waste deflects public attention from the emerging problem of disposing of nuclear facilities themselves after they have outlived their usefulness.

Decommissioning Problems

Once a civilian or military nuclear facility has finished its useful life, the NRC and the DOE require that the owners decommission the facility by removing from the site the radioactive materials, including land, groundwater, buildings, contents, and equipment and by reducing residual radioactivity to a level permitting the property to be used for any other purpose.[33] Because a commercial reactor's life span is expected to be fifty years, an increasing number of the nation's reactors had to be decommissioned beginning in the 1990s. Sixteen nuclear power plants are currently undergoing decommissioning and five have completed the process. However, no utility has yet completely decommissioned a large plant, and none expect to do so until a permanent high-level waste depository is available. Instead, the utilities plan to partially decommission their facilities and put them in so-called safe storage while awaiting the completion of a permanent repository.

Little is known about how large facilities can be taken apart and rendered safe. Few of the nation's utilities have done much practical planning for decommissioning their own plants. No reliable estimates are available for decommissioning costs, which have been calculated to range from tens of millions to $3 billion for each facility.[34] The NRC currently requires utilities to set aside $105 million to $135 million for decommissioning, but many experts believe these estimates are too low. Utilities are also required to have decommissioning plans, cost estimates, or written certification that they will meet the NRC's cost estimates. Still, no utility has yet created a decommissioning fund, assessed its rate payers for the costs, or filed a complete decommissioning plan with the NRC in the absence of a permanent high-level waste repository.

The DOE's responsibility for decommissioning the nation's military reactors presents even more formidable problems. Investigations of the nation's military nuclear facility management beginning in the late 1980s revealed appalling negligence in waste storage and management, leaks of dangerous radioactive materials for decades into the surrounding environment and civilian settlements, and deceit and secrecy in managing information about the lethal dangers created both onsite and offsite from waste mismanagement. This legacy of negligence leaves the DOE with a conservatively estimated cost of $230 billion to decontaminate and decommission its nuclear facilities.[35] Many experts believe the costs will climb much higher, so intolerably high that the sites will be, as some plant engineers privately predict, "national sacrifice zones" never decontaminated adequately.[36]

Waste management and nuclear plant decommissioning problems will trouble Americans for centuries and remain a reminder of the technological optimism and mission fixation that inspired Washington, D.C.'s approach to nuclear technology development. Indeed, the politics of civilian nuclear power development has been as important as its science in shaping the economic, ecological, and technological character of the industry. So it will continue to be. The future of commercial nuclear power will be determined, in good part, by how Congress, the White House, and the NRC respond to its present ills and challenges. The battle for the nuclear future is still being fought in these political arenas.

The Nuclear Regulatory Commission in the Middle

The NRC works in the vortex of controversy over commercial nuclear power regulation. Critics of the nuclear power industry almost ritually indict the NRC for its regulatory failures. But even its proponents recognize a problem. It was an NRC commissioner newly appointed by President Reagan, a pronuclear spokesperson for a pronuclear administration, who publicly complained shortly after assuming office about the "surprising lack of professionalism in the construction and preparation . . . of nuclear facilities" and "lapses of many kinds—in design analysis resulting in built-in design errors, in poor construction practices, in falsified documents. . . ."[37] The NRC's regulatory deficiencies arise, in large part, from the political circumstances of its origin and the outlook of its professional staff. The NRC was created in 1974 when Congress abolished the AEC and vested that agency's regulatory authority in the new NRC. The new agency could not readily dissolve the strong, congenial professional and institutional relationships linking former AEC staff to the nuclear power industry, nor could it eliminate the impulse to promote and protect the industry so deeply rooted in the AEC's history. In addition, the NRC remains unapologetic about its commitment to nuclear power. "People who serve on this commission and on its staff do believe in the nuclear industry," retorted one staff member to a critic.[38] Successive NRC commissioners and their staffs often tried to regulate without prejudice and sometimes succeeded, but institutional history and professional experience often—the critics say *usually*— prevailed against regulatory rigor.

In the aftermath of Three Mile Island, the NRC has made an effort to be a more aggressive and foresighted regulator, and its relationship to the industry has become more complex. The NRC required a multitude of changes in plant management that cost utilities an average of $50 million. It has been quicker and harsher in assessing regulatory penalties, but the commission is still cited for serious regulatory lapses. For example, a GAO study of five nuclear facilities between 1986 and 1987 disclosed that "despite records of chronic safety violations, NRC did not close them. With only one exception, a safety incident occurred that made continued operation impossible or the utilities shut them down when the problems grew severe." Regarding plant safety standards, the study noted that the "NRC may take from several months to 10 or more years to resolve . . . generic issues, including those NRC believes pose the highest safety risk."[39] A GAO investigation of the NRC's supervision for the decommissioning of eight small reactors in 1987 found that the "NRC fully or partially released two sites for unrestricted use where contamination at one was up to 4 times, and at the other up to 320 times higher than NRC's guidelines allowed. . . . Also, among five facilities that buried waste, NRC does not know the types and amounts of radioactive waste that have been buried at four of the sites."[40]

Defenders of the NRC assert that many of its regulatory lapses result from understaffing and underfunding, and that the regulatory changes required by the NRC often take years for utilities to accomplish. Some observers argue that the NRC must be doing its job reasonably well because it is also a frequent target of criticism from the nuclear power industry itself. One certainty is that the NRC operates in a radically different political environment from that prior to the accident at Three Mile Island. Relentless public exposure, politically potent and organized critics from the scientific and environmental communities, fading congressional enthusiasm for nuclear power, and technical controversy over the safety and economic prospects of nuclear power all produce a politically volatile regulatory climate in which the NRC must expect to operate. The transcendent political question for the NRC at the beginning of the twenty-first century, however, is whether it will be presiding over the death of the Nuclear Dream.

Stubborn Hope: Breakthrough Technology, the White House, and the Greenhouse

In mid-2006, one of the nation's most prominent environmentalists made a startling admission. Patrick Moore, a founder of the militant international environmental organization Greenpeace and persistent critic of nuclear electric power, had changed his mind. "In the early 1970s," he wrote in the *Washington Post,* "when I helped found Greenpeace, I believed that nuclear energy was synonymous with nuclear holocaust, as did most of my compatriots. . . . Thirty years on, my views have changed, and the rest of the environmental movement needs to update its views, too, because nuclear energy may just be the energy source that can save our planet from another possible disaster: catastrophic climate change."[41] What changed his mind? He cited many reasons: the potential of newer, safer, reactor technologies; the nuclear reactor's lack of climate warming emissions; increasing nuclear reactor safety; and—perhaps most important—the urgency to renounce dependence on fossil fuel. This was heresy to a great many environmentalists. Still, Moore's admission pointed toward a policy pathway slowly but persistently attracting increased public and political attention. Despite the nuclear power industry's tarnished past, public opinion polls in recent years reveal an eroding public resistance to renewed nuclear power development while the Bush administration's relentless advocacy has kept nuclear power open to political debate. If the nuclear power industry has cause for optimism about the future, it lies in this possibly transforming political sea change.

Spokespersons for the industry assert that the lessons learned from five decades of experience with commercial nuclear power are being applied in the design of a new generation of smaller, safer reactors free from the technical and economic ills of the present ones.[42] The advanced light-water reactor presently at design stage is alleged to be ten times safer than current reactors in terms of severe accident prevention. Two other promising technologies, the modular high-temperature gas-cooled reactor, sometimes called the pebble-bed reactor, and the liquid metal reactor, are also at design stage. The nuclear industry asserts that this new generation of reactors, while smaller than present ones, could be used in combination (as modules) to produce as much power as needed much more safely and economically in future power plants. Moreover, the industry now supports the adoption of a standard design for all future commercial reactors instead of the multiple designs now in use. This strategy would facilitate the rapid development and application of safety standards for the whole industry.

The commercialization of this new generation of reactors will require a huge investment in research and development. The nuclear power industry, unable to raise capital on this scale in light of its past experience, must

depend on the federal government for aid. Congress, reluctant to preclude the nuclear option, has helped to keep the industry alive by renew-
ing the Price-Anderson Act, which limits the insurance liability of utility
operators, now to a maximum of $7 billion for any single commercial reac-
tor accident. This new liability limit is still much smaller than a nuclear
utility would ordinarily expect to pay in liability for an accident without
the act in place.

Advocates for continued reactor development argue that should an
alternative for fossil fuels be needed in the future, the nation cannot afford
to have only the present flawed reactor technologies available. After
reviewing the considerable uncertainties over future availability of fossil
fuels and other energy alternatives, science policy specialists Joseph G.
Morone and Edward J. Woodhouse concluded that the nuclear option still
makes sense:

> We cannot predict what energy the nation and world will want or need, nor
> what options will be available to meet the demands. . . . It is conceivable that
> there will be enough options to render nuclear power unnecessary in many
> nations, but equally conceivable that there will not be. And if such difficul-
> ties as the greenhouse effect do force a shift away from coal, and financially
> feasible energy alternatives are not available, much of the world may be
> backed into a corner: either rapidly construct a new generation of giant light
> water reactors, feared by a substantial portion of the population, or face the
> economic and other consequences of extremely tight energy supplies.[43]

The Cold War's Wasteland: Nuclear Weapons Facilities

At the dawn of the twenty-first century, it appears that the largest environmental program in U.S. history will be the environmental restoration
of military facilities, especially the numerous sites now administered by the
DOE in which military nuclear weapons research, production, and testing
have been conducted since the 1950s. The luckless DOE had inherited the
weapons facilities from the AEC when the commission was abolished in
1974. However, private corporations continued to operate the facilities
under contract to the DOE, which was assumed to be exercising regulatory oversight. Some of the resulting environmental problems were accidents or mistakes, perhaps inevitable. But contractors and their federal
watchdogs alike too often behaved as if regulations were irrelevant. The
legacy is environmental damage on a scale inviting disbelief.

Carelessness, incompetence, and willful evasion of regulations compounded with criminal negligence afflicted the weapons program from its
inception, tainting public and private participants alike. Most of these acts
were concealed by a wall of military secrecy until the 1970s. By the early
1990s, however, the wall was thoroughly breached. In 1992, for example,
the federal government admitted a shared responsibility with its contrac-

tors for environmental crimes at the Rocky Flats weapons facility. One contractor, Rockwell International, admitted guilt for ten crimes, including five felonies, and paid an $18.5 million fine. The DOE itself admitted that during the 1980s it had deliberately resisted any effort by the U.S. Environmental Protection Agency (EPA) or state environmental agencies to make its weapons facilities comply with environmental laws.[44] The DOE's evasions were inspired, in good part, by fear of multiple lawsuits from state governments, facility employees, and other private interests if Washington, D.C., admitted liability for environmental negligence or crimes. The suits came anyway.

"The Toughest, Most Dangerous Work in the World"

Site restoration now involves seventeen major locations in twelve states and more than fifty smaller sites—in all, more than 122 facilities in thirty states and the Marshall Islands. The DOE estimates suggest that cleanup of all sites—if the appropriate technologies can be created—will take at least seventy-five years and require at least $230 billion, or more than the Mercury, Gemini, and Apollo space programs combined, and could exceed $300 billion. Alone, the nuclear weapons cleanup would become the largest public works program in U.S. history. If it is extended to the more than eleven thousand other military facilities where various kinds of mixed (that is, radioactive and chemical) hazardous waste currently exist, the total cost of environmental restoration of national military facilities could exceed a half-trillion dollars and require the better part of a century. However, cost and time estimates are educated guesses, the bottom line of which has been increasing steadily since the late 1980s.

Former Secretary of Energy Hazel O'Leary's description of the cleanup as the "toughest, most dangerous work in the world" seems appropriate in light of the DOE's own grim appraisal of its task:

> Many facilities are old and deteriorating and present serious threats to those who work in and around them. The complex is regulated under a mix of internal and external regulatory and advisory bodies that administer a maze of laws, regulations, directives, orders, and guidance. The result is intense frustration through DOE's workforce, serious overlaps and gaps in regulatory requirements, and a failure to address hazards according to their relative risks, costs and benefits.[45]

The Wastes

The radioactive and chemical wastes now contaminating the DOE facilities have been accumulating since the beginning of World War II. Some of the most dangerous wastes, such as liquid radioactive chemicals at the Hanford site and at the Rocky Flats facility have been stored since the early

1940s in badly deteriorating containment tanks designed to last less than twenty years. Only after George H. W. Bush's administration initiated an aggressive investigation did the extent of the environmental contamination begin to appear. As the investigation widened under the Clinton administration, it became clear that accurate estimates about the extent of chemical contamination remaining on the sites and migrating offsite were difficult to make. The DOE has estimated that at least five hundred waste streams, or flows of waste from weapons sites, exist together with at least 500,000 cubic meters of mixed wastes.[46] Many of the liquid and solid chemical wastes, particularly high-level and transuranic substances, can be dangerous to humans and the environment for 100,000 years or more.

Damage estimates are problematic because accurate records at the weapons sites are elusive—in some cases, for instance, monitoring of waste streams moving off military reservations created in the 1940s was not initiated until the early 1990s. The DOE may be only partially responsible for these conditions, but it bears most of the legal and administrative liability for site restoration and becomes the lightning rod in the political turbulence sure to arise. The DOE must characterize the wastes involved, stabilize any dangerous waste-containment structures, remove all nuclear and hazardous materials from the sites, and sequester them in safe repositories. Many of the highly dangerous radioactive liquid and solid wastes are not well understood. Technologies for managing many wastes have not been developed. Safe and permanent repositories for the most dangerous wastes do not yet exist. Site cleanup will also require prolonged collaboration with a multitude of other agencies, including the Department of Defense, the EPA, the DOI, and all the state governments whose jurisdictions are affected by site work. Figure 8-4 depicts the past and projected magnitude of the high-level wastes accumulating at the four major DOE nuclear facilities.

The DOE, with desperate optimism, describes its task as the "vigorous challenge of cleaning up and safely containing waste for a thousand years. Scientific, environmental, and technical professionals must work closely with managers, educators, lawyers, innovators, and communicators to find the best solutions for cleaning up the environment and safely managing waste now and in the future. DOE's cleanup goal is one of the most difficult and vital tasks of our time."[47] A brief examination of conditions at the most thoroughly investigated site, the Hanford Nuclear Reservation near Richland, Washington, suggests how intimidating the challenge will be.

Billion-Dollar Burps and Cleanup Careers

The Hanford Nuclear Reservation is almost half the size of Rhode Island. Its highly radioactive military wastes dating from the early days of World War II will become the costliest, most complex, and most technically

Figure 8-4   Historical and Projected Cumulative Volumes of Untreated High-Level Waste in Storage

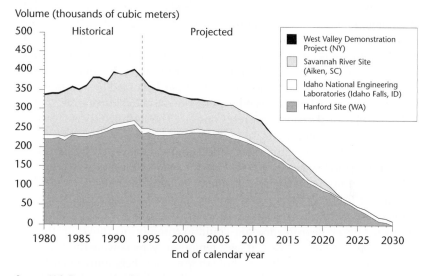

Source: U.S. Department of Energy, *Spent Fuel Storage Requirements 1993–2040* (Washington, D.C.: Government Printing Office, 1996), 38.

challenging restoration facing the DOE. The most dangerous of Hanford's wastes are fifty-four million gallons of highly corrosive liquid radioactive materials stored in 177 tanks designed in the early 1940s to last for no more than several decades. About one million gallons of these materials have leaked from sixty-six of the tanks since 1960, most of it into sub-surface soil and groundwater.[48] Much of this waste has migrated to major surface waters, including the Columbia River. Federal investigation has revealed a long history of administrative and technical bungling by the prime contractor, Westinghouse, largely concealed with bureaucratic obfuscation. In 1968, for instance, a major safety lapse involving an over-heating and partial fuel melting at a nuclear weapons assembly plant was reported as "an improbable mechanical failure."[49] The DOE reports indicated that workers at the facility were exposed to toxic gas leaking from the liquid containment tanks at least sixteen times since 1987, and some workers suffered permanent lung damage. Cleanup at the site was origi-nally predicted to cost perhaps $50 billion, but estimates climb inexorably. The cost of a treatment plant begun in 2001 to stabilize and prepare the site's liquid radioactive wastes for safe disposal for instance, has soared from $4.3 to $11 billion.[50] "People's careers are going to be over before this is done," remarked a spokesperson for Westinghouse.[51]

The witch's brew of problems posed by Hanford can be appreciated by considering Tank 101-SY, one of the most dangerous of the numerous liquid waste containments dating from the 1940s. Tank 101-SY holds 1.14 million gallons of extremely unstable, high-level radioactive waste stored so long that its chemistry and behavior are no longer well understood. The tank is known to contain potentially explosive concentrations of hydrogen gas that must be "burped" from the containment every hundred days. In 1991, videos revealed what looked like "a partly cooled lava inside a volcano, seething and lurching as it burps noxious and explosive gases . . . produced by chemical and nuclear reactions. . . . The shifting wastes splash the walls and bend metal parts . . . a narrator describes 'rollover events' in which the tank agitates itself."[52] By the century's end, the chemical mixture was said at the time to resemble "a giant radioactive soufflé." The tank wastes also offer unwelcome excitement: "Whipped up unexpectedly by a pump that was supposed to dissipate pockets of hydrogen gas," observed one reporter, "the waste has smothered one tube for vapor sampling, threatens other instruments and could eventually overflow. . . . In May workers stopped the growth, at least temporarily, by lancing the crust with high-pressure waste jets, but the hole they made is beginning to close."[53]

The state of Washington, suspicious of both the DOE and its Hanford contractors, has insisted on site inspection by its own regulators. At Tank 101-SY, an inspector in early 1992 found "three separate leak-detection systems, all inoperable: a sump pit that would detect liquids but was already flooded with water, an instrument for measuring radiation that was broken, and a liquid detector that was supposed to be suspended just above the floor between the inner and outer walls of the tank, but instead was hanging two and a half feet up, so it would not detect anything until wastes reached that level."[54] The federal government has been sued by the state of Washington, Westinghouse employees, environmental organizations, and private citizens for environmental contamination alleged to have been created throughout the Hanford site's history. Cleanup will require close collaboration not only with state and local interests but also with the EPA, because wastes onsite and offsite are subject to regulation under almost all major environmental laws, including the Clean Air Act, the Toxic Substances Control Act, the Resource Conservation and Recovery Act, the Clean Water Act, and Superfund legislation. By 2001, however, the DOE had just begun to identify the nature and location of the wastes to which these various regulations apply. "I don't make any claims about this tank," admitted one DOE energy expert. "I'm not convinced anyone understands the chemistry and physics involved. . . ."[55]

Hanford is the DOE's worst problem, but the complexities of site restoration are alike at most of the DOE weapons sites. Many experts believe that full restoration of all the DOE sites will be technically and economically impossible, forcing Congress or the DOE to practice administrative triage by selecting the priority sites (a responsibility the DOE fervently wishes to avoid, so nasty would be the congressional infighting).

A Perverse Economic Boon

If there is any political good news at the DOE sites, it is that restoration should be an economic windfall for communities and counties surrounding the facilities. DOE site cleanups will likely be a national growth industry. In Richland, Washington, and the neighboring cities of Pasco and Kenniwick, a real estate boom has been under way since 1991, and employment at the Hanford site is expected to exceed the largest workforce during the site's operating years. The cleanup has doubled the workforce required to manage sites such as Tank 101-SY. Spending for environmental cleanup in two other states meant no net loss of income for areas surrounding the weapons sites. The DOE's Savannah River site, presently employing 24,000 persons, is South Carolina's largest employer, and the workforce is expected to grow.[56] The economics of the DOE's cleanup has also complicated its restoration job, for site cleanup has become a coveted local expenditure that attracts considerable congressional attention, generating a minefield of political pressures and calculations to which the DOE must respond in making any important site decisions.

Black Gold

The George W. Bush administration's aggressive promotion of increased coal mining and consumption is a new chapter in an old story. Every U.S. president from Richard Nixon to Ronald Reagan tried to dam the flow of imported oil into the United States with a wall of coal. Coal is the nation's most plentiful fossil fuel. With reserves sufficient for 250 years at current consumption rates, it is inevitable that federal energy planners should repeatedly attempt to substitute abundant domestic coal for expensive, insecure imported oil. Economic and environmental problems, however, continue to inhibit a massive national conversion to coal combustion. The Reagan administration, convinced that excessive environmental regulation impeded coal consumption, was determined to have more coal and less environmental regulation. Reagan's successor, however, could not afford to regard coal so cordially. Most of the highly publicized environmental problems confronting George H. W. Bush's administration had "coal" written all over them: acid precipitation, climate warming, and more than one hundred major American cities with severe smog problems. Nonetheless, coal will remain for many decades a major fossil fuel and a continuing environmental problem.

The Saudi Arabia of Coal

Coal represents about 90 percent of the remaining U.S. hydrocarbon reserves. The coal industry liked to remind Americans during the energy crisis of the 1970s that the nation had the equivalent of Saudi petroleum reserves in coal. This coal rests in three geologic reserves: Appalachia's wooded hills and hollows sprawling across parts of seven southeastern states, the midwestern plains, and the western plains and grasslands.

In the late 1990s coal accounted for about 22 percent of U.S. energy consumption. Electric utilities, the prime coal consumers, generate more than half their power from coal-fired boilers and have been increasing their coal consumption. Although U.S. coal production stays at record levels, the industry has been afflicted since the 1950s with declining employment, chronic labor violence, and boom-or-bust economic cycles. The industry's economic fortunes are closely tied to the electric power and metallurgical industries, which consume, respectively, 85 and 13 percent of annual coal production. Because more than eight of every ten tons of mined coal are transported by rail, many railroads have become heavily dependent on coal production for revenue.

Presidential coal policies have always been rationalized by great expectations. The Nixon and Ford administrations' largely fanciful Project Independence promised that the United States could become almost independent of imported petroleum by 1980 through reliance on coal and conservation. President Carter, ignoring the chimera of "energy independence," still proposed in his 1977 energy plan to diminish U.S. dependence on petroleum through a 66 percent increase in domestic coal combustion within a decade and the creation of a massive new synthetic fuels industry based on coal feedstocks. The Reagan administration announced its intention to sell new coal mining leases in western public lands containing five billion tons of coal as a means of encouraging more production. The coal industry, sensing a possible reversal of its fortunes, was quick to proclaim coal the "great black hope of America" and to shift its political weight behind new White House coal initiatives.

There were several plausible reasons for coal's continuing attraction to energy planners despite related economic and environmental problems. According to some estimates, accelerated coal combustion might displace as much as 2.5 million barrels of imported petroleum consumed by the United States daily. A coal boom might bring 100,000 new workers to Appalachia, reviving its stagnant economy, and perhaps 50,000 more workers to the West; coal-related income in the West and Great Plains might rise by $850 million to $1 billion. Large "mine-mouth" electricity-generating plants, located adjacent to coal seams to reduce transportation costs, could provide dependable, secure electric power for the growing West and Midwest. The Carter energy plan might have increased railroad coal loadings by 350 percent between 1978 and 1985. Coal was secure energy, without menace from Middle Eastern politics and unpredictable world petroleum markets. Coal could glitter as gold if only the new coal boom could be made environmentally and economically tolerable.

Can Surface Mining Be Regulated?

The most significant adverse environmental impacts associated with coal use are created by surface mining and combustion. Many of the problems associated with coal combustion were examined in Chapter 6. The regulation of surface mining has been no less contentious.

Virtually all coal mined west of the Mississippi River and half the coal produced in Appalachia is surface mined. Surface mining rapidly has replaced underground mining because it is cheaper, more efficient, more profitable, and less labor intensive. Unless rigorously regulated, however, surface mining is environmentally catastrophic. More than 1.5 million acres of American land have been disturbed by coal surface mining; more than a million of these acres remain a wrecked and ravaged waste, long abandoned by their destroyers. More than one thousand additional acres are disturbed each week by surface mining, and more than thirty states have been scarred by unreclaimed surface mines.

In Appalachia, surface miners roamed the hills virtually uncontrolled for decades. The evidence is written in thousands of sterile acres, acidified streams and rivers, decapitated hills, and slopes scarred by abandoned mine highwalls. In western prairies and grasslands, unregulated surface mining left thousands of barren, furrowed acres buried under spoil banks so hostile to revegetation that they seemed like moonscapes to observers. After decades of resistance, the mining industry has come to recognize the necessity of environmental regulation of surface mining, but vigorous controversy continues over the manner of this regulation and its effectiveness.

President Carter, fulfilling a promise made during his election campaign, signed the Surface Mining Control and Reclamation Act (SMCRA) of 1977 and thereby created the first federal surface mining regulatory program. The act, strongly promoted by environmentalists against fierce resistance from the mining industry and two vetoes by President Ford, was intended to control the environmental ravages of surface mining by restoring surface-mined land to productivity whenever possible. The act's major features included the following:

• Environmental performance standards with which all surface miners were to comply in order to operate. Standards were to be established to regulate the removal, storage, and redistribution of topsoil; siting and erosion control; drainage and protection of water quality; and many other matters affecting environmental quality.

• Requirements that mined land be returned, insofar as possible, to its original contours and to a use equal or superior to that before mining commenced.

• Special performance and reclamation standards for mining on alluvial valley floors in arid and semiarid areas, on prime farmland, and on steep slopes.

• Enforcement of the act through a mining permit program administered jointly by the federal government and the states, according to federal regulations.

• Protection of land unsuitable for mining from any mine activity.

• Creation of a special fund, financed from a tax on existing surface mining, to reclaim so-called orphan mine sites.

• Creation of an agency, currently the Office of Surface Mining Reclamation and Enforcement (OSMRE) within the DOI, to enforce the act.

Few federal regulations were more directly and consistently attacked by the Reagan administration than those arising from SMCRA. The attack fell squarely on the OSMRE and on the regulations it wrote. OSMRE's field offices were reduced drastically, and its full-time staff inspectors diminished by half. Estimates suggest that Watt's office may have rewritten more than 90 percent of the regulations originally formulated by the DOI under President Carter.[57]

Despite improvements after 1985, SMCRA remains a troubled and underfunded program. The OSMRE and the states confront a hugely expensive and complex problem in protecting public health and safety on America's abandoned coal mine lands. Estimates suggest the total cost of restoring these ravaged and deserted acres is $8.6 billion.[58] Among other tasks, this requires remediation of 9,000 acres of unstable waste piles and embankments, 4 million linear feet of dangerous highwalls, 8,200 acres of subsiding soil, and 23,000 acres of clogged stream lands.[59] A succession of directors continues through the OSMRE's revolving door. The amount of improvement in program administration remains questionable. The OSMRE struggles at improving its public image (perhaps in desperation, its Web site now includes a children's link where young viewers can download a coloring book and poster depicting surface mines).[60] It seems apparent, at least, that the OSMRE cannot or will not exercise dependable, vigorous administrative oversight of state enforcement programs.[61] Still, some observers believe that the controversies surrounding SMCRA have had constructive results, including greater sensitivity in Washington, D.C., to the needs of the states and greater economic efficiency through more flexibility in program regulations.

One important test of surface mine regulations is whether they result in an environmentally safer mining industry and a significant restoration of the many thousand orphan mine sites across the United States. An answer is elusive, partially because the restoration of surface mine sites is difficult under the best of circumstances and public resources to underwrite much of the restoration cost remain unpredictable.

The Restoration Gamble

Obscured in the controversy over SMCRA's enforcement has been an issue even more important to the future of surface mining: Is restoration of mined lands in the manner contemplated by the act achievable? Technical studies suggest that the capacity of mining companies to restore mined land to conditions equal or superior to their original condition is likely to be site specific, that is, dependent on the particular biological and geological character of each mining site. Western mining sites are often ecologically fragile; relatively limited varieties of sustainable vegetation and scarce rainfall make ecological regeneration of the land difficult. With only limited experience in the restoration of western mine sites, most experts are reluctant to predict that mine sites can be restored to ecological vitality even with good intentions, generous funding, and high-quality technical resources.

The prospects for restoration are less forbidding in Appalachia, where an abundance of precipitation, richer soil, and a greater diversity of native flora and fauna are available. Nonetheless, many experts believe that disruption of subsurface hydrology and the drainage of acids and salts from the mines' spoil heaps may not be controlled easily even when surface revegetation is achieved. Restoration remains a gamble with nature. If restoration proves difficult, confronting public officials with the prospect that a major portion of all surface-mined land may remain virtually sterile for centuries, a further national controversy may erupt over continuing surface mining.

More than a decade of experience with SMCRA leaves only fragmentary evidence of its success. After studying SMCRA's enforcement among many states, for instance, political scientist Uday Desai concluded that the consequences have been mixed, at best. Environmentally safe conditions apparently were being maintained at active mine sites in Montana, Pennsylvania, and Wyoming. But in Kentucky, a major mining state, the law appeared to have had only a "marginal" impact, and in West Virginia, another important coal state, it "had not been thoroughly and rigorously enforced in many areas."[62] Desai's conclusion suggests how far SMCRA's enforcement has yet to go in achieving its purpose:

> It is not possible to make an unqualified overall national assessment, but the evidence . . . indicates that, in most (but by no means all) cases, surface coal mining is being carried out in environmentally less destructive ways than

before the Act. However, accomplishment of its ultimate objective has fallen far short of the expectations of many. In addition, there has been a serious deterioration of the situation on the ground in some states such as Kentucky.[63]

Despite the formidable challenges involved, OSMRE resolutely casts restoration in a benign light. But while the nation's coal production is constantly increasing, its future is still uncertain at the turn of the twenty-first century.

The nation's coal production was never greater, nor its future more uncertain, than at the turn of the twenty-first century. Amendments to the Clean Air Act added in the 1990s require that national sulfur oxide and nitrogen oxide emissions be reduced, respectively, by about 50 percent and 10 percent—a policy that could bring economic recession to Appalachia's troubled coal fields. Increasing emission control costs will create strong incentives for utilities to seek alternative fuel sources when possible. Policies to mitigate global climate warming, such as the Kyoto climate treaty supported by President Clinton, all contemplate major reductions in U.S. fossil fuel combustion—another assault on Old King Coal. However, the new Bush administration committed itself early to reducing domestic emission controls on carbon dioxide, encouraging new coal consumption, and abandoning U.S. support for the Kyoto agreement. Encouraged by this political support, the coal industry also nourishes a tenuous hope that it might be able to commercialize the now experimental "clean coal" technologies, such as fluidized bed combustion, which could reduce coal's sulfur content before combustion. The commercial prospects for these technologies remain unproved. The industry's continued vitality is tethered precariously to the uncertain fate of the Bush administration's energy policies. Only the ecological devastation of coal mining is ensured. It will be the inheritance of unborn generations, a legacy written in Appalachia's scarred hills and acidified streams and in sterile mine waste plowed into moonscapes across the western plains and deserts.

Conclusion

Coal combustion and civilian nuclear power are two examples of the implicit and inevitable association between environmental quality and patterns of energy development. The United States is currently following a path of energy development that can make vast, and possibly irreversible, changes in the nation's environment. Continuing coal use perpetuates surface mining, along with all its environmental risks, across Appalachia and the West. Industrial and utility coal combustion can intensify problems of air pollution, acid precipitation, and possibly the greenhouse effect through the first decade of the twenty-first century. Even if civilian nuclear power should fail to develop beyond facilities currently operating or under construction, the risks of accidents and the institutional difficulties in managing nuclear waste and decommissioning plants will remain significant well into the new century. Serious technical, administrative, and political difficulties exist in the enforcement of legislation intended to protect the nation from the most environmentally malignant impacts of these technologies.

Equally important are the environmental implications of current energy policy for the future. First, the United States today has no explicit, comprehensive program of energy conservation, nor does it have any governmental commitment to promoting the development and proliferation of energy-conserving technologies beyond what may be accomplished through the deregulation of energy prices. This implies that energy development is likely to place growing stress on environmental quality and nonrenewable resources such as fossil fuels.

Second, the continuing U.S. dependence on nonrenewable energy resources, along with the adverse environmental impacts often associated with these resources, is slowly but resolutely moving the United States into a position where it may have to contemplate a severe energy-environment trade-off should a new energy crisis emerge. Public opinion polls have long suggested that environmental quality is most politically vulnerable to an energy crisis. Should the public and its officials feel they must choose between more energy and continuing environmental protection, there seems to be a strong disposition to opt for energy development. Continued reliance on environmentally threatening energy sources leaves U.S. policy makers with few options but environmentally dangerous ones in the face of another energy crisis.

Third, it should be apparent from discussions of coal and nuclear power development that many of the environmental risks associated with these energy sources are created or exacerbated by failure of institutional management or design. Stated somewhat differently, the problems of decommissioning reactors or finding a safe and publicly acceptable repository for nuclear waste illustrate the failure of policy makers to anticipate the institutional arrangements essential to ensuring the safety of energy technologies. An essential aspect in planning the future development of energy technologies through government, whether they be synthetic fuel technologies, nuclear fusion, or something else, should be careful and prolonged consideration of the institutional arrangements essential to ensure the technologies' safety—a sort of institutional risk assessment that raises tough and realistic questions about the impact of technologies on governmental institutions and their capacities to manage such technologies in an environmentally sound way.

Suggested Readings

Duffy, Robert J. *Nuclear Politics in America.* Lawrence: University Press of Kansas, 1997.
Freese, Barbara. *Coal: A Human History.* New York: Perseus Books Group, 2003.
Flynn, James, et al. *One Hundred Centuries of Solitude: Redirecting America's High-Level Nuclear Waste Policy.* Boulder, Colo.: Westview Press, 1995.
Nye, David E. *Consuming Power: A Social History of American Energies.* Cambridge: MIT Press, 1997.

Notes

1. Thomas Doggett, "Bush Tapped Solar Energy Funds to Print Energy Plan," Reuters News Service, www.solar-energy.net/bushtappedsolarenergyfunds.htm, March 29, 2002.
2. Zachary Coile, "Schwarzenegger's Guiltless Green," *San Francisco Chronicle,* April 12, 2007, A4.
3. Natural Resources Defense Council, "Summary of the Harmful Provisions in the Energy Bill, July 26, 2005," www.nrdc.org/legislation/factsheets/050726_energy.pdf, March 29, 2007.
4. Mark Holt and Carol Glover, "Energy Policy Act of 2005: Summary and Analysis of Enacted Provisions," Congressional Research Service Report, March 8, 2006, www.cnie.org/NLE/CRS/abstract.cfm?NLEid=1593, March 28, 2007.
5. Jeffrey M. Jones, April 17, 2007, "Public Favors Environmental Protection over Energy Production as Priority for U.S.," www.galluppoll.com/content/?ci=26941, May 3, 2007.
6. U.S. Department of Commerce, Bureau of the Census, *Statistical Abstract of the United States, 2000* (Washington, D.C.: U.S. Government Printing Office, 2001), 584.
7. U.S. Energy Information Administration, "Energy Basics 101," www.eia.doe.gov/basics/energybasics101.html, January 3, 2007.
8. Council on Environmental Quality, *Environmental Quality, 1992* (Washington, D.C.: U.S. Government Printing Office, 1993), 331.
9. U.S. Department of Commerce, Bureau of the Census, *Statistical Abstract of the United States, 1997* (Washington, D.C.: U.S. Government Printing Office, 1998), 273.
10. U.S. Energy Information, "Overview of U.S. Petroleum Trade," *Monthly Energy Review,* March 2007, 17.
11. U.S Energy Information Administration, *U.S. Crude Oil, Natural Gas, and Natural Gas Liquids Reserves: 2005 Annual Report* (Washington, D.C.: U.S. Government Printing Office, 2006), chap. 3.
12. International Energy Agency, *World Energy Outlook, 2002* (Paris: International Energy Agency, 2002), tab. 3.1, p. 90.
13. Doggett, "Bush Tapped Solar Energy Funds."
14. U.S. Department of Energy/Nuclear Power Industry, *Strategic Plan for Light Water Reactor Research and Development* (Washington, D.C.: U.S. Department of Energy, February 2004), executive summary.
15. Ibid., 8.
16. On the history of U.S. commercial nuclear power, see Irvin C. Bupp and Jean-Claude Derian, *The Failed Promise of Nuclear Power* (New York: Basic Books, 1978); and Steven L. Del Sesto, *Science, Politics and Controversy: Civilian Nuclear Power in the United States, 1946–1974* (Boulder, Colo.: Westview Press, 1979).
17. Bupp and Derian, *The Failed Promise of Nuclear Power,* chap. 5.
18. Christopher Flavin, *Nuclear Power: The Market Test* (Washington, D.C.: Worldwatch Institute, 1983), 27.
19. National Desk, "Off by $4 Billion and 14 Years, Michigan Nuclear Plant Starts," *New York Times,* January 24, 1988, 1(28).
20. Barnaby J. Feder, "Nation's Biggest Atomic Utility to Shut Two Units,"*Wall Street Journal,* January 16, 1998, A10.
21. U.S. Department of Energy, Energy Information Administration, *Annual Energy Review 2002* (Washington, D.C.: U.S. Government Printing Office, 2002), 254. See also Max Schulz, "Nuclear Power Is the Future," *The Wilson Quarterly* (autumn 2006): 98–107.

22. Matthew L. Wald, "As Nuclear Reactors Show Age, Owners Seek to Add to Usable Life,"*New York Times*, June 22, 1989, A1.
23. Associated Press, "Safety Rating for Nation's Biggest Nuclear Plant Lowered," www.cnn.com/Nuke%20Safety%20Problem07.html, February 22, 2007.
24. David Lochbaum, *Nuclear Tightrope: Unlearned Lessons of Year-plus Reactor Outages* (Washington, D.C.: Union of Concerned Scientists, 2006), 1.
25. Walter A. Rosenbaum, "Nuclear Wastes and Federalism: The Institutional Impacts of Technology Development," in *Western Public Lands: The Management of Natural Resources in a Time of Declining Federalism*, ed. John G. Frances and Richard Ganzel (Totowa, N.J.: Rowman and Allanheld, 1984). See also Luther J. Carter, *Nuclear Imperatives and Public Trust* (Washington, D.C.: Resources for the Future, 1987), chaps. 4 and 5; and Edward J. Woodhouse, "The Politics of Nuclear Waste Management," in *Too Hot to Handle? Social and Policy Issues in the Management of Radioactive Waste*, ed. Charles A. Walker, Leroy C. Gould, and Edward J. Woodhouse (New Haven: Yale University Press, 1983), 151–83.
26. Quoted in "Nevada to Get Nuclear Waste, Everyone Else 'Off the Hook,'" *Congressional Quarterly Weekly Report*, December 19, 1987, 3136–37.
27. Ibid.
28. "Nuclear Waste: House Approves Temporary Storage Bill,"*Greenwire*, April 16, 1997.
29. Matthew L. Wald, "U.S. Will Start over in Planning for Nuclear Waste Dump,"*New York Times*, November 29, 1989, A1.
30. U.S. General Accounting Office, "Nuclear Waste: Yucca Mountain Project behind Schedule and Facing Major Scientific Uncertainties," Report No. GAO/RCED 93-124 (May 1993), 4.
31. Keith Schneider, "Nuclear Waste Dump Faces Another Potential Problem," *New York Times*, June 3, 1989, 1(8). See also U.S. General Accounting Office, "Nuclear Waste: Storage Issues at DOE's Waste Isolation Pilot Plant in New Mexico," Report No. GAO/RCED 90-1 (December 1989).
32. National Desk, "Limited Reopening of Plutonium Plant in Washington State,"*New York Times*, December 15, 1989, B14. See also U.S. General Accounting Office, "Nuclear Energy: Environmental Issues at DOE's Nuclear Defense Facilities," Report No. GAO/RCED 86-192 (September 1986), 2–4.
33. U.S. General Accounting Office, "Nuclear Regulation: NRC's Decommissioning Procedures and Criteria Need to Be Strengthened," Report No. GAO/RCED 89-119 (May 1989), 2–3. On decommissioning problems generally, see Cynthia Pollock, *Decommissioning: Nuclear Power's Missing Link* (Washington, D.C.: Worldwatch Institute, 1986).
34. Pollock, *Decommissioning*, 25–33.
35. U.S. Department of Energy, *Estimating the Cold War: The 1995 Baseline Environmental Management Report* (Washington, D.C.: U.S. Government Printing Office, 1996).
36. Keith Schneider, "The 29-Year Ordeal to Tear Down One Building,"*New York Times*, October 31, 1988, A14.
37. Quoted in National Desk, "U.S. Nuclear Official Criticizes Industry Planning," *New York Times*, December 12, 1981, B12.
38. Quoted in Matthew L. Wald, "Shoreham: Arguing over the Next Step,"*New York Times*, January 21, 1985, L1.
39. U.S. General Accounting Office, "Nuclear Regulation: Efforts to Ensure Nuclear Power Plant Safety Can Be Strengthened," Report No. GAO/RCED 87-141 (August 1987), 2–3.
40. U.S. General Accounting Office, "Nuclear Regulation: NRC's Decommissioning Procedures," 2–3.
41. Patrick Moore, "Going Nuclear: A Green Makes the Case," *Washington Post*, April 16, 2006, B1.
42. Richard E. Balzhiser, "Future Consequences of Nuclear Nonpolicy," in *Energy: Production, Consumption and Consequences*, ed. John L. Helm (Washington, D.C.: National Academies Press, 1990), 184–204. See also Christopher Flavin, *Reassessing Nuclear Power: The Fallout from Chernobyl* (Washington, D.C.: Worldwatch Institute, 1987), 62–74.
43. Joseph G. Morone and Edward J. Woodhouse, *The Demise of Nuclear Energy? Lessons for Democratic Control of Technology* (New Haven: Yale University Press, 1989), 147.

44. Matthew L. Wald, "Bomb Plant Case Draws More Fire,"*New York Times,* November 2, 1993, A18.
45. Lawnie H. Taylor Sr., *Ten Year Cleanup of U.S. Department of Energy Waste Sites: The Changing Roles of Technology Development in an Era of Privatization* (Washington, D.C.: U.S. Department of Energy, 1996), chap. 1.
46. U.S. Department of Energy, Office of Environmental Restoration and Waste Management, *Fact Sheets: Environmental Restoration and Management* (Washington, D.C.: U.S. Government Printing Office, 1991), 21.
47. Ibid., 2.
48. U.S. General Accounting Office, "Understanding of Waste Migration at Hanford Is Inadequate for Key Decisions," Report No. GAO/RCED 98-80 (March 1998), 3.
49. *New York Times,* January 25, 1992. See also U.S. General Accounting Office, "Nuclear Waste: Problems and Delays with Characterizing Hanford's Single-Shell Tank Waste," Report No. GAO/RCED 91-118 (April 1991).
50. U.S. Government Accountability Office, *Hanford Waste Treatment Plant: Contractor and DOE Management Problems Have Lead to Higher Costs, Construction Delays, and Safety Concerns,* Report No. GAO-06-602T (April 2006), 1.
51. Matthew L. Wald, "At Old A-Plant, One Sure Thing Is the Volatility,"*New York Times,* June 21, 1993, A1.
52. Matthew L. Wald, "Hazards at Nuclear Plant Festering Eight Years after Warning," *New York Times,* December 24, 1992, A11.
53. Matthew L. Wald, "Nuclear Site Is Battling a Rising Tide of Waste," *New York Times,* September 27, 1999, A14.
54. "Quoted in "Better 'Up' Than 'Boom,'"*New York Times,* June 21, 1993.
55. Wald, "Nuclear Site Is Battling a Rising Tide of Waste."
56. Matthew L. Wald, "Carolina Plant to Encase Atomic Wastes in Glass," *New York Times,* November 28 , 1990, B6; *New York Times,* August 5, 1993.
57. Changes in OSMRE regulations during this period are discussed in Conservation Foundation, *State of the Environment, 1982* (Washington, D.C.: Conservation Foundation, 1984), 303–410. Estimates of the number of regulations rewritten are found in Philip Shabecoff, "Many Are Divided on Watt's Legacy,"*New York Times,* October 12, 1983, A20.
58. U.S. Department of the Interior, Office of Surface Mining Reclamation and Enforcement, *Abandoned Mine Land Reclamation: Update on the Reclamation of Abandoned Mine Land Affected by Mining That Took Place Before the Surface Mining Law Was Passed in 1977* (Washington, D.C.: Office of Surface Mining Reclamation and Enforcement, 2003), 20. Available at http://www.osmre.gov/aml/remain/zintroun.htm.
59. Ibid.
60. U.S. Department of the Interior, Office of Surface Mining, "Mining and Reclamation Coloring Book," January 23, 2002, www.osmre.gov/coloring.htm, April 7, 2004; U.S. Department of the Interior, Office of Surface Mining, "Mining and Reclamation Poster," February 28, 2002, www.osmre.gov/poster.htm, April 7, 2004.
61. U.S. General Accounting Office, "Surface Mining: Interior Department and States Could Improve Inspection Programs," Report No. GAO/RCED 87-40 (December 1986), 3. See also Richard Miller, "Implementing a Program of Cooperative Federalism in Surface Mining Policy," *Policy Studies Review* 9 (autumn 1989): 79–87; and Richard Harris, "Federal-State Relations in the Implementation of Surface Mining Policy," *Policy Studies Review* 9 (autumn 1989): 69–78.
62. Uday Desai, "Assessing the Impacts of the Surface Mining Control and Reclamation Act," *Policy Studies Review* 9 (autumn 1989): 104–05.
63. Ibid., 105.

Chapter 9

635 Million Acres of Politics:
The Battle for Public Lands

*For many westerners, particularly those in the Rocky Mountain states,
the sport appeals to the urge for unfettered—and fast—exploration of
large swaths of terrain. But environmentalists say the snowmobile's
continued presence [in Yosemite Park] represents the triumph of commercial interests over conservation.*

*Representatives of both camps were standing within 50 feet of each
other on Tuesday afternoon as Old Faithful spewed velvety veils of
water into the cold, sunny air. O'Neal Browder, 63, an accountant
from Birmingham, Ala., who has snowmobiled into the park half a
dozen times in the past 25 years, called those who would ban the
machines "'a bunch of elitists." Nearby, Norman Ashcraft, a former
Manhattanite now living in Connecticut, rested on his ski poles. Told
that [Secretary of the Interior] Norton was nearby, he grimaced and
said, "'She's the enemy."*

—New York Times, February 17, 2005[1]

Buried toward the back of the 200-page-thick national energy plan conceived by the George W. Bush administration was a proposal guaranteed
to embroil the White House, Congress, energy developers, and environmental advocates in a national controversy smoldering for more than a
decade and involving millions of acres of land most Americans will never
see and could not locate on a map. The conflict swirls about the Arctic
National Wildlife Refuge (ANWR), 19.6 million acres of pristine polar
wilderness in the remote northeastern corner of Alaska, among the wildest
and most inaccessible of U.S. public lands. ANWR is huge and resplen-
dently wild, a sprawling panorama of tundra marshes and lagoons, inter-
laced with glacier-fed rivers and lodged between the foothills of the soaring Brooks Range and the expansive, frigid Beaufort Sea. All parties to the
conflict agree: It is stunningly beautiful. They agree on little else.

289

ANWR is also another flashpoint of political conflict over access to the nation's public lands. Such conflicts have flared repeatedly throughout U.S. history. In many ways, ANWR is a microcosm of the larger political forces, actors, and institutions historically drawn into these unrelenting conflicts over the use of vast natural resources held in trust by the federal government for the people of the United States. Beginning with a brief description of the actors and issues involved in the Alaskan dispute, this chapter explains why the nation's public lands have always been a battleground between advocates of contending, and often sharply conflicting, uses for the natural resources involved. The explanation involves the ambiguous, and often confusing, congressional legislation intended to determine which interests shall have access to these resources; the impact of the environmental movement upon public land politics; and the constantly embattled federal agencies, especially the Department of the Interior (DOI) and the U.S. Forest Service, responsible for the politically arduous job of simultaneously preserving these lands, promoting use of their resources, and protecting their most valuable ecological functions. Using the national forests and wilderness areas as examples, the narrative illuminates currently significant public lands controversies.

ANWR: Public Land Politics at a Boil

The national energy plan had recommended that the "President direct the Secretary of the Interior to work with Congress to authorize exploration and, if resources are discovered, development of the 1002 area of ANWR."[2] But Congress should "also require the use of the best available technologies and should require that activities will result in no significant adverse impact to the surrounding environment." To the U.S. energy production industries and their allies, this proposal seemed reasonable and plausible, a long overdue, practical remedy to the nation's dangerously growing dependence on imported oil. The proposal infuriated environmentalists, conservationists, and their allies. Environmentalists frequently characterize ANWR as "the crown jewel of America's refuge system" and predict that further energy exploration there will result in catastrophic air pollution, habitat destruction, wildlife decimation, and ecological degradation. Arrayed among these colliding forces were a multitude of other interests who, in differing combination, are commonly drawn into disputes over the use of the public lands.

"The Biological Heart" of a Wilderness

As with most public lands owned by the federal government, ANWR's size and purpose are defined by Congress, and responsibility for its oversight is vested in the DOI. ANWR was created in 1980 from federal lands within Alaska for the purposes of wildlife conservation, habitat preservation, wilderness protection, promotion of recreation, and energy exploration—an example of a "multiple-use" designation that almost ensures a constant battle among contenders for different uses. Much of ANWR's 19.6 million acres has been opened to oil and natural gas exploration. The Trans-Alaskan pipeline, created in 1971, has been producing almost a million barrels of petroleum daily from Prudhoe Bay on Alaska's North Slope, and 90 percent of the adjacent coastal lands remain open for gas and oil leasing. However, about 1.5 million acres of the coastal plain, considered to be the most biologically rich and vulnerable within ANWR, was restricted from energy exploration unless such activity is specifically authorized by Congress. This region, often called the 1002 Area in reference to its authorizing legislation, is the epicenter of the political conflict over ANWR.

The ecological riches of the 1002 Area are undisputed. This natural endowment includes 160 bird species; the most important onshore denning area in the United States for polar bears; the principal calving ground for 130,000 migratory porcupine caribou; habitat for grizzly bears, arctic foxes, wolves, wolverine, and numerous whales; and many endangered plant and animal species. Ruggedly beautiful wilderness and vast Arctic panoramas invite recreation and tourism. This language of ecological values, biological conservation, and environmental aesthetics resonates powerfully among environmentalists. Much of this, they believe, would be sacrificed to produce exaggerated quantities of petroleum unlikely to alleviate significantly the nation's energy problems.[3]

At Stake: America's Energy Security?

Proponents of energy exploration in the 1002 Area speak primarily about national security, energy supply, and coexistence between energy production and environmental protection. They assert, for instance, that drilling in the area could yield as much as sixteen billion barrels of oil, an amount equal to thirty years of oil imports from Saudi Arabia. They also assert that newer, more efficient energy production technologies will limit the amount of land to be disturbed by energy production to a few thousand acres and, in any case, that the ecological disruption involved is vastly exaggerated by environmental opponents. Most important, proponents of further energy production argue that the reserves now untapped under the 1002 Area will significantly improve U.S. security by decreasing dependence on imported oil, which threatens to increase in the future. All these arguments speak to the nation's sensitivity to petroleum dependency, rising energy needs, and domestic security awakened in the aftermath of the September 11, 2001, terrorist attacks.[4]

The Play of Politics

Since 1980 the DOI has been ready to sell energy exploration leases on the 1002 Area, but, because Congress must first agree, the political battle over exploration has been waged largely within Congress and the White House. In 1996 President Bill Clinton vetoed congressional authorization to permit the leasing. Since then, similar legislation has been approved in the House of Representatives eight times and then defeated, usually in the Senate.[5] In July 2003, the Senate unexpectedly rejected an ANWR leasing proposal vigorously promoted by the Bush administration. Still, the White House ANWR campaign persisted with dependable support from the entire Alaskan congressional delegation and from the Department of the Interior (whose ANWR Web site, for instance, pointedly includes a "How Long Would Your State Run on ANWR Oil?" chart to demonstrate the value of ANWR to each state).[6] And the Bush administrations FY 2008 budget assumed that legislation would be approved to open the ANWR to energy exploration. Thus, the fate of the 1002 Area remains insecure and destined for continual contention among a multitude of political and economic interests.

Some of the stakeholders in the ANWR conflict have been highly visible: Congress, the White House, the DOI, environmental advocates, and energy industries rarely escape national attention. Another important stakeholder is the state of Alaska. Many states benefit through economic royalties received from resource exploitation on public lands in their jurisdiction, but Alaska's situation is unique. Royalties from energy production are the state's economic foundation. Every Alaskan resident—man, woman, or child—is reminded about this economic dependence by an annual check (currently about $1,100) representing his or her share of more than $660 million in annual dividends from state oil royalties.[7] Alaskans largely support energy exploration in the 1002 Area, believing energy production and environmental protection are compatible. Many resent what they consider interference by Washington, D.C., and other interests, including environmentalists, in what they believe should be Alaska's own affair. Not surprisingly, Alaska's Republican governor Frank Murkowski complained about "America's extreme environmental community" after the Senate's rejection of ANWR energy leasing in 2003 and promised that he would open as much as a million acres of state-owned offshore waters to energy exploration.[8] Many of Alaska's Native Americans, however, were unlikely to cheer. The Inupiat Eskimos and an indigenous subsistence culture, the Gwich'in Indians, are among the native tribes heavily dependent on the

1002 Area's continued ecological vitality for food and fuel. The state's commercial fishing interests were also disturbed by possible degradation of their offshore stocks.

The stakeholders in ANWR's resources include local, state, and federal governments; the federal bureaucracies administering the public lands; the economic interests seeking to exploit resources and the interests determined to protect them; as well as foreign governments, including Japan and China, that might become large consumers for the petroleum produced from the 1002 Area. In brief, ANWR epitomizes the pluralistic political struggles over natural resources in the public domain that have erupted continually throughout U.S. history.

A History of Contested Access

The controversy over ANWR renews an environmental struggle begun long before the concept of environmentalism was imagined. Fierce political contention over the use of the public domain runs like a dark and tangled thread throughout the fabric of U.S. history, reaching to the republic's inception. During the first century of American independence, the conflict was largely between the states and private economic interests to obtain as much public land as possible for their own advantage. Only in 1976, in fact, did the government of the United States officially end its policy of conveying huge expanses of public lands to private control. By then, more than 1.1 billion acres of land, an expanse larger than Western Europe, had been surrendered to the states, farmers and trappers, railroads, veterans, loggers and miners, and canal builders—in other words, to any interest with the political strength to make a persuasive claim to Congress. Land shaped American character more decisively than did any other aspect of the nation's environment. With the mobilization of the conservation movement in the early twentieth century, the federal government began to restrict private control of the public domain in the interest of the American people. Though vastly reduced, the public domain remains an enormous physical expanse embracing within its continental sprawl, often accidentally, some of the nation's most economically and ecologically significant resources, a biological and physical reserve still largely unexploited. The struggle to determine how this last great legacy shall be used constitutes, in large part, the substance of the political struggle over public lands.

At one time, most of the land in the United States was public domain. Over the past two centuries, the federal government has owned almost four of every five acres on the continental United States. This land, held in trust for the people of the nation, is governed by Congress, in whom the Constitution vests the power to "dispose and make all needful Rules and Regulations respecting the Territory or other Property belonging to the

United States."[9] Until the beginning of the twentieth century, Congress had been concerned primarily with rapidly divesting itself of the lands, turning them over to the states or to private interests in huge grants at bargain-basement prices. Only belatedly did Congress, powerfully pressured by the new American conservation movement, awaken to the necessity of preserving the remaining natural resources in the public domain before they were wholly lost. By this time, most of the remaining public lands lay west of the Mississippi River; much was wilderness too remote and inaccessible to be exploited easily or grasslands and rangelands seemingly devoid of economic attraction.

The Public Domain

Today the federal government owns approximately 635 million acres of land, about 28 percent of the total U.S. land area. Many western states are largely public domain: More than half of Alaska, Idaho, Nevada, Oregon, Utah, and Wyoming are federally owned; public lands constitute more than one-third of Arizona, California, Colorado, and New Mexico (Table 9-1). Much of this land, originally ceded to the western states when they joined the Union, was rejected by the states as useless for timbering, grazing, or farming; some was held in trust for Native American tribes by the federal government. Only later, well into the twentieth century, did exploration reveal that vast energy and mineral resources might reside under the tribal reservations, wilderness, timberland, and grasslands remaining in the public domain. The economic value of public lands was increased greatly in 1953, when the United States joined other nations in redefining the limits of national authority over offshore waters. Before 1953 the traditional standard had limited national sovereignty to three miles offshore. In 1953 Congress passed the Outer Continental Shelf Lands Act despite the vigorous opposition of coastal states such as Florida and California. The act declared federal government ownership of outer continental shelf (OCS) lands extending as far as two hundred miles offshore. The legislation, ratifying an international treaty negotiated by the State Department, ended a long-standing dispute between the federal and state governments over control of offshore energy resources by immediately vesting in the federal government control over almost all of the 1.1 billion acres of submerged continental shelf land. By accident and design, that third of the nation, together with its spacious offshore lands, now controlled by the federal government, has become a public trust of potentially huge economic value. And the land is a moneymaker. In recent years, for example, federal collections from user fees, mineral and fossil fuel extraction, land sales, timber production, and other economic activities added more than $1 billion annually to federal government income.

Table 9-1 Total and Federally Owned Land, by State, 2000

State	Total (1,000 acres)	Not owned by federal government (1,000 acres)	Owned by federal government[a] Acres (1,000)	%
Alabama	32,678	31,353	1,326	4.1
Alaska	365,482	144,630	220,852	60.4
Arizona	72,688	40,309	32,379	44.5
Arkansas	33,599	30,190	3,410	10.1
California	100,207	52,318	47,889	47.8
Colorado	66,486	42,377	24,108	36.3
Connecticut	3,135	3,121	14	0.5
Delaware	1,266	1,250	16	1.2
District of Columbia	39	30	9	23.2
Florida	34,721	30,122	4,599	13.2
Georgia	37,295	35,268	2,027	5.4
Hawaii	4,106	3,467	639	15.6
Idaho	52,933	19,827	33,106	62.5
Illinois	35,795	35,205	590	1.6
Indiana	23,158	22,648	510	2.2
Iowa	35,860	35,631	230	0.6
Kansas	52,511	51,837	674	1.3
Kentucky	25,512	24,066	1,447	5.7
Louisiana	28,868	27,669	1,199	4.2
Maine	19,848	19,675	173	0.9
Maryland	6,319	6,153	166	2.6
Massachusetts	5,035	4,964	71	1.4
Michigan	36,492	32,417	4,076	11.2
Minnesota	51,206	46,989	4,217	8.2
Mississippi	30,223	28,551	1,672	5.5
Missouri	44,248	39,450	4,798	10.8
Montana	93,271	65,843	27,428	29.4
Nebraska	49,032	48,381	651	1.3
Nevada	70,264	11,945	58,319	83.0
New Hampshire	5,769	5,010	759	13.2
New Jersey	4,813	4,690	124	2.6
New Mexico	77,766	51,194	26,572	34.2
New York	30,681	30,459	222	0.7
North Carolina	31,403	29,414	1,989	6.3
North Dakota	44,452	42,137	2,316	5.2
Ohio	26,222	25,781	441	1.7
Oklahoma	44,088	42,422	1,666	3.8
Oregon	61,599	29,243	32,356	52.5
Pennsylvania	28,804	28,088	717	2.5
Rhode Island	677	674	4	0.5
South Carolina	19,374	18,265	1,110	5.7
South Dakota	48,882	45,762	3,120	6.4
Tennessee	26,728	24,613	2,115	7.9
Texas	168,218	165,910	2,307	1.4
Utah	52,697	18,696	34,001	64.5

[a] Excludes trust properties.

(Table continues on next page)

Table 9-1 Continued

State	Total (1,000 acres)	Not owned by federal government (1,000 acres)	Owned by federal government[a] Acres (1,000)	%
Vermont	5,937	5,562	375	6.3
Virginia	25,496	23,217	2,280	8.9
Washington	42,694	30,518	12,176	28.5
West Virginia	15,411	14,188	1,222	7.9
Wisconsin	35,011	33,192	1,819	5.2
Wyoming	62,343	31,273	31,070	49.8
United States	2,271,343	1,635,989	635,355	28.0

Source: U.S. Department of Commerce, Bureau of the Census, *Statistical Abstract of the United States, 2002* (Washington, D.C.: Government Printing Office, 2003), 211.

[a] Excludes trust properties.

An Unanticipated Bounty

The magnitude of mineral, timber, and energy reserves in the public domain remains uncertain. Many areas, including much of the gigantic Alaskan wilderness, have yet to be inventoried fully. Estimates of resources on more accessible lands also can be controversial. However, commonly cited figures suggest the reasons why public lands have assumed such importance to major economic interests in the United States:[10]

• About 32 percent of U.S. petroleum, 35 percent of U.S. natural gas, and 37 percent of U.S. coal production originate on the public lands.

• About 60 percent of low-sulfur U.S. coal resides on federal lands west of the Mississippi River.

• About 68 percent of undiscovered U.S. petroleum reserves and 74 percent of natural gas reserves are estimated to reside on federal lands.

• About 30 percent of the nation's forests remain untimbered on federal wilderness land or in national forest areas.

Beyond those resources on which a price can be placed, the public domain contains both incalculable natural treasures whose worth has become evident to generations—Yosemite, Yellowstone, the Grand Canyon, and the other national parks—and nameless wild and free places, the wilderness that the naturalist Aldo Leopold has called "the raw material out of which man has hammered the artifact called civilization" and to which, he reminds us, we need often return, in fact and imagination, as to a sanctuary.[11] Indeed, much of what remains undisturbed on the American earth, still available to this generation in something like its original condition, can be found only in federal wilderness areas. Whether wilderness is or should be a thing beyond price and beyond exploitation remains among the most bitterly controversial of all environmental issues.

Diversity within the Public Domain

The public domain has been divided by Congress into different units committed to different uses and administered by different executive agencies. The most important of these uses are the following:[12]

• *National Wilderness Preservation System.* Created by Congress in 1964, the system currently comprises 105.8 million acres of land, including more than 50 million acres of Alaskan wilderness added in 1979. By legislative mandate, wilderness lands are to be set aside forever as undeveloped areas.

• *National Park System.* Created in 1872 with the designation of Yellowstone National Park, the system currently constitutes 66 national parks and 388 national monuments, historic sites, recreational areas, near-wilderness areas, seashores, and lake shores, altogether embracing more than 83 million acres. Closed to mining, timbering, grazing, and most other economic uses, the system is to be available to the public for recreational purposes.

• *National Wildlife Refuge System.* The system currently includes more than 96 million acres, two-thirds in Alaska but also distributed among all fifty states. The more than five hundred refuges are to provide habitat for migratory waterfowl and mammals, fish and waterfowl hatcheries, research stations, and related facilities.

• *National Forests.* Since 1897 Congress has reserved large forested areas of the public domain and has authorized the purchase of additional timberlands to create a forest reserve, to furnish continuous timber supplies for the nation, and to protect mountain watersheds. Forest lands are to be managed by a multiple-use formula that requires a balance of recreation, timber, grazing, and conservation activities. Currently exceeding 190 million acres, national forests are found principally in the far western states, the Southeast, and Alaska.

• *National Rangelands.* The largest portion of the public domain, located primarily in the West and Alaska, is made up of grassland and prairie land, desert, scrub forest, and other open space collectively known as rangelands. Although often barren, a substantial portion of the 404.7 million acres of rangeland is suitable for grazing. Federal agencies issue permits to ranchers for this purpose.

Such a classification implies an orderly definition of the uses for the public domain and a supporting political consensus that do not exist. Behind the facade of congressionally assigned uses stretches a political terrain strewn with conflicts of historical proportions over which lands shall be placed in different categories, which uses shall prevail among competing demands on the land, how much economic exploitation should be permitted in the public domain, and how large the public domain should be.

Since 1970 two national public land policies have provoked the most significant of these conflicts: the congressionally mandated practices of multiple use, or balanced use, for much of the public domain and the creation of vast tracts of highly restricted wilderness areas and roadless areas precluding all or almost all human development. This chapter examines the ecological and political context in which multiple-use and wilderness conflicts arise and the participants who are drawn into the struggles. These conflicts characteristically pit federal resource management agencies, state and local governments, commodity producers and users, and environmentalists against one another over issues that long predate the first Earth Day.

Conflicts over Multiple Use

Disputes over multiple use of the public domain customarily evolve in roughly similar political settings. Conflict focuses on land administered by one of the federal resource agencies, usually the DOI's Bureau of Land Management (BLM) or the Agriculture Department's Forest Service, charged with the stewardship of millions of acres of the public domain under a multiple-use mandate.

Struggling to interpret an ambiguous congressional mandate for land management, the resource agency will commonly find several parties in conflict over the interpretation of multiple use. These parties include the states within whose jurisdictions the land resides, the various private economic interests with a stake in the decision, congressional committees with jurisdiction over the agency's programs, and perhaps the White House. Especially since 1980, environmental interests have been important and predictable participants. Sometimes the issues are resolved—that is, if they are resolved—only by congressional reformulation of land-use policy.

The Land-Use Agencies

Management of the public domain is vested principally in four federal agencies whose collective jurisdiction, more than a million square miles, exceeds the size of Mexico. The Forest Service, the National Park Service, the BLM, and the Fish and Wildlife Service control about 90 percent of all the land currently in the public domain. The Forest Service and the BLM control by far the largest portion of this collective jurisdiction. Unlike the National Park Service and the Fish and Wildlife Service, the Forest Service and the BLM are required by Congress to administer their huge public trusts under the doctrine of multiple use. The two agencies come to this task with strikingly different political histories and territorial responsibilities.

The Forest Service. Created as part of the Agriculture Department in 1905, the Forest Service is one of the proudest and most enduring monuments to America's first important conservation movement. Founded by Gifford Pinchot, one of the nation's greatest conservationists, the service has a long and distinguished history of forest management. Widely recognized and publicly respected, the service has been adept at cultivating vigorous congressional support and a favorable public image—who is not familiar with Smokey the Bear and other service symbols of forest preservation? The service's jurisdiction covers 191 million acres of the land, including some grasslands, within the U.S. forest system. With more than 38,000 employees and a budget exceeding $2.0 billion, the Forest Service historically has possessed a strong sense of mission and high professional standards. "While the Forest Service has frequently been at the center of political maelstroms," political scientist Paul J. Culhane wrote, "it has also been regarded as one of the most professional, best managed agencies in the federal government."[13] Operating through a highly decentralized system of forest administration, local forest rangers are vested with great discretion in interpreting how multiple-use principles will apply to specific forests within their jurisdictions.

The Bureau of Land Management. The BLM manages more than 264 million acres of public domain and leases another 200 million acres in national forests and private lands, but the bureau remains obscure outside the West. The BLM's massive presence throughout the West is suggested by Figure 9-1, which identifies the proportion of state lands currently managed by the agency and suggests, as well, why western political interests have been so deeply implicated in the BLM's political history. The BLM has struggled to establish standards of professionalism and conservation that would free it from its own long history of indifference to conservation values and from unflattering comparisons with the Forest Service.

The BLM was created in 1946, when President Harry S. Truman combined the DOI's old Grazing Service and General Land Office to form the new bureau with the largest land jurisdiction of any federal agency. Starting with responsibility for managing federal grasslands and grazing lands, the BLM gradually added to its jurisdiction other lands with mineral resources and, more recently, 78 million acres of Alaskan lands, including many large wilderness areas. The BLM has inherited a great diversity of lands with different dominant uses: the Alaskan wilderness, more than 2.5 million acres of prime Douglas timber in western Oregon, and 146.9 million acres of grazing lands. The BLM also is responsible for arranging the leases for mineral exploration on all public domain lands and on the OCS.

Figure 9-1   Percentage of State Acreage Managed by the U.S. Bureau of
             Land Management, 2003

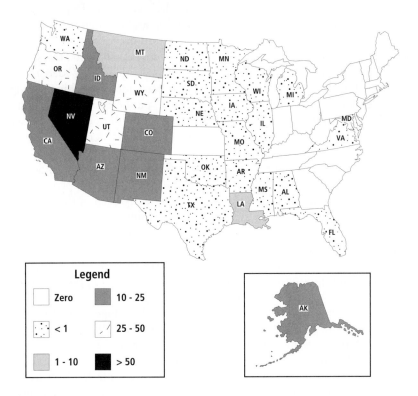

Graphic courtesy of the Bureau of Land Management.

Source: U.S. Department of the Interior, Bureau of Land Management, *Fiscal Year
2003 Annual Report: Shared Community Stewardship for America's Public Lands*
(Washington, D.C.: Government Printing Office, 2003), 73.

   Lacking the prestige of the Forest Service and burdened with a long history of deference to the ranching and mining interests that form a major
portion of its constituency, the BLM has struggled to create greater professionalism, more sensitivity to conservation, and more aggressive
enforcement of land-use regulations within its jurisdiction. Throughout its
history it has suffered from chronic understaffing and underfunding—its
budget and staff are less than a third of that of the Forest Service despite
its greater jurisdiction. And the BLM has never enjoyed the relative insulation from top departmental management that the Forest Service has

experienced. This, to many environmentalists, is one of its chronic problems. According to resource expert James Baker, "The multiple-use concept suffers at the BLM because management decisions are influenced by top policy personnel appointed by the administration in power, who inherently focus on one single use, such as mining, and ignore or give short shrift to such other legitimate uses as wildlife and recreation."[14]

The BLM and the Forest Service work in a political milieu the character of which is shaped by the ambiguous, and sometimes inconsistent, requirements of multiple-use land management; by pressures from the private interests seeking access to resources on land within agency jurisdictions; by conflicts with environmentalists over the appropriate balance between environmental protection and resource use—both of which the agencies are expected to promote; by frequent conflicts between the president and Congress over their respective authority over the agencies; and by state governments, particularly in the West, determined to press on the agencies, Congress, and the White House the states' claims for preference in policy making. All these conflicts were exacerbated in the 1980s by the determination of the White House to force major changes in existing understandings about such issues and in the 1990s by the growing political strength of the so-called wise use movement in opposition to environmentalist pressures on federal land management agencies.

An Ambiguous Mandate

In carrying out their assigned tasks, managers in these agencies often must walk an administrative tightrope fashioned from the inconsistencies and vagaries of their legislatively defined missions. Three different federal statutes charge the BLM and the Forest Service with administering the lands in their trust according to multiple-use principles. The most elaborate definition of the doctrine, ripe with the ambiguities that create so many problems in its implementation, is found in section 530 of the Multiple Use–Sustained Yield Act (1960):

> "Multiple use" means: the management of all the various renewable surface resources of the national forest so that they are utilized in the combination that will best meet the needs of the American people; making the most judicious use of the land for some or all of these resources or related services over areas large enough to provide sufficient latitude for periodic adjustments in use to conform to changing needs and conditions; that some land will be used for less than all of the resources; and harmonious and coordinated management of the various resources, each with the other, without impairment of the productivity of the land, with consideration being given to the relative values of the various resources, and not necessarily the combination of uses that will give the greatest dollar return or the greatest unit output.[15]

The intent of this complicated mandate is to make sure that in land management "any use should be carried out to minimize interference with other uses of the same area and, if possible, to complement those other uses."[16] But it provides to agency managers scant information concerning how these differing values are to be defined and balanced when differing claims on land use must be resolved. Because almost 60 percent of all public lands are held by federal agencies under some form of multiple-use law, such problems are commonplace and conflict over their resolution is predictable. The BLM, for instance, has wrestled for years with managing desert areas east and north of Los Angeles to the satisfaction of both conservationists and vehicle-racing enthusiasts. Each year the BLM processes more than one hundred applications for motorcycle races, some annual events with as many as 3,000 competitors. Conservationists have argued that the races permanently scar the land, alter native ecological balances, and create noise and other disruptions for other recreationists.[17] In trying to reduce the impact of such racing, the BLM must determine the proper balance between recreation and conservation values in terms of these specific desert lands. Any decision becomes controversial.

The agencies frequently discover that multiple use also leads to a conflicting mandate. The Forest Service is expected to protect the national forests from excessive timbering but at the same time assist state and private forest owners in obtaining access to federal forests. Wildlife refuges are supposed to protect and preserve the ecologically viable habitat for endangered species but also provide grazing, hunting, and perhaps mining opportunities to private interests.

But the multiple-use doctrine also gives both agencies, and particularly the local resource managers who must often translate the doctrine into operational terms, a means of managing the conflicting interest pressures on the land. Multiple use requires a balancing of uses, and concern for a variety of claims, without ensuring any one dominance. This formula leaves resource managers with the opportunity to balance and negotiate among interests claiming use of public resources. It also promises constant pressure on the agencies to create or alter interpretations of multiple use by whatever interests feel that existing interpretations discriminate against their claims on the land.

The Pluralistic Politics of the Public Lands

Multiple-use legislation is a mirror to U.S. resource politics, capturing the continual competition between a multitude of public and private interests for access to the public domain. The balance of forces changes over time, as we shall continually observe, but the conflict plays out across lines of political cleavage created by federalism, the separation of powers, and interest group liberalism so deeply embedded in U.S. political culture.

State, Regional, and Private Interests

State governments, particularly in the West, historically have been deeply concerned with federal land-use policies and for more than a century have pressed Washington, D.C., for greater control over public lands within their boundaries. Because the public domain constitutes so large a portion of many western states, decisions made at the federal level affecting land use can have an enormous economic, political, and social impact on the western governments. The states have a direct economic stake in multiple-use management. Approximately 20 percent of Forest Service receipts for timber sales are returned to local governments in lieu of property taxes on federal lands. More than a third of the BLM's annual receipts for mining royalties and other uses of its land is returned to the states.

The Sagebrush Rebels. Regional politics is also deeply implicated in resource controversies. In general, the western states have long believed that they have been denied a properly influential voice in decisions affecting their lands. They often perceive themselves to be governed by a remote and unresponsive bureaucracy insensitive to their special concerns. In particular, the western states want a louder voice in determining grazing rights, in setting conditions for mineral exploration, in establishing timbering quotas, and in deciding how revenues from resource use in the public domain will be allocated. Many states, such as Utah, have insisted that the federal government ought to divest itself of much land within the state borders, turning the land and all its resources over to the states. By the 1980s the western determination to assert greater state and regional control over federal lands had assumed a political identity known as the Sagebrush Rebellion. The rebellion found powerful spokesmen in President Ronald Reagan, a former California governor, and James Watt, his combative Secretary of the Interior, who promised—but eventually could not deliver—the liberation from Washington's public land controls so long coveted in the West.

President Clinton reignited the volatile mix of political resentments that had fueled the earlier western Sagebrush Rebellion by his decision, without congressional cooperation, to designate 43 million acres of western national forest lands as roadless areas, thereby virtually precluding any form of economic development. Western political interests again found a presidential champion in newly elected George W. Bush, himself a westerner, an oil man deeply committed to domestic energy development, and a political conservative unsympathetic to the Clinton administration's restrictive public lands policies. Bush left no doubts about his political inclination by appointing Gale Norton as Secretary of the Interior. Norton was another westerner with a political pedigree strongly reminiscent of Watt's, the *beau ideal* of the Sagebrush Rebels. (Norton and Watt had even worked for the same conservative public interest law firm in Colorado.) Congressional conservatives, especially Republicans, were strongly encouraged by these congenial presidential signals to mount an aggressive legislative assault on the roadless area designations and related Clinton land-use regulations. The situation foreshadowed numerous early, barbed confrontations between the new Bush administration and environmentalist interests that were a prelude to Bush's turbulent relationship with environmentalism following his inauguration.

Energy Conflicts. Recalling the conflict over ANWR described at the chapter's outset, it is understandable how the concepts of "energy" and "energy crisis" evoke particularly intense political emotions among environmentalists concerned with public lands. They also raise federal-state resource conflicts in yet another context. A long historical shadow reaching back to the 1980s falls over any current discussions of either issue. The 1980s were characterized by unusually open and bitter conflict over management of the public domain, particularly energy resources, triggered by the Reagan administration's vigorous attempts to change land policies in a manner that angered conservationist and environmental groups throughout the United States while attracting support from many western states. The protracted controversy profoundly alarmed environmentalists and many more traditional conservationists. It left the environmental movement with a lingering suspicion about Republican energy policies, a lingering paranoia about western political intentions, and a deeply embedded antipathy toward any individuals or political impulses even faintly reminiscent of resource politics during the Reagan years.

Energy development has been historically inseparable from U.S. public lands politics since the beginning of the twentieth century. Energy exploration and production have been powerful justifications for the development of public lands, and the related array of organized economic interests embraces many of the nation's largest and most powerful corporations and politically potent state and regional political coalitions, especially those historically identified with the midwestern and western "oil patch." Between 1981 and 1988 the Reagan administration and its opponents waged a conflict of historic proportions over the fate of energy and related resources on public lands. The administration began the 1980s with a determination to open public lands to energy and mineral exploration and to transfer tracts of public lands to state and private control on a scale unmatched by any other administration in the twentieth century. These grand designs for resource development were frustrated by resistance from moderates of both congressional parties, a fierce opposition campaign by environmentalists and their conservationist allies, and inept political promotion by Reagan administration spokesmen. Perhaps most important, domestic energy supplies recovered rapidly with the collapse of the OPEC oil embargo, petroleum prices fell, and public concern for an energy crisis evaporated. Reagan's Republican successor, George H. W. Bush, largely avoided confrontations with the environmental community over resource management. Clinton, in contrast to Reagan and Bush, deliberately and repeatedly frustrated efforts by energy developers to expand their access to fossil fuel resources on continental public lands and on the OCS. Clinton's sweeping designation of new roadless areas and other restrictions on public land development during his final years in office, described earlier in this chapter, especially antagonized domestic energy producers who looked to George W. Bush for redress. And so, it was left for Bush to propose aggressive new energy development in his national energy plan and thereby demonstrate how close to the surface of American life the political tensions of the Reagan years remain.

When Bush announced within a few weeks of assuming the presidency that the nation faced another energy crisis, it was inevitable that environmentalists would respond as if another Republican-led assault on public lands was forthcoming, particularly because energy interests had contributed substantially to Bush's presidential campaign. Moreover, Bush was also a westerner and his energy policies tilted strongly toward the interests of western states. The Bush national energy plan, and its subsequent legislative proposals, seemed to confirm environmentalist suspicions that Bush was enthusiastically resurrecting Reagan's public lands policies with further embellishments. Environmentalists pointed to initiatives such as the acceleration of oil and gas exploration permits on public lands, a drastic slowdown in designation of new wilderness areas, the relaxation of environmental restrictions on mineral mining on federal land, and a revocation of limits on off-highway recreation vehicles on public lands to demonstrate that Bush "threatens to do more damage to our environmental protections than any other [president] in U.S. history."[18] Although environmentalists and their allies were able to defeat some of these initiatives in Congress, many other administration initiatives were accomplished because they could be implemented entirely by the White House or bureaucratic agencies.

The Ambivalent States. Despite Sagebrush Rebellion rhetoric, the states are often guilty of doublethink about resources in the public domain, as the controversy over land policy in the 1980s illustrates. Eager to reap the economic advantages of greater resource use on lands within their domain—more royalties, more severance taxes, greater industrial development, and the like—the states were equally determined not to pay calamitous ecological and economic costs for rapid resource exploitation. The federal government's new public lands policies often aroused not enthusiasm but hostility among the western states. These states wanted resource development *and* environmental protection.

Conflict between the federal government and the states was focused most sharply on the federal government's proposal for accelerated leasing of exploration rights to oil and gas on the OCS. In 1978 Congress had passed the Outer Continental Shelf Lands Act Amendments to increase greatly the environmental safeguards required for OCS exploration. To this end, extensive federal consultation with the states was required prior to any lease sales off their shores. The federal government's announced intention to sell thirty-two oil lease tracts off the central California coast sent California to the federal courts seeking an injunction to prevent the leasing. Citing federal failure to consult with the state under terms of the 1978 legislation, the court issued the injunction and the DOI subsequently withdrew most of the disputed tracts from auction.

Responding to pressure from California state officials, including the new Republican governor, most environmental groups, and most of the state's congressional delegation, Congress in 1982 and 1983 further restricted lease sales off the northern and central California coast by denying appropriations to implement the leasing. In 1984 Congress banned leasing in several OCS basins off Florida and Massachusetts. Often, states have taken unilateral action to impede or prevent development of OCS lands. Even Bush family values could not prevail against state interests on energy matters when, in mid-2002, Governor Jeb Bush of Florida successfully opposed federal efforts to commence oil exploration in Florida OCS waters, which his brother, the president, had supported. Thus the OCS states have largely succeeded in substantially reducing, at least temporarily, the scope of offshore energy exploration through a combination of legal and political strategies. Environmentalists, however, remain uneasy about the future because substantial OCS leasing is still permitted.[19] As if to confirm the worst environmentalist suspicions, Congress passed new legislation in late 2006 opening about 8.3 million acres of OCS to exploration in the eastern Gulf of Mexico and rewarding Louisiana, Mississippi, Alabama, and Texas with 37.5 percent of all new energy production revenues.

Resource conflicts at the boundaries between federal and state power are inevitable, grounded in the bedrock of the U.S. constitutional system itself. As long as the federal government continues to push aggressively for greater energy exploration and production on public lands, or asserts its regulatory control over the public domain, the states will continue to press with equal determination for greater influence, if not control, over decisions about such activities within their own borders.

Private Resource Users

Interests using resources in the public domain, or ambitious to be among the elect, are important participants in the process of making public land-use policy. Each of the major federal land-use agencies has its "clientele," that coalition of organized groups with a major economic or ideological stake in the agency's programs. In general, resource users want to expand their access to resources in the public domain, to use the resources as cheaply as possible, to protect the continuing availability of renewable resources, and to maintain or enhance their influence within the agencies making decisions about resources strategic to them. For example, sheep and cattle ranchers customarily participate actively in the political struggles over BLM rangeland regulations; individual timber companies, such as Weyerhaeuser and Crown Zellerbach, and timber trade associations, such as the National Forest Products Association, are involved in Forest Service determinations about allowable timber harvests; and Peabody Coal and Climax Coal, two of the largest coal-mining companies in the United States, will be found with the spokesperson for the National Coal Association actively attempting to influence the BLM or the Fish and Wildlife Service in writing regulations for coal leasing on land within their agency jurisdictions.

This intimate and historical involvement of clientele in land agency politics often has been criticized sharply, first by the earlier conservation movement and currently by environmentalists. Critics have asserted that agencies are easily "captured" by the clientele, who then promote resource exploitation at the sacrifice of balanced use and, particularly, with little regard for environmental values. Conservationists once dismissed the BLM as the "Bureau of Livestock and Mining." Similarly, environmentalists routinely sued the BLM in the 1980s for allegedly failing to enforce surface mining regulations on coal lessees in New Mexico and Wyoming. The Forest Service's exemplary reputation has been no shield from accusations that it sanctions clear cutting and other timber practices abhorrent to environmentalists because the service allegedly has come to define its mission largely as timber production in response to commercial timber company demands. Agency administrators, however, often have a legislative mandate to promote resource use within their jurisdictions, and, as a consequence, some community of interest with resource users is inevitable. As we have often observed, the right of access by affected private groups to those administrators making decisions affecting such groups is regarded as a fundamental principle in U.S. politics. Both tradition and law make the continued involvement of resource users in agency decisions inevitable and their self-interested pressures on the agencies a continual threat to the concept of balanced use. Often environmental and conservation groups constitute practically the only politically active and effective force for balanced use within the private pressure group system.

Congress and the Public Domain

Congress ultimately decides how the public domain will be used. Although it cautiously shares some of this authority with the president, Congress traditionally has been a jealous and vigilant guardian of its prerogatives to decide finally how the states, federal land management agencies, private resource users, and others shall use the lands it holds in trust for the people of the United States. This authority flows from Article IV of the Constitution and from numerous Supreme Court decisions affirming the primacy of legislative authority in determining the character of the federal lands. Recent Supreme Court decisions have compelled Congress to share with the president the power to withdraw public lands from private use, but Congress has been quick to challenge presidents and their executive agencies when it felt they were usurping a legislative prerogative in land management.

As in other policy areas, congressional control over the public domain is exercised through the committees and subcommittees in each chamber with jurisdiction over federal land management agencies. Although Congress vigorously defends its authority to define agency programs, it has also left the agencies with enormous discretion in deciding how lands within their jurisdictions will be used; the many multiple-use laws enacted in the past several decades leave to local land managers great latitude in establishing the character of specific land uses. These agencies, as a result, operate in a politically risky milieu, in which discretion is always subject to congressional challenge. When the presidency and Congress are controlled by the same party, conflicts between the two branches over agency decisions are seldom prolonged or serious. But the situation becomes ripe for conflict when differing parties control the White House and one, or both, congressional chambers. Then agency managers, exercising what they believe to be their discretionary authority on behalf of the president's program, may find themselves and their agency under congressional attack. Many of the most publicized conflicts over the Reagan administration's land-use policies erupted as battles between the Secretary of the Interior and Democratic-controlled House committees with jurisdiction over the department's land programs. During the Clinton presidency the situation was reversed, with a Democratic president and Secretary of the Interior usually defending the administration public lands policies against a largely critical Republican majority in both congressional chambers. Feeding the conflict were partisan disagreements over which programs the department should implement and traditional disputes over the limits of executive discretion.

In the past several decades, Congress has demonstrated an increasing concern for environmental values by enacting legislation requiring federal land management agencies to give conservation greater importance in land-use decisions. The Wilderness Act of 1964, an early manifestation of this growing ecological sensibility, designated by statute for the first time more than nine million acres of public lands as wilderness and provided for additional future designations. Later, the National Environmental Policy Act (NEPA) of 1970 required federal land management agencies, among many other executive agencies, to create environmental impact statements (EISs) in which the environmental consequences of land-use decisions had to be identified and considered in decisions affecting the public domain. Other major multiple-use laws passed in the 1970s, to be examined later in this chapter, explicitly required the relevant federal agencies to incorporate ecological protection among the uses to be protected in the affected public domain. This concern for environmental value demonstrated in good part the rising political strength of environmental groups in the legislative process. Congress, particularly the House, came to be the principal institutional bastion within the federal government from which environmentalists mounted their attack on Reagan's land-use policies at the DOI.

The Environmental Movement and Public Lands

Environmentalists always have given the management of public lands a high priority. Both the National Park Service and the Forest Service were created near the beginning of the twentieth century in response to vigorous promotion by the great American conservation movement, the ideological and political predecessor of the existing environmental movement. Historical legal and political battles had been waged by the Sierra Club, the Audubon Society, and other environmental groups against ecologically reckless projects promoted by federal water resource agencies long before the environmental era was named. In the 1970s environmentalists achieved a number of legislative and judicial victories that vastly expanded their influence in federal land management activities and compelled even the ecologically primitive BLM to develop, at least fitfully, an environmental conscience.

Among the most important of these achievements was passage of NEPA. As defined by the Council on Environmental Quality, which is responsible for its implementation, NEPA required that EISs be prepared by federal land management agencies for major land-use decisions affecting the environment—in effect, for most major land management planning. Draft statements had to be circulated for public review and comment prior to completion, and agency officials were obligated to give the statements careful consideration in all relevant decisions.

In practical terms, the EISs became an early warning system for environmental groups, alerting them to the implications of numerous agency policies whose importance might otherwise have gone unnoticed. Environmentalists had opportunity to organize a political strategy for influencing land management decisions. Further, the statements often forced agencies, such as the BLM, to give greater attention to the ecological impacts of their management practices. Not least important, the EIS was a legally enforceable procedure; environmental groups skillfully exploited many opportunities to use the federal courts to delay or frustrate agency decisions they opposed by challenging the adequacy of impact statements.

Federal courts, often with the explicit approval of Congress, greatly expanded the environmentalists' standing to sue federal agencies for alleged failures to give environmental values sufficient attention in land-use planning. This greatly liberalized standing often enabled environmental interests to compel federal agencies to give them a voice in agency proceedings. Critics charged, sometimes justifiably, that environmentalists were seizing on these new strategies primarily to disrupt administrative procedures and thereby to harass their opponents even when their case lacked merit. But the environmental activities inspired by enhanced standing, as well as the impact statement procedures, quite often resulted in valuable ecological improvements in federal land management and greater federal attention to the balanced use of land, to which many agency managers previously had given little more than lip service.

Finally, congressional attempts to encourage greater public involvement in the making of land management decisions by the Forest Service, the National Park Service, and the BLM also provided environmentalists with effective strategies for influencing federal policies, particularly at the local level at which so many land-use decisions were made. Indeed, environmental groups have perceived correctly that generous provision for public involvement in federal land-use planning has been among the most effective structural means of giving them access and influence in the administrative process generally. For this reason, they have been acutely concerned about the enforcement of these participation provisions in federal land law and convinced that any attempts to narrow such opportunities, by law or administrative manipulation, were covert attacks on their political bases.

In many respects, the 96 million acres of pristine federal land now congressionally protected from development under the Wilderness Act are a monument to environmentalist activism and to the laws and administrative regulations that enormously enlarged the environmentalists' administrative and congressional influence. As political scientist Craig W. Allin observed, provisions for public involvement in federal land-use planning at the local level provided wilderness advocates with the incentive and resources to expand their power at the congressional grassroots.

Wilderness advocates quickly overcame their initial organizational disadvantage in local areas. Grassroots organizations sprang up, meeting the demands for public participation and pressing for inclusions of favored areas [in the National Wilderness Preservation System]. National conservation organizations assisted through local chapters and by publishing information about successful tactics.[20]

In a political system in which localism dominates congressional life, this ascent of environmentalist power from the grassroots was an instance of capturing the political base from the opposition.

The Wise Use Movement Emerged, Submerged, and Revived

Out of the political turbulence inspired by the Reagan administration's aggressive attempt to promote greater private access to public lands there emerged in 1988 the wise use movement. The movement is a loose alliance of public lands user groups: resource developers seeking more public resources such as timber and fossil fuels; grazing and ranching interests opposed to increased user fees on public lands; and a multitude of other economic, regional, and political interests whose assorted agendas share a desire to diminish severely the federal government's restrictions on access to the public domain. Under the wise use banner march groups in other respects as dissimilar as the National Inholders Association (private property owners within public lands), the National Farm Bureau Federation, the Western Cattlemen's Association, the American Freedom Coalition (a part of the Reverend Sun Myung Moon's Unification Church), the Blue Ribbon Coalition (off-road vehicle manufacturers), off-road vehicle owners, timber interests, petroleum companies, and many others. It is not, however, simply another incarnation of the Sagebrush Rebellion. The idea of property rights as a legal and philosophical basis for action—a strategy that greatly expanded the movement's political appeal beyond the West—gave the wise use movement a national atmosphere and an intellectual depth. As political scientist Sandra K. Davis explained,

> The idea of protection of property rights was borrowed from the property rights movement, which originated in eastern states, and derived its basic concept from the libertarian party. It has been nurtured by intellectual leaders such as Richard Epstein, a law professor at the University of Chicago, and Roger Pilon of the Cato Institute. The Wise Use Movement's adoption of the property rights issue has facilitated its appeals for political support and its likelihood of succeeding in legal cases.[21]

The ideological underpinning of the movement is provided by various economic theories and theorists who argue that private use of many presently protected natural resources—timber, fossil fuels, and grazing lands especially—would constitute a more economically efficient and nationally beneficial policy (or wise use) than the present restrictions on public resource exploitation. In this respect, wise use is in many ways a modern reprise of the progressive movement's conviction that the "highest and best use" of the public domain often implied its economic development. By grounding its arguments in economic theory, moreover, the movement gains a measure of intellectual respectability and a breadth of appeal to political and economic conservatives that is lacking in arguments based solely on often-arcane disputes over specific resource economics. The movement also shares a hearty dislike for environmentalists that occasionally erupts into vitriol such as one leader's assertion that the movement intended "to destroy the environmental movement once and for all."[22]

The wise use movement packed a potentially powerful appeal but lacked a charismatic national political leader and proven political impact at the polls. It also lost much of the financial support provided by large resource-dependent corporations, such as Boise Cascade, Coors, and Weyerhaeuser, which were disappointed by the movement's feeble political impact and overheated rhetoric. Instead, corporate promoters of wise use have turned increasingly to think tanks such as the Cato Institute, the Heritage Foundation, and the Heartland Institute, which appeal to a much broader intellectual and social constituency while offering greater promise of political return on their investments. Nonetheless, the environmental movement regards the wise use idea with considerable apprehension. Many environmentalists believe that "wise use" ideas, if not the name, have been revived in the land use philosophy of important Bush administration land managers such as former Secretary of the Interior Gale Norton, Secretary of Agriculture Ann Veneman (whose political background and land use philosophy closely resembled Norton's) and many of their subordinate administrative appointees.[23]

The Department in the Middle

The DOI was inevitably the focus of controversy over energy exploration in the public domain. More than 200 billion tons of coal, perhaps a fourth of the nation's coal reserves, lie below western lands under the DOI's jurisdiction. Since passage of the Mineral Leasing Act of 1920, the Secretary of the Interior has had the discretionary authority to sell leases and to establish conditions for private mineral and energy exploration on public lands. Such leases, to be sold at "fair market value," must be "diligently developed" into mining operations within a decade; both federal and state governments charge royalties for coal production within their boundaries. Until the 1980s, however, the department promoted coal and other resource exploration on its lands rather indifferently, and during the 1970s, leasing was virtually suspended while the DOI, Congress, and the White House struggled to fashion a comprehensive leasing program. One finally emerged in the late 1970s but soon was challenged by the Reagan administration's new coal programs.

The change in coal leasing philosophy under the Reagan administration was immediate and dramatic. In 1981 alone, the DOI leased more than 400 times the acreage for coal exploration than it had the previous year. Proponents of a greatly accelerated leasing program asserted that the nation needed the energy resources lying unused in the public domain, that federal regulations could protect the lands from the ravages of surface mining, and that the economic productivity created by private use of the energy resources would generate more jobs and greater prosperity. Many of those within the DOI's political leadership would have said a hearty, if perhaps private, "amen" to the summary conclusion on the subject by the president of the American Mining Congress: "Our society is built on the stuff that comes out of the hole in the ground and if we don't unplug the red tape stuffing the hole, this country is going to be in one hell of a mess."[24]

The DOI's announced intentions to accelerate the sale of leases for oil and gas exploration on the OCS and its interest in leasing when legally possible even wilderness areas for exploration convinced environmental groups and congressional opponents of the Reagan programs that a massive public campaign to counteract the new policies was imperative. Congress became the institutional weapon.

The Politics of Checks and Balances

"The probability of our developing any meaningful dialogue with this Administration is low indeed," Russell Peterson, the politically seasoned president of the National Audubon Society, lamented after talking with White House officials less than a year after President Reagan's inauguration.[25] Most environmentalists agreed and turned instead to Congress, as they often did during those times, to exploit constitutional and partisan rivalries to their advantage in seeking an institutional restraint on the president's land policies. For environmentalists, constitutional checks and balances can become a lever with which to move the executive branch, or to frustrate presidential intentions, on resource matters. Such issues can easily arouse the institutional rivalries at the heart of the constitutional order. During the Reagan years, the White House programs awakened among many legislators, particularly those on House and Senate committees with oversight of the DOI's programs, a conviction that the department, with the White House's blessing, was abusing its delegated authority and subverting congressional intent in handling the new energy programs. Democrats on the oversight committees, especially in the House, sought opportunities to challenge and embarrass the White House by attacking its land programs. In the battle over land policy, the House Committee on Interior and Insular Affairs became the most aggressive congressional antagonist to the White House.

During the latter years of the Clinton administration, however, environmental and conservation interests frequently played the game of constitutional checks and balances in reverse. Republicans controlled both congressional chambers, and Alaskan legislators, among the most aggressive promoters of energy exploration on public lands, were chairs of major Senate and House natural resource and energy committees. Then the environmental lobbies used presidential influence to thwart numerous efforts by these Republican-controlled committees to expand oil, natural gas, and timber production in ANWR, the Tongass National Forest, and Alaskan OCS areas.

With George W. Bush in the White House, environmentalists confronted yet a different situation through most of this administration, with Republicans controlling the presidency and, for most of the time, both congressional chambers. In this situation, environmentalists found that a strong bipartisan environmentalist bloc in the Senate could be used to counter aggressive energy development plans favored by the president and House Republicans. With the return of Democratic congressional control following the 2006 elections, environmentalists expected much more aggressive congressional efforts to constrain the Bush administration's efforts to open the public lands to more commercial use and energy exploration.

The Politics of Presidential Leadership

The balance of political party strength in Congress may affect the environmentalists' agenda for good or ill, but the presidency is also a repository of formidable, independent constitutional and political resources to promote or frustrate that agenda. The presidency offers opportunities for policy initiatives, for dramatizing and popularizing issues, and for invoking the constitutional prerogatives of the chief executive and his administrative authority in ways enabling the president—or his administrative appointees—often to achieve the president's environmental goals with little, if any, congressional collaboration. Presidential history from Reagan to George W. Bush amply illustrates the impact of this executive presence on public lands management.

Watt's resignation as DOI secretary in October 1983 did not end the conflict over land policies initiated by the Reagan administration, nor did it diminish the administration's determination to open up the public domain to further energy exploration. Through the use of existing budgetary authority, established discretionary freedom, and "a thousand small changes," Watt had managed, in the face of formidable opposition, to move federal policy strongly toward more resource development on public lands. Watt's successors created less public stir than their predecessor while pursuing the same land policies more successfully throughout the tenure of the Reagan administration. Pressure to develop energy resources persisted.

George H. W. Bush's administration began on a more conciliatory note, with the president committing himself to an active environmental agenda and implicitly distancing himself from Reagan's public lands policies. But the environmental community was not pleased with the administration's new Secretary of the Interior. The president's choice, Manuel Lujan Jr., a former congressional representative from New Mexico, had been identified closely with mining, timber, and other corporate resource users during his legislative tenure. He was widely perceived within the environmental community as more antagonist than ally. Lujan's early pronouncements, including advocacy of greater energy exploration on OCS lands, did little to dissipate this image.

The Clinton administration arrived in Washington freighted with environmentalist expectations of a major reversal in public lands policies that never occurred. Despite the appointment of Bruce Babbitt, an environmentalist paragon, as Secretary of the Interior and his outspoken commitment to turn away from the pro-development policies of the Reagan and Bush administrations, the White House seemed indecisive and uncertain in its land-use policies. As a result, Babbitt was frequently left without the president's apparent support in major clashes with Congress over forest management, energy exploration licenses, and grazing fees on public lands—all major concerns to public lands activists of all political persuasions. Further, Babbitt's, and Clinton's, environmentalist reputation was progressively deflated. For a time, it appeared that the Clinton administration had been considerably more successful in stifling the pro-developmental momentum of the previous two presidents than in promoting a vigorous, strongly environmentalist land-use program of its own. However, Clinton's performance, especially during his final months in office, proved immensely gratifying to environmentalists and, in his final days, a spectacular demonstration of presidential authority over the public lands.

In December 2000 Clinton declared formally the creation of the largest nature preserve in U.S. history and thereby achieved a record unique to U.S. politics. With the addition of the new Northwestern Hawaiian Islands Coral Reef Ecosystem Reserve—a huge South Pacific expanse as large as Florida and Georgia combined and containing more than 70 percent of the nation's existing coral reefs—Clinton's administration had created more public lands for recreational and conservation purposes than any other presidency in U.S. history. The Hawaiian designation was the final flourish to an ongoing presidential performance moving at breakneck speed through the final year of the administration in Clinton's determination to leave Americans what he called his land legacy. Altogether, Clinton's land legacy would be more than 50 million acres of new or newly protected public domain and the designation of 65 million acres of existing public forest land in Washington, Oregon, Idaho, and Montana as roadless areas, thereafter off-limits to commercial timbering.

Clinton's action left behind a lingering, bitter controversy. Wherever commercial access to natural or biological resources was prohibited, and that was virtually everywhere, the resource developers—timber companies, petroleum and natural gas corporations, ranchers, coal and mineral miners, and commercial fishermen among them—complained of national assets being locked up. Many members of Congress, and Republicans especially, were infuriated because Clinton's land-use decisions, especially during that last frantic year, were frequently made without congressional approval, through authority granted unilaterally to the president by the American Antiquities Act of 1906. Moreover, Clinton was quick to blame Congress for its inaction. "Where Congress has been unable or unwilling to act," his spokesperson pointedly noted about the Hawaiian preserve, "this administration had not hesitated to use its full Executive authority to protect public health and the environment."[26]

Many western political leaders found additional reason to complain, particularly about the new roadless areas. Clinton's designation, for instance, had removed almost 20 percent of Idaho's land area from commercial timbering. "It's the kind of unilateral land management decision by the federal government that further deepens the distrust and skepticism that comes naturally to those of us in the West," protested Idaho governor Dirk Kempthorne.[27] Western ranchers denied access to grazing land by the same policy were incensed. "I think we Pacific Northwesterners," went one characteristic complaint, "ought to tell them Easterners to get the hell out of our area. Clinton, Gore, and whoever else is managing things back there: leave us alone!"[28] The U.S. Forest Service found the reaction of western resource developers so hostile that the service's Web site summarized the response as "Roadless Rage." Hawaiian commercial fishermen protested about the prohibition on their activity in the new ocean reserve. "The President's order," went one sarcasm, "gives the Great White Father in Washington control of Hawaiian resources."[29]

The Fate of the Forests

More than one in every ten acres in the public domain could be used for commercial timber production. This land, about 89 million acres, lies mostly within the jurisdiction of the Agriculture Department's Forest Service. Since the end of World War II, pressure has been unremitting on the Forest Service to increase the size of the annual timber harvest (discussed below) from national forests to satisfy the nation's growing demand for wood products. Recently, there has been increased pressure to open many undisturbed old-growth timber stands and wilderness areas to commercial logging. Against this economic pressure, the Forest Service is required not only to enforce the doctrine of multiple use, which forbids the service from allowing timber cutting to preclude other forest uses, but also to manage timber cutting to ensure a sustained yield from any forest reserve used for commercial timbering. Congress has left to the Forest Service the difficult and politically contentious responsibility of defining how much timber cutting is compatible with multiple use and sustained yield.

The struggle over competing timber uses is fought in the arcane language of forest economics—"nondeclining, even-flow" formulas, "allowable cuts," and "allowable-cut effects"—but the larger interests and issues at stake are apparent. The struggle represents a collision between preservationist and developmental priorities for timber, between competing definitions of the nation's economic needs, and between differing definitions of the Forest Service's mission. It is a struggle likely to intensify well into the future.

A Disputed Treasure in Timber

About half of the nation's softwood sawtimber reserves and a substantial portion of its remaining hardwoods grow today in the national forests. The Pacific Coast region, particularly the timbered hills and lowlands of the Pacific Northwest, contains the largest of these timber stands within the public domain; the area contains almost half the pine, spruce, fir, and other softwoods in the national forests. These timber reserves, more than three times the size of all the private commercial forests in the United States and currently worth more than $20 billion, will increase in value.

Although timber cutting was permitted in the national forests from their inception, the demand for commercial timber in the forests assumed major proportions only after World War II. In the early 1940s the Forest Service sold about 1.5 billion board-feet of timber per year; by 1973 the cut exceeded 12.3 billion board-feet. Driven by the nation's ravenous postwar desire for new housing, the demand for wood products rose steadily in the three decades following 1945. Private timber companies, approaching the limits of their own production, began to look increasingly to the national forests as an untapped timber reserve. This demand, if wholly satisfied, would likely result in a doubling of the annual timber harvest from the national forests, in keeping with the industry's estimates that the U.S. demand for wood products would double by the early twenty-first century.

Pressure to expand the allowable timber cut has been particularly intense in the Pacific Northwest. Many of the Douglas fir forests in Oregon and Washington are old-growth stands, virgin forests never touched by a logger's saw, growing in a continuity of development many centuries old. These forests are among the most ecologically diverse and historically unique of all timber stands in North America, reminders of a continent once largely timbered with a profusion of species greater than all of Europe's. Many virgin forests, together with other less spectacular timberlands, are on Forest Service lands still classified, or eligible for classification, as wilderness. To many environmentalists and to organized preservation groups such as the Sierra Club and the Wilderness Society, these lands are the living expression of the preservationist ethic, the values of the movement made visible. They are, in political terms, "gut issues."

The Greening of Forest Policy

The environmental movement has profoundly changed forest management policies since 1970 by altering its political underpinnings. Before the 1970s, as political scientist George Hoberg observed, "the forest policy regime was characterized by a dominant administrative agency, a strong orientation toward the development of timber resources, and little input from the public."[30] By the early 1970s the organized environmental movement had acquired political muscle and, together with its political allies, had promoted new environmental laws and new federal agencies to implement them. Environmentalists aggressively used their newly expanded judicial access to fashion litigation into a potent political weapon. New statutory and administrative provisions for public involvement in the implementation of forest policy and greater congressional oversight of Forest Service policies expanded environmentalist influence in day-to-day forest management. These changes meant a new pluralism in forest management politics in which resource developers no longer dominated and in which environmentalists had become major players whose interests had to be acknowledged, along with their allies, in policy making at all governmental levels.

Once again, as in other aspects of environmental policy, environmental organizations found the courts during the 1970s and early 1980s to be an effective ally. Especially important was the growing trend among federal courts to scrutinize carefully the Forest Service's management decisions to ensure they were compatible with newly enacted environmental laws rather than to defer, as the courts had done traditionally, to the Forest Service's professional expertise in cases in which the service's decisions were

challenged. It was success in overturning the historic Forest Service practice of clear cutting in the early 1970s, observed Hoberg, that demonstrated what this shift in judicial attitudes meant for environmentalists:

> Conservationists found an obscure provision of the original authorizing
> statute of the Forest Service ... requiring that harvested trees had to be
> "dead or matured" and that they had to be marked before being cut.
> Although these requirements were legislated even before the development of
> the forestry profession in the United States, the court refused to defer to the
> Forest Service's interpretation of the statute's meaning and enjoined clear-
> cutting in the Monongahela National Forest in West Virginia and the Ton-
> gass National Forest in Alaska. By outlawing the most common method for
> harvesting timber, these rules created a crisis of timber management. Con-
> gress was forced to rewrite management laws.[31]

The Forest Service did not respond warmly to most of these early provo-
cations. Professional foresters and the Forest Service's rank and file often
resented the challenge to their professional judgment and the environmentalist insinuations that they were ecologically unenlightened. The rise
of politically organized and powerful environmentalism, moreover, spelled
the end of the Forest Service's administrative autonomy, especially the
customary judicial deference and the congenial congressional oversight it
had come to expect. When Congress passed the National Forest Management Act (NFMA) in 1976, it compelled the Forest Service to open its forest management planning process from the lowest levels to environmentalist involvement and set new standards for multiple-use decisions in
which ecological values had to be given major consideration. Gradually,
however, the Forest Service adapted to the new environmental realities,
with the considerable assistance of progressive leaders within professional
forestry itself. The academic training and recruitment of Forest Service professionals was transformed to include much greater emphasis on environmental values and ecologically supportive practices in job preparation. The
Forest Service adjusted its organizational structure and decision-making
procedures to the new requirements of NEPA, the NFMA, and other judicial and congressional mandates to better incorporate environmental values in its policy making.

Still, the Forest Service, like other federal land management agencies,
must live with multiple-use laws as the fundamental calculus for its land-
use decision making, environmentalism notwithstanding. Thus, forest managers are never free of conflicting forces and values pressing constantly on
them whenever major forest management policy must be formulated or
implemented. Indeed, multiple-use legislation creates the fundamental political order out of which all forest management decisions must ultimately
arise.

Multiple Use and Sustained Yield

Because Congress has chosen not to specify how it expects foresters to define multiple use or sustained yield in specific jurisdictions, the Forest Service has been left with enormous discretion in translating these formulas into practice. As with the multiple-use doctrine, the congressional definition of sustained yield is open to diverse interpretations, as section 531 of the Multiple Use–Sustained Yield Act suggests, "Sustained yield . . . means the achievement and maintenance in perpetuity of a high-level annual or regular periodic output of the various renewable resources of the national forests without impairment of the productivity of the land."[32]

Conflict over interpretation of multiple-use mandates has been intensified by requirements in the Resource Planning Act of 1974, as amended by the NFMA, that the Forest Service prepare comprehensive development and management plans for each of the more than 120 management units it operates. The Forest Service began this process in the late 1970s and still has not adopted final plans for all its management units. These management plans often become a catalyst for controversy among interests with competitive demands on particular planning units. Final adoption of a management plan does not necessarily end the controversy, however, for arguments often continue over whether the plan is being implemented properly. The Forest Service often finds itself in the middle of a continuing, and often unresolvable, conflict over what pattern of multiple use is, or should be, implemented in a given forest tract.

Both sustained-yield and multiple-use doctrines are important to the commercial timber industry because they provide the basis for the Forest Service's determination of the allowable cut in a given timber reserve—the amount of timber that can be removed from a particular resource area in a given time period. The Forest Service has interpreted sustained yield to require a nondeclining, even-flow policy, which limits the timber cut in a given area to a constant, or increasing rate—but never a declining one. In effect, this has limited severely the cutting of old-growth forests, particularly in the Pacific Northwest, to the ire of the timber industry, local communities, and those economists who believe a larger cut of old-growth timber is more economically efficient and compatible with the multiple-use doctrine. Environmentalists generally support protection of old-growth forests and advocate further reductions on the allowable cut elsewhere.[33]

In response to pressure from the timber industry and the Reagan administration's own preferences, the Forest Service began to increase the timber harvest substantially in the mid-1980s and to plan for increasing harvests through the 1990s. Between 1982 and 1989 the total timber cut in the national forests grew from 6.7 to 12.7 million board-feet.[34] Forest Service professionals contend that this expansion is consistent with the statutory mandate to maintain a sustained yield. But the timber industry wants more production. With its own reserves being depleted rapidly, the industry contends that only a timber harvest from the national forests significantly above the currently projected levels will provide enough wood for the U.S. economy in the next several decades.

Jimmy Carter's administration, responding to the rising cost of new housing, had ordered the Forest Service to depart "in a limited and temporary way" from its general sustained-yield principles and to open up some wilderness areas not specifically included in the National Wilderness Preservation System for timber harvesting. The Reagan administration, more sympathetic to the viewpoint of the National Forest Products Association, advocated that the Forest Service permanently modify its sustained-yield practices to permit greater timber cuts without violating the balanced-use principle. In keeping with this production bias, the Reagan administration's budgets substantially increased spending for Forest Service activities closely associated with timber production, such as new forest road construction.

The Forest Service asserted that it could meet the higher timber production levels demanded by the Reagan administration only by cutting deeply into the Pacific Northwest old-growth timber, including many of the nation's remaining virgin forests. Although towering stands of old Douglas fir and associated species within these forests provide incomparable vistas and sustain a great variety of plant and animal life, they are not particularly productive from an economic viewpoint. About a quarter of the trees will rot once they mature. Most of these forests have already matured, and most timber has ceased to grow: The trees cover highly productive land on which second- and third-growth timber would flourish, producing much greater income during the twenty-first century than could be realized from current use. Professional foresters associated with the commercial timber industry have asserted that protecting most of the old-growth forests from commercial cutting largely prevents decaying old forests from being converted to more productive young stands. Moreover, the Forest Service's critics note, higher timber cuts do not mean an end to all, or even most, of the old-growth stands but a selective cutting of some and the conversion of others to second-growth production.

Environmentalists have long opposed the logging of old-growth forests, citing the soil destabilization and ecosystem disruption they assert is almost inevitable. Nor do they find the economic arguments persuasive. The battles tend to be fought on a forest-by-forest basis, as the Forest Service proposes the required long-range plans for each forest and then files the necessary EISs. Environmentalists often challenge the overall adequacy of the impact statements and the specific timber production goals. The struggle over timber use spills into the related issue of wilderness designation, where the Forest Service also exercises discretionary authority. George H. W. Bush's administration inherited one of these struggles, an especially emotional and public dispute provoked by Forest Service plans to permit greatly expanded timber cutting in old-growth northwestern forests. The plan might have succeeded, except for ecological serendipity in the form of the northern spotted owl.

The Northern Spotted Owl versus the Timber Industry

The spotted owl is now an icon of American resource politics, a symbol of the clash between competing approaches to valuing natural resources. In the mid-1980s the Forest Service had planned to permit commercial timber companies to make substantial cuts in the old-growth Oregon forests, whose 2.3 million acres represent the last 1 percent of the nation's original forest cover. In 1985, biologists in the DOI's Fish and Wildlife Service reported to the departmental leadership that the northern spotted owl, whose habitat was almost exclusively northwestern old-growth forests, was fast disappearing and should be designated an endangered species. Estimates indicated that about fifteen hundred nesting pairs of owls remained, all in the first-growth stands. One consequence of this designation would be to protect this habitat, if geographically unique, from almost all forms of development. The DOI's leadership initially overruled this recommendation under considerable pressure from the timber industry and a variety of local Oregon and Washington interests, including timber mills, community leaders, unions, local congressional representatives, and timber industry workers.

Spokespersons for these interests argued that designating the northern spotted owl an endangered species would virtually end logging on 1.5 million acres of old-growth timber in Oregon and Washington. The federal government estimated that between 4,500 and 9,500 jobs would be lost, but the timber industry asserted that the actual figure was ten times that amount. "You're talking about complete devastation of communities," protested then-senator Slade Gorton, R-Wash. The president of the Northwest Forestry Association, a trade group, repeated a familiar refrain among local economic interests in Washington and Oregon: "To devastate a regional economy over the spotted owl seems absurd. You're talking about affecting half our industry."[35] The timber industry's outrage was exacerbated further because much of the old-growth, softwood timber was exported, primarily to Japan, where it could command several times the domestic price.

Environmentalists had opposed commercial logging in old-growth forests long before the specific tracts in Oregon and Washington entered the dispute. Environmentalists have argued that intensive logging in old-growth forests, with the building of logging roads and disruptive soil practices sure to attend it, greatly reduce the forest's ability to conserve water and to prevent soil erosion, thus violating the principle of balanced use. Spokespersons for environmental organizations have also contended that much of the old-growth timber is found in poor soil—at high elevations and on steep slopes—and exposure to weathering will cause rapid erosion after logging begins. Moreover, they assert, these forests support a unique ecosystem with a great variety of important and irreplaceable flora and fauna. Finally, environmentalists challenge the presumption that a major increase in the timber harvest would significantly decrease housing costs. In any case, many acceptable substitutes for wood exist in the U.S. economy that can be had without sacrificing virgin forests, they note.

But for the northern spotted owl, these arguments might have succumbed to the political weight of local, regional, and national interests defending commercial access to first-growth timber. In the fall of 1988, environmental organizations obtained a federal court order that instructed the Secretary of the Interior to list the northern spotted owl as endangered, and in mid-1989 the DOI complied with the court's demand. The designation appeared almost to end commercial logging in northwestern first-growth forests, but it did nothing to diminish the rancor, or the economic stakes, involved in the continuing controversy over the appropriate use of the national forests.

Timber Sales Reform

George H. W. Bush's administration came into office committed to an active environmental agenda, implicitly distancing itself from the Reagan–Watt era in its goals for public lands. Although the environmental community had been displeased with the administration's choice of Lujan as the new Secretary of the Interior, it was considerably more receptive to the administration's proposal in early 1990 to reduce timber sales substantially in twelve national forests. The new proposal seemed to repudiate the previous administration's resource policies and to signal a major effort to reform traditional Forest Service sales practices, which had long been criticized by environmentalists. The sales-below-cost controversy—political dynamite in the western states—seemed to set the new administration's public lands policy on a collision course with vast segments of the Forest Service's constituency. The controversy had been simmering for decades. As the Conservation Foundation noted,

> The Forest Service typically constructs the roads and assumes other management and administrative responsibilities that allow private companies to

harvest [public forest timber] economically. . . . However, several studies have alleged that the nation actually loses money (as well as valuable wilderness and wildlife habitat) in many cases, particularly in the Rocky Mountain region, because the Forest Service must spend more to allow the harvesting to occur than it receives from the harvests. The Forest Service denies that the economics of sales such as those in the Rocky Mountains and the Northwest are as unfavorable as many critics claim.[36]

Environmentalists, as well as critics within the Forest Service, had long asserted that this practice amounted to public subsidies for the commercial timber industry and a sacrifice of all other multiple-use values, such as recreation or wildlife habitat, to timber sales. "We think the Forest Service overestimates what is sustainable," argued a spokesperson for the National Wildlife Federation. "They overestimate how much timber a given area can produce, they overestimate the potential for the lands to be reforested and they underestimate the impacts on fish and wildlife. The bottom line is they are timber-dominated."[37]

When the Forest Service initiated a new bookkeeping system in 1987, the system appeared to demonstrate that the service was losing money on about two-thirds of its timber sales.[38] Critics cited Alaska's Tongass National Forest as an example of the losses disclosed by the new bookkeeping: The Forest Service had spent about $50 million annually to finance the cutting of 450 million board-feet of timber that brought less than $1 million to the government in revenue.[39] Nonetheless, the new proposal had many formidable opponents, including loggers, timber companies, state and congressional political spokespersons for the affected areas, and the Forest Service itself. Because much of the Forest Service budget was spent on preparing and auctioning acreage for commercial logging, a reduction in these sales would mean a substantial budget reduction for the service. In effect, the administration's plan represented the first major assault on a forest management practice that had endured for more than a half century, fortified by a powerful coalition of political and economic interests and defended by one of the federal government's most successful and respected public agencies.

The Clinton administration used the new bookkeeping system to considerable advantage in its efforts to restrain continuing efforts by the commercial timber industry and western state governors to expand allowable timber cuts in the national forests. The new system also worked to the advantage of conservation elements within the Forest Service who had been pressing for greater timber conservation for many decades. It was now possible to demonstrate not only that federal timber sales were not the financial asset they were asserted to be but also that increased road building and logging in the national forests would often increase the federal timbering deficit.

How Much Wilderness Is Enough?

A substantial portion of the 65 million undeveloped acres under the jurisdiction of the Forest Service—the roadless regions—could become part of the National Wilderness Preservation System and thereby be forever excluded from timbering. A large portion of this roadless area is eligible for assignment to timber production. Timber producers, environmentalists, the Forest Service, and Congress have disagreed since the 1980s over how much of this roadless area should be designated for multiple use—in other words, how much of the area should be open to timbering, mineral exploration, and other nonrecreational and nonconservation uses. Perhaps as much as a third of the whole national forest system, including many old-growth stands, is in these roadless areas.

Environmentalists have been apprehensive that any multiple-use designation for large undeveloped tracts will be an invitation not only to aggressive timbering but also to oil, natural gas, and coal exploration. They predict that energy industries, on locating energy reserves, will seek exceptions to environmental regulations. Air pollution from electric power plants and energy refining operations adjacent to public lands with energy reserves will result, predict environmentalists, and the quality of the lands will be degraded irreversibly. They would prefer that most of the roadless areas under the Forest Service's jurisdiction be included in the National Wilderness Preservation System.

With some justification, environmentalists also allege that the Forest Service's strong commitment to its traditional multiple-use doctrine makes it reluctant to turn large tracts of roadless areas over to a single dominant use such as wilderness preservation. This conviction led environmentalists to criticize the manner in which the Forest Service conducted its first major inventory of roadless areas within its jurisdiction in the early 1970s.

Nonetheless, the Multiple Use–Sustained Yield Act requires the Forest Service to include wilderness protection among other multiple uses of land within its jurisdiction. The NFMA also requires the Forest Service to draw up a master plan for the use of land under its jurisdiction that includes consideration of wilderness designation. Thus, the Forest Service was given both ample authority and explicit responsibility to recommend to Congress additional roadless areas for inclusion in the National Wilderness Preservation System. Although Congress alone possesses the authority to assign land to the system formally, the Forest Service's recommendations frequently influence the decisions. The White House, however, often has proposed its own plans for the roadless areas, sometimes at variance with Forest Service initiatives.

The Carter and Reagan administrations offered proposals to Congress for allocating the roadless areas between wilderness and multiple-use categories; both proposals departed in significant ways from the Forest Service's own proposals. The Carter administration's plan, the more conservative, would have allocated about 10 million acres to wilderness and reserved another 10 million for further study. The Reagan administration, committed to increasing the size of territory open to timbering and energy exploration, rejected the Carter proposal. Congress, as it has often done, chose to follow its own agenda for wilderness preservation. Since the Reagan administration, relatively few new areas have been designated for wilderness because Congress and the White House could reach no agreement on priorities.

Conclusion

The struggles over energy exploration, mining, and timbering on public lands reveal a durable structure to the political conflicts over the use of public resources in the United States. The pattern tends to be repeated because it grows from political realities inherent in the U.S. governmental system.

At the center of the conflict is a federal executive agency guarding the resource as a public trust and wrestling with an ambiguous mandate for its management. Most often this agency will be part of the DOI or the Forest Service. The mandates will be vague because Congress must rely on the professional administrator to make expert resource decisions—hence the generality of the mandates—and ambiguous because Congress often shrinks from choosing between conflicting claims on resources. Thus, multiple-use prescriptions for forest or range management appear to offer something to recreationists, conservationists, and resource developers without really settling competing claims. The administrative managers for the public resource inevitably will find their professional decisions politicized as conflicting interests seek to influence technical decisions to their advantage. Technical decisions themselves can often be made and justified in different scientifically defensible ways. All this means that resource administrators sometimes can exercise their professional judgment in the service of their own group and political loyalties. In all these ways, the resource management agency finds itself at the center of a political conflict over the public domain.

Further, both the White House and Congress will become partisan advocates of resource management policy, attempting to influence administrative decisions relevant to resource management and responding to pressure from organized interests with a stake in resource management. We have observed in timber, wilderness, and energy development policies the predictable tendency of Congress to intervene in administrative management in order to protect interests important to legislators. So, too, Presidents Carter, Reagan, Bush, Clinton, George W. Bush, and indeed every president before them for a half century, have directed the DOI and the Forest Service to pursue specific objectives in resource management compatible with their ideological biases and political commitments. Indeed, Congress and the White House often compete in attempting to influence administrative determinations affecting the public domain. The president, despite the illusory title of chief executive, has no guarantee of success in the struggle.

The plurality of organized interests involved in resource decisions means that Congress, the White House, and the administrative agencies are enmeshed in a process of coalition building with organized groups during resource policy making. These organized interests, moreover, involve not only private interests but also the states within which the public domain resides and for which the use of the domain's resources have significant political and economic consequences.

Finally, policy struggles quite often are waged in the technical language of resource economics and scientific management. Perhaps more than most environmental issues, public resource management is an arcane business to most Americans, particularly those living where few public lands exist. In such circumstances, specialized private groups, such as environmentalists and resource users, tend to operate almost invisibly to the public. The outcome of the policy struggles depends particularly on the groups' organizational resources, technical expertise, and political adeptness in the administrative infighting and legal wrangling that often characterize resource policy making. It is a political arena, more particularly, in which organized environmental groups often constitute practically the only expression of viewpoints not associated with resource users or administrators.

Suggested Readings

Clark, Jeanne N., and Daniel McCool. *Staking out the Terrain: Power Differentials among Natural Resource Management Agencies.* 2d ed. Albany: State University of New York Press, 2000.

Davis, Charles, ed. *Western Public Lands and Environmental Politics.* Boulder: Westview Press, 1997.

Lowry, William R. *Dam Politics: Restoring America's Rivers.* Washington, D.C.: Georgetown University Press, 2003.

Reisner, Marc. *Cadillac Desert.* Rev. ed. New York: Penguin Books, 2001.

Scott, Doug. *The Enduring Wilderness: Protecting Our National Heritage through the Wilderness Act.* Golden, CO: Fulcrum Press, 2004.

Vaughn, Jacqueline, and Hanna Cortner, *George W. Bush's Healthy Forests: Reframing the Environmental Debate.* Boulder: University Presses of Colorado, 2005.

Notes

1. Felicity Barringer, "Secretary Tours Yellowstone on Snowmobile, *New York Times*, February 17, 2005, A18.

2. National Energy Policy Group, *National Energy Policy* (Washington, D.C.: Office of the President, 2001), 5–9.
3. Defenders of Wildlife, *Arctic National Wildlife Refuge,* http: www.savearcticrefuge.org, May 1, 2007.
4. C. Coon, "Tapping Oil Reserves in a Small Part of the ANWR: Environmentally Sound, Energy Wise," August 1, 2001, www.heritage.org/research/energyandenvironment/em763.cfm, April 14, 2004.
5. For a legislative history of ANWR, see M. Lynne Corn and Bernard A. Gelb, "Arctic National Wildlife Refuge (ANWR): Controversies for the 108th Congress," *Congressional Research Service Report No. 1B10111* (Washington, D.C.: Congressional Research Service, 2003).
6. U.S. Department of the Interior, "Environmentally Responsible Energy Production in Alaska's Arctic National Wildlife Refuge (ANWR)," www.doi.gov/anwr/index.html, April 15, 2007.
7. Rachael D'Oro, "Alaska Environment, Development Co-Exist," www.lists.envirolink.org/pipermail/ar-news/Week-of-Mon-20031117/010930.html, May 1, 2007.
8. Mike Chambers, "Alaska Governor Invites U.S. Oil Drilling," *AP Online,* April 1, 2004, www.highbeam.com/library/doc3.asp?DOCID=1P1:929982, April 6, 2004.
9. Article IV, section 3, clause 2.
10. Congressional Quarterly, *The Battle for Natural Resources* (Washington, D.C.: Congressional Quarterly, 1983), chap. 1; see also U.S. Department of the Interior, Bureau of Land Management, "Energy: Fuel for Thought," www.blm.gov/education/00_resources/articles/energy/energy2.html, April 16, 2007.
11. Aldo Leopold, *A Sand County Almanac* (New York: Oxford University Press, 1949), 222.
12. A useful survey of public lands may be found in U.S. Department of the Interior, Bureau of Land Management, *Managing the Nation's Public Lands* (Washington, D.C.: U.S. Government Printing Office, 1983).
13. Paul J. Culhane, *Public Lands Politics* (Baltimore: Johns Hopkins University Press, 1981), 60.
14. James Baker, "The Frustrations of FLPMA," *Wilderness* 47 (winter 1983): 11. See also Jeanne N. Clarke and Daniel McCool, *Staking Out the Terrain: Power Differentials among Natural Resource Agencies* (Albany: State University of New York Press, 1985), chaps. 4 and 5.
15. 16 U.S.C. § 530, 74 Stat. 215 (1960). On the impact of sustained use on the Forest Service, see Culhane, *Public Lands Politics,* chap. 2.
16. 16 U.S.C. § 530, 74 Stat. 215 (1960).
17. Council on Environmental Quality, *Environmental Quality, 1979* (Washington, D.C.: U.S. Government Printing Office, 1980), 309.
18. Natural Resources Defense Council, "The Bush Record," http://www.nrdc.org/bushrecord/default.asp, May 15, 2004.
19. On the history of recent federal OCS legislation, see Marc Humphries, "Outer Continental Shelf: Debate over Oil and Gas Leasing," *Congressional Research Service Report to Congress,* August 14, 2006.
20. Craig W. Allin, "Wilderness Policy," in *Western Public Lands and Environmental Politics,* ed. Charles Davis (Boulder: Westview Press, 1997), 179.
21. Sandra K. Davis, "Fighting over Public Lands: Interest Groups, States, and the Federal Government," in *Western Public Lands and Environmental Politics,* ed.Charles Davis, (Boulder: Westview Press, 1997), 23.
22. Quoted in World Resources Institute, *The 1994 Information Please Environmental Almanac* (New York: Houghton Mifflin, 1993), 159.
23. Sheldon Rampton, "Fish out of Water: Behind the Wise Use Movement's Victory at Klamath," *PR Watch,* (April-June 2003): 117–26.
24. Philip Shabecoff, "Debate over Wilderness Area Leasing Intensifies,"*New York Times,* February 15, 1982, D6.
25. Ibid.

26. Quoted in Douglas Jehl, "In Idaho a Howl against Roadless Forests," *New York Times,* July 5, 2000, A10.
27. Ibid.
28. Ibid.
29. *New York Times,* December 5, 2000.
30. George Hoberg, "From Localism to Legalism," in *Western Public Lands and Environmental Politics,* ed. Charles Davis (Boulder: Westview Press, 1997), 48.
31. Ibid., 53.
32. 16 U.S.C. § 530, 74 Stat. 215 (1960).
33. Culhane, *Public Lands Politics,* chap. 2.
34. U.S. Department of Commerce, Bureau of the Census, *Statistical Abstract of the United States, 1989* (Washington, D.C.: U.S. Government Printing Office, 1990), 656.
35. Timothy Egan, "U.S. Stand on Owl Seen Saving Trees in West," *New York Times,* April 27, 1989, A18.
36. Conservation Foundation, *State of the Environment: A View toward the Nineties* (Washington, D.C.: Conservation Foundation, 1987), 220.
37. Margaret E. Kriz, "Last Stand on Timber," *National Journal,* March 3, 1990, 509.
38. Philip Shabecoff, "Aid Is Asked on Recreation in Forests," *New York Times,* February 17, 1988, B5.
39. Timothy Egan, "Logging in Lush Alaskan Forest Profits Companies and Costs U.S.," *New York Times,* May 29, 1989, 1(1).

Chapter 10

The United States and
Climate Diplomacy:
The Emerging Politics of
Global Environmentalism

*Some experts argue the entire notion of what constitutes national
security should be redefined, believing that environmental "catastrophe" is as likely to cause chaos in the future as ideological and ethnic
conflicts of the past. In response, the CIA, State Department, National
Security Council, Defense Department, and the National Intelligence
Council have all established "high-level" positions to deal with
environmental issues. . . .*
—Wall Street Journal, *September 25, 1997*

*The environment continues to rank in the middle of the list of "most
important issues facing the U.S. today." However, among 10 environmental problems, global warming (or climate change) now tops the
list: Almost half the respondents put global warming in first or second
place. In 2003, the destruction of ecosystems, water pollution and
toxic waste were far higher priorities. . . .*
—MIT Tech Talk, *November 1, 2006*[1]

Newly inaugurated president George W. Bush had barely settled into the
White House in January 2001 before he was entangled in an increasingly
common and politically treacherous policy predicament for the presidency:
a conflict between domestic economic policy and international environmental protection. Scarcely had he maneuvered through the first entangle-
ment when he was caught again in a similar one, this time for the duration
of his presidency.

330

Prologue: The Greenhouse Visits the White House

The first problem was a surprise. A sudden electric power shortfall in early 2000, wholly unanticipated by Bush's policy planners, had created major economic disruption in California. The president was expected to do something—or at least appear to be doing something. Bush announced in early March 2001 that he would not approve new reductions in carbon dioxide emissions from major U.S. electric utilities—a refutation of his earlier campaign commitment to implement the new regulations intended to reduce U.S. production of greenhouse gases. The president explained that he now believed the nation was facing an energy crisis requiring new economic incentives for more electric power production, not more costly utility regulations. Moreover, he did not wish to upset the consumer economy. "At a time when California has already experienced energy shortages," he explained, "and other Western states are worried about price and availability of energy this summer, we must be very careful not to take actions that would harm consumers."[2] That decision was doubly irritating to environmentalists, who considered it both a defeat for domestic air pollution regulation and for international efforts to combat global climate warming.

The second issue was no surprise. A week after the first announcement, a White House spokesperson declared that the Bush administration had "no interest in implementing the Kyoto Protocol"—the international treaty signed by the United States and thirty-seven other industrialized nations in 1997 to reduce their emissions of the greenhouse gases believed to be a major cause of global climate warming. This announcement infuriated environmentalists. It also provoked severe criticism from Western European nations that had also signed the Kyoto Protocol and now considered the president's action "arrogant," "irresponsible," and "sabotage." "Completely provocative and irresponsible," snapped France's minister for the environment.[3] But in fact, the president's treaty rejection should have been expected because Bush had repeatedly declared his objections to the agreement during his presidential campaign. In Bush's opinion the treaty was an unnecessary burden on the U.S. economy, and he seemed unapologetic. "We will not do anything that harms our economy, because first things first are the people who live in America."[4]

In less than a month, however, the president was apparently reconsidering the whole climate warming issue. By the end of April the Bush administration was conspicuously convening numerous conferences among the president; his cabinet; and a variety of scientists, economists, and business leaders to discuss the scientific basis for the climate warming theory and to consider alternative solutions. One senior government official involved in the discussions conceded that the president might be reconsidering his decisions about the Kyoto Protocol. "The decisions six weeks ago were made in an appalling vacuum of information," he noted. "A substantial portion of the people involved wish they had it to do over again. They might still have rejected Kyoto, but probably in a different way."[5] Critics quickly blamed the president's early environmental difficulties on what they deemed his incompetent—or worse—leadership.

Thus evolved another collision between domestic economic and global environmental issues, unsettling its policy agenda throughout George W. Bush's administration. The White House repeatedly foundered in finding a satisfactory resolution to the climate issue. Almost from the president's first inauguration, the White House veered between stubborn rejection of the Kyoto agreement and alternatives cobbled from tentative acceptance of the theory of climate warming with various responses that avoided governmental regulation of U.S. greenhouse gas emissions. Whatever the White House response, the climate warming issue would not go away.

Every American president since Richard Nixon at times has struggled in a similar manner with one environmental problem or another posing an apparent conflict between domestic economic development and global ecological conservation. Bush's rapid progression from domestic crisis through global controversy to indecision over global climate warming illuminates the inherent political and scientific complexity of such issues, their unprecedented scale, and their uniqueness.

That Bush should have confronted issues of global climate warming so early and often in his presidency testifies to an ongoing transformation in U.S. environmental governance. The domestic and international environments are now inextricably interrelated ecologically and politically. However the Bush administration reconciled—or tried to reconcile—the immediate conflict between domestic economic policy and international efforts to control climate warming, global environmentalism was sure to intrude again, insistently and unavoidably, on future policy deliberations. Indeed, the distinction between domestic and international environmental policy is rapidly eroding, as both science and diplomacy force the recognition of their increasing interdependence. Although international environmental issues such as climate warming are increasingly common on the U.S. policy agenda, the political path leading to that agenda differs from that for most domestic issues in ways important in shaping their political characteristics.

Unlike domestic environmental issues, climate warming, like most other global environmental issues, ascended the national policy agenda unaccompanied by a threatened reactor meltdown, a dangerously leaching toxic waste site, or other dramatizing events and despite an apathetic public. Global warming did not, until after 2005 provoke a sense of urgency or compelling concern among most of the U.S. public. For instance, in 2001, only 28 percent of the American public reported knowledge of

Bush's reversal about carbon dioxide emissions, and only 20 percent were aware of his Kyoto Protocol decision, despite generous media coverage of both matters.[6] Climate warming, in fact, has never appeared on the public's list of the "most important problems facing the country" compiled periodically by the Gallup Organization.[7] Neither did the discovery of a possible greenhouse effect in the early 1980s inspire the traditionally powerful U.S. pressure groups, such as business, labor, or education, to demand some governmental response. Even the environmental movement was slow to seize on the issue.

Science, not aroused public opinion or economic interest groups, has been the prime political mover behind most global environmental issues. In this respect, the global environmental issues advancing on the domestic policy agenda since the 1990s differ from the environmental problems that crowded it in previous decades. As global issues assume greater political and economic importance to Americans, however, the institutions, actors, and processes characteristic of international environmental politics will become increasingly influential in domestic environmental politics. This confluence of domestic and global political forces creates a distinctive transboundary, or cross-national, politics—a style of national environmental decision making likely to grow in importance as the twenty-first century continues to unfold.

Transboundary Environmental Politics

Since the 1990s three global issues—acid precipitation, stratospheric ozone depletion, and global climate warming—have dominated the nation's international ecological agenda and increasingly affected its domestic environmental policies. More than any others, these issues exemplify the internationalization of national environmental politics evolving almost from the first Earth Day.

The United States has been a party to international environmental agreements since 1921, but the scope and pace of this global ecological involvement have increased significantly since the 1960s. Among the 152 multilateral environmental treaties and agreements adopted by the United States through 1990, 20 were signed between 1921 and 1959, 26 during the 1960s, 49 during the 1970s, and 48 in the 1980s.[8] Before the 1980s, most of these ecological agreements, like the UN Law of the Sea Convention signed in 1984, dealt with protection and preservation of the marine environment and fisheries or, like agreements relating to Antarctica and outer space, with freedom of access to common global resources. Transboundary air and water pollution, and especially human-induced (anthropogenic) changes in global climate, received little, if any, diplomatic attention and remained a largely arcane matter for scientists and public health experts.

The rapid rise after the 1970s of scientific concern about cross-national pollution and human-induced climate change, together with a growing volume of information, increasingly sophisticated global environmental monitoring, and the mounting political strength of global environmental organizations, encouraged increased worldwide governmental attention to transboundary pollution problems. As the geographic and climatologic scale of scientific analysis expanded, the politics of international environmentalism was transformed. By the mid-1980s the cross-national transport of pollutants and its global impact had become a major, distinctive issue.

Historic Markers: Stockholm, Rio, and Kyoto

The rapid growth of U.S. involvement in global environmental diplomacy, and especially the nation's increasing engagement in problems of transboundary pollution, can be documented by three historic markers: the Stockholm, Rio, and Kyoto environmental conferences spanning the years between 1972 and 1997. Growing U.S. activism began with the 1972 Conference on the Human Environment in Stockholm, Sweden, the first truly international conference devoted exclusively to environmental issues, attended by 113 states and representatives from 19 international organizations. The theme "Only One Earth" dramatized internationally for the first time the growing gravity and scale of global environmental problems ranging from population growth to outer space pollution. Among the other significant accomplishments of the Stockholm meeting were the creation of the UN Environmental Program, initially supported vigorously by the United States, and the enactment of many other, largely symbolic measures that committed the United States to a major role in future international environmental activities.[9]

The second major international meeting, the 1992 Conference on Environment and Development, popularly called the Earth Summit and held in Rio de Janeiro, was attended by an even larger international delegation of representatives from 179 countries, including 116 heads of state. The new conference theme, "Our Last Chance to Save the Earth," invoked the growing sense of urgency about global environmental degradation that characterized the meeting, which focused special attention on the environmental concerns of developing countries. The Rio Declaration on Environment and Development, probably the most widely known of all the conference statements, proclaimed twenty-eight guiding principles to strengthen global environmental governance. Although U.S. delegates attended the conference and actively participated in almost all of its proceedings, the official U.S. delegation, representing the viewpoint of President George H. W. Bush and his Republican administration, was widely and severely criticized for its reluctance to lead in conference policy making and, in particular, for its refusal to join other industrial nations in agreeing to timetables and reduction goals for the greenhouse gas emissions assumed responsible for global climate warming.

Although environmentalists were deeply disappointed in the U.S. delegation's lackluster performance in Rio, in a broader perspective the Rio conference resulted in a multitude of lesser U.S. commitments to increasing international environmental activism. Most notably, it unleashed powerful domestic and international political pressures on the United States that resulted in the Clinton administration's commitments to the timetables and emission targets for greenhouse gas reduction incorporated into the 1997 Kyoto Protocol.

By the time of the Kyoto meeting, the United States had also signed the 1987 Montreal Protocol on Substances that Deplete the Ozone Layer, limiting domestic production and consumption of chlorofluorocarbons (CFCs) and related chemicals destroying the global stratospheric ozone layer; it had resumed financial support for the UN Fund for Population Activities, earlier halted by the Reagan and Bush administrations; and it had ratified the Biodiversity Treaty and the UN Law of the Sea Convention, again reversing Reagan-Bush presidential policies. Although the United States seemed unlikely to sign the original Kyoto agreement in light of George W. Bush's outspoken opposition and continued Senate disagreement over its details, worldwide diplomatic pressure virtually compelled the United States to remain involved in global climate warming treaty negotiations. Thus, the U.S. diplomatic trajectory from Stockholm to Kyoto was leading the country steadily, if unevenly, toward a broadening and deepening commitment to international environmental governance.

Environmental Diplomacy: Incentives and Disincentives

A multitude of events in the last quarter of the twentieth century, such as the development of satellite monitoring of the earth, computer technology, new environmental sciences, and, especially, the growth of an international scientific community deeply engaged in ecological research, all have compelled national governments to recognize the reality of transboundary pollution while raising a new global consciousness of its scope and impact. Transboundary pollution eludes the jurisdiction of any national government. Its management—combating pollution of the Mediterranean Sea, for example—often requires local or regional collaboration among governments. But as science becomes more sophisticated in its ability to monitor and to understand pollution processes, it increasingly frames transboundary environmental problems in terms of complex, intricately related, virtually global causes and effects. This impulse toward comprehensive conceptions of international pollution also animates modern science, however unintentionally, to continually push prospective solutions up the scale of international management.

State Sovereignty versus Ecological Stewardship. All international diplomacy occurs in a global setting that is frequently considered anarchic in the sense that there is no sovereign political regime—no determinate governmental institutions, laws, processes, or principles—to which national governments give dependable allegiance. In this sovereignless political arena, national relations are governed at different times and places by many principles in various combinations—political or economic power, cultural affinities, historical antagonisms, a regional or global superpower, technological and geographic resources, the rule of law, and much else— the nature of which is a source of unending preoccupation for diplomats and scholars. It is no surprise that the political foundation on which modern nations are expected to ground their international environmental diplomacy is at best precarious, a structure currently designed to satisfy two dissonant principles—the concepts of national sovereignty over indigenous resources and national responsibility for environmental stewardship—and so inherently insecure.

Embedded in modern environmental diplomacy, therefore, is the fundamental tension between these two principles. Today the United States and other nations recognize both principles as stated in Article 21 of the Stockholm Declaration (1972) and later reaffirmed by the Rio Declaration:

> States have in accordance with the Charter of the United Nations and the principles of international law, the sovereign right to exploit their own resources pursuant to their own environmental policies, and the responsibility to insure that activities within their jurisdiction or control do not cause damage to the environment of other states or of areas beyond the limits of national jurisdiction.

Article 21 prudently recognizes the reality of state sovereignty and self-interest and implicitly its primacy in international politics. Virtually all national policy makers, in any case, act as if state sovereignty and self-interest were a higher principle, even while genuflecting in the direction of environmental responsibility toward their neighbors. In effect, the United States conducts its international environmental diplomacy in a global political arena where its own self-interest and sovereignty, and those of every other nation with which it negotiates, are always at risk of conflict with U.S. environmental goals or with the global policies deemed essential to resolve satisfactorily an international environmental problem. Moreover, the U.S. government, superpower or not, cannot routinely or legally assert a sovereign will over other nations in environmental matters as it can often do in domestic political dealings with the states and other domestic political institutions.

National Costs and Benefits. Transboundary environmental issues, like domestic ones, involve an uneven distribution of costs and benefits, ones calculated in regional, international, and global metrics that involve money, sovereignty, national prestige, and historical experience.

Virtually all transboundary problems, such as acid deposition, entail upstream-downstream relations in which one nation, or group of nations, disproportionately bears the impact of pollution migration while the polluter is likely to reap the benefits—or to believe it does. This upstream-downstream disjunction is rich in political, social, and economic cleavages sure to erupt whenever issues of pollution management arise.[10] The United States plays both roles in international politics. It is a major source of greenhouse gas emissions associated with global climate warming and the airborne chemicals responsible for stratospheric ozone depletion, but it also shares the ecological and human health risks from both problems with other nations. The United States is also producer and recipient of transboundary acid deposition. International environmental issues are typically first raised, often exclusively, by the downstream pollution recipients, as happened in the case of acid deposition. The problem of acid rain was first brought to international attention in the 1970s by Scandinavian countries experiencing widespread lake and stream damage never previously encountered. European nations, such as Great Britain and Germany, which appeared to be major sources for the chemical precursors of Scandinavia's acid precipitation, resolutely resisted diplomatic efforts to reduce their acid rain emissions until new environmental assessments revealed that they, too, were significantly affected by acid precipitation.[11]

Many international environmental problems—climate change or the depletion of commercial fishing species, for example—also involve significant cross-generational costs. The cost of this generation's failure to abate the rising depletion of commercial ocean species will be fully experienced by another generation that may be unable to earn a living at all from once-thriving Atlantic tuna or cod fisheries. Rising global sea levels, shifting temperate climate zones, and other major impacts predicted from climate warming may not create significant human problems for several decades or a generation. As with domestic issues, observed political scientist Lynton Caldwell, "policies are made or affirmed and implemented by people accountable to the present, not to the future generations. Therefore, the urgency of an issue as an object of policymaking is not necessarily a measure of its ultimate significance."[12] In the case of international issues, the problem of cross-generational impacts is further complicated because many of the most severe cross-generational consequences will be experienced by the world's smaller, or most economically or culturally disadvantaged, nations—those with comparatively meager political leverage on international affairs and least able to mitigate or adapt to prospective ecological change.

Moreover, so-called developing or underdeveloped nations habitually view international ecological issues through the lens of their political history, infusing their environmental diplomacy with ideologies, passions, and assumptions drawn from their colonial experience or from past diplomatic, political, or economic associations with Western, industrialized countries. The United States invariably wears distinctive mantles in the perceptions of such nations engaged in environmental diplomacy. It is "Western," "colonial," or "capitalist," a "superpower," "Northern," or "white"—all perceptions, along with many others similarly derived, that inevitably affect the conduct of any ecological negotiations involving not only the United States but also other Western and industrialized nations. Postcolonial and other developing nations, for instance, are likely to suspect initially that U.S. or other Western diplomatic initiatives concerning the environment are covert attempts at exploitation or subjugation. Latin American nations may suspect that U.S. environmental initiatives are a newer version of the deeply resented "big stick" diplomacy the United States employed toward its southern neighbors earlier in the twentieth century. Nonetheless, people in developing societies are increasingly aware of and concerned about environmental problems.

Even if history casts no long shadow over environmental diplomacy, the natural rivalries and tensions among sovereign states, and the omnipresent impulse to national power and sovereignty, always threaten a chokehold on national environmental sensibilities; all nations appraise prospective environmental policy first by its apparent impact on their own sovereignty and power. The surest poison for any international environmental agreement is a national leadership's conviction that their country's sovereignty will be compromised. Thus, opponents launching an early attack on a possible U.S. agreement in Kyoto to limits on U.S. domestic greenhouse gas emissions were quick to conjure images of imperiled national autonomy. "We are taking national sovereignty away from every nation that signs this treaty," charged Republican senator Chuck Hagel of Nebraska. "Would [a binding treaty] mean a United Nations multinational bureaucracy could come in and close down industry in the United States?" he queried, adding meddling bureaucrats to the menace.[13]

Almost as potent in shaping environmental diplomacy is national prestige and image: Leaders recoil from negotiations that imply national responsibility for an environmental offense or that attack the legitimacy of domestic environmental practices. "Any attempt by states or international bodies to alter national [policy] regimes immediately brings into play questions of sovereignty and the competence of a national bureaucracy. Once allegations are made against countries or their subjects, powerful defensive impulses from those identified as polluters may be expected," noted European scholars Sonja Boehmer-Christansen and Jim Skea.[14] Negotiations get prickly when issues, or apparently impartial scientific data, are construed in a good guy–bad guy style that appears to create national villains and victims. As a cautionary tale, political scientist Marc Levy described the result of this strategy during the 1993 negotiations among European countries over a treaty to reduce acid-rain-producing emissions. Using environmental monitoring data, "Swedish and Norwegian officials branded the United Kingdom an irresponsible renegade guilty of damaging Scandinavian resources. In one heated moment, Norwegian environment minister Thorbjorn Berntsen publicly called his British counterpart, John Gummer, a shitbag."[15] Negotiations will be far less impassioned, and usually more productive, when issues and technical data are constructively interpreted to emphasize problem solutions and alternative strategies.

Given the many risks and costs perceived in international environmental diplomacy, national governments are strongly motivated to assume a wait-and-see attitude toward environmental initiatives generated elsewhere, especially if they can become "free riders" to multilateral agreements made by other countries when—as in the case of acid rain abatement—benefits cannot be reserved only for those countries signing the treaty. International environmental agreements often require some sort of new implementation structure, perhaps a regional or global monitoring system for a pollutant, and this may also be an inducement to stay on the diplomatic sidelines. This is particularly likely when the scientific evidence supporting action is not compelling. The evidence may be disputed among experts or suspected of some political or diplomatic taint, or dramatic proof of a problem may be absent—all situations common to many contemporary international environmental issues such as climate warming, global energy resources, or the ecological vitality of coral reefs and their related ecosystems.

Even so, hundreds of environmental treaties exist, and more are being negotiated despite the disincentives. In addition, a large and complex array of international institutions functions to implement these agreements. Clearly, powerful incentives compel nations to participate in international environmental diplomacy.

Incentives to Cooperation. Perhaps the most compelling and common incentive for nations to negotiate environmental agreements is recognition of a shared problem or the possibility of mutual advantage. The Montreal Protocol, the 1987 agreement in which forty-seven nations, including the United States, pledged themselves to specific targets and timetables for reducing their production and use of ozone-destroying CFCs, was driven largely by persuasive scientific evidence of a large hole in the ozone layer above the Antarctic and predictions of a disastrous depletion of atmospheric ozone in less than a century. Significantly, the original signatories negotiated further agreements in 1990 and 1992 to accelerate the pace and scale of CFC reductions when additional scientific data indicated that global ozone depletion was even more serious than originally assumed. These agreements were greatly facilitated by a broad scientific consensus on the problem, by the appearance of a vivid ozone hole, and by recognition that the serious human health and ecological risks of continued stratospheric ozone depletion would be shared globally. Nonetheless, developing nations such as China, India, and the African states were initially reluctant to join the Montreal accords. They were persuaded by a ten-year extension of their compliance deadline and an assurance of financial assistance in finding CFC substitutes through a special multilateral fund established for that purpose. This instance of so-called side payments—incentives designed to encourage reluctant nations to join in multilateral agreements—illustrates a strategy often used in environmental, as well as other, international agreements.[16]

Like expediency, prestige also works to the advantage of environmental diplomacy. Nations often join international agreements—especially when the apparent costs are minimal—when the perceived gain is prestige, improved national image, or political advantage. France, Belgium, and Italy, for example, signed the 1979 Convention on Long Range Transboundary Air Pollution not only to wear the halo of a good environmental citizen in Europe but also because they anticipated that the national emission reduction goals to which they agreed would be achieved even without the agreement.[17] In a similar vein, the Clinton administration agreed in 1992 to stabilize greenhouse gas emissions at 1990 levels by the year 2000, thereby reversing the Bush administration's policy, which won approval of environmentalists and obscured much of the international censure of the United States for its opposition at the Rio conference to such goals. However, the administration's implementation plan relied largely on voluntary compliance and other nonregulatory strategies, which many domestic critics charged were relatively costless economically or politically and were ultimately ineffective.

National security and other military considerations can become potent incentives for international environmental cooperation. The United States, like almost all other nuclear powers, has entered into a variety of international weapons management and disarmament agreements, such as limits on the above-ground testing of atomic weapons and the placement of nuclear missiles, largely for strategic military purposes. Even before environmentalism became a global issue, other, practical considerations had reduced the likelihood of nuclear war, accidental nuclear explosions, and the proliferation of weapons-grade nuclear materials. More recently, U.S. initiatives and agreements to limit the global dispersion of nuclear wastes and to develop technologies for the safe storage of such material or its conversion to peaceful uses have been motivated as much by military security as by environmental considerations. In a broader perspective, the growing evidence of global environmental degradation and the concurrent recognition of the mounting capability of technologies to profoundly alter the physical and biological bases of all global life—indeed, to eliminate it in some instances—are promoting a growing perception among policy makers that national security and environmental protection are becoming inextricably linked for virtually all nations.

Political and economic power, often wielded not so subtly, are also common weapons in environmental diplomacy. With its huge presence in the global economy, for instance, the United States can use access to its domestic market as a potent inducement for agricultural exporting nations to accept U.S.–promoted controls on pesticides and other potentially toxic chemicals on commodities shipped abroad. Nor has the United States been reluctant to use foreign aid or the promise of other kinds of economic or technical assistance to facilitate environmental agreements on climate diplomacy, hazardous waste management, the protection of Antarctica, and many other diverse matters.

The Crucial Role of Science. Scientists and science have assumed an important and sometimes (in the case of current global climate issues) decisive role in promoting environmental issues to international significance. The relatively recent ascent of environmental science as a crucial force in setting the international environmental agenda has many explanations: the proliferation of and collaboration among scientific organizations at all international levels; the growing technical capability and sophistication of the physical and biological sciences, abetted by increasing national investments in environmental research among the technologically advanced countries; the rapid elaboration of highly efficient global communications systems; and the exponential growth of global environmental monitoring and assessment data.[18]

A striking aspect of contemporary science is not only its capacity to compel international attention to environmental issues but also its success in doing so on the basis of predictions, computer models, and other extrapolations, the effect of which is to project politics and policy issues far into the future, thereby linking present-day decision making in concrete and explicable ways to what has been traditionally treated as a remote, and quite frequently irrelevant, social world. This amounts to a subtle but ongoing and pervasive redefinition of political time and space for the world's key policy makers, a lengthening of the conceptual horizons in policy thinking, and a frequently forced and not necessarily welcome confrontation with the long-term consequences of today's decisions defined in the more or less authoritative language of science.

The resources and authority of modern environmental science originate primarily among the world's technologically advanced and largely Western societies, especially in the United States, Western Europe, and Japan. Because of its enormous scientific infrastructure, American science frequently assumes a major, often dominating, role in Western scientific undertakings. Although the environmental science driving global ecological concerns draws considerable strength from its pervasive American and Western character, this becomes an impediment to global environmental diplomacy when non-Western and developing nations suspect, as they often do, that Western science is manipulated to serve Western political and economic interests. As the United States, with other industrialized nations, increasingly strives to include developing and non-Western countries in multilateral agreements concerning climate warming, acid precipitation, and many other matters, establishing the credibility of the scientific assessments on which such negotiations depend has become a predictable task.

Environmental Diplomacy: The International Structure

U.S. environmental diplomacy occurs within a regime of regional and international organizations, many created specifically to implement environmental agreements, and often-tenuous principles of international law established by treaty or precedent by which nations are expected to abide. International negotiations on transboundary pollution have historically been based on two principles of international law: the polluter-pays principle and the precautionary principle. The governance that this international structure exerts over the conduct of U.S. international environmental affairs is highly variable and often problematic, as it is with all other sovereign nations. Generally, international law and organization exert as much influence on American ecological policy as the United States chooses to accept. But the fabric of law and organization from which international environmental politics is constituted is not threadbare. The United States and other nations do recognize and accept some measure of global environmental governance, and international environmental organizations exercise a continuing, if often subtle, influence on the daily conduct of world affairs.

Environmental Principles. Several standards of international law are widely acknowledged in defining national obligations in environmental matters. First, the polluter-pays principle is generally applied. This is interpreted in Principle 16 of the Rio Declaration to mean that

> national authorities should endeavor to promote the internalization of environmental costs . . . taking into account the approach that the polluter should, in principle, bear the cost of pollution, with due regard for the public interest and without distorting international trade and investment.

Second, the precautionary principle dictates that nations take action, even when there is a degree of scientific uncertainty, to abate any potentially harmful pollutants. In recent decades, the rise of international environmental consciousness has led the United States, among other nations, to predicate ecological diplomacy on appealing, if not predictably compelling, assertions about an international responsibility to "protect the Global Commons," consider intergenerational equity, and respect various "environmental rights" in international affairs. Such principles are, in fact, often recognized and respected in international diplomacy even if they are not yet a constant normative force. Of more practical importance are the explicit obligations to which the United States and other nations agree in specialized environmental treaties, protocols, and other understandings. One measure of the potency of such obligations is the extent to which they are translated domestically into appropriate law and governmental practice. Another measure is the consistency with which such agreements are honored over significant time periods. That the United States and other nations have accepted the CFC emission controls involved in the Montreal Protocol, for example, or have observed the UN Law of the Sea regarding national fishing rights in international waters, whatever the reasons, is a reminder that international principles cannot be marginalized as diplomatic window dressing.

Multilateral Agencies. The many permanent organizations implicated in environmental diplomacy are clearer evidence of international environmental governance. Among the most important to the United States are the major decision-making bodies of the United Nations (UN), in particular those UN entities with a primarily environmental mission: the UN Environmental Program, the UN Development Program, and the UN Commission on Sustainable Development. The UN Environmental Program was created in 1972 by the Stockholm Conference to "monitor, coordinate and catalyze" international environmental activities. Its most significant activities include environmental management, information dissemination, and environmental monitoring and assessment, such as that undertaken in its highly regarded Earthwatch Program. The UN Development Program, created in 1965, has become an important distributor of multilateral funds to promote biological diversity, aid in the cleanup of international waters, and combat global warming and stratospheric ozone depletion. The UN Commission on Sustainable Development, created in 1992 with a membership of fifty-two nations, is charged with monitoring the implementation of programs initiated by the 1992 Rio conference, particularly the transfer of financial and technical resources to developing nations.[19]

Besides these UN agencies, a multitude of other multilateral international organizations are important to U.S. environmental diplomacy. Created mostly since World War II, these organizations facilitate and coordinate scientific, economic, and humanitarian activities that have environmental implications. Among them are the World Meteorological Organization, the Food and Agriculture Organization, and the International Atomic Energy Association. In recent decades, European multilateral organizations, particularly the European Union, have assumed great importance in the conduct of environmental diplomacy among industrialized Western nations and the Organization for Economic Cooperation and Development. To these can be added hundreds of more specialized and regional entities, often created specifically to implement and monitor the progress of various international and regional agreements. Especially important in shaping the ecological impact of global economic development, particularly among Asian and African nations, are the powerful multilateral economic development agencies such as the World Bank, the Agency for International Development, and many private agencies such as the Ford Foundation.

NGOs and Multinational Corporations. By the second day of the crucial Kyoto conference in late 1997, observers reported, a carnival atmosphere prevailed, in good part because more than 10,000 persons were crammed into its public meeting space in anticipation of a speech by U.S. vice president Al Gore. More than a third of this human crush represented nongovernmental organizations (NGOs), mostly industry and environmental groups from around the world attempting to influence the deliberating national delegations.[20] Hundreds of organizations constructed displays and information booths encircling the proceedings. Most were competing to capture an audience, as, for example, the five-million-member international environmental organization Greenpeace, which erected a giant solar array in the parking lot to power an "environmentally correct kitchen." Environmental NGOs created their own daily newspaper for delegates and visitors. Spokespersons for environmental groups, who ordinarily couldn't get a phone call to the media returned, were courted by reporters. For environmental NGOs it was a grand and gratifying demonstration of their importance in international environmental affairs.

The Kyoto conference was a testimony to the global importance of the NGO sector as a whole in environmental diplomacy. "The importance of NGOs in environmental policymaking can hardly be overemphasized," observed Lynton Caldwell. "NGOs have been essential from its beginning, both within and without nations, and they have been instigators of numerous treaties and international cooperative arrangements." Much of their influence, he noted, rises from their freedom from the constraints of diplomatic protocol and bureaucratic procedure. "In both the forming and execution of international policy," he concluded, "they may act more rapidly and directly, with less risk to national sensitivities, than can official intergovernmental agencies."[21] The number of NGOs of all kinds active in global environmental affairs has continually mounted. Current estimates suggest the number of NGOs has grown from perhaps 15,000 in the early 1980s to more than 100,000 in 2007, including a notable rise in the number of non-Western and grassroots organizations representing indigenous peoples. The special importance of proliferating scientific NGOs has already been noted. The rapid emergence of environmental NGOs has somewhat overshadowed the continuing influence and vigor of corporate NGOs, particularly the crucial role of multinational corporations in environmental diplomacy. Multinational corporate NGOs, a great many originating or based in the United States, represent a rough counterpart to national corporations and other regulated interests in domestic affairs, except that they are often far more powerful and resourceful. This is no surprise considering that the multinational corporations they serve, including numerous petroleum, industrial, and manufacturing interests, annually produce goods and services valued above the gross national products of all but a handful of the world's nations.

Global Politics Is Different

Even a brief depiction of the global political arena illuminates vast differences from the domestic setting of U.S. environmental politics. Unlike the constitutionally sorted and ordered division of U.S. domestic governmental power, no sovereign authority—no widely understood, accepted, or explicit apportionment of power—predictably directs international affairs. Rather, it is a world of competing national sovereignties where power in all forms is customarily the real legitimating and coercive force in international agreements. It is a world of highly pluralized political interests becoming yet more fragmented as traditional nation states are increasingly forced to accommodate, and often compete with, NGOs, multinational corporations, regional and international governmental bodies, and other entities for diplomatic influence. It is also a world as yet untouched by the moderating influence of a liberal, democratic civic culture or of any common cultural grounding at all. It is a world of dangerous ideological and cultural cleavage, where the hold of environmental governance is still tenuous. In this setting, environmental diplomacy has only just begun to temper the force of power and sovereignty, and a global environmental consciousness is but recently emergent.

Still, since 1980 three of the most significant environmental agreements in world history, to be discussed throughout this chapter, have been negotiated. The Convention on Long Range Transboundry Air Pollution (LRTAP) was enacted in 1979, the Montreal Protocol on Substances that Deplete the Ozone Layer (Montreal Protocol) was signed in 1987, and the Kyoto Protocol to the United Nations Framework Convention on Climate Change (Kyoto Agreement) negotiated in 1997 was officially implemented in 2006. In each case, the United States has assumed, albeit sometimes reluctantly, a major role. If these agreements achieve their purpose in significant measure, they are likely to be the grounding for an unprecedented climate diplomacy later this century.

Climate Diplomacy: Ozone Politics and the Montreal Protocols

No issue in climate diplomacy has been driven harder, or more successfully, to international attention by science than has stratospheric ozone depletion. Virtually all national governments now implicitly accept the dominant scientific characterization of the problem. The rapidity with which international agreements have been negotiated to reverse the stratospheric depletion of ozone represents a degree of accord rare to climate diplomacy. Even nature seemed a conspirator, producing a remarkably timely ozone hole for a diplomatic backdrop.

The Ozone Issue Emerges

The most common chemicals implicated in stratospheric ozone depletion, CFCs, were originally developed in 1931 as a refrigerant safe for humans to handle and subsequently became one of the great success stories in industrial chemistry. For almost a half century thereafter, CFCs were used to make flexible urethane foam for carpeting and furniture; rigid polyurethane foam to insulate homes and refrigeration units; foam for trays, fast-food wrappers, and other convenience items; and, most important, automobile, industrial, and commercial refrigerants. At the time controls were initiated, annual world production approached two billion pounds. The United States produced about 30 percent of the world's supply.[22] Other chemicals now known to contribute to the ozone problem include halogenated hydrocarbons (halons), used as a flame suppressant; another close chemical relative, hydrochlorofluorocarbons (HCFCs); and possibly methyl bromide, a widespread agricultural chemical used as a soil fumigant.

The first significant scientific warning about the possible danger of CFCs was raised in 1974 by U.S. scientists whose research suggested that CFCs released active chlorine into the upper atmosphere, destroying ambient ozone. If this were true, they warned, adverse consequences would ensue. Upper-atmospheric ozone had long been recognized as important to global human and ecological health, primarily because it reduced the amount of ultraviolet light striking the earth's surface, thus protecting humans from high exposures believed to promote skin cancer and cataracts, among other problems, and because it affected terrestrial and aquatic plant photosynthesis. The publicity that this announcement provoked among scientists and the mass media encouraged an immediate, sharp increase in public and private support for research, which eventually convinced the United States to ban CFCs from all domestic aerosol products in 1978 and to press other nations to take similar action. Concurrently, a new wave of international research and communication about stratospheric ozone among climate scientists began.

In 1985 British scientists in Antarctica were surprised when their research revealed an ozone hole over the South Polar region. The ozone hole was political serendipity, arming proponents of an ozone treaty with a powerful psychological weapon. Subsequent analysis of satellite data between 1980 and 1992 indicated an increase in the size and depth of the Antarctic hole of 2.5 percent, plus or minus 1.4 percent, per decade. In 1993 scientists also documented ozone levels 2 to 3 percent below any previously recorded by satellite in both the Northern and Southern Hemispheres. In 1995 the World Meteorological Organization reported that its North American monitoring stations had measured ozone levels 10 to 15 percent below the long-term averages, including a significant decline over the Arctic and a 35 percent decline over Siberia. By 1994 most climate scientists were prepared to accept the verdict from the World Meteorological Organization's major report, *Scientific Assessment of Stratospheric Ozone*: "Anthropogenic chlorine and bromine compounds, coupled with surface chemistry on natural polar stratospheric particles, are the cause of polar ozone depletion."[23] But not all experts agree about the cause of ozone depletion. Additional causes have been proposed for the ozone depletion, including natural phenomena and other, more benign consequences. Measured stratospheric ozone decline is apparently nonlinear, at times showing short-run stabilization and even reversal, leading some scientists to assert that the ozone hole is a transient matter.[24] Nonetheless, the politics of ozone diplomacy have fallen quickly in step with the prevailing scientific consensus.

Montreal and Beyond

By the mid-1980s other major global producers of CFCs were persuaded by the scientific evidence to follow the lead of the United States in controlling CFC production and distribution. With considerable support from the UN Environmental Program, which acted as a clearinghouse for worldwide data about ozone depletion, the Montreal Protocol was signed in 1987 by forty-seven nations, including the United States. Since then, 120 more nations have signed on. It was among the first international agreements to establish target dates and emission reduction levels for chemical substances believed to harm the global climate. The Montreal Protocol was actually a supplement to the Vienna Convention for the Protection of the

Ozone Layer, the first of several such protocols to speed the phase-out of ozone-depleting chemicals.

In its original form, the United States and other signatories to the Montreal Protocol agreed to

- Reduce annual production of CFCs by 50 percent from 1986 levels by June 1999,
- Stabilize CFC production within seven months after the protocol came into force and reduce by 20 percent by June 1994,
- Stabilize at 1986 levels the production of halons and other chemicals assumed to be ozone depleting by early 1992,
- Allow developing countries up to ten additional years to comply with the deadlines and to increase their domestic use of the controlled chemicals,
- Restrict trade in restricted chemicals with nonsignatories to the treaty,
- Create a multilateral fund to assist developing countries in complying with the treaty. The United States provides about 25 percent of the fund's current budget.

As scientific evidence about the scale of global ozone depletion mounted, the United States agreed to two additional protocols, the London (1990) and Copenhagen (1992) agreements, initiated by Germany and Switzerland, both of which had unilaterally begun to phase out additional chemicals. These agreements accelerated the phase-out of CFCs, methyl chloroform, and carbon tetrachloride to early 1996 and halon to 1995 and established a freeze on methyl bromide consumption for all developing countries. An unusual feature of all these protocols was the extent to which they committed the United States and other signatories to a moving target for chemical phase-outs, with the goals changing as scientific research prompted new understandings about reduction schedules. More recently, a working group of Montreal Protocol signatories has recommended a phase-out of all methyl bromide and HCFC production and other measures to which the United States has not yet agreed.

The primary domestic regulatory instrument for compliance with the Montreal Protocol is Title VI of the Clean Air Act Amendments of 1990, which initially contained chemical phase-out schedules keyed to the original Montreal Protocol and now incorporates the most recent modifications, the Copenhagen Protocol, which the United States signed in 1992.

Implementation Issues

Enforcing the domestic regulation of ozone-depleting chemicals has not been easy. Congress passed excise taxes on Freon in the late 1980s and early 1990s that drove the price of CFC-12, commonly used in auto air conditioners, from 60 cents per pound to about $25 per pound by 2001, with further increases expected. A highly profitable international and domestic smuggling business has been created by the regulations, and an estimated 10,000 to 20,000 tons of smuggled CFC-12 and related gases now enter the United States annually. A second major problem involves international negotiations to ban metered-dose inhalers, a major source of CFCs used by more than 100 million people internationally to control asthma and other chronic obstructive pulmonary diseases, a rate increasing globally. A number of countries, as well as some influential domestic interests, have objected to this prospective ban. Domestic agricultural interests also opposed the total phase-out of methyl bromide, arguing that it should be permitted nationally and internationally for essential use as a soil fumigant.

Despite these objections, the Clinton administration vigorously promoted a more aggressive domestic and international approach to the phase-out of CFCs. Congress in 1997 ratified amendments to the Vienna Protocol (1995) that accelerated the original schedule for the phase-out of methyl bromide to a new target date of 2005. In 1999 the United States also agreed to the Beijing Protocol, an amendment to the original Montreal Protocol that advanced the date for the developing nations to eliminate all HCFC production to 2020. George W. Bush's administration, early enmeshed in political controversy over its opposition to the Kyoto agreement, appeared unenthusiastic about an additional climate battle and hardly mentioned the Montreal agreement in its environmental discourse. Still, annoyance about the steadily rising domestic price of substitutes for CFC-12, especially in the air conditioning industry, ticked like a political time bomb waiting to detonate.[25]

Climate Diplomacy: Acid Precipitation

In the early 1990s a national opinion poll estimated that more than three fourths of the public ranked atmospheric damage, forest destruction, and air pollution among the nation's "very serious or extremely serious" environmental problems.[26] By the early twenty-first century acid precipitation had become commonplace on the public's agenda of environmental ills. A decade earlier, acid precipitation lacked not only public visibility but also scientific credibility and political force. The transformation of acid precipitation into a salient public issue demonstrates clearly how scientific advocacy allied to national media capable of magnifying and dramatizing the scientific issues can powerfully shape the public's environmental sensibilities and, thereby, the public policy agenda. The politics of acid precipitation, as much as the science, has advanced the issue from scientific speculation to a matter of public policy. Despite continuing scientific debate about the character and severity of the ecological impact of acid precipitation, the weight of the political constituency demanding public measures to abate it made a policy response inevitable. As James L. Regens observed in his careful study of the issue's development, once acid precipitation became politically sensitive, other aspects of the issue become secondary. "Sensitive environmental issues, by their very nature, create controversy. Once they find a niche in the policy-making process, the existence of scientific, technical, or economic uncertainty may forestall action but ultimately is not likely to preclude regulatory interventions."[27]

The Scientific Evidence

There is now little disagreement among all concerned over the existence of acid precipitation. But disagreement persists about practically every other aspect of the matter, including how much industry, utilities, and automobiles contribute to the problem; how injurious such precipitation is to humans and the environment; and who should bear the costs for abating air emissions causing acid precipitation—if, in fact, abatement is necessary.

The most common chemical precursors of acid precipitation are sulfur and nitrogen oxides emissions from fossil fuel combustion and metal smelting. These gases can be captured by high-altitude winds and transported hundreds of miles from their point of origin. In the process, these gases become sulfate and nitrate aerosols, then join with other airborne chemical compounds, including ozone and hydrogen peroxide, volatile organic compounds, and water, to become the complex chemicals that return to earth dissolved in water or fixed in ice crystals. Microscopic solids of heavy metals, termed microparticulates, may also become acid deposition. Based on estimates made in several eastern U.S. watersheds, between 60 and 70 percent of acid precipitation found in rain or snow is sulfuric acid and the remainder mostly nitric acid.[28]

Scientists have been aware since the late 1800s that some acid precipitation occurs naturally, without human involvement.. However, acid precipitation has since become increasingly widespread and acidic over the last two centuries, leading to growing scientific concern that human (anthropomophoric) sources may account for these increases.. Acid precipitation now occurring throughout much of the world, including the United States, is believed to be ten to thirty times more acidic in many U.S. industrialized regions than it would be naturally.[29] Scientists attribute most of the increase in range and intensity of acid precipitation to growing fossil fuel combustion, particularly by electric utilities and industry. The United States, currently discharging about 41 metric tons of nitrogen and sulfur oxides annually, is the global leader in human-induced acid precipitation, but acid precipitation is a world issue because all industrialized nations and many developing ones discharge significant amounts of the precursors of acid precipitation.

The first warning that acid precipitation might be an impending global problem came in the early 1970s, when scientists discovered that hundreds of previously normal Swedish lakes had become too acidic to maintain normal biological processes: The usual plant and animal life was absent or dying. Many lakes were deceptively beautiful: "The water is sparkling clear because acid had destroyed everything in it, including the color. It is abnormally peaceful because its natural aquatic life, from fish to crayfish to snails, has ceased."[30] Much of the acid precipitation in Sweden's lakes originated in Eastern and Western Europe and other parts of Scandinavia. By the mid-1980s evidence had accumulated rapidly that lake acidification and other ecologically disruptive effects of acid precipitation were increasing at an alarming rate in Scandinavia, Eastern and Western Europe, Great Britain, and North America. By the late 1980s high levels of acid precipitation had been discovered for the first time over rain forests in Central Africa. Moreover, wherever acid precipitation was significant, it appeared to be damaging forests, forest soils, agricultural lands, and their related ecosystems. Large-scale forest dieback can be extremely costly. As a report by the UN Environmental Program noted, "A 1990 study put the cost of pollution damage to European forests at roughly $30 billion per year—about equal to the revenues from Germany's steel industry, and three times as much as Europe's current financial commitment to air pollution abatement."[31]

By the 1990s evidence was mounting that acid precipitation was economically as well as ecologically costly and increasingly pervasive throughout the United States. The evidence became daily news: "A massive dying of red spruce and other trees was documented in 1988 along the crest of the Appalachians from Maine to Georgia. Researchers asserted it was '90 percent certain' that the pollution originated in the Ohio and Tennessee River valleys."[32]

After surveying almost half the twenty-seven hundred lakes in New York's Adirondack Mountains, a New York state environmental agency reported in 1989 that one quarter were so acidic that the vast majority could not support fish and an additional one fifth were so acidified they were "endangered."[33]

Scientists employed by the Environmental Defense Fund reported in 1988 that acid precipitation, primarily oxides of nitrogen from automobiles and utilities, accounted for one quarter of the nitrates entering the Chesapeake Bay. Nitrogen oxides were found to be degrading not only the bay but also the waters of Long Island Sound, the New York Bight, and North Carolina's Albemarle–Pamlico Sound.[34]

The Politics

The Reagan administration, asserting that insufficient evidence existed about the distribution and dangers of acid precipitation, initially refused to propose more than additional research on the issue. Political pressure continued to build, however, not only from environmentalists but also from northeastern states claiming environmental damage from midwestern air emissions. Complaints also came from Canada, where 20 to 40 percent of the acid precursors appeared to come from the United States. The Reagan administration belatedly conceded the seriousness of the acid precipitation problem by signing an international protocol in 1988 that committed the United States to limit its nitrogen oxide emissions in 1994 to 1987 levels. The George H. W. Bush administration—taking an aggressive stance that earned the president a rare accolade from environmentalists—agreed to provisions in Title IV of the Clean Air Act Amendments of 1990 that committed the United States to reducing sulfur dioxide emissions from electric-generating plants by ten million tons per year and nitrogen oxides by two million tons per year, and set a cap on the amount of sulfur oxides emitted by the year 2000—altogether a potential 50 percent reduction of 1990 emission levels. An innovative feature of Title IV was the creation of a market-based system (discussed in Chapter 5) for trading emission allowances among regulated interests to finance cleanup costs.[35]

Although the U.S. decision to initiate controls of its sulfur oxide emissions was welcomed in Canada and other nations, a long-term solution to acid precipitation domestically and internationally is not yet assured. Regulating the other major precursor of acid precipitation, nitrogen oxides, has been far more difficult because the domestic political costs are steep. Most of the nitrogen precursors arise from mobile sources—automobiles, utility vehicles, and light trucks—cherished by average Americans. The mounting number of these vehicles, even with required pollution control devices, is a major reason why nitrogen oxides remain a major urban air-quality problem. In contrast, sulfur oxides are emitted from a relatively small number of large sources, such as electric power plants and industrial smelters, which are, as economist John E. Carroll remarked, "a regulator's dream" because a culprit can be named. But nitrogen oxide control "threatens politically unacceptable changes in lifestyles and points an accusing finger at most of the population vis-à-vis its lifestyle. . . . Lawmakers who are also politicians invariably see opportunities in [sulfur dioxide] control and only political danger in any effort toward [nitrogen oxide] control."[36]

The Clinton administration was content with cautious promotion of further regulation for acid precipitation in the face of the inevitable political controversies latent in any effort to move beyond the regulatory limits of the Clean Air Act. The administration's most significant advances occurred during Clinton's last year in office. In October 2000 the United States tentatively agreed to a bilateral treaty with Canada that would eventually diminish domestic nitrogen oxide emissions from eastern U.S. electric utilities by 50 to 75 percent, thereby reducing a major source of cross-border acid precipitation highly resented by Canadians. Two months later, the Environmental Protection Agency (EPA) announced new auto-mobile pollution rules, strongly promoted by Clinton, that would virtually eliminate nitrogen oxide and sulfur oxide emissions by diesel engines. The new emission standards, considered a major advance in controlling the pre-cursors of acid precipitation, were finally enacted only after a protracted and bitter political struggle with the automobile industry domestically and internationally.

Environmentalists were pleased when George W. Bush's administra-tion affirmed support for the new diesel standards. The president's first energy plan, however, was another matter. The new plan seemed too ripe with proposals for increased fossil fuel production and combustion likely to promote further acid precipitation: a plea for the construction of eigh-teen hundred new electric power plants, a proposal to relax regulatory con-trols on new fossil-fuel-burning electric utilities, and a generous subsidy for the industrial development of so-called clean coal technologies, among other ideas. The administration's ambitious energy programs seemed, in many respects, to create another debate over acid precipitation with a dif-ferent name.

Climate Diplomacy: Climate Warming

In mid-1988 James E. Hansen, director of the National Aeronautics and Space Administration (NASA) Goddard Institute for Space Studies, testi-fied to members of the Senate Energy and Natural Resources Committee that it was "99 percent certain" that the unusually hot summer of 1988 was evidence that a global climate warming was under way.[37] That remark instantly caught the attention of Congress and the media. Suddenly, global warming, often called the greenhouse effect, bore the imprimatur of NASA science; it was speculation no more. Hansen accomplished what the envi-ronmental movement could not despite many years of labor. Global warm-ing had acquired political credibility. "The scientific evidence is com-pelling," concluded Sen. Tim Wirth, D-Colo. "Now the Congress must begin to consider how we are going to slow or halt that warming trend."[38]

In fact, the scientific evidence was less than compelling at the time, but global climate warming had arrived politically on a wave of international scientific advocacy, and presidents were compelled to act as if it were immi-nent. Both the George H.W. Bush and Clinton administrations, uneasy with

the science and politics of climate warming, initiated measures, albeit irres-
olutely, to mitigate the impact of global warming. Because the United
States is the leading producer of the carbon dioxide emissions believed to
be the biggest human contributor to global warming, a U.S. initiative to
reduce significantly its own greenhouse gas emissions is essential to any
worldwide scheme to prevent climate warming.

Is the Climate Warming? Yes

Predictions of impending global warming are based primarily on evidence that the amount of carbon dioxide in the atmosphere has been
steadily increasing since the Industrial Revolution in the mid-nineteenth
century and that average global temperatures have been rising significantly since the mid-1950s.. Until the middle of the twentieth century, fossil fuel combustion, mostly from worldwide coal burning and motor vehicles, was the principal source of these emissions. Since 1970, deforestation
(particularly in the South American and Asian tropics) is estimated to
have annually created additional carbon dioxide emissions by removing
dense forests that absorb carbon dioxide naturally.[39] The greenhouse theory asserts that increasing levels of carbon dioxide, methane, nitrogen
oxides, and other gases accumulating in the earth's atmosphere will progressively trap more of the earth's heat; various studies project that global
climate will warm by an annual average of 1° to 4°F in the 21st century.

A 1997 report from the Intergovernmental Panel on Climate Change
(IPCC), the most internationally influential scientific entity currently
involved with climate change research, provided what many experts considered the most prudent and authoritative assessment of future climate
alterations, including

- An annual mean global surface temperature rise of 1° to 4°F by the
year 2100,
- A global mean sea level rise of approximately one foot, largely from
the melting of polar ice caps,
- A shift in spatial and temporal patterns of precipitation globally,
with a net increase of about 7 percent globally.[40]

Changes of this magnitude without mitigation would profoundly, and
possibly catastrophically, affect much of the world. Low-lying areas,
including many economically underdeveloped countries in Africa and Asia
as well as island nations, would be inundated by seawater, their economic
and ecological sustainability severely jeopardized. Economically and technologically advanced nations with exposed seacoasts or levee-protected
lowlands would also confront formidable economic, engineering, and logis-
tical problems in adjusting to rising seas. Generally, the world's temperate

zones would likely shift further north, accelerating the desertification and deforestation of many continental areas in Asia, Africa, Europe, and North America, while transforming agricultural production in many others. Along with these transformations would come predictable but difficult-to-predict shifts in regional ecology and a multitude of other natural changes. Not all the predicted changes would necessarily be adverse. Some experts have also predicted longer and more productive growing seasons for many crops as a result of increased ambient carbon dioxide, the transformation of some northern latitudes into new agricultural "breadbaskets," and other benign consequences. In any event, the profound global alterations attending significant climate warming, however characterized, would apparently create a relatively swift, pervasive transformation of human societies and world ecosystems unprecedented in modern human history.

In early 2007 an updated IPCC report, based on rapidly accumulating new scientific studies, confirmed the IPCC's earlier prediction of global climate warming and provided ominous new data. The new report doubled the top end of the predicted climate warming globally to 11°F over the coming century and predicted an acceleration of the trends causing concern earlier. According to the IPCC report, the twentieth century was the warmest in the past thousand years. During that period, sea level rose ten times faster than the average rate over the past 3,000 years. While continuing to acknowledge the tentativeness of many conclusions, the latest IPCC report seemed to confirm a growing scientific consensus about the imminence of climate warming and to strengthen political pressure for international governmental responses.[41]

Will There Be a Climate Warming? No and Maybe

Not all atmospheric scientists or other experts find predictions of an imminent climate warming convincing. The ongoing scientific debate swirls around a multitude of complex technical issues certain to confuse the public. The critics' favorite target has been the computer models used to generate climate warming predictions, which have been assailed continually for faulty assumptions and inadequate data about current climate trends. Some experts have asserted that many computer models are based on inaccurate measures of historical temperature change, that climate warming models fail to describe the long-range physics of climate change, that other historical climate data are misconstrued or misapplied in climate modeling, and much more. Some experts cite other causes, such as solar activity and terrestrial volcanoes, to explain climate warming. Others rely on different models suggesting that the greenhouse effect is not inevitable. Still others do not believe sufficient evidence exists to make *any* responsible judgment about future climate warming. Media reports often mystify.

In November 1997, for instance, national news media reported that a Columbia University scientist had discovered evidence in ancient ocean sediments that global warming might be part of a longer natural climate cycle. The same day, another report in the same paper described findings by federal government scientists that satellite data indicated, contrary to most climate warming predictions, a current increase in Antarctic water. In early 1998, however, another federal agency reported that global temperatures in the previous year reached their highest levels since records were kept, adding credibility to the warming hypothesis.[42]

The Evolving Politics

The United States produces about one third of the total global carbon gas emissions believed responsible for climate warming and must therefore be an active participant in any global agreements intended to mitigate the greenhouse effect. A great diversity of domestic political interests are caught up in the regulatory battle over greenhouse gas emissions, including electric utilities, which account for 80 percent of all domestic coal combustion; automobile manufacturers and petroleum producers, whose products create significant carbon emissions; agricultural crop and livestock producers; and almost any other fossil-fuel-consuming industries. Throughout the 1990s the domestic campaign for national and international controls on greenhouse gas emissions was led primarily by scientists, environmentalists, and segments of the national media. They were strongly supported by most European nations and Japan, which were prepared to negotiate a tough climate treaty by the early 1990s and brought considerable diplomatic pressure on the United States to act similarly.

Most potentially regulated segments of the U.S. economy, led by the utilities, car manufacturers, and petroleum producers, were joined by organized labor in early opposition to any domestic or international agreements setting compulsory timetables and targets for cutbacks in fossil fuel emissions associated with climate warming. This domestic opposition was joined by most developing nations, which collectively account for 30 to 40 percent of current global greenhouse gas emissions. Some developing countries believed that the largely Western scientific community advocating climate controls could not speak to the interests of the developing world. Some poorer nations, for instance, resented calculations produced by the IPCC indicating that deforestation and livestock in developing nations contributed to global climate warming. From the perspective of developing countries, this unfairly stigmatized their difficult economic circumstances. In their view, "deforestation is a matter of desperation, not choice, and subsistence animals who provide a variety of useful functions cannot be compared with surplus, overfed stock in rich countries."[43] Developing countries also asserted that greenhouse gas abatement should be the industrialized nations' responsibility because developing nations needed all their resources for survival. "How can we devote our precious resources toward reducing emissions," asked Malawi's minister of Forestry, Fisheries and Environmental Affairs at the Kyoto conference, "when we are struggling every day just to feed, clothe and house our citizens?"[44] Nor did the developing countries find most economists helpful. Economists who asserted that developing countries could abate their fossil fuel emissions far more cheaply than could developed ones seemed to be feeding the appetites of privileged nations for thrusting the abatement burden as much as possible onto others.

In any event, the estimated costs to the United States alone to reduce its carbon dioxide emissions would be enormous. The cost of abating carbon dioxide emissions in the United States would fall heavily on coal users and producers, particularly electric utilities, and the auto industry. The capital cost of installing control technologies for carbon dioxide emissions—and no commercially proven technology yet exists—is estimated to be 70 to 150 percent of the entire cost of a new electric-generating facility. This cost could raise the average American's electric bill by 75 percent.[45] Every American would feel some impact of abatement policies on his or her lifestyle and pocketbook.

Until the early 1990s scientific disagreement and public passivity forced policy makers to become scientific judges and scientists to become salespeople in the struggle to determine whose data would govern policy decisions. By the end of George H. W. Bush's administration, however, the combined scientific and diplomatic pressures, together with gradually emerging public concern about climate warming, forced the White House to confront the greenhouse effect diplomatically. At the 1992 Rio conference, the U.S. delegation reluctantly agreed to reduce voluntarily its greenhouse gas emissions to 1990 levels by the year 2000. It was evident two years later that neither the United States nor several other industrialized nations would meet the voluntary emission abatement targets they had set in Rio. President Clinton later agreed to negotiate a binding treaty at the 1997 Kyoto conference, convened at the initiative of the parties to the UN Framework Convention on Climate Change. Thus, the United States for the first time was apparently committed to a compulsory target-and-timetable agreement. But no consensus on the need for such a treaty existed within either congressional party or among the public as the negotiations began, leaving the outcome very much in doubt.

The Kyoto Agreement

By the time the Kyoto conference convened in December 1997, national opinion polls indicated strong public support for U.S. action to limit climate warming, even unilaterally if necessary, and the IPCC report released that year added further impetus for action.[46] Nonetheless, the Clinton administration, facing an unsympathetic Republican congressional majority and continued domestic opposition from almost all the prospective regulated interests, seemed irresolute and confused, leading environmentalists and their allies to doubt that the United States would agree to tough greenhouse gas emission controls despite previous promises. Because any agreement signed at Kyoto would require Senate approval, the congressional mood constantly occupied the U.S. negotiators. The Senate characteristically viewed the proceedings through political bifocals, continually scrutinizing the international implications for U.S. sovereignty and then the likely domestic economic impacts, particularly in home states. With Senate Republicans generally skeptical and Democrats divided on the treaty's merits, the U.S. delegation knew that eventual Senate approval of any agreement would be problematic.

With 120 nations attending and worldwide media coverage, Kyoto became one of the century's historic international environmental conferences. To the considerable surprise of environmentalists and others expecting an indecisive performance, the U.S. delegation eventually committed to what many observers considered a rigorous schedule of emission reductions. By agreeing to the draft treaty, the United States had pledged to

• Join other industrialized nations in a set of binding emission targets for all six major greenhouse gases, which for the United States amounted to a 7 percent overall emission reduction;

• Achieve emission targets over a set of five-year "budget periods" beginning with the years 2008–2012;

• Join with other countries accepting emission targets in an "emissions trading" regime through which such nations could buy and sell emission allowances for greenhouse gas as long as all kept within the overall emission targets to which they agreed;

• Permit joint implementation through which countries with emission targets could get credit toward their targets through project-based emission reductions in other such countries;

• Encourage developing countries to join voluntarily in the emissions trading program and, through other parts of the protocol, to secure a meaningful commitment from developing countries to set timetables and targets for their own emission reductions.[47]

The Kyoto Protocol would enter into force when at least fifty-five countries, accounting for at least 55 percent of the total 1990 carbon dioxide emissions of developed countries, ratified the agreement.

After Kyoto

The Kyoto Protocol is freighted with many uncertainties for the United States. It will have little domestic impact unless the Senate ratifies it. President Clinton had promised to submit the agreement for ratification within three years of signing the draft. However, the Senate voted 95–0 not to consider the treaty in 1998, primarily because developing nations such as India and mainland China were not bound by its terms. Proponents hoped that Clinton might rally the necessary two-thirds Senate majority for the treaty, but the prognosis became so bleak that Clinton abandoned any serious effort to promote the protocol in the closing years of his administration.

George W. Bush's early opposition to the agreement seemed assurance—if more were needed—that the protocol would never survive Congress in its original form. Moreover, public concern about climate warming, while rising, still lacked the intensity to elevate the matter to high-priority among the nation's most important public issues, even though it was increasingly identified as a major *environmental* problem. The Gallup Poll reported in mid-2004, for instance, that the proportion of the public that reported worrying about climate warming "a great deal or a fair amount" had declined from 72 percent in mid-2000 to 51 percent by Earth Day 2004.[48] On Earth Day 2007, Gallup noted that "overall, Americans' concern about global warming has not generally shown much fluctuation since Gallup first asked the question in 1989."[49] Numerous members of both parties have pledged their opposition unless the developing nations also agree to mandatory domestic emission cutbacks, which they have so far vigorously rejected. Other major senatorial concerns involve fears of lost sovereignty and adverse domestic economic impacts. Somewhat unexpectedly, tentative support emerged for the agreement among some segments of the automobile manufacturing, petroleum, and electric utility industries, but powerful opposition remains. Further, many scientists believe that the Kyoto Protocol is at best a first step toward what must be a greatly accelerated timetable, with much greater emission reductions among all major industrial nations, if the worst impacts of a future climate warming are to be averted.

The Emerging Politics of Sustainability

Internationally, the ideal of unrestrained global economic growth, fueled by a pervasive and ambitious nationalism, has increasingly seemed to be a prescription for a future ecological catastrophe of global proportions. In the United States, the urgent environmental problems driving climate diplomacy have made it apparent domestically, as well, that national economic and technological development must somehow be reconciled with environmental conservation. As Chapter 1 noted, "sustainablility" has increasingly become a catalytic policy concept linking economic development, environmental conservation, and social equity in global environmental policy discourse. The creation of the President's Council on Sustainable Development in 1993 appeared to confirm the ascendance of sustainability to the national public policy agenda. By the time George W. Bush entered the White House, virtually all U.S. institutions engaged in global environmental diplomacy were associating their mission in some manner with rapidly emerging world attention to sustainable development.

"Sustainability" resonates powerfully with environmentalists, who respond enthusiastically to its call for restraint on environmental exploitation, and with the leadership of developing countries struggling to reconcile ecological conservation with the insistent drive for economic and social development. Sustainability also appeals to the developed world's political leaders by a semantic alchemy enabling the idea—at least abstractly—to reconcile what often seems irreconcilable: sustained economic growth and environmental conservation, free market economics and ecological protection, the developing world's craving for development and the developed world's apprehension about global resource depletion.

Moreover, *Our Common Future* (the "Brundt Report")—the United Nation's globally important 1987 report on sustainability discussed in Chapter 1—was acclaimed for advocating development "that meets the needs of the present without compromising the ability of future generations to meet their own needs" but, like most general definitions of sustainability, this can be interpreted very differently, and incompatibly, by different observers. Thus, sustainability (or "sustainable development") easily becomes so conceptually murky that policy makers peer into its depths and report quite different visions. And so politicians learn a hard political lesson: However beguiling the principle, translating sustainability into international and national policy is ultimately difficult and contentious.

The Implementation Challenge

The U.S. domestic and international commitment to sustainability policies seems incontrovertible when measured by the mission statements of federal agencies. Most federal environmental and diplomatic agencies now have a dedicated policy office or department, and at least a mid-level administrator committed to promoting sustainability policies in some form. In the U.S. State Department the responsibility rests with an assistant secretary of State, in the EPA with an "Environmental Innovation" division, in the Department of Energy with its national "Smart Growth Network," and so on. All these agencies, however, face a constant struggle in securing the budgetary resources and White House attention necessary to underwrite a vigorous, continuing diplomatic investment in global sustainable policies.

White House and Congressional support for domestic and global initiatives in sustainability policy, however well-intentioned, have so far been problematic. By the end of the Clinton administration in 2000, for example, the President's Council on Sustainable Development had become moribund, a symptom of a gradually eroding U.S. commitment of resources to global environmental policy beginning in the mid-1990s and continuing through the George W. Bush administration.[50] In contrast, much of the energy and imagination invested in promoting domestic sustainability policies has originated with state and local governments, environmental groups, and a rapidly proliferating cadre of "smart growth" community activists and organizations.

The White House commitment to global initiatives about sustainable development has always been hostage to many competing, more compelling political and economic priorities, often arising from confounding events. Thus, the Clinton administration's sustainable policy agenda largely evaporated after the election of an unsympathetic Republican congressional majority in 1994 and Clinton's later impeachment battle. George W. Bush's more modest agenda of sustainable development policies were often frustrated by shrinking budget resources attributable to the soaring cost of the Iraq war and domestic tax policies. The Bush plan, for example, creating a "Millennium Challenge Corporation" that would distribute $5 billion annually to promote in developing states many projects congenial to sustainability was badly hobbled by the Iraq conflict.

White House agendas about global sustainability, moreover, often betray conflicting ideological and partisan viewpoints. Early signals are often prophetic. The Clinton administration's 1993 creation of the President's Council on Sustainable Development created what the environmental community interpreted to be a welcome gesture of continuing support for additional sustainability initiatives from the White House and the Democratic Party. President George W. Bush's failure to attend the 2002 World Summit on Sustainability in Johannesburg, South Africa, also seemed to send a message that Bush and the Republican Party considered environmental issues, and sustainability in particular, a marginal concern.

Implementing global sustainability policies is also complicated by the inherent need for tough, contentious governmental choices that translate lofty abstractions into operative policies at local levels nationally and internationally. As foreign policy scholar David G. Victor warns, sustainability can often dissolve into a "cocktail-party concept," ignoring difficult trade-offs during local implementation. The cocktail version "gleams with the promises of harmony and globalism: economic growth, environmental protection, and social justice . . . achieved fully and simultaneously. . . ."[51] Victor suggests some practical problems in implementing sustainability-related policies at the local level in many developing nations:

> Cocktail-party visions of sustainability properly laud the benefits of electricity, for example, as a cure for darkness and a substitute for costly candles. Yet the diesel generators that bring electric lighting to the most remote

areas are, in some respects, a paragon of unsustainability: diesel, which is derived from oil, is an exhaustible and polluting resource. Poor communities love diesel-generated electricity nonetheless: it has brought them television, high-quality lighting, and refrigeration, which were unavailable before. Similarly, whenever multinational environmentalists have sought to ban DDT worldwide, developing countries have resisted, wisely pointing out that the pesticide is crucial to controlling mosquitoes and other disease carriers in poor regions such as West Africa.[52]

The idea of sustainable development is also freighted with a strong moral imperative: Sustainability is not only desirable, it is ethically mandatory. Those who argue for some version of sustainability thereby can often seize a moral high ground and readily cast critics and dissenters of one sort or another as moral or ethical delinquents. Moreover, once a policy prescription is enshrined as a moral or ethical principle, negotiation or compromise becomes extremely unpalatable for the proponents. Because the idea of inherent limits to economic growth and natural resource consumption is far from universally accepted among policy makers and their advisers, the normative undertones to sustainable development advocacy may often become an implicit, and often unrecognized, frustration to productive negotiations.

Finally—to consider sustainability at the level of micromanagement—uncertainties and disagreements are certain to occur over the proper indicators for various policy decisions. What should policy makers take into account, for example, when measuring economic growth? What is the proper metric to use in estimating national, state, or local natural resource consumption? Air quality? Species diversity or extinction? Answers to indicator problems can be found, and have often been provided, when communities in the United States or elsewhere begin to tackle the practical aspects of measuring sustainability. In most cases, however, the development of indicators on which policy makers can agree as a basis for crafting specific measures to implement sustainable development has become a negotiating and bargaining process—in effect, a politics of indicator development.

Because one can easily imagine numerous other impediments, it is understandable that the implementation of sustainable development policies proceeds glacially at the national and international levels. But it does proceed, and out of the resulting scientific vagaries, political complexities, and economic debates, policy makers are beginning to translate, albeit tentatively, many of the grand principles of sustainability into practical policy—or policy experiments—across the globe. In the United States, the most vigorous efforts to turn sustainability theory into policy practice have been among local governments.

Sustainable Development in American Politics

The impact of sustainable development is only beginning to appear in American political practice and public policy. Although the term itself has been popularized almost into a cliché, efforts to translate its implicit principles into political practice have been relatively uncoordinated and inconsistent. At the federal, state, regional, and local levels, however, evidence is growing that many of the ideas that the proponents of sustainability advocate are being applied, often experimentally, in many different policy domains.

The federal government continues to promote the concept of sustainable development through incremental, modest innovations in its own structure, such as the Interagency Working Group on Sustainable Development Indicators and numerous study initiatives within virtually all major federal departments. Among federal agencies, the ecological precepts on which sustainability ideas are grounded are being most aggressively tested and implemented by the major land management agencies—the Bureau of Land Management, the Forest Service, the National Park Service, and the Fish and Wildlife Service—through the development of *ecosystem management.*

The ecosystem approach to national resource management became a significant scientific and political force itself in the late 1980s, supported by an influential coalition of federal agency officials, natural scientists, ecologists, and policy analysts. The affinity of the approaches to ecological planning of advocates of sustainable development and proponents of ecosystem development created a political synergy helpful to both movements. In many respects, ecosystem management has become a laboratory in which many theories about planning for ecological sustainability are being tested.

Domestic Ecosystem Management

Ecosytem management assumes that natural systems should be maintained, as much as possible, on the basis of their natural boundaries, and the various biological and physical systems within these boundaries, together with their constituent parts, should be managed with awareness of their interdependence. Ecosystem management should not be balkanized among a number of different federal agencies with different missions, resource priorities, and land authority.

This approach to ecological planning, as Chapter 1 emphasized, attracts advocates of sustainable development for several reasons. It emphasizes the goal of long-term sustainability rather than shorter-term economic productivity from ecological resources. It promotes a sensitivity to ecosystems as interdependent natural entities whose vitality depends on a mutually productive relationship with their human environment. It promotes comprehensive and coordinated planning of ecosystems to minimize conflict and confusion among competing agency managers responsible for elements of the ecosystems. Perhaps most important, it places great reliance on ecological and socioeconomic data, rather than economic indicators, in assessing the value of ecosystems and their desirable status. At the same time, the ecosystem approach requires federal land management agencies to address their traditional missions in a new way and to adopt a new organizational culture different from their historical experience. Not least important, ecosystem management requires the creation and adoption of new scientific and social data and new conceptual approaches to resource development.

By the time George W. Bush assumed the presidency, the federal government was actively involved in four major efforts at ecosystem management: They concerned the old-growth forests in the Pacific Northwest, the South Florida (Everglades) Restoration Project, the urban watershed incorporating the Anacostia River in Maryland and the District of Columbia, and the restoration of Alaska's Prince William Sound after the *Exxon Valdez* oil spill in 1989. The challenges involved in applying an ambitious ecosystem management strategy are suggested by the Florida experience. As noted earlier in this book, the Everglades activity has become the largest ecosystem restoration project internationally, involving an ecosystem extending from mid-Florida to the southern end of the Florida Keys. It will require the collaboration of eleven federal agencies, the state of Florida, ten counties, and hundreds of regional and local governments for a period estimated to exceed thirty years and cost a conservatively estimated $10.9 billion. Because of its scale, the Everglades restoration will be intensely observed worldwide as an experiment in sustainable ecological management of historic proportions.

Sustainable Politics and Communities

Although the federal ecosystem projects attract considerable attention, the most widespread, vigorous, hands-on effort to transform the ideas of sustainability into practical public policy appears to be emerging at the community level in the United States. The federal government has encouraged this evolution of community planning through initiatives such as the EPA's continuing Community Based Environmental Protection program and the President's Council for Sustainable Development, both of which encourage the development of resources and leadership for sustainability in local government. The vigor of local sustainability politics, however, appears to be as much a spontaneous expression of grassroots political reform as an offspring of federal innovations.

The movements for community sustainable development march under a variety of names, an indication that some are fusions of several older, local reform movements; others are new entities succeeding older reform organizations; and some are existing organizations expanding their agendas to embrace a version of sustainability alongside other reforms. Typically, they call themselves "Sustainable [Hometown]," "Sustainable [County]," perhaps a "Healthy Community" movement, or possibly "Keep [Hometown] Green." These organizations are often inspired by a historically powerful reform impulse in local American politics, which since the Progressive Era has been a potent source of urban political reform and renewal. By whatever name, they share some vision of comprehensive, community-based growth management predicated on the planning principles implied by advocates of sustainability.

Community-based sustainability is so recent that it remains largely a reform without a record, a civic impulse yet to prove its resilience. Despite its intuitive appeal to environmentalists and civic activists, intense political and economic conflicts are as predictable at the local level as at the national and international levels and are just as refractory, when implementation is attempted, because the same troublesome issues arise, albeit on different scales. Moreover, local sustainable development movements are vulnerable to becoming another example of "This Year's Look in Civic Improvement"—a beguiling political reform momentarily attracting the tenuous loyalty of well-intentioned reformers soon disenchanted when progress begins to slacken.

Conclusion

Something profound, and as yet but vaguely conceived, happened to political cognition in the latter third of the twentieth century. To this phenomenon we have ascribed the inadequate word "environmentalism." The artifacts are the most visible and, ultimately, the least important. Beginning with Earth Day 1970 in the United States and comparable political stirrings elsewhere in the industrialized world, a structure of domestic laws, institutions, and cultural practices has evolved in the United States to translate "environmentalism" into a social force and presence. This already large and elaborate national structure—the focus of most of this book—has become one national pediment among many throughout the world on which a new regional and international regime of environmental management—the focus of this chapter—is emerging. This incipient globalization of environmental management is extremely tenuous and as yet largely unproven, still more symbol than monument. Yet it does exist, and it has never existed before in the history of human civilization. It is worth reflecting on the profound historic implications of an international protocol to manage climate change in the twilight of the twentieth century.

At the beginning of the new century, however, a better perspective on the future path of environmentalism might be gained by looking beyond its current political and governmental architecture, important as that may be, to its implications for our evolving national conceptions of political time, space, and causality. From this perspective, one of environmentalism's most profound impacts has been to accelerate the way in which science is transforming public policy making. Environmental science, embodied in the technical underpinnings of current understandings of climate warming, ozone depletion, and intergenerational equity, is compelling policy makers to think in terms of policy problems and impacts, of the consequences of present decisions and future undertakings, and on a time scale almost unthinkable a few decades ago and unavoidable in the future. The genie of anticipatory environmental science is out of the bottle and, like the secrets of nuclear power, cannot now be ignored, however disconcerting it may be. Although our national political language has always been afflicted with vaporous rhetoric about "the future" or "concern for future generations," science today is providing policy makers with the intellectual tools and a scientific metric for characterizing the future impact of present public decision making that impose a responsibility quite new to public life.

Added to this increasingly sophisticated ability to describe and anticipate the environmental consequences of present policies, environmentalism has also made us aware, sometimes acutely, of the need to think deliberately about the long-term risks of technological innovation. As the U.S. experience with nuclear power amply demonstrates, it is not only the scientific risks of technology development that need to be appraised but also the institutional risks—the questions about whether we have, or can develop in appropriate ways, the institutional means of managing satisfactorily the technologies we create domestically and internationally.

Most important, the evolving impact of environmentalism on our politics and culture has made an especially persuasive case, for those who will listen, that we are beginning a new century not only with the technological ability to destroy the cultural and biological conditions for the survival of human life on earth but also with the capability to alter the genetic foundations of human life and thus consciously shape human evolution in materially and spiritually beneficial ways. Environmentalism at its best is a challenge to develop the moral and ethical sensibilities to leaven this power with an enlightened stewardship of the earth.

Suggested Readings

Chasek, Pamela S., ed. *The Global Environment in the Twenty-First Century.* Washington, D.C.: Brookings Institution Press, 2001.

Haas, Peter, ed. *Institutions of the Earth.* Cambridge: MIT Press, 1994.

Kutting, Gabriela. *Environment, Society, and International Relations.* New York: Routledge, 2000.

Porter, Gareth, and Janet Welsh Brown. *Global Environmental Politics.* 3d ed. Boulder: Westview Press, 2000.

Schreurs, Mianda A. *Environmental Politics in Japan, Germany, and the United States.* Cambridge: Cambridge University Press, 2002.

Susskind, Lawrence E. *Environmental Diplomacy: Negotiating More Effective Global Agreements.* Washington, D.C.: Island Press, 1999.

Notes

1. Nancy Stauffer, "MIT Survey: Climate Change Tops Americans' Environmental Concerns," *Tech Talk,* November 1, 2006, http://web.mit.edu/newsoffice/2006/survey.html, April 20, 2007.
2. Douglas Jehl and Andrew C. Revkin, "Bush, in Reversal, Won't Seek Cut in Emissions on Carbon Dioxide," *New York Times,* March 14, 2001, 1.
3. Edmund L. Andrews, "Bush Angers Europe by Eroding Pact on Warming," *New York Times,* April 1, 2001, 1.
4. Ibid.
5. Andrew C. Revkin, "Bush Calls in Experts to Help Set Course on Climate," *New York Times,* April 28, 2001, 9.
6. Pew Research Center, www.people-press.org/apri01rpt.htg/img2.gif, May 10, 2001.
7. Darren K. Carlson, "Scientists Deliver Serious Warning about Effects of Global Warming," *Gallup News Service,* January 23, 2001, www.gallup.com/poll/releases/ pr010123. asp, May 10, 2001.
8. Marvin S. Soroos, "From Stockholm to Rio and Beyond: The Evolution of Global Environmental Governance," in *Environmental Policy in the 1990s,* 3d ed., ed. Norman J. Vig and Michael E. Kraft (Washington, D.C.: CQ Press, 1997), 283.
9. For the history of international environmental negotiations, see Lynton Keith Caldwell, *International Environmental Policy: Emergence and Dimensions,* 2d rev. ed. (Durham: Duke University Press, 1990).
10. See, for example, Jill Jager and Tim O'Riordan, *The History of Climate Change Science and Politics* (London: Routledge, 1996); Sonja Boehmer-Christansen and Jim Skea, *Acid Politics* (New York: Belhaven Press, 1991); Duncan Liefferink, *Environment and the Nation State: The Netherlands, the EU and Acid Rain* (New York: Manchester University Press, 1996); and Oran Young, *International Governance: Protecting the Environment in a Stateless Society* (Ithaca: Cornell University Press, 1994).
11. Boehmer-Christansen and Skea, *Acid Politics,* pt. II.
12. Caldwell, *International Environmental Policy,* 14.
13. "Four U.S. Senators Lobbying in Kyoto," *Washington Post,* December 3, 1997, A35, A42.
14. Boehmer-Christansen and Skea, *Acid Politics,* 19–20.
15. Marc A. Levy, "International Co-operation to Combat Acid Rain," in *Green Globe Yearbook 1995,* ed. Helge Ole Bergesen and Georg Parmanis (New York: Oxford University Press, 1996), 63.
16. See Richard Elliot Benedick, *Ozone Diplomacy: New Directions in Safeguarding the Planet* (Cambridge: Harvard University Press, 1991).
17. Levy, "International Co-operation," 60.
18. On the role of science in international climate diplomacy, see Bert Bolin, "Science and Policy Making," *Ambio* 23 (February 1994): 25–29; Peter Haas, "Introduction: Epistemic Communities and International Policy Coordination," *International Organization* 46 (winter 1992): 1–35; Joseph Alcamo, Roderick Shaw, and Leen Hordik, ed., *The RAINS Model of Acidification* (Boston: Kluwer Academic, 1990); and John E. Carroll, ed., *International Environmental Diplomacy: The Management of Transfrontier Environmental Problems* (New York: Cambridge University Press, 1988).
19. On the UN Environmental Program, see Peter M. Haas, "United Nations Environmental Program," in *Conservation and Environmentalism: An Encyclopedia,* ed. Robert Paehlke (New York: Garland, 1995), 653–56; for UN environmental organizations generally, see Caldwell, *International Environmental Policy,* chap. 4.

20. Traci Watson, "It's a Full-on Circus in Kyoto,"*USA Today,* December 4, 1997, A04.
21. Caldwell, *International Environmental Policy,* 313.
22. Larry Parker and David E. Gushee, "Stratospheric Ozone Depletion: Implementation Issues," *CRS Issue Brief for Congress,* No. 97003 (Washington, D.C.: Congressional Research Service, January 16, 1998).
23. Cited in Parker and Gushee, "Stratospheric Ozone Depletion," 6.
24. See, for example, S. Fred Singer, "(N)O3 Problem," *National Interest* (summer 1994): 73–76; Pamela S. Zurer, "Complexities of Ozone Loss Continue to Challenge Scientists," *Chemical and Engineering News,* June 12, 1995, 20–23; and U.S. Congress, House Committee on Science, Subcommittee on Energy and the Environment, *Stratospheric Ozone: Myths and Realities,* Hearings, 104th Cong., 1st sess., September 20, 1995.
25. Parker and Gushee, "Stratospheric Ozone Depletion," 7.
26. The poll, conducted by Environmental Opinion Survey in June 1991, is cited in Environmental Protection Agency, *Securing Our Legacy* (Washington, D.C.: Environmental Protection Agency, 1992). See also National Desk, "U.S. Launches Satellite to Study Weather and to Make Spy Photos," *New York Times,* September 25, 1988, 1(32).
27. James L. Regens, "Acid Deposition," in *Keeping Pace with Science and Engineering: Case Studies in Environmental Regulation,* ed. Myron F. Ulman (Washington, D.C.: National Academy Press, 1993), 185.
28. General Accounting Office, "The Debate over Acid Precipitation: Opposing Views, Status of Research," Report No. CMD 81-113 (September 11, 1981). See also Sandra Postel, *Altering the Earth's Chemistry: Assessing the Risks* (Washington, D.C.: Worldwatch Institute, 1986), 25–33; and James L. Regens and Robert W. Rycroft, *The Acid Rain Controversy* (Pittsburgh: University of Pittsburgh Press, 1988), chap. 2.
29. Sandra Postel, *Air Pollution, Acid Rain, and the Future of the Forests* (Washington, D.C.: Worldwatch Institute, 1984), 18.
30. Ross Howard and Michael Perley, *Acid Rain* (New York: McGraw Hill, 1982), 19.
31. World Resources Institute, *World Resources: 1992–93* (New York: Oxford University Press, 1992), 193.
32. Philip Shabecoff, "Deadly Combination Felling Trees in East," *New York Times,* July 24, 1988. 1(1).
33. Elizabeth Kolbert, "Acid Rain Emperils Adirondacks Fish,"*New York Times,* July 7, 1989, A1.
34. William K. Stevens "To Treat the Attack of Acid Rain, Add Limestone to Water and Wait,"*New York Times,* April 25, 1988, C4.
35. For an analysis of Title IV's political history, see Gary C. Bryner, *Blue Skies, Green Politics,* 2d ed. (Washington, D.C.: CQ Press, 1995), chaps. 3, 4.
36. John E. Carroll, "Acid Precipitation: Legislative Initiatives," in *Conservation and Environmentalism: An Encyclopedia,* ed. Robert Paehlke (New York: Garland, 1995), 6.
37. Philip Shabecoff, "Global Warming Has Begun Expert Tells Senate,"*New York Times,* June 24, 1988, A1.
38. Ibid.
39. Postel, *Altering the Earth's Chemistry,* 8.
40. *New York Times,* December 1, 1997, F4.
41. Intergovernmental Panel on Climate Change, Working Group 1, "Summary for Policymakers," *Climate Change 2001: Synthesis Report,* ed. Robert T. Watson (New York: Cambridge University Press, 2001).
42. These stories were reported in William Stevens, "From Under the Sea, Climate Jolts," *New York Times,* November 18, 1997, F1; Malcolm Brown, "Ice Shifts Confound Warming Models," *New York Times,* November 18, 1997, F8; and "Scientists See Weather Trend as Powerful Proof of Global Warming," *Washington Post,* January 9, 1998, A8.
43. Jill Jaeger and Tim O'Riordan, "The History of Climate Change Science and Politics," in *Politics of Climate Change,* ed. Tim O'Riordan and Jill Jaeger (London: Routledge, 1996), 5.
44. Calvin Sims, "Poor Nations Reject Role in Warming," *New York Times,* December 13, 1997, A7.

45. Matthew L. Wald, "Fighting the Greenhouse Effect," *New York Times,* August 28, 1988, 3(1).

46. John Cushman, "Polls Show Public Support for Treaty," *New York Times,* November 11, 1997, A1; see also "Public Backs Tough Steps for a Treaty on Warming," *New York Times,* November 28, 1997, A36.

47. U.S. Environmental Protection Agency, "The Kyoto Protocol on Climate Change." Fact sheet released by the U.S. Department of State, Bureau of Oceans and International Environmental and Scientific Affairs, January 15, 1998, www.state.gov/www/global/global_issues/climate/index.html/ s/fs_kyoto_climate_980115.html. June 4, 2001.

48. David W. Moore, "Americans Tepid on Global Warming Accord," *The Gallup Poll Tuesday Briefing,* April 13, 2004, www.gallup.com, April 16, 2004.

49. Environmental News Service, "Polls: Water, Warming, Travel, Youth and Green Guilt," www.ens-newswire.com/ens/apr2007/2007-04-23-03.asp, May 1, 2007.

50. Paul E. Hagen, "The Green Diplomacy Gap," *Environmental Forum* (July/August 2000): 28–38.

51. David G. Victor, "Recovering Sustainable Development," *Foreign Affairs* (January/February 2006): 92.

52. Ibid, 97.

List of Abbreviations

AEC	Atomic Energy Commission
AFOs	animal feeding operations
AID	Agency for International Development
ANWR	Arctic National Wildlife Refuge
AQCR	Air Quality Control Region
BCA	benefit-cost analysis
BLM	Bureau of Land Management
CAA	Clean Air Act of 1970
CAFOs	concentrated animal feeding operations
CAGW	Citizens Against Government Waste
CEQ	Council on Environmental Quality
CERCLA	Comprehensive Environmental Response, Compensation, and Liability Act of 1980 ("Superfund")
CFCs	chlorofluorocarbons
CPI	consumer price index
CPSC	Consumer Product Safety Commission
CWA	Clean Water Act
DEHP	diethylhexyl phthalate
DINP	diisononyl phthalate
DOD	Department of Defense
DOE	Department of Energy
DOI	Department of the Interior
EDS	Endangered Species List
EIS	environmental impact statement
EO	executive order
EPA	Environmental Protection Agency
EPAt	Energy Policy Act of 2005
ESA	Endangered Species Act of 1973
FAO	Food and Agricultural Organization
FIFRA	Federal Insecticide, Fungicide, and Rodenticide Act of 1947
FQPA	Food Quality Protection Act of 1996
FWPCAA	Federal Water Pollution Control Act Amendments of 1972

FWS	Fish and Wildlife Service
GAO	Governmental Accountability Office
GNP	gross national product
HCFCs	hydrochlorofluorocarbons
IAEA	International Atomic Energy Agency
IPCC	Intergovernmental Panel on Climate Change
LRTAP	International Convention on Long Range Transboundary Air Pollution
LUST	liquid underground storage tank
MCL	maximum contaminant limit
NAAQS	National Ambient Air Quality Standards
NAFTA	North American Free Trade Agreement
NASA	National Aeronautics and Space Administration
NAWQ	National Water-Quality Assessment
NEPA	National Environmental Policy Act of 1969
NFMA	National Forest Management Act
NGOs	nongovernmental organizations
NIEHS	National Institute for Environmental Health Sciences
NIMBY	"not in my backyard"
NOx	nitrogen oxides
NOAA	National Oceanic and Atmospheric Administration
NPDES	National Pollution Discharge Elimination System
NPL	National Priority List
NRC	Nuclear Regulatory Commission; National Research Council
NRDC	Natural Resources Defense Council
NSPS	New Source Performance Standards
NSR	New Source Review (Clean Air Act of 1970)
NWPA	Nuclear Waste Policy Act of 1982
OCS	outer continental shelf
OECD	Organization for Economic Cooperation and Development
OIRA	Office of Information and Regulatory Affairs
OMB	Office of Management and Budget
OSHA	Occupational Safety and Health Administration
OSH Act	Occupational Safety and Health Act
OSMRE	Office of Surface Mining Reclamation and Enforcement
PCBs	polychlorinated biphenyls
POTWs	Publicly Owned Treatment Works
PPM	parts per million
PSD	prevention of significant deterioration
R&D	research and development
RARE	Roadless Area Review and Evaluation
RARG	Regulatory Analysis Review Group

RCRA	Resource Conservation and Recovery Act
RIA	regulatory impact analysis
SARA	Superfund Amendments and Reauthorization Act of 1986
SDWA	Safe Drinking Water Act
SIP	State Implementation Plan
SMCRA	Surface Mining Control and Reclamation Act
SOx	sulfur oxides
SNF	spent nuclear fuel
SUVs	sport utility vehicles
TCDD	2,3,7,8-tetrachloridibenzodioxin
TMDL	total maximum daily load
TRI	Toxic Release Inventory
TSCA	Toxic Substances Control Act
UNCS	United Nations Commission on Sustainable Development
UNDP	United Nations Development Program
UNEP	United Nations Environmental Program
USTs	underground storage tanks
VOCs	volatile organic compounds
WIPP	Waste Isolation Pilot Project
WMO	World Meteorological Organization

Index